CW01304731

Contents

Preface 5

1 The Portable Antiquities Scheme: An Overview 6

2 Dress Fittings 32
Brooches, Buckles, Buckle Clasps, Strap Ends, Buttons, Button and Loop Fasteners, Toggles, Cufflinks, Pins, Hooked Tags and Dress Hooks, Beads, Lace Tags, Sleeve Clasps, Girdle Hangers.

3 Ornaments 86
Dress pendants, Badges, Finger Rings, Bracelets and Arm Rings, Torcs, Ear Rings, Bodkins, Staff Terminals.

4 Personal Care 104
Combs, Tweezers, Ear Scoops, Nail Cleaners, Cosmetic Mortars, Razors, Mirrors, Chatelaines, Dental Implements, Wig Curlers.

5 Religion and Belief 116
Ampullae, Bullae, Figurines, Crucifixes and Crosses, Reliquaries, Statues, Monumental Brasses, Votive Models and Miniature Objects.

6 Literacy and Learning 134
Book Fittings, Seal Matrices, Seal Boxes, Writing Implements, Wax Spatulae, Parchment Prickers, Aestels, Inscribed Objects, Sundials.

7 Domestic Life 148
Household and Furnishings: Locks and Keys, Padlocks, Decorative Fittings, Fire Steels and Strike-a-Lights, Candlesticks and Candle Holders, Lamp Hangers. **Food and Drink:** Cauldrons, Hanging Bowls, Pans and Skillets, Buckets, Ewers and Wine Jugs, Mortars, Knives, Whetstones, Spoons, Chafing Dishes, Taps, Tankards. **Pastimes and Entertainment:** Toys, Gaming Pieces and Dice, Pipes, Pipe Tampers, Musical Instruments, Bells.

8 Tools and Manufacture 200
Axes, Adzes, Axe Hammers, Perforated Implements, Flint Implements, Metal Tools, Metalworking Tools, Die Stamps, Moulds, Ingots, Casting Waste. **Textile Working:** Spindle Whorls, Needles, Thimbles, Loom Weights, Pin Beaters, Weaving Combs, Weaving Battens, Scissors and Shears, Linen Smoothers, Textile Dressing. **Agriculture:** Ploughs, Querns, Sickles.

9 Trade and Commerce 244
Purses, Coins (Iron Age, Roman, Early Medieval, Anglo-Saxon, Medieval, Post Medieval, Early Modern), Coin Weights, Tumbrels, Balances, Weights, Jettons, Tokens, Cloth Seals.

10 Horses and Transport 282
Horseshoes, Spurs, Saddles, Stirrups, Bridles and Bridle Bits, Strap Fittings, Harness Pendants, Vehicle Fittings, Terrets and Linch Pins.

11 Warfare and Hunting 312
Spearheads, Arrowheads, Daggers and Dirks, Rapiers, Swords, Chapes, Maces, Battleaxes, Shields, Helmets, Armour, Firearms and Gun Related Finds, Hunting and Hawking.

12 Where to Find Out More 352

13 Further Reading 357

The British Museum's
Portable Antiquities Scheme

Finds Identified

An illustrated guide to metal
detecting and archaeological finds

by Kevin Leahy and Michael Lewis

The authors and their colleagues at the Portable Antiquities Scheme dedicate this work to Professor Roger Bland, OBE, FSA by whose inspiration and dedication the Scheme was created.

The British Museum

Portable Antiquities Scheme
www.finds.org.uk

Front cover image The handle from a Roman wine jug (page 169)

Back cover image Anglo-Saxon cruciform brooch (page 40)

Design and layout Christine Jennett

Published by Greenlight Publishing
119a Newland Street, Witham,
Essex CM8 1WF
Tel: 01376 521900

www.greenlightpublishing.co.uk

Printed by Gutenberg Press

ISBN 978-1-897738-63-4

© 2018 Portable Antiquities Scheme

All rights reserved

No part of this publication may be reproduced, stored in a retrieval system, or transmitted in any form by any means, electronic, mechanical photocopying, recording or otherwise, without the prior permission of Greenlight Publishing.

Preface

About the Authors

Dr Kevin Leahy is a National Finds Adviser for the Portable Antiquities Scheme. He has been liaising with metal detectorists and recording their finds for over 40 years. He has an expert knowledge of many periods of archaeological finds, but is probably best known for his interest in the Early Medieval period; he excavated the important Anglo-Saxon cemetery site at Cleatham, Lincolnshire and also undertook the initial cataloguing of the Staffordshire Hoard.

Dr Michael Lewis is Head of the Portable Antiquities Scheme, and has been working for the Scheme since 2001. He has a particular interest in the material culture of the Middle Ages, especially objects associated with personal devotion and religious reform. He is also well known for his work on the Bayeux Tapestry, particularly in relation to Late Anglo-Saxon manuscript illuminations.

Both authors are Fellows of the Society of Antiquaries of London (FSA) and Members of the Chartered Institute for Archaeologists (CIfA).

About the Book

This book is organised on a thematic basis with similar types of objects being placed together, rather than separated by period. We progress from objects associated with the individual, such as dress fittings, to items connected with wider aspects of society, such as trade and industry. It is hoped that this will allow readers to see how object types changed over time with the introduction of new materials, techniques and styles. In each case, the PAS database number is given (e.g. PAS-F1ND3S) which will allow readers to go to the original record. There they will see a full description of the find along with images of other similar objects recorded by the Scheme. The PAS database has enormous depth and it is possible to see everything that has been recorded, and to generate maps showing where they have been found. For reasons of confidentiality the findspots are not given in detail but the mapping is sufficiently detailed to show each area's archaeology. Most of the material recorded by the PAS is metal, particularly copper-alloy, which represents 93% of what has been logged. If not otherwise stated, all the objects described below are copper-alloy and all dates are AD unless BC is indicated. No scale bars have been used, but the maximum dimension of each object is stated. Emphasis is given to some important classes of object, such as brooches and coins, which are commonly found and, after much study, well dated.

Chapter 1
The Portable Antiquities Scheme
An Overview

Portable Antiquities Scheme
www.finds.org.uk

Recent years have seen a renewed interest in archaeological finds, which had long been deeply unfashionable. Perhaps as a reaction against object-centred antiquarian collecting, much 20th century archaeology was concentrated on sites, with less interest in finds in their own right. We are now starting to look again at finds or 'material culture' with revitalised interest, and are discovering what they can tell us. Specialist groups have been set up to study finds, and technological advances allow us to examine and record objects in ways previously unimagined. Every object has its story to tell – its 'object biography' – starting from the materials used to make it, to how it was made, used and finally abandoned or lost. The study of finds brings us into direct contact with past generations.

The British Museum's Portable Antiquities Scheme (PAS) is part of the bedrock on which this revolution stands. The Scheme began in 1997, with the aim of advancing archaeological knowledge and understanding by recording finds discovered by the public: a vison which remains true to this day. Working with colleagues in Wales (where the Scheme is run independently) and our partners in local museums and heritage organisations across the land, the PAS recorded

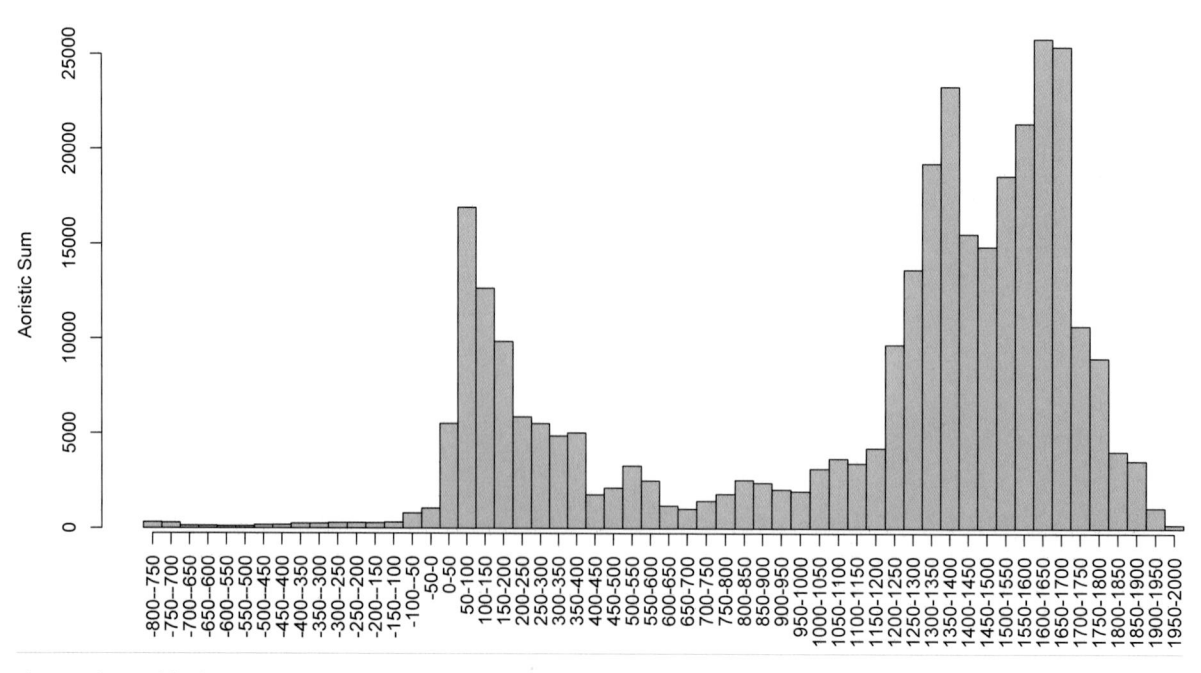

The numbers of finds recorded by the PAS, tabulated by date. This table does not include coins, where the numbers found would distort the pattern. The rise in the quantity of finds following the Roman Conquest is clearly shown, as is their rapid decline with the collapse of Roman Britain. (Image: Eljas Oksanen)

1.3 million archaeological finds during its first 20 years, giving an unparalleled view of the past. Many important objects have been recorded, but the Scheme's strength has been the depth of knowledge that it has produced, showing the changing pattern of human life over time.

The PAS has been made possible by advances in technology, most of which are computer based. Fundamental to the Scheme's record of the past is its database – www.finds.org.uk/database. The Internet has allowed the Scheme to make its records widely and publicly available and advances in digital photography have made it possible to produce and distribute high quality images. The development of GIS (Geographic Information Systems) means that the data can be plotted electronically, and searches, which would have once taken months to carry out, can be done in a moment. Almost all of what has been recorded with the PAS comes from the plough-soil and is unstratified (not found in an undisturbed archaeological context).

Once an object enters the plough-soil its survival will be measured in years, not decades, and if not found (and recorded) it will be rapidly destroyed and lost forever. Many findspots are now being recorded using GPS (Global Positioning System) devices, allowing us to see the spatial relationship between finds and study the movement of settlement across the landscape.

The PAS database is now large enough to be analysed in a statistically meaningful way, setting it alongside other (more traditional) archaeological and historical datasets. It is good to see PAS data being used for archaeological research in universities and as a first point of call by people with an interest in the past.

All this technology would be useless, however, without the human element, in particular the many finders (most of whom are metal detectorists) who have allowed their discoveries to be recorded, as well as those who have recorded the finds: the Scheme's locally based Finds Liaison Officers (FLOs), and the volunteers and self-recorders who help them. This book is a testament to their work. We would also like to thank Dianne Leahy, Margaret Broomfield and the late David Williams, (whose wisdom will be sorely missed) for checking the text, and Andrew Brown and John Naylor who advised on the coins section and Laura Burnett and Rob Webley who advised on Medieval and Post Medieval finds.

The Scheme's geographical coverage appears comprehensive, with finds being recorded from most areas, but there are gaps. In some areas metal detecting is prohibited, whilst in others the topography makes searching impossible (or less fruitful). Urbanisation restricts what land can be searched, though we do see remarkable finds from the Thames in London where 'mudlarking' on the foreshore is licensed. Some areas are much richer in archaeology than others – the heat-map (page 11) shows that finds are overwhelmingly concentrated in eastern England. This seems to reflect the division of England into two zones: the lowland zone of the south and east, and the highland zones of north and west. This division is marked in many other ways. The highland zone, with its hard rock geology and higher rainfall is suitable for farming cattle and sheep. On the soft, geologically more recent, rocks of the south east, farming focuses on growing crops.

It is important to be cautious in analysing these differences; is the lowland zone really richer in finds, or are we simply seeing large amounts of archaeological material being collected from sites destroyed by ploughing? The pattern revealed by recorded finds is supported by the Domesday survey of 1086, where it is apparent that finds are more common in areas with the greatest population densities. There are exceptions though; there is a marked concentration of finds in East Yorkshire, where Domesday records a low population in 1086. This is probably explained by William the Conqueror's 'Harrying of the North' in the aftermath of rebellion against his rule. The PAS has tried to look systematically at these biases in its data and consider them in an analytical way, setting them alongside other sources of evidence.

Metal objects buried in the soil corrode, but eventually reach an equilibrium where they can survive, unchanged, for thousands of years. However, once they enter the plough soil their decay will be rapid. This early Medieval buckle is pitted by 'bronze disease' and will eventually be reduced to greenish powder, its iron pin is already represented only by rust. To stop this happening, finds must be kept dry, in a sealed box, with silica gel as a desiccant. **(IOW-F6C490, 28mm, Gatcombe, Isle of Wight, 400-600)**

THE PORTABLE ANTIQUITIES SCHEME: AN OVERVIEW

The English landscape has been intensively occupied for millennia with the activities of each generation overlying those of the past. On this aerial photograph, taken at Haxey, North Lincolnshire, the ripening crops show the ditches of probable Roman fields overlaid by rectangular 'retting pits' used in the preparation of flax. (Image: Mike Felcey)

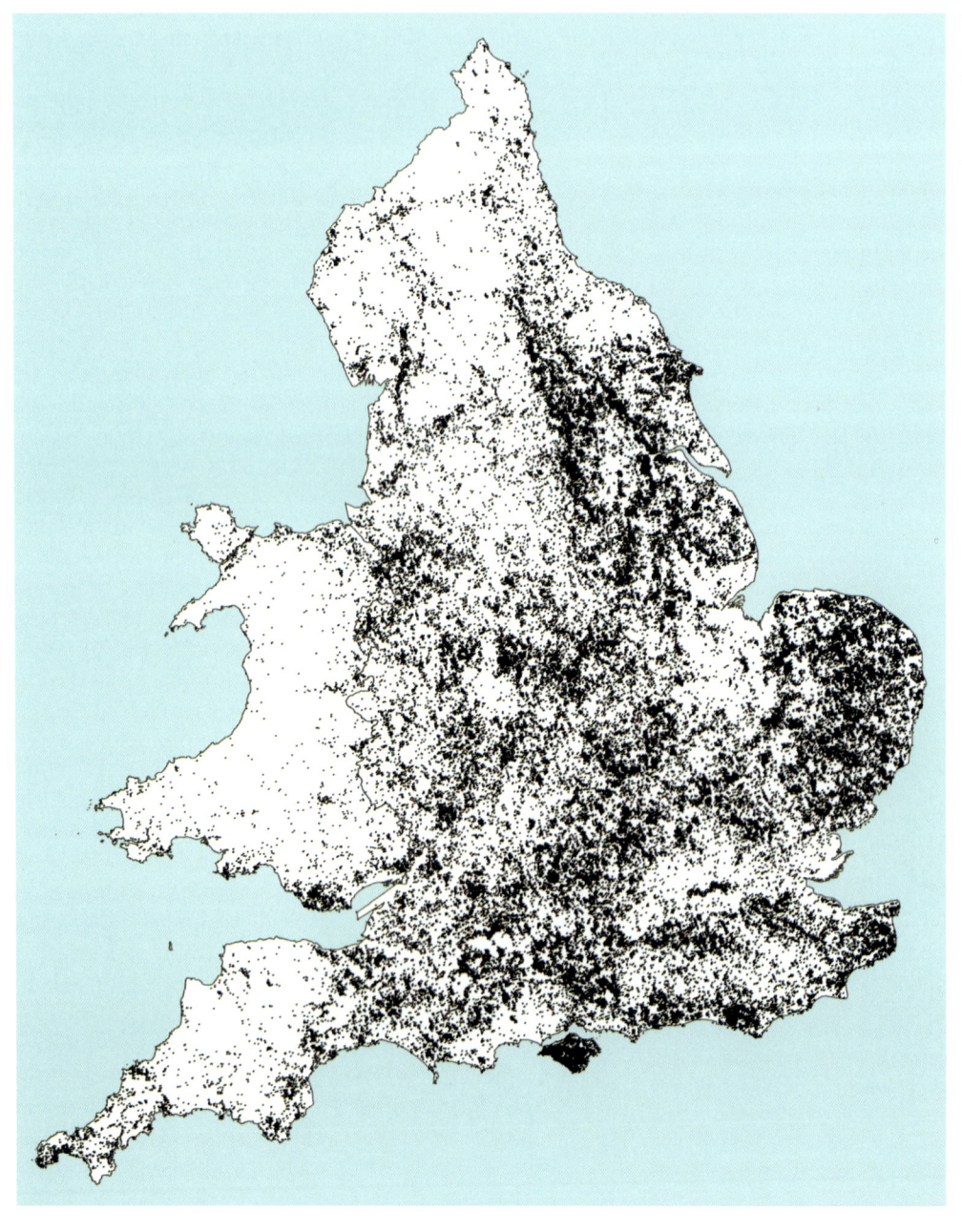

The overall distribution of finds recorded by the PAS. (Image: Eljas Oksanen)

THE PORTABLE ANTIQUITIES SCHEME: AN OVERVIEW

Heat map showing the areas where the greatest numbers of finds have been recorded by the PAS. It can be seen that finds are concentrated in the 'lowland zone' of the south and east.
(Image: Eljas Oksanen)

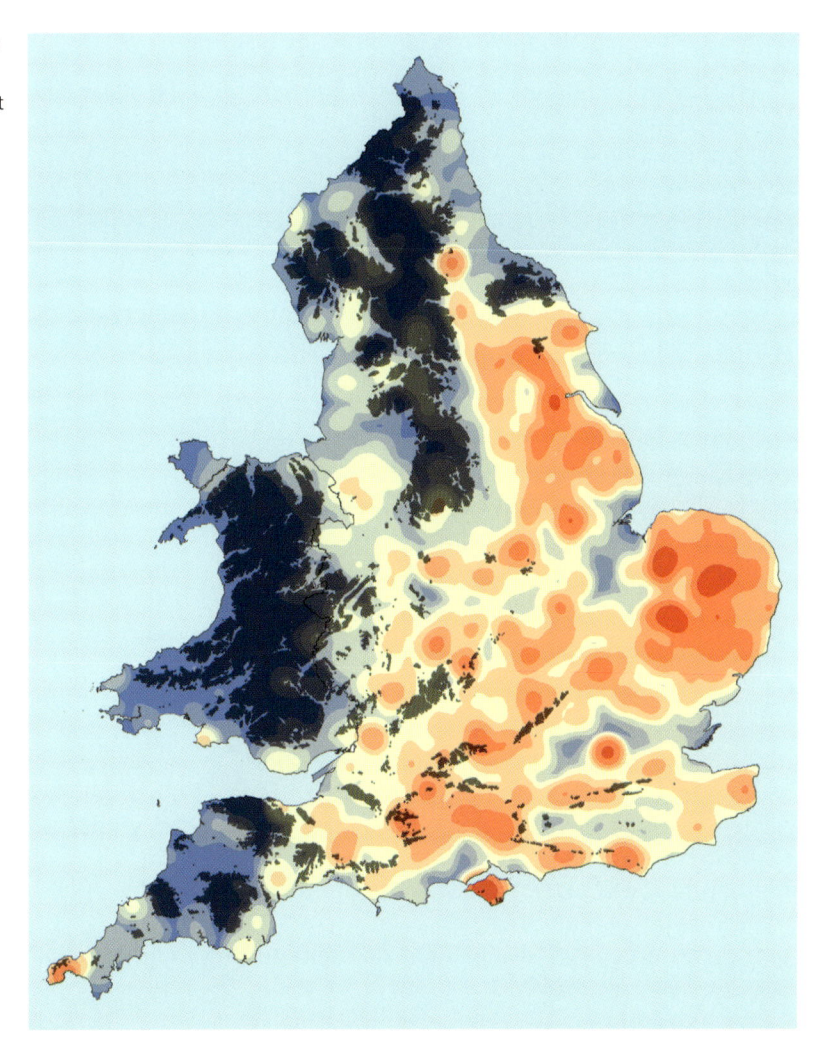

Metal detecting has produced large amounts of finds, many of which are of recent date. This group from South Ferriby, North Lincolnshire shows the quantity and range of material being found.
(Image: Kevin Leahy)

THE PORTABLE ANTIQUITIES SCHEME: AN OVERVIEW

It is also important to think about how the material recorded by the PAS got into the ground. Some of it was undoubtedly lost accidentally, but other items were probably deposited for ritual or religious reasons. People in the past lived in a world that they understood to be controlled by the arbitrary acts of gods who needed to be placated; what might seem to us as irrational behaviour made perfect sense to them. An advantage of the PAS dataset is that it can be used as a self-check: if there are no Early Medieval finds from an area but Roman and Medieval material is being found, it suggests that the gap is real – there was no Early Medieval activity in that area.

It is useful to summarise the archaeology of each period of the past as revealed by finds recorded by the PAS as of 2017, the 20th year of the Scheme's existence. In 2017 there were over 800,000 records on the database, some containing multiple objects, giving a total of 1,250,000 finds. While this figure will quickly become out of date, it is unlikely that the proportion of each type of find will change: this is the advantage of a large dataset. While an attempt has been made to suggest the numbers of each type of find that has been recorded, along with a general idea of their distribution, this has not always been possible. In some instances, complex terminology and uncertainty in identifying particular finds has led to object types being recorded on the PAS database in a number of different ways (e.g. badge and pilgrim badge) making it difficult to determine exactly how many have been recorded.

Flint and Stone, c.800,000-c.2,500 BC: 33,000 Records

Human beings have been intermittently present in Britain for over 800,000 years, and for much of this time finds of flint and stone are almost all the evidence we have for them. The PAS has recorded 350 Lower Palaeolithic handaxes, most of which date from between 800,000 to 180,000 years ago, when Britain enjoyed a temperate, wooded, environment in which elephants, hippos, rhino and lions roamed. Then came the Ice Ages, when northern Britain was covered by glaciers, with harsh periglacial conditions over the rest of the country. At this time, human habitation came to an end. Lower Palaeolithic finds recorded by the PAS reflect this, coming mainly from south of the Humber and Severn Estuary where the landscape had not been scoured by the ice. A retreat of the ice, around 60,000 years ago, allowed hunters to return to Britain, although the PAS has recorded few implements from this period. Britain then had a tundra-like environment which lasted until 24,000 years ago, when the ice again advanced. Around 13,000 BC an improving climate allowed humans to return, this time permanently. While the hunters on the tundra had focused on a few species, such as horses, rising temperatures allowed the spread of trees across the landscape, making such hunting difficult. This called for a wider based strategy which included the pursuit of smaller prey. During this period, known as the Mesolithic, small flint microliths were made, of which many examples have been recorded by the PAS.

The Neolithic period started around 6,000 years ago, with farming introduced into Britain for the first time. This period also witnessed the construction of stone and earth monuments for burial and ritual. Pottery appeared, along with new tools and weapons, such as leaf-shaped arrowheads and polished stone axes, examples of which are recorded on the PAS database. Finds of later prehistoric flint and stone implements seem particularly dense in some areas, particularly Cornwall, Lincolnshire and East Anglia, but care is needed in interpreting the data; these concentrations may be due, not to intense prehistoric activity, but fieldwork being focused in these parts of the country.

For most of the past, the presence of human beings in Britain is represented only by flint handaxes like this example from Ramsey and Parkeston, Essex.
(ESS-88730B, 140mm c.500,000-180,000 BP)

THE PORTABLE ANTIQUITIES SCHEME: AN OVERVIEW

Hominid footprints revealed in 2013 after heavy seas had washed sand from the beach at Happisburgh, Norfolk. These footprints have been dated to c.800,000 BP and form an evocative link with the deep past. Within two weeks they were washed away by the sea; an extreme, but not unusual example of the fragility of the past. (Image: Simon Parfitt)

The Neolithic period saw the construction of the first monuments in the landscape. Trees on the skyline mark the Minninglow, Derbyshire Neolithic chambered tomb. (Image: Kevin Leahy)

THE PORTABLE ANTIQUITIES SCHEME: AN OVERVIEW

Bronze Age, c.2,500-c.600 BC: 10,000 Records

The appearance of metalworking appears to have made little difference at first, with flint and stone continuing to be used alongside metal throughout prehistory. By 2017 the PAS database included almost 6,000 finds of Bronze Age metalwork along with 2,700 flint and stone objects and some 250 pieces of gold. These finds are concentrated in the eastern counties, but the distribution extends across lowland England. Most important are Bronze Age hoards, containing weapons, tools, ornaments and ingots of which more than 200 have now been recorded by the PAS as Treasure. In the past these have been interpreted as 'founders' hoards (scrap objects that were to be melted down), but some archaeologists are now suggesting that they were buried for ritual purposes. New finds recorded through the PAS are of crucial importance, particularly when they are recorded in situ, allowing us to consider why this metalwork was buried.

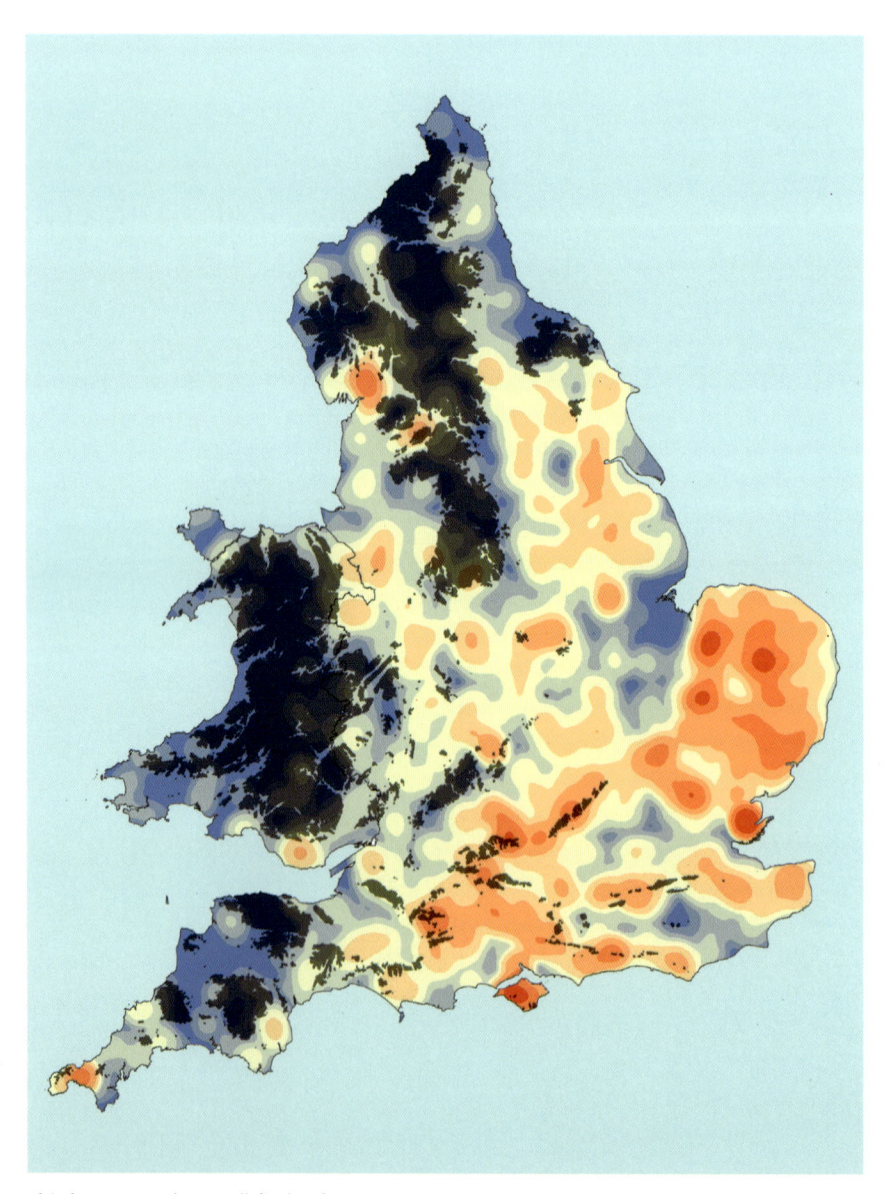

This heat map shows all finds of Bronze Age metalwork recorded by the PAS. There appear to be major concentrations in East Anglia and Hampshire, but it must be remembered that the finds covered a period of more than a thousand years and things are likely to have changed over time. The smaller concentrations would no doubt be worth examining in detail. (Image: Eljas Oksanen)

THE PORTABLE ANTIQUITIES SCHEME: AN OVERVIEW

No book on Britain's archaeology is complete without a picture of Stonehenge. While we have all seen it before, this iconic late Neolithic-Early Bronze Age monument shows what the makers of the finds we are recording could achieve.
(Image: Michael Lewis)

Contemporary with Stonehenge is this Early Bronze Age round barrow at Kirmond le Mire, Lincolnshire. The survival of a few superb burial mounds like this show just how much has been lost from Britain's landscape.
(Image: Kevin Leahy)

THE PORTABLE ANTIQUITIES SCHEME: AN OVERVIEW

Above: hoards are telling us much about the Bronze Age – this example contains an early spearhead, an axe and part of a broken axe: damaged objects are a feature of many Bronze Age hoards. Hoards show the type of objects available at the time they were buried and, by comparing hoards, we can build up a sequence showing how bronze implements developed. **(NMGW-0B9997, 196mm (spearhead), Wenvoe, Vale of Glamorgan, 1700-1500BC)**

Left: while most finds come from the plough soil, some are undisturbed and it is vital to record their context. The prompt action of the finder of two Bronze Age hoards near Driffield, East Yorkshire allowed PAS staff and volunteers to excavate them and record the position of each axe and ingot fragment.
(Images: Dianne Leahy)

THE PORTABLE ANTIQUITIES SCHEME: AN OVERVIEW

Iron Age c.600 BC-AD c.50: 54,000 Records

Like the introduction of bronze, the appearance of iron does not appear to have made an immediate difference to people's lives. Significant changes had occurred in the later Bronze Age, around 1,000 BC, when society seems to have become organised on a larger scale, building hillforts and dividing land into units for rearing livestock. The Iron Age is not represented by finds of iron in the PAS dataset – only 94 of the 54,000 Iron Age finds recorded with the PAS are iron. This is explained by the fact that many detectorists set their machines to discriminate against iron, which is usually poorly preserved and impossible to date. Within the PAS dataset are 45,000 Iron Age coins, many of which were incorporated into the PAS database from the Celtic Coins Index. The large scale issuing of coins again points to society becoming organised and sophisticated. Their distribution helps define the Iron Age tribal areas, and their economic and political contacts.

Late Iron Age tribal areas, known from historical documents – coin finds help define the extent of these tribal lands. The distribution of hill forts (indicated by red dots) is interesting as they show different needs and traditions across England and Wales during later prehistory. (Image: Kevin Leahy)

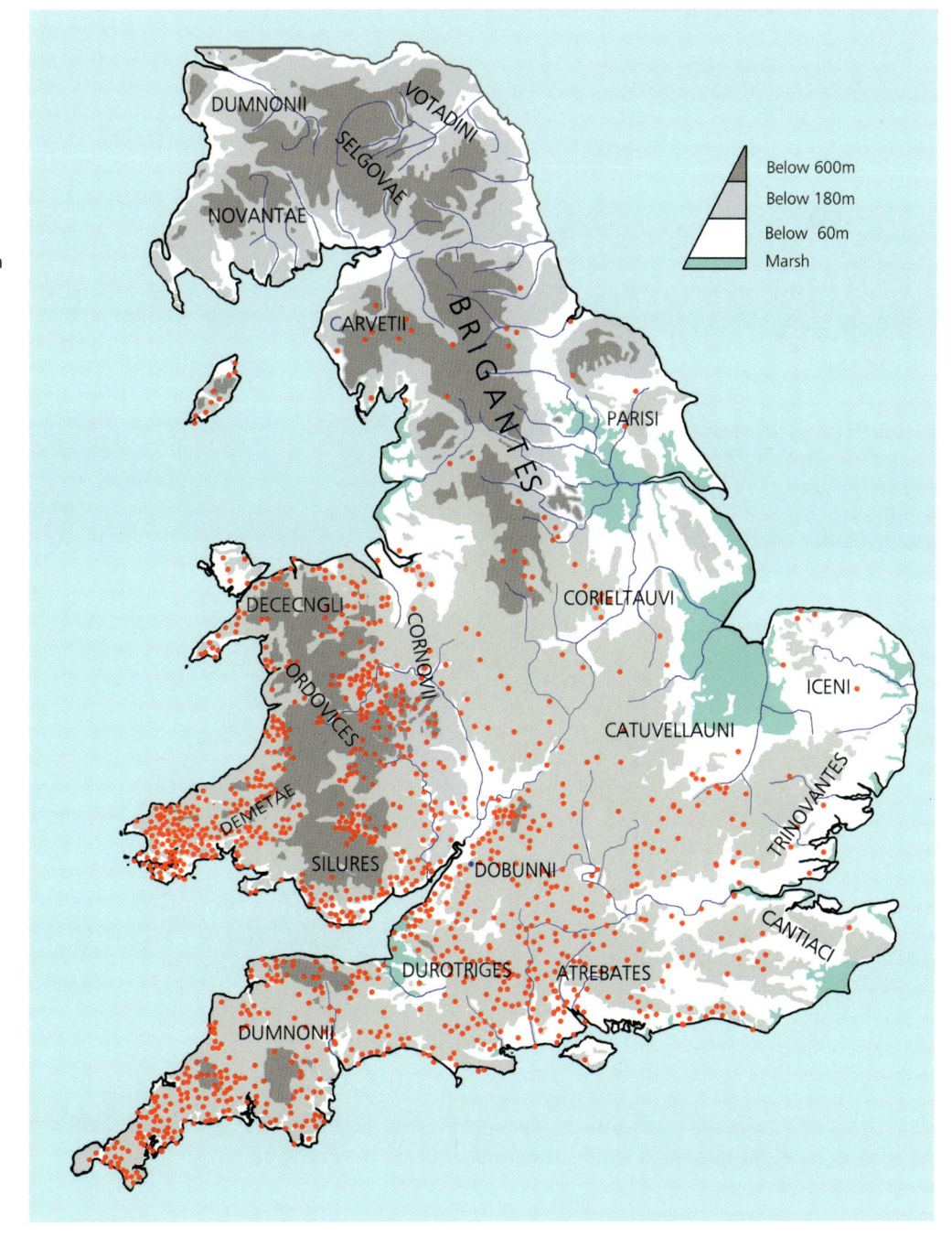

THE PORTABLE ANTIQUITIES SCHEME: AN OVERVIEW

Huggate Wold, Prehistoric triple ditch system. The Later Bronze Age to Early Iron Age saw great changes, with the construction of the first hill forts and the division of the landscape with the digging of massive, long distance, boundaries as shown here. (Image: Peter Halkon).

The characteristic building of the Iron Age was the round house. This example was reconstructed on its original site at Weelsby Avenue, Grimsby, North-East Lincolnshire. It was found within a small enclosure with human skulls in the ditch either side of its gateway. (Image: Kevin Leahy)

THE PORTABLE ANTIQUITIES SCHEME: AN OVERVIEW

A cache of late Iron Age weapons being excavated following its discovery by detectorists near South Cave, East Yorkshire. It contained five swords and 33 spearheads covered by amphora sherds. They were probably buried following the arrival of the Romans around AD70.
(Image: Kevin Leahy)

This find consisted of three gold torcs (two twisted and one plain) together with a gold bracelet, which were probably imported from the continent. The discovery of continental type, Early Iron Age, material in the West Midlands is significant, leading us to wonder about the contacts involved. **(WMID-FD08 146mm, (torc) Leekfrith, Staffordshire, c.400-300 BC)**

THE PORTABLE ANTIQUITIES SCHEME: AN OVERVIEW

Roman Period AD c.43-c.410: 328,000 Records

Roman finds represent the largest single group on the PAS database. The 328,000 records contain a total of 628,000 finds of which 253,000 are coins – a striking total for a period lasting only 367 years. The number of finds must reflect the size of the population of Roman Britain which has been placed at around two to four million people, with PAS data supporting the higher figure. The Roman conquest in AD 43 had taken Britain into the world of Mediterranean civilisation. Cities, villas and forts are well known, but the material recorded by the PAS casts a new light on life in the Roman province of Britannia, showing the extent and nature of rural settlement. Roman Britain looks remarkably prosperous, the large numbers of small metal objects suggesting that this material was widely available and that people had disposable wealth. The reasons for this apparent affluence are likely to be complex; the Roman army would have put an end to the endemic tribal warfare and stimulated what had been a subsistence economy – it was now worth producing, not just for home use, but for a growing market leading to a rise in prosperity.

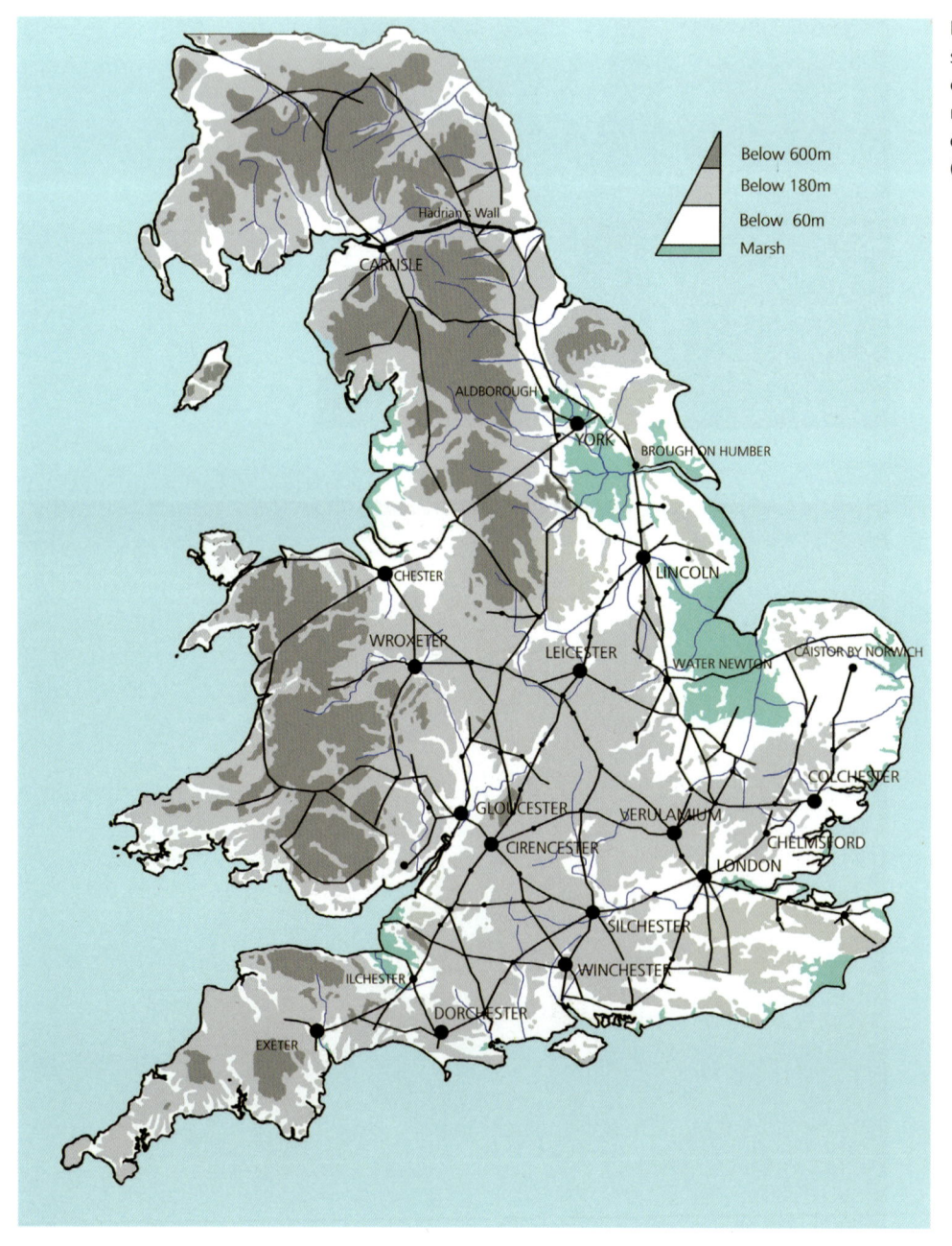

Roman Britain showing the major cities, towns and the road network, an ordered landscape. (Image: Kevin Leahy)

THE PORTABLE ANTIQUITIES SCHEME: AN OVERVIEW

Roman remains have long fascinated antiquarians who were able to recognise and date them even if everything else remained a mystery. This antiquarian illustration shows the mile castle at Castle Nick, on Hadrian's Wall.
(Image from Collingwood Bruce *The Hand-Book to the Roman Wall*, 7th edition, 1914)

The landscape is itself a historic document over which each generation writes its story. These crop-marks at Hougham, Lincolnshire, show the intensity of Roman settlement and the need to link finds to their context. (Image: Historic England)

THE PORTABLE ANTIQUITIES SCHEME: AN OVERVIEW

A map of the Roman finds recorded by the PAS shows them to be strongly concentrated in East Anglia, East Yorkshire and Lincolnshire, extending along the Trent Valley. There are gaps in the distribution which can be explained by topography: the Fens, inland from the Wash, and the highland zone to the West. Some gaps seem odd – there are, for example, fewer finds from Kent than might be expected. Such anomalies offer opportunities for further investigation and analysis to add to our understanding. An important aspect of the PAS record is that it is possible to look at clusters of certain object types and consider what they might mean: for example, why are large numbers of a particular Roman buckle type or brooch found in a certain area? Nowhere else in the Roman Empire has material been recorded on the scale achieved by the PAS. It is possible to see the rise, and eventual decline, of the Roman economy in Britain, with large numbers of small, low value coins being found, reflecting an active economy which collapsed in the early 5th century. Coin hoards are being reconsidered due to PAS data. The 3rd century Frome hoard contained 52,523 coins and weighed 350 pounds, which, since it was found in a single pot, would have been impossible to move. Archaeologists now think that some such coin hoards were deposited with no intention that they would ever be recovered, but were instead buried as offerings to the gods. It is all so much more complicated and interesting than ever suspected.

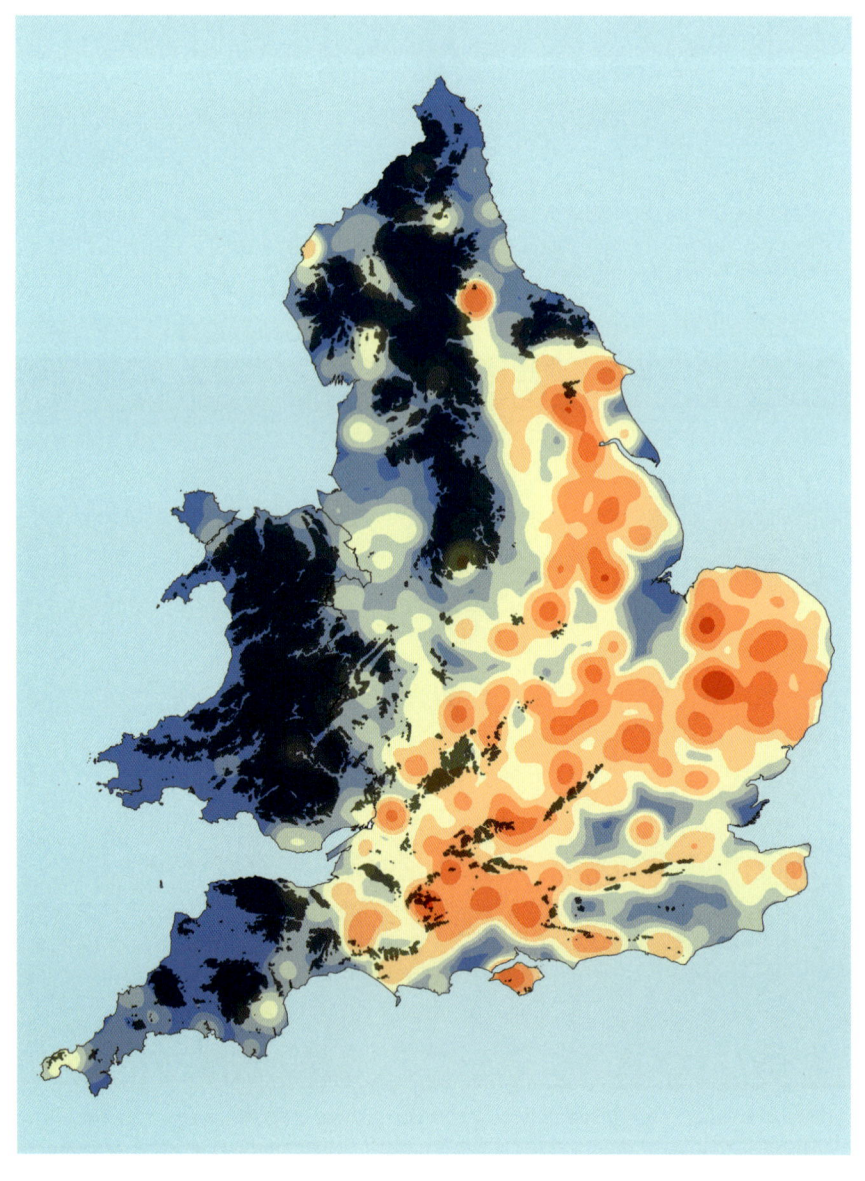

Heat map showing the density of Roman finds in Britain, where the richness of eastern England is clear. Some of the gaps can be explained by topography (marshlands around the Wash) but others are more difficult to understand.
(Image: Eljas Oksanen)

THE PORTABLE ANTIQUITIES SCHEME: AN OVERVIEW

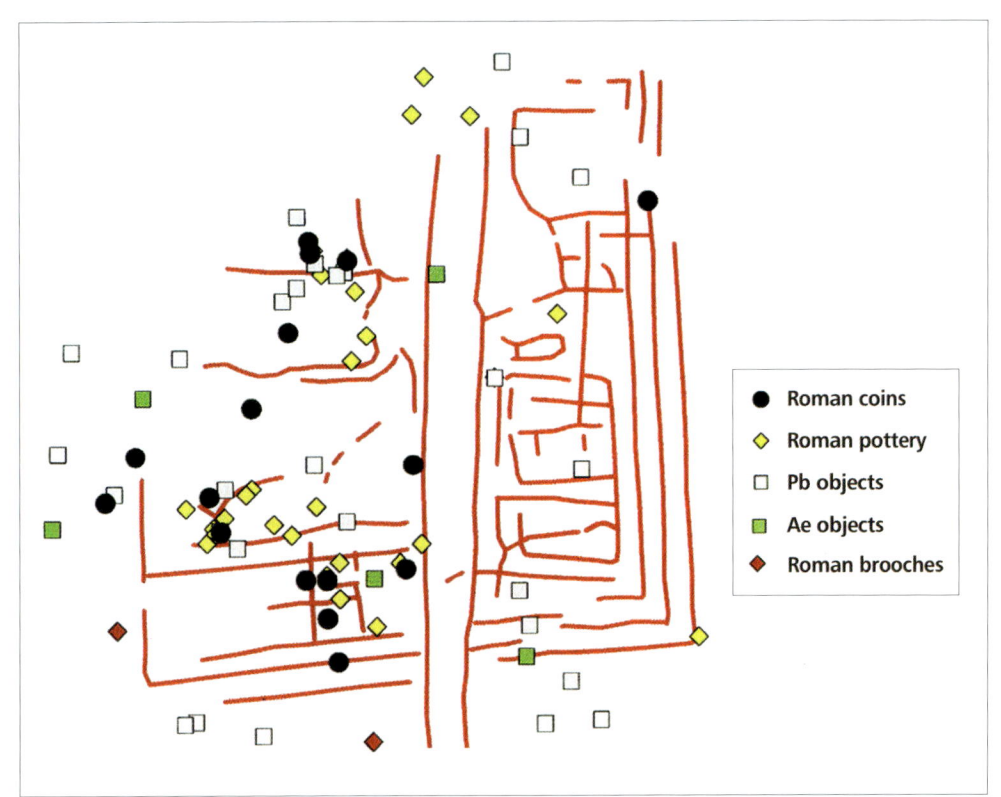

The careful logging of finds during metal detecting can reveal important evidence of past landscapes and land use. This survey is interesting in that the detector finds did not come from the area where the ditches had been recorded. Perhaps the houses were in the more open area with the ditches representing paddocks, or are we looking at finds getting onto fields with manure? (Image: Mike Hemblade)

A surprising amount of Roman building survives above ground. The Late Roman Saxon Shore Fort at Burgh Castle, Norfolk remains a massive and impressive structure. (Image: Kevin Leahy)

THE PORTABLE ANTIQUITIES SCHEME: AN OVERVIEW

Early Medieval Period AD c.410-c.1066: 31,000 Records

The Roman administration collapsed during the early 5th century and was replaced by small scale tribal societies. Cities and villas appear to have been abandoned, coins went out of use, and the large-scale Roman pottery industry ended. The Anglo-Saxons came from northern Europe and southern Scandinavia and are recognisable from their distinctive cemeteries and the grave goods that these contained. The PAS has added to our knowledge of this period with over 7,500 records of the early Anglo-Saxon finds (AD 400-700), and the discovery of many new, but alas, plough-damaged, cemeteries. These finds mainly came from Norfolk, Lincolnshire and East Yorkshire, which were the core areas of Anglo-Saxon settlement.

The Early Medieval period saw many changes, with England moving from being a tribal society to becoming (over time) a united, centralised kingdom – the first king of all England being Æthelstan (r.927-39). Christianity, arriving in the late 6th century, brought material associated with the new faith, as well as important links with Christian Europe. The Anglo-Saxons also interacted with their Celtic neighbours in Ireland, Scotland and Wales, and later, the Vikings from Scandinavia brought their art and culture to these isles. These changes affected the things that people used and the way they dressed, which can be seen in the material recorded by the PAS.

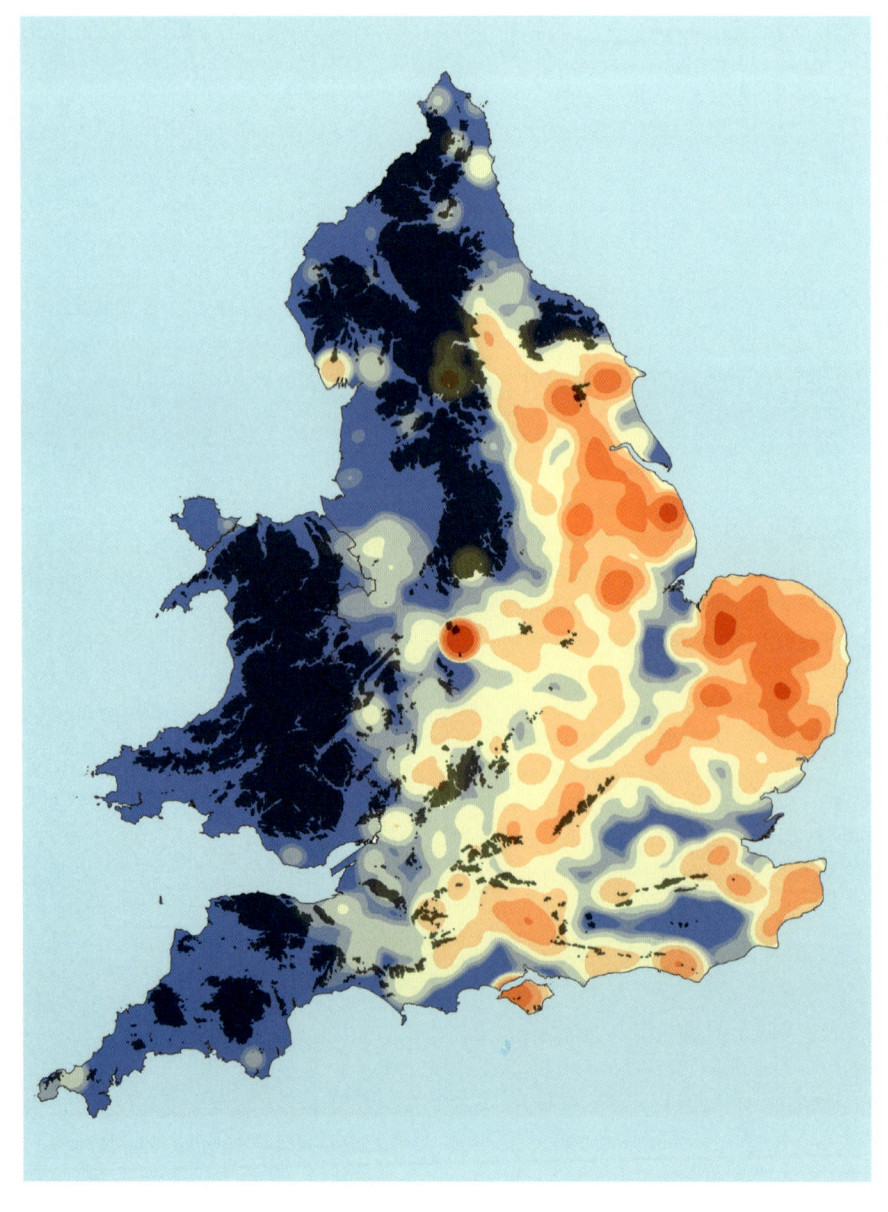

Heat map showing all Early Medieval finds. These cover a period of over 600 years, during which great changes took place. The situation in the 5th century was quite unlike that of the 11th century. The massive concentration in the Midlands represents a single find: the Staffordshire Hoard. (Image: Eljas Oksanen)

THE PORTABLE ANTIQUITIES SCHEME: AN OVERVIEW

Discovered in 2009 the Staffordshire Hoard of Early Anglo-Saxon treasure generated world-wide interest. Consisting mainly of gold and silver war-gear and Christian objects, it gave new insights into 7th century aristocratic life.
(Image © Birmingham Museums Trust)

It is vital to record finds in detail. Work underway to prepare the first catalogue of the Staffordshire Hoard, the weight, measurement and description of each fragment recorded and placed onto a computer database. (Image: Kevin Leahy)

THE PORTABLE ANTIQUITIES SCHEME: AN OVERVIEW

Groups of finds like these are common in Eastern England and mark the sites of ploughed-out Anglo-Saxon cemeteries. Fragments include parts of cruciform brooches, sleeve clasps, girdle hangers and, bottom right, a mount from a hanging bowl. (Image: Kevin Leahy)

While large numbers of finds are discovered by detectorists, archaeological excavations are producing massive amounts of material. The excavation of the Flixborough Anglo-Saxon settlement produced thousands of finds. (Image: Kevin Leahy)

THE PORTABLE ANTIQUITIES SCHEME: AN OVERVIEW

The use of grave goods in cemeteries ended around AD 670, leaving us without this source of evidence. Until recently, the Middle and Later Anglo-Saxon periods were known only from a few casual finds – when, in 1964, Sir David Wilson published his catalogue of the British Museum's collection of later Anglo-Saxon metalwork he was only able to list 155 items collected since the museum's foundation in 1753. By 2017 the PAS had recorded over 23,000 items of Late and Middle Anglo-Saxon date, revolutionising our understanding of later Anglo-Saxon England. This period can now be seen as rich and prosperous, supporting what we knew from documentary sources. The PAS has also recorded more than 250 single pieces of Viking metalwork and almost 2,000 items that are described as 'Anglo-Scandinavian' – a term used to describe material made in England under Viking influence. This is significant as it suggests that the Viking conquest was more than just a change of management, but a movement of people from Scandinavia.

Anglo-Saxon stone cross in Eyam, Derbyshire, churchyard. Now incomplete (its middle section missing), it still stands eight feet tall and retains its carved head. The decoration on this fine cross reminds us that the metalwork of the Early Medieval period should not be considered in isolation, but as part of an artistic tradition involving sculpture, wood carving and illuminated manuscripts.
(Image: Kevin Leahy)

THE PORTABLE ANTIQUITIES SCHEME: AN OVERVIEW

The finds recorded by the PAS represent only one aspect of the 650 year Anglo-Saxon period. When looking at Portable Antiquities we must not forget that the Anglo-Saxons left some larger objects, like the magnificent late 10th century All Saints' Church, Earls Barton, Northamptonshire. (Image: Kevin Leahy)

Medieval Period AD c.1066-c.1539: 185,000 Records

There is no doubt that the Norman Conquest of 1066 marked a pivotal point in British history, but this divide (between the Early Medieval and Medieval periods) is seemingly invisible in the record of finds found by detectorists – the Normans left their mark in our language, and through the construction of great castles and cathedrals, but not much in everyday artefacts recorded by the PAS, or so it seems. Throughout the 11th century, England (in particular) became culturally closer to Europe, which is reflected in the design, form and style of artefacts found. The PAS dataset shows a notable spike in the number of finds from the 13th century until the Black Death (1348), when the population of Britain declined by as much as 60%. This, though a great tragedy, benefited those who survived, as wages rose and working conditions improved in the face of a shortage of labour. The Middle Ages also saw increased urbanisation, as people moved from the countryside into towns, and there was a growth in markets and fairs, with craftsmen and merchants using navigable rivers, roads and the sea to trade their wares and exchange goods. England benefited from a sophisticated monetary system, inherited from the Late Anglo-Saxon period.

Most notable during the Middle Ages was the increasing influence, wealth and power of the Christian church, particularly of the Pope (as its head) and the Roman curia (the bureaucracy of the Roman Catholic Church) that supported him. Almost all who lived in these isles believed their life (and after-life) was influenced by the divine; people looked to God for direction, comfort and protection. This reverence to God, the Virgin, and the Saints, is clear in the objects recorded by the PAS.

Magnificent churches like Beverley Minster, East Yorkshire, show both the power of the Church and its overwhelming presence in people's lives. These buildings still have the power to impress, but to people living in tiny cottages they must have been awesome. (Image: Kevin Leahy)

THE PORTABLE ANTIQUITIES SCHEME: AN OVERVIEW

The quality of building was superb. This splendid vault at Fountains Abbey, North Yorkshire formed, not part of the church, but an undercroft beneath the Lay Brothers' dormitory. (Image: Michael Lewis)

While many deserted Medieval villages have now been destroyed by ploughing, Gainsthorpe, North Lincolnshire represents a remarkable survival, with the village streets and houses still visible. (Image: Kevin Leahy)

THE PORTABLE ANTIQUITIES SCHEME: AN OVERVIEW

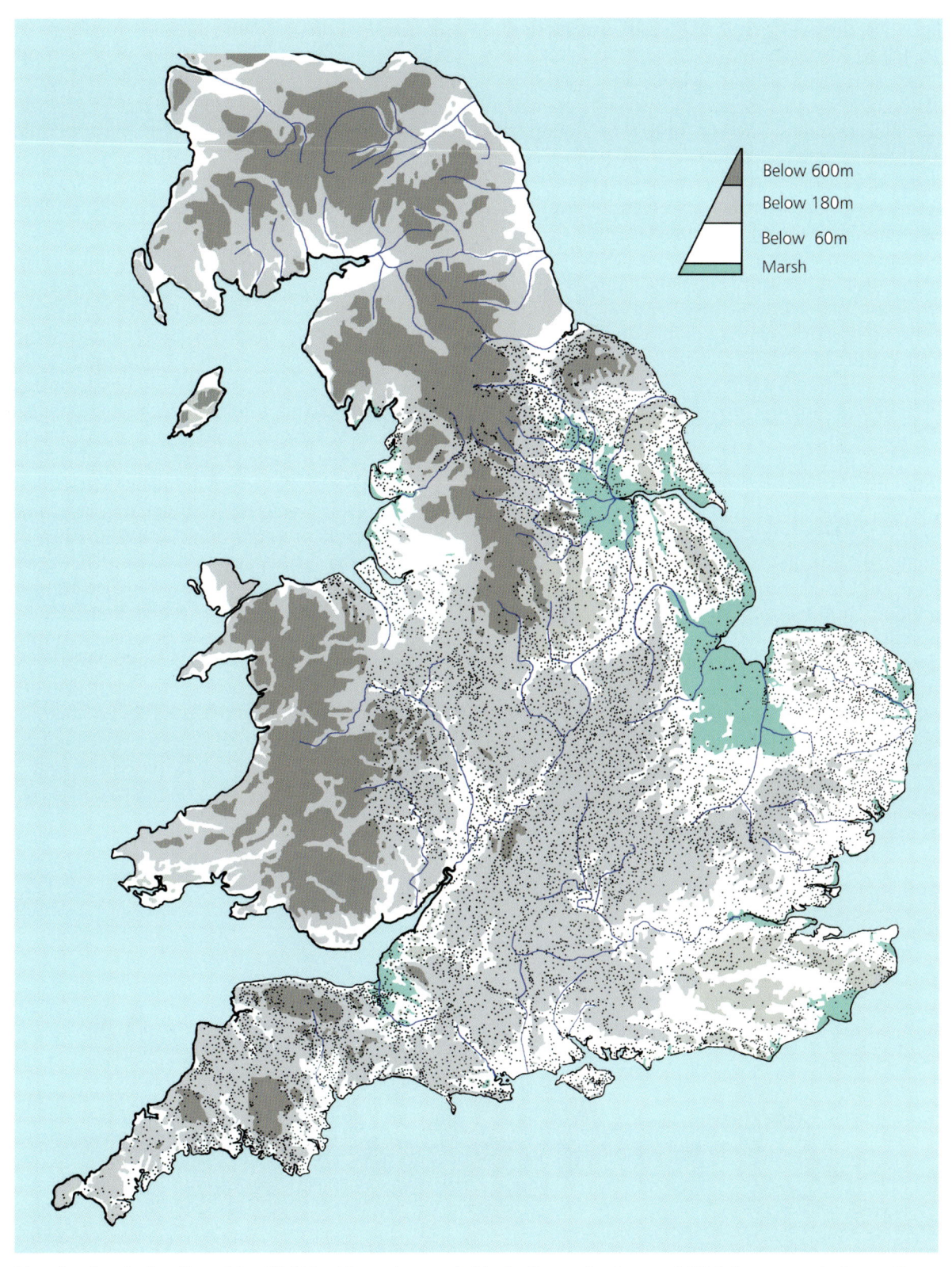

Map showing the location of the 13,418 settlements recorded in the Domesday Survey of 1086. Some areas in the north-west were not completed but the overall coverage is remarkable and provides a background against which we can look at the PAS finds. (Image: Kevin Leahy)

THE PORTABLE ANTIQUITIES SCHEME: AN OVERVIEW

Post Medieval Period AD 1540-onwards: 154,000 Records

'Post Medieval' is an odd term, used by archaeologists to describe the period between the Reformation (of the mid-16th century) and the present day. The period is a long one, and saw massive change, especially in terms of human thought and technology. The Dissolution of the Monasteries, 1536-41, led to fundamental changes in society. The old order, which (for all its corruption) had provided for the poor and sick, was gone, and the beautiful church buildings that had dominated the towns and countryside were destroyed. Henry VIII's sale of the monasteries released large amounts of land and capital which led to a quickening of the economy.

The printing press was undoubtedly influential, enabling public consumption of written works (both old and new) that both reaffirmed and challenged traditional thinking; much like the Internet has done today. Those who protested (Protestants) against 'the old religion' (Catholicism) believed that religious practice had obscured the word of God, and they sought to cleanse churches of the objects that distracted clear thinking; many Medieval religious objects found by detectorists might have entered the ground at this time. Whilst England only experienced a short time as a republic – the Commonwealth of England (1649-59) – the scars of the English Civil War (that led to this period of rule without a king) are found across the country. Charles I was the last king to believe he had a divine right to rule, and paid the price with his head! His son, and namesake (Charles II) oversaw the Restoration of the monarchy (in 1660), and objects from that time not only celebrate his coronation but also the king's reputation as the party-loving 'merry monarch'.

Technological advances saw the introduction of machine-made coins (in 1662), and a large increase in the number of machine-made objects. Most of this modern material, unless unusual, does not interest archaeologists, but the PAS database does include over 4,500 objects of more modern date. It can be tricky for the FLOs working for the PAS to decide what (and what not) to record, especially as it is apparent that the junk of today may be of interest to people in the future, and it is likely that we do not know as much about the recent past as we think we do. Such decisions are guided by their local knowledge of the past, an understanding of the rarity of certain artefact types, and new directions in archaeological research. People who record their finds with the PAS are helping to set new directions in research and taking us into previously unconsidered areas of the past.

Whitby Abbey, North Yorkshire, is typical of the great monastic houses that were dissolved and substantially destroyed at the time of the English Reformation. (Image: Michael Lewis)

THE PORTABLE ANTIQUITIES SCHEME: AN OVERVIEW

Silver medallion commemorating Charles I's return to London after his Scottish Coronation in 1633. This shows a view over the city from the south with the old Saint Paul's cathedral (lost in the Great Fire of 1666) and London Bridge with its covering of buildings and traitors' heads on pikes. The course of the Thames, from which so many finds have come, is clearly shown. (Image: Kevin Leahy)

The Industrial Revolution led to a massive increase in manufacturing production as evidenced by these blast furnaces, dated to 1780 and 1818, at Morley Park, Derbyshire. The massive quantity of material resulting from this expansion lies outside the limit of PAS recording: the PAS is selective in recording Post Medieval finds. (Image: Kevin Leahy)

Chapter 2
Dress Fittings

BROOCHES

After coins and buckles, brooches are the most common objects found – by 2017, the PAS had recorded 42,000 of them. While nowadays brooches are purely decorative, in the past they were much more significant, forming a vital part of dress, holding clothing in place. Variations in brooch design and decoration has led to them being studied in detail, making it possible to date many of them. Brooches are useful for understanding changes in the way people were attired and fashions in dress. When worn, they conveyed messages about the wearer, showing their social status and ethnicity. Fine, highly decorated brooches reflected wearer's wealth and status. Brooches were sometimes characteristic of different peoples; a Viking woman, for example, could be recognised by her brooches, as much as by her style of dress. The distribution of brooch finds recorded by the PAS allows us to look at where particular groups of people settled. Brooches show the styles of art characteristic of their period and also carry symbolic messages, now lost to us.

Brooches come in two basic forms: the bow brooch, with a sprung pin like a modern safety pin, and annular and penannular types, in which the cloth was pulled through a ring and then caught on the pin. In the case of the latter, pulling the cloth back locks the pin against the ring, ensuring a secure attachment.

Pre-Roman

The PAS had recorded over 3,200 Iron Age brooches by 2017, a small number in comparison to the 28,000 recorded from the much shorter Roman period (about 600 years compared with 367 years). This could reflect the quickening of the economy brought about by the Romans, although brooch numbers appear to have been increasing in the years prior to the Roman Conquest. Iron Age brooches are widespread, but they seem most common in eastern and southern Britain, areas occupied by important pre-Roman tribes. The terms 'Hallstatt' and 'La Tène' refer to Continental sub-divisions of the Iron Age.

Roman brooches recovered from a Lincolnshire site. Brooches were common in the 1st and 2nd centuries but become less frequent in later centuries. (Image: Kevin Leahy)

DRESS FITTINGS

WILT-9C4C4A, 46mm, Wylye, Wiltshire (400-200 BC)
Iron Age brooch of La Tène I type. Its up-turned foot is not joined to the bow, a feature of early La Tène brooches. The brooch was made from a single piece of bronze, one end of which was hammered out to form a wire spring.

HAMP-24E208, 49mm, Soberton, Hampshire (150-50 BC)
Middle to Late Iron Age bow brooch, which seems to copy the form of an early Iron Age, Hallstatt 'leech-shaped brooch'. The way in which its foot curves up to join the bow on this brooch suggests a later date.

YORYM-6C1BCA, 52mm, Yapham, East Yorkshire (200-1 BC)
With their broken-backed appearance La Tène II 'involute' brooches are a strange type, this is an excellent example being both complete and having scrolled Celtic decoration on its foot plate. These brooches are widely, but thinly, spread throughout England, but with a concentration in graves in East Yorkshire.

YORYM-1AE283, 66mm, Rowley, East Yorkshire (AD 25-100)
A late Iron Age brooch of La Tène III type, its upturned foot absorbed into the catch plate. It is interesting to see the way in which objects like these brooches evolve over time.

BH-B9AD33, 31mm, Braughing, Hertfordshire (100 BC-100 AD)
Penannular brooches, such as this, are marked by a gap in the ring through which the pin passes. The ring was then twisted to lock the brooch and secure the cloth. These brooches appear to pre-date the simpler annular type.

Roman

The Roman Conquest brought a phenomenal increase in the use of brooches, with over 28,000 examples of this period on the PAS database. It seems incredible that so many brooches came to be lost, but this number must be seen in the context of the length of the Roman occupation of Britain (367 years) which gives a loss rate of 76 brooches per year, from a population that may have been as high as four million. Even if we take account of brooches not being used consistently throughout the Roman period, the number of these, being easily lost objects, is not unreasonable. The distribution of Roman brooches does not appear to have been random, with some types being concentrated in certain areas; this might represent tribal areas that survived as civitas (administrative districts) into the Roman period.

DRESS FITTINGS

WILT-CE93D8, 34mm, East Ilsley, Berkshire (43-70)
Bow brooches of Hod Hill type were a Continental brooch type brought into Britain by the Romans in AD 43. Despite their early date they are widely distributed through lowland Britain.

LVPL-51A341, 73mm, Sandbach, Cheshire (43-65)
Oddly, for a Roman brooch, this fine example of dolphin type had an iron pin which might have been a replacement. These brooches are fairly common and widespread across England with concentrations in Lincolnshire and Norfolk.

YORYM-1DEC97, 50mm, Darrington, West Yorkshire (75-200)
As is often the case, the eponymous headstud is missing from this brooch, instead represented by its seating and a hole. This brooch type has a hinged pin rather than a coiled spring. Headstud brooches are particularly common in Lincolnshire and up into East Yorkshire, the areas of the Corieltauvi and Parisi Iron Age tribes, which became Roman civitas.

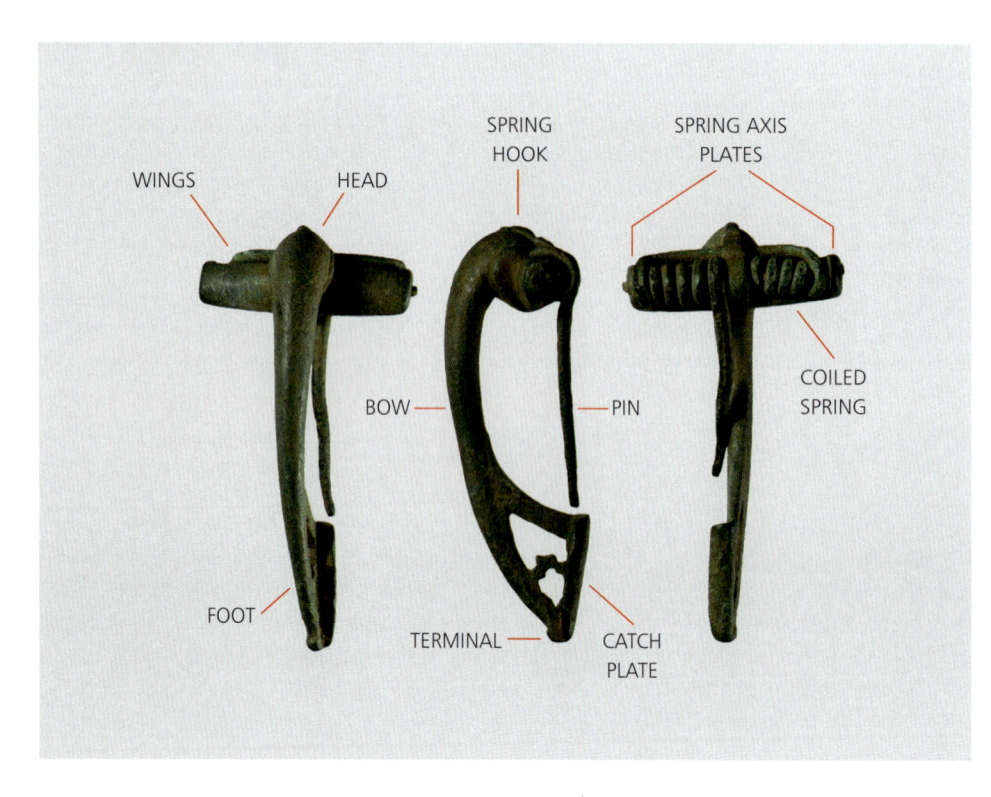

BH-DA5013, 57mm, Milton under Wychwood, Oxfordshire (43-100)
Brooches of Polden Hill type are characterised by their coiled pin springs seated beneath a grooved cross bar. This spring was secured by a bar running through perforated plates on each end of the wings. The PAS data shows these brooches to be concentrated in the West Midlands and Welsh Marches with an odd outlying cluster in Suffolk.

Labels: WINGS, HEAD, SPRING HOOK, SPRING AXIS PLATES, BOW, PIN, COILED SPRING, FOOT, TERMINAL, CATCH PLATE

DRESS FITTINGS

LVPL-1FD141, 73mm, Bickley, Cheshire (25-60)
Bow brooches of Colchester type were in use during the time of the Roman Conquest and headed a series of developments in brooch design.

HAMP-FFB09A, 50mm, Winchester, Hampshire (75-175)
Trumpet brooches are a British type and are often highly decorated; this example bears traces of tin plating. These are one of the most common brooch types with over 3,000 being recorded. Most come from Lincolnshire and Yorkshire, although they are also frequently found in the western counties of England.

WAW-10D806, 54mm, near Evesham, Worcestershire (60-80)
This fine, tin-plated brooch is what is known as an 'Aesica type' taking its name from a fort on Hadrian's wall. Many Roman brooches have been named after sites where they were first recognised such as the 'Colchester type' or from a distinguishing feature: 'trumpet brooch'.

WMID-DDA2BD, 73mm, Loppington, Shropshire (320-400)
Crossbow brooches are of a late Roman type, which seems to have been associated with army officers and civil servants. Some include the use of screw threads, which were rarely seen in antiquity.

WILT-212A28, 27mm, Deverills, Wiltshire (40-400)
Penannular brooches were used in Iron Age Britain and remained in use into the early Roman period, after which they passed out of use. They reappear in the 4th century, perhaps as a native revival. Widespread, they are more common in the north with a small concentration in the south of Lincolnshire.

DRESS FITTINGS

YORYM-1BB5BA, 34mm, Kilham, East Yorkshire (100-300)
With its original gilding, this brooch would have been a striking object. A strand of beads may have been attached to the loop and linked to another brooch. Despite differences in appearance, the pin mechanism on the underside of plate brooches is similar to that found on bow brooches. Plate brooches are most common in East Anglia but are found elsewhere.

NMGW-6A45F4, 30mm, Bronington, Wrexham (100-300)
Oval brooches are not uncommon but rarely retain their glass setting. In this case the surviving setting contains a glass copy of an intaglio gem stone showing a standing figure and a tree.

DOR-8A9B68, 45mm, Puddletown, Dorset (100-300)
Pieces of multi-coloured millefiori glass were used to produce an intricate design on the face of this plate brooch.

SOM-7ED8B2, 40mm, Somerton, Somerset (100-300)
Plate brooches were often inlaid with enamel and many are in the form of birds and animals; this brooch represents a two-headed monster.

SUR-F4F606, 37mm, Harting, West Sussex (100-300)
Enamel decorated chicken brooch. We can only wonder if the bird was associated with the god Mercury or was just for fun?

SWYOR-0E2A45, 35mm, Spofforth with Stockeld, North Yorkshire (100-300)
Originally tinned, this lion brooch would have had a silvery appearance. Traces of an iron pin survive on its back.

DRESS FITTINGS

WMID-D81166, 28mm, Cranford, Northamptonshire (100-300)
Enamel inlaid axe brooch. These are known from all over the Roman Empire and may have been related to religious cults.

SWYOR-4B5519, 58mm, Misterton, Nottinghamshire (100-300)
Dragonesque brooches are Celtic (Iron Age) in inspiration. They are widespread, but most common in East and South Yorkshire. These brooches operated in an unusual way: unlike the pins on bow and penannular brooches, their pin was twisted around one of the narrow necks and passed through the cloth, before being hooked through the other neck.

Early Medieval

The Early Anglo-Saxon period is dominated by cemeteries where the dead were buried with grave goods. During this time the deceased were interred fully clothed, showing how brooches were worn and who was wearing them. Early Anglo-Saxon brooches seem to represent national dress, with Anglian women wearing cruciform brooches and Saxon women preferring circular varieties. It is a difference which ends in the 7th century, after which brooches became smaller and more uniform, and pins were more commonly used to secure clothing. This change was perhaps due to Continental influence that came with Christianity. Dressed burial came to an end around 670 with objects no longer appearing in graves, and archaeologists have to rely on stray finds, along with scant evidence from manuscript illuminations and other art. The Middle Anglo-Saxon period, saw the formation of the Christian Anglo-Saxon kingdoms, such as East Anglia, Kent, Mercia, Northumbria and Wessex. The Viking conquest of much of England, around 878, marks the start of the Late Anglo-Saxon period. This disaster, and the subsequent re-conquest of the Danelaw by the kings of Wessex, heralded what has been described as a Golden Age; England was prosperous and stable, although the Vikings continued to be a nuisance. The abrupt end of the Anglo-Saxon state came with the Norman Conquest of 1066, though, for most people, life continued much as before: trudging through the mud behind the plough, the view of the oxen's back-sides would have remained depressingly familiar.

Cruciform Brooches

These cross-shaped brooches have nothing to do with Christianity; their form is derived from knobs fitted to the ends of a pin holding the coiled spring in place. Cruciform brooches developed over time from small, simple brooches to large, highly decorated forms bearing the strange disjointed animals of the so-called Anglo-Saxon 'Style I', zoomorphic art. In contrast to the copper-alloy pins and springs on Roman brooches, the fittings on Anglo-Saxon brooches were made from iron. In graves, cruciform brooches, great square-headed brooches and small long brooches are usually found with the 'foot' uppermost. As the decoration only appears coherent when the brooch is viewed with the wings and knobs at the top (as shown below) it is possible that they were to be primarily enjoyed by the wearer, not the spectator. There are over 2,000 cruciform brooches on the PAS database with a distribution that extends from East Anglia up into Yorkshire and Northumberland and across into the East Midlands but with an outlying group in Kent.

The excavation of the grave of a 6th century Anglian woman at Walesby, Lincolnshire. She was wearing a pair of annular brooches, one on each shoulder, to support her gown. In the middle of her chest is a large cruciform brooch. A pair of sleeve clasps can be seen on her right wrist. (Image: Kevin Leahy)

DRESS FITTINGS

NMS-0E8C32, 64mm, Scole, Norfolk (400-450)
Its small size and the round-sectioned knob show this brooch to be early. The two side knobs, originally on the ends of the iron bar holding the spring, have become detached and lost.

NMS-D48874, 14mm, Loddon, Norfolk (400-450)
Detached knob from a cruciform brooch; the iron pin passed through the hole along its length and the groove fitted over the edge of the brooch's head plate. The knob's flattened D-section shows it to have been a later type.

SF-3C3EF6, 95mm, Barham, Suffolk (475-525)
A more developed cruciform brooch; the foot, in the form of an animal head, has expanded with scroll-shaped nostrils and the D-sectioned knobs are now cast in one piece with the head plate.

NMS-60A394, 94mm, Great Cressingham, Norfolk (500-550)
The development of the cruciform brooch continues with the addition, below the arched bow, of two eagle head 'lappets'. The use of stamp marks is a common feature on Early Anglo-Saxon metalwork.

SF-464732, 28mm, Kenninghall, Norfolk (520-570)
Knob from a late cruciform brooch. Some late brooches still had separately cast knobs. The knob was aligned by loops on its underside which slipped over pins on the sides of the brooch.

DRESS FITTINGS

FAKL-BD5E61, 154mm, North Kesteven, Lincolnshire (520-570)
Cruciform brooches became increasingly large and flamboyant with the addition of 'lappets' and expanded knobs. This large 'florid' brooch was gilded and bears silver appliqués. Cast in one piece, it is decorated in a devolved version of Anglo-Saxon Style I animal art.

Small Long Brooches
These brooches appear to have been simplified versions of the larger cruciform and great square-headed brooches. They were worn in pairs and secured a woman's tubular dress at the shoulders, the weight of her skirt being taken by a belt. Over 1,400 small long brooches are recorded on the PAS database and show a similar distribution to that of cruciform brooches.

YORYM-C33D41, 71mm, Driffield, East Yorkshire (400-520)
This small long brooch has simple, incised, decoration. While common on Early Medieval metalwork, ring and dot decoration was also used in other periods.

DRESS FITTINGS

CAM-FC9EE2, 71mm, Longstanton, Cambridgeshire (400-520)
This small long brooch appears to have been based on a great square-headed brooch but is undecorated.

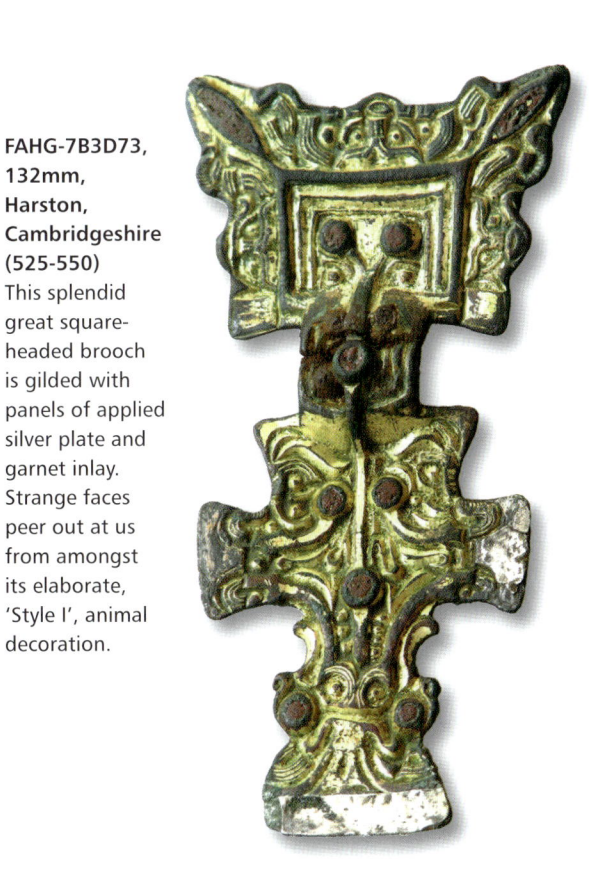

LIN-4EB8E0, 79mm, Greetham area, Lincolnshire (400-520)
A common type of small long brooch, decorated with rows of small, semi-circular, stamp impressions.

Great Square-Headed Brooches

Such brooches are considered the pinnacle, or (depending on taste) the depths, of Early Anglo-Saxon brooch design. Often gilded and decorated with devolved animals they can be striking objects. Great square-headed brooches are much less common than other brooches, with only around 250 of them on the PAS database. They are widespread, but with a concentration of finds in East Anglia which extends across into the Midlands. Each Anglo-Saxon cemetery usually contains only a few of them, suggesting they were just worn by members of principal families, perhaps only the matriarch in each generation.

FAHG-7B3D73, 132mm, Harston, Cambridgeshire (525-550)
This splendid great square-headed brooch is gilded with panels of applied silver plate and garnet inlay. Strange faces peer out at us from amongst its elaborate, 'Style I', animal decoration.

NCL-82EDE3, 136mm, Tanby, North Yorkshire (510-550)
Cruder version of a great square-headed brooch, with greatly simplified decoration.

DRESS FITTINGS

FAKL-0F4D67, 122mm, North Kesteven, Lincolnshire (525-570)
Despite the flamboyant decoration on the face of this great square-headed brooch, the fittings for the pin and spring are typically small and insubstantial; hardly looking strong enough to support the brooch, let alone hold clothing in place.

Circular Brooches

While cruciform and small long brooches were concentrated in the east, north and midlands (the areas of England settled by Angles) the Saxons (in the south) preferred circular brooches, like the saucer and button brooches. As with small long brooches, circular brooches were worn in pairs on the shoulders or breast. The pin mechanism on these was usually made of iron and consisted of the same safety pin arrangement as was used on cruciform brooches.

BERK-B4ED99, 35mm, Dorchester, Oxfordshire (400-450)
This decorative foil was originally soldered on the face of an applied brooch. It was made using a *Pressblech* die (see page 227).

SUR-1C82C9, 44mm, Long Compton, Warwickshire (500-550)
Typical saucer brooch, with raised rim and gilded Anglo-Saxon Style I animal decoration. While highly stylised, it is possible see a beast's head at 12 o'clock.

NCL-08F6E7, 56mm, Catterick, North Yorkshire (500-600)
Applied brooches are not well represented amongst PAS records. Cut from sheet metal they are fragile and failed to survive in the ground. They predated saucer brooches but remained in use alongside them.

42

DRESS FITTINGS

WMID-CE6945, 46mm, Ryton on Dunsmore, Warwickshire (475-550)
This saucer brooch bears geometric, rather than animal decoration. Unlike the sheet metal applied brooches, saucer brooches were cast in one piece, with the decoration, pin fittings and dished rim already in place.

WILT-947963, 41mm, Salisbury, Wiltshire (475-550)
While it resembles basketwork, some features of this saucer brooch, like the 'jaws' and pellet 'eye' at 12 o'clock suggest that it was based on a zoomorphic design.

BERK-BE69FE, 31mm, Souldern, Oxfordshire (475-525)
The decoration on this brooch is based on a ring of running spirals, a motif commonly seen on saucer brooches.

HAMP-914D62, 21mm, Soberton, Hampshire (450-550)
Button brooches look like small versions of saucer brooches, but finds from graves show that while saucer brooches were worn in pairs, button brooches were usually worn singly. The glowering, moustached face, is typical of them.

SUR-D3EF81, 17.2mm, Whitchurch, Hampshire (450-550)
A more stylised face can be seen on this button brooch, and its pin fittings seem very robust.

BERK-725B84, 28mm, Boxford, West Berkshire (500-570)
A disc brooch showing the use of cast, moulded decoration. The iron pin is marked by rust marks on the back.

IOW-1654A1, 26mm, Calbourne, Isle of Wight (500-570)
Disc brooches like this are distinguished by their restrained decoration, stamped or incised onto the surface. Notching is common around their edges and many examples were tin plated.

DRESS FITTINGS

YORYM-866606, 53mm, Riccall, North Yorkshire (590-670)
This jewelled 'keystone' brooch was the 12th example of its class to be found but the first one from outside Kent, and the first to be made of gilt copper-alloy rather than gilded silver. The empty cell in the centre originally contained a white material, probably sea-shell.

YORYM-285423, 51mm, Naburn, North Yorkshire (450-550)
Openwork brooches are mainly found in the midlands but northern examples are known. The swastika is an ancient sun symbol which only took on its more sinister meaning in the 20th century.

Annular and Penannular Brooches

These brooches had a long history stretching back into the Iron Age. They are simple in shape but highly effective, holding the cloth much more securely than the 'safety pin' bow brooches. Annular brooches were commonly used in Medieval England. Penannular brooches were not used, although they remained fashionable in Ireland and Scotland. While they are frequently found in Anglo-Saxon graves, the PAS has, surprisingly, only recorded 56 Early Medieval annular brooches. It is possible that their fragile nature has given them a poor survival rate in the plough soil. Penannular brooches are still less common finds.

YORYM-507065, 26mm, Brantingham, East Yorkshire (575-640)
Annular brooches decorated with opposed animal heads occur in Kent and the north-east of England suggesting links between the two regions.

SF-965DBD, 19mm, Hilborough, Norfolk (475-570)
This annular brooch is decorated with incised stab marks. Annular brooches are most common in Anglian areas of eastern England, but are known as far west as the upper Thames valley and up into Yorkshire.

LEIC-B8E5C1, 42mm, Hickling, Nottinghamshire (475-570)
Annular brooch with an oval-sectioned ring and moulded decoration, its iron pin is missing. These brooches were worn in pairs at the shoulders to support a tubular gown (see page 38).

IOW-4ECBF1, 24mm, Calbourne, Isle of Wight (400-700)
Like the following example, this penannular brooch is of British type representing a survival of native culture after the arrival of the Anglo-Saxons. It bears traces of enamel inlay.

DRESS FITTINGS

FAKL-A05256, 73mm, Hooton Pagnell, South Yorkshire (400-700)
This penannular brooch was originally inlaid with enamel. It is of British (Welsh) type and suggests the survival of the original population after the arrival of the Anglo-Saxons. These brooches are most common in Lincolnshire, where there is other evidence for a Celtic survival.

Strip and Ansate Brooches

These brooches date from the Middle Anglo-Saxon period. Strip brooches can be traced back into the 7th century. Many are plain and difficult to date, particularly as they are not found in graves. Ansate brooches are a northern European type and can be dated by Continental finds.

CAM-A4DEEE, 55mm, Folksworth and Washingley, Cambridgeshire (720-820)
This is an interesting example of a gilt copper-alloy strip brooch. Many of these brooches are plain, but the decoration on this example allows it to be dated to the middle part of the Early Medieval period.

DENO-3FD883, 57mm, Perlethorpe cum Budby, Nottinghamshire (720-820)
Plain strip brooches were once assigned to earlier periods, but are now believed to be of Middle Anglo-Saxon date.

HAMP-CEBED7, 52mm, Wellow, Hampshire (720-820)
This gilded strip brooch bears a finely executed animal surrounded by interlace, a style typical of the 8th century. The spring, pin and catch plate were cast in one piece with the brooch.

DRESS FITTINGS

NMS-DC2A2E, 40mm, Raynham, Norfolk (720-850)
Middle Anglo-Saxon ansate brooch, of a type which originated in northern Europe. The PAS has recorded over 300 of these brooches, with finds focused in East Anglia, Lincolnshire and up into Yorkshire.

NMS-2F75FB, 47mm, Fincham, Norfolk (650-750)
Further example of the wide range of ansate brooches being found in England, reflecting trade across the North Sea.

DUR-6E265A, 54mm, Upper Poppleton, North Yorkshire (700-900)
Ornate ansate brooch set with silver studs.

Late Anglo-Saxon Brooches

The Late Anglo-Saxon period saw the continued use of disc brooches, which illustrated manuscripts show being worn by men.

Brooches of this period include small disc brooches bearing the figure of a lion – these appear crude, but the lion is generally surrounded by 28 pellets suggesting that this was an important number. These brooches are an East Anglian type, but occur as far north as York. Lead brooches come in a range of styles and were probably based on silver originals, which have not survived. It has been recently suggested these brooches typify London fashion that then became popular elsewhere. A delightful feature of the Late Anglo-Saxon period is a series of gilt copper-alloy brooches with cloisonné enamel inlay. The PAS has recorded over 500 Late Anglo-Saxon brooches, which are widespread but with an emphasis on eastern England.

YORYM-B664E6, 27mm, Paull, East Yorkshire (900-1100)
There appears to have been a fashion for lead jewellery in the Late Anglo-Saxon and early Anglo-Norman periods with both brooches and strap ends being made. The PAS has recorded over 80 Late Anglo-Saxon lead brooches with most finds coming from Norfolk, Lincolnshire and East Yorkshire.

LIN-0D8085, 41mm, Bardney, Lincolnshire (900-1065)
It has been suggested these were models used in the making of copper-alloy brooches, but this example bears traces of its iron pin showing that it was used as a brooch.

DRESS FITTINGS

LON-C39171, 26mm, Harrietsham, Kent (900-1100)
Early Medieval cloisonné enamel brooches bear a superficial resemblance to Roman enamel brooches, but there are important differences: on Anglo-Saxon brooches the enamel is set in cloisonné cells separated by narrow walls, whilst Roman brooches use champlevé enamel with the glass laid in cast cells.

NLM-01ECC1, 26mm, Broughton, North Lincolnshire (900-1100)
Fine polychrome late Saxon brooch of the Saunderton type, the most commonly found in England. The PAS has recorded 90 of these brooches which are widespread through England.

SUR-AB3160, 40mm, Effingham, Surrey (900-1100)
A remarkable piece of enamel work depicting a face. Like many of these brooches, it was gilded. On its back are fittings for the pin and a loop which may have been for a safety cord.

Viking Brooches

These can be recognised by their decoration, which is in characteristic Scandinavian style, and in some cases by their shape, with trefoil and lozenge forms being immediately recognisable. Viking brooches are important as they show the movement of Scandinavian peasant women into England during the late 9th and early 10th centuries, indicating that the Danelaw involved the arrival of settlers and was not just a military conquest. More than 50 Viking brooches have been recorded by the PAS, most of which come from Lincolnshire, Norfolk, and Yorkshire, areas of known Viking settlement. The styles of Viking metalwork have been defined by modern scholars, not by the Vikings, and are named from places where objects in these styles were found; for example, the Jellinge style is named after the designs on a small silver cup from the royal site of Jelling, Denmark.

NMS-53A3B4, 30mm, Burnham Market, Norfolk (900-1000)
Viking brooch with Terslev decoration. Interestingly, the metalwork in England continued to follow the changing fashions seen in Scandinavia.

LIN-F00E1B, 28mm, Tetney, Lincolnshire (900-950)
Viking brooch decorated in the Jellinge style, showing two, typical S-shaped intertwined animals. The additional loop fitting on the back of the brooch is often seen on Viking brooches.

DRESS FITTINGS

WILT-9A5AE7, 59mm, Longbridge Deverill, Wiltshire (875-950)
Fine Viking trefoil brooch decorated in the Borre style, upon which some animals' heads can be seen. Trefoil brooches were based on Carolingian horse harness fittings which the Vikings adopted and adapted as brooches for their womenfolk.

NMS-E84328, 27mm, Caistor St Edmund, Norfolk (900-1000)
Viking brooch bearing three Borre style animals' heads. The deep dome of this brooch suggests that it might be an import from Scandinavia rather than a local, Anglo-Scandinavian, copy, which tend to be flat, rather than domed.

LEIC-A43E83, 41mm, West Barkwith, Lincolnshire (850-950)
The oak-leaf design on this Viking trefoil brooch is a much devolved version of Carolingian acanthus leaf decoration.

CAM-371E87, 32mm, Weston Colville, Cambridgeshire (900-950)
An openwork disc brooch decorated in the Jelling style.

NMS-5A6FD9, 27mm, Shipmeadow, Suffolk (900-1000)
Viking lozenge brooch, with each arm ending in a typical Borre style animal head.

BERK-39FCC8, 22mm, Wantage, Oxfordshire (924-39)
Brooches made from silver coins were only gilded on the display side, as on this example made from a penny of King Athelstan.

WILT-C94353, 19mm, Nether Wallop, Hampshire (1050-53)
The reverse of this brooch, made from a penny of Edward the Confessor, retains part of the mechanism that held the pin.

DRESS FITTINGS

Medieval

Brooches in the Middle Ages take a wide variety of forms, with those of copper-alloy and pewter imitating (with varying degrees of success) those of precious metal, particularly silver; some of these might have been gilded. Nowadays these base-metal brooches look tarnished, but when first made they would have appeared more like those copied. Most common are annular brooches, but also recorded with the PAS are brooches made from coins (a phenomenon of the Late Anglo-Saxon and Anglo-Norman periods). The PAS has recorded over 3,500 Medieval brooches. These are widespread, but are most common in the populous lowland zone to the south and east of a line from the Humber to Severn. Many Medieval brooches bore inscriptions; these were often pious, such as the popular 'AVE MARIA' (Hail Mary) legend, but some took the everyday world for inspiration; a particular favourite is a 13th century brooch from Writtle, which bears an inscription translated as 'I am a brooch to guard the breast, so that no ruffian may put his hand there'.

IOW-506491, 19mm, Arreton, Isle of Wight (1400-1500)
On this chunky brooch is a star with letters between each point reading 'bien va', meaning 'be well'.

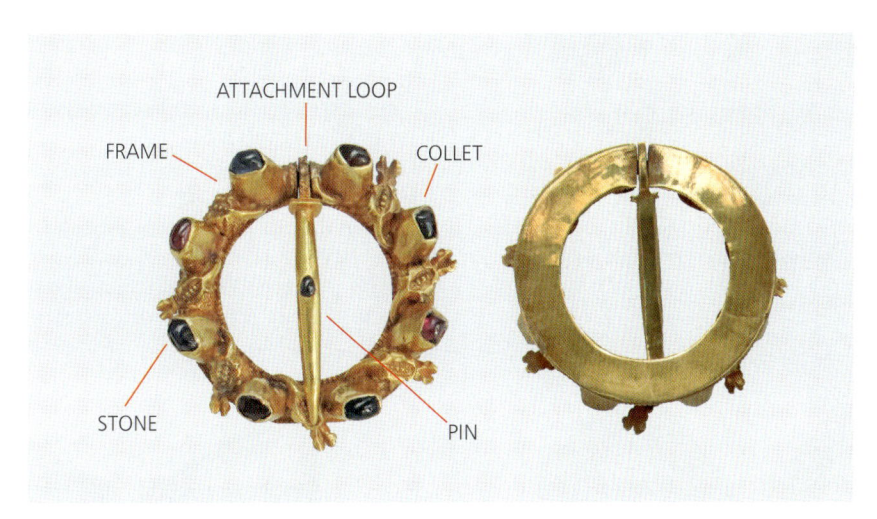

LVPL-039CF2, 41mm, Manchester (1280-1320)
Gold annular brooch, probably French in origin, with collets, each containing a red garnet or blue sapphire. It has been suggested this ornate form of annular brooch represents the fruit of the broom (*Genista sagittalis*) adopted as a badge by Geoffrey of Anjou (1113-51), the father of Henry II.

KENT-964818, 23mm, Little Chart, Kent (1250-1400)
The collets on this brooch contain enamel instead of stones and form an eight-pointed star.

NMGW-9C3A27, 22mm, Penllyn, Vale of Glamorgan (1427-34)
This annular coin brooch is of later date than most, being cut from a groat of Henry VI minted at Calais.

DRESS FITTINGS

LON-05FA00, 30mm, City of London (1200-1400)
Lead brooches, such as this, are unusual discoveries. This example is inscribed with the first words of the Ave Maria prayer, in veneration of the Virgin Mary.

LIN-9A4B26, 17mm, Kirton in Holland, Lincolnshire (1200-1400)
In the form of clasped hands, this gold annular brooch has a nonsensical inscription: VILVIVILIVLI.

IOW-336352, 27mm, Brighstone, Isle of Wight (1300-1400)
Silver annular brooch of quatrefoil form which gives the names of the magi (three wise men) in Lombardic script. IACEPARMELCHIORBALTASA (Jaspar, Melchior, Balthasar). It is interesting that its reverse (the non-display side) is also decorated.

WILT-CFEC24, 19mm, St Paul Malmesbury Without, Wiltshire (1200-1400)
This silver, star-shaped, brooch is full of meaning. One of its sides is inscribed: AMOR VINC, for 'love conquers all', and on the other IE SV CI EN, probably for 'I am here in the place of a friend'. The second legend suggests this might have been a love gift, though it also invokes the name of Christ; IESV is a shortened form for Jesus.

SWYOR-185E03, 17mm, Folkton, North Yorkshire (1250-1400)
Base-metal brooches could be crafted with care, such as this annular brooch of lozenge form. It has decorated bands of square 'dots' and is gilded.

DOR-417FA2, 15mm, Gussage All Saints, Dorset (1200-1400)
Silver-gilt brooch with an unusual, triangular form. The gilding would have been applied as an amalgam of gold and mercury which was heated, evaporating the mercury to leave a thin layer of gold.

SF-2C11E5, 46mm, Stanstead, Suffolk (1200-1400)
This rectangular brooch, perhaps used as a buckle, has upon it a prayer for the Virgin Mary which appears to be blundered; AVE MARIA RIAS PR (rossette) MEL, which does not make sense. It shows craftsmen of such items might not necessarily understand the words they wrote.

Post Medieval and Later

A wide variety of Post Medieval brooches were made, both in terms of form and decoration, as well as the materials and techniques used. Brooches ceased to be only functional, being replaced by buttons. This meant that brooches became lighter and purely decorative.

With the Reformation, religious images and inscriptions went out of use. Wire became more widely available, as did the use of sheet metal decorated by pressing. The PAS is selective in recording modern items, but an array of base-metal alloy brooches occur in the examples recorded, though few (mostly only items of potential Treasure) have been scientifically tested.

IOW-78B105, 25mm, Shorwell, Isle of Wight (1500-1600)
The form of this silver annular brooch harks back to the Middle Ages, only its stamp (taken to be the maker's mark) - EL - shows it to be of more recent manufacture.

NLM-91300B, 26mm, Hibaldstow, North Lincolnshire (1820-80)
This leaf-shaped brooch has the remains of the lugs for a hinged pin and a groove for the catch plate. Its central setting, perhaps glass or a semi-precious gem, is missing.

NLM-451F2E, 23mm, Bottesford, North Lincolnshire (1850-1900)
Originally, this brooch was extremely gaudy. It shows a cross, thought to represent a flower garden, composed of glass tiles and millefiori inlay: perhaps millefiori (meaning 'thousands of flowers') was used intentionally because of the dual meaning. Solder marks on the back show the position of the pin.

DUR-FD8848, 41mm, Ferryhill, County Durham (1942-1943)
This brooch bears the insignia of the 8th Kings Royal Irish Hussars but has a clasp in the form of a riding crop which, with the use of sterling silver, suggests that it is a 'sweetheart brooch' worn as a keepsake of a soldier serving in the regiment in World War II.

DRESS FITTINGS

BUCKLES

Buckles are common finds, with over 44,000 of them on the PAS database, most of which are simple but can still be dated. Some buckles were used with a plate, but in many cases the strap simply went around the buckle frame. Buckles were sometimes decorated and represented an important item of jewellery, particularly for men, although they were also worn by women. They also had many other roles such as on horse harnesses and baggage. They were used in conjunction with other items of metalwork, particularly strap ends and strap sliders, which secured the loose ends of belts.

Roman

Buckles were introduced into Britain by the Roman army, being used for securing armour and fastening sword belts and do not appear to have been adopted by the civilian population. Early buckles are not common, with fewer than 40 of them on the PAS database. The 4th century saw a massive increase in the use of buckles and related strap ends, with over 220 Late Roman buckles recorded. There has been a great deal of discussion about these items, which are seen as historically important. Decorated with animals' heads, they can be paralleled by finds from the Continent, where they are found along the Rhine-Danube frontier between the Empire and the barbarians to the east. This has led them to be associated with the Roman army, which by

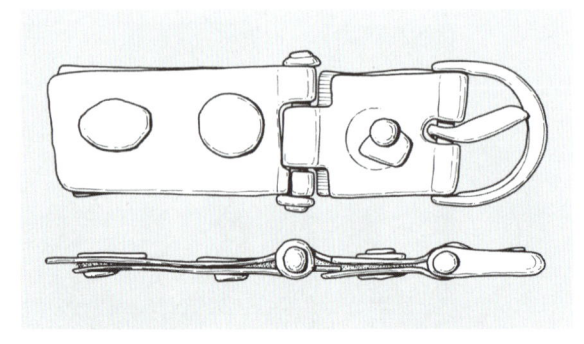

SF-26D9F1, 55mm, Barham (Suffolk, 50-200)
This Early Roman buckle, with its two-part hinged plate, was probably used to secure armour in place (see page 343).

SF-51227A, 36mm, Barnardiston, Suffolk (43-100)
Attached to a buckle plate by a hinge mechanism this buckle is typical of those worn at the time of the Roman Conquest.

LANCUM-117F81, 57mm, Arnside, Cumbria (43-200)
With its leaf and tendril design and enamel inlay this ornate Early Roman buckle plate represents a lovely piece of Classical decoration.

LANCUM-123688, 37mm, Arnside, Cumbria (43-200)
Simple Roman buckle on which the strap went through the T-shaped slot and the pin went around the short bar between the scrolls. Some areas of the buckle show wear through use.

SF-8144A8, 30mm, Worlington, Suffolk (50-150)
Part of a buckle from a Roman soldier's armour. These simple C-shaped buckles can be misdated since they are identical to some Medieval buckles.

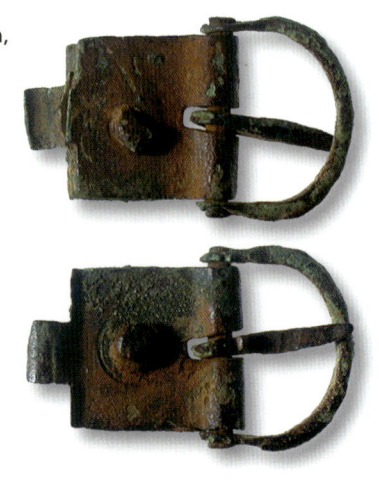

the 4th century, was dominated by Germanic soldiers. The discovery of these buckles in Britain led to the suggestion that Romans had posted Germanic soldiers (*foederati*) in Britannia and it was these men who subsequently rebelled and took control of what became England. Interestingly, the Late Roman buckles recorded by the PAS do not come from the threatened frontier zone along Hadrian's Wall or the vulnerable coastline, but from the lowland zone with its towns and villas. This suggests that these belt fittings were worn, not by frontier troops, but by '*bucellarii*', militias organised by local magnates.

Later Roman

SUSS-FDFE86, 31mm, Amberley, West Sussex (325-425)
Cast in one piece, this is a simplified local copy of a continental buckle on which the loop and plate were made separately. It is possible to make out the animal head decoration.

HAMP-6636CF, 32mm, Ropley Hampshire (325-425)
Elaborate openwork belt plates formed part of late Roman buckle sets. The buckle was attached to the plate by a hinge-like mechanism, with a pin passing through the rings on the end of the plate.

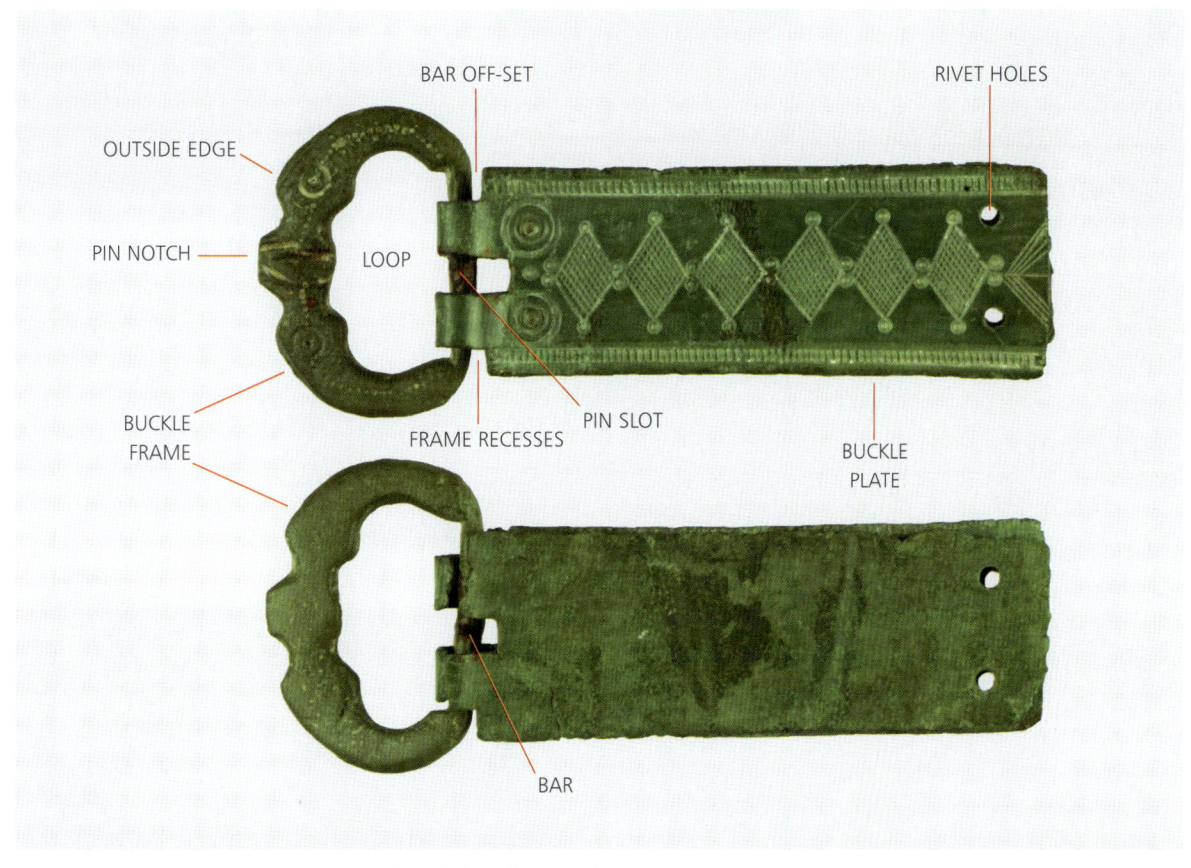

WILT-741DAF, 56mm, Kingston Deverill, Wiltshire (325-425)
The animal head decoration on this Late Roman buckle has been highly simplified, but it was paired with a carefully decorated plate. Buckle plates seldom survive, but this one, with its incised decoration, is typical.

DRESS FITTINGS

HAMP-F6FC56, 42mm, Twyford, Hampshire (325-425)
The two confronted animals forming the loop of this late Roman buckle are based on Continental originals, but the birds sitting on the animals' backs are seen to be a local, British addition, perhaps drawing on Iron Age traditions.

BERK-C9AC82, 43mm, Bourton on the Water, Gloucestershire (325-400)
Clearly local, if not home-made, this copy of a late Roman buckle still reflects a Classical design from the Imperial workshops along the Rhine-Danube frontier.

HAMP-8C3C28, 30mm, Alresford, Hampshire (350-450)
These tiny buckles with horse head decoration are of late Roman type, but are found in the graves of Anglo-Saxon women.

LVPL-71B7F1, 38mm, Horton cum Peel, Cheshire (300-450)
This buckle is a good copy, but the decoration has been cast, not chisel cut, as seen on the Continental originals. Buckles of this type formed part of elaborate, chip carved, belt sets which were worn by officers in the late Roman army and senior civil servants.

BH-996262, 25mm, Ravensden, Bedfordshire (325-400)
The decoration on this object combines two facing, classical, dolphins with horses' heads on top of them.

Early Medieval

The PAS has recorded more than 1,250 Early Medieval buckles made from copper-alloy, iron, silver and gold. These are found in the graves of both Anglo-Saxon men and women, showing them to have been worn by both sexes. Many are plain and simple, making dating difficult, especially if they are not found in an archaeological context. Other buckles are more diagnostic, with some magnificent examples which can be dated by their type, style or decoration. Over 70 Viking and Anglo-Scandinavian buckles have been recorded with the PAS making a useful addition to our knowledge of the use of Viking decoration in England.

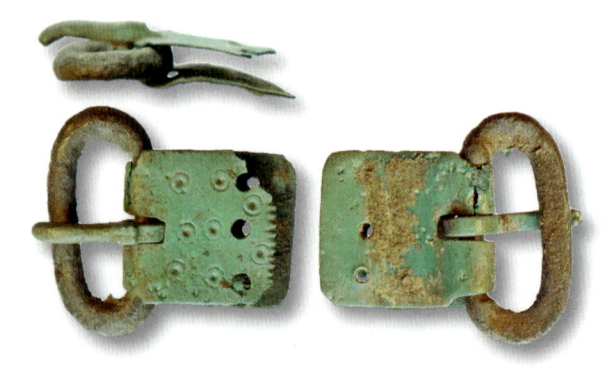

SUR-3B44D7, 20mm, Bletchingley, Surrey (600-850)
Buckle and plate of a simple form, but one that can be assigned to the Anglo-Saxon period. This is the most commonly found type of Early Medieval buckle.

54

DRESS FITTINGS

WILT-81EB00, 37mm, Bremhill, Wiltshire (700-900)
The style of the decoration and the use of enamel suggest that this buckle plate is of Irish origin. There are over 90 Early Medieval Irish objects on the PAS database most of which came into England during the Viking period.

YORYM-BA8B84, 53mm, Cropton, North Yorkshire (600-720)
This 'lyre shaped' buckle plate is Visigothic, being made in Spain by the Germanic peoples who migrated there during the 5th century. It was based on a Late Roman, Byzantine, style and was repaired in antiquity. It is one of three Visigothic buckles recorded on the PAS database and shows contacts with an area not normally associated with Anglo-Saxon England.

PUBLIC-E50572, 35mm, near Kirmington, North Lincolnshire (500-600)
This gilt copper-alloy buckle can be dated by the early Anglo-Saxon style eagles' heads set either side of the bar, as well as the stamp decoration.

PUBLIC-BB0F91, 41mm, Elham, Kent (500-600)
This finely cast Anglo-Saxon buckle is of a type found across western Europe and the Mediterranean from the 5th century onwards. In England, many of them have been discovered in the graves of women. The complex form of the pin is typical.

FAKL-A943E9, 39mm, Skirpenbeck, East Yorkshire (570-670)
Small, but elaborate, Anglo-Saxon buckle, with a buckle plate and pin, set with blue glass. It is not known what the cavity within the plate contained. Buckles with plates bearing three rivets (like this) date from the late 6th into the 7th century.

DRESS FITTINGS

GLO-51DC59, 32mm, Cold Ashton, Gloucestershire (550-650)
Superb Anglo-Saxon, silver-gilt buckle pin, set with cloisonné garnets and blue glass. These stones were laid on gridded gold foils to scatter the light that shone back through the gemstones.

YORYM-245698, 19mm, Saxton with Scarthingwell, North Yorkshire (1000-1100)
Buckle decorated with two highly stylised animals' heads facing each other over the bar. This buckle type appears to have been in use during the 11th century, the animals being in late Viking style.

GLO-20D4FE, 37mm, Churchdown, Gloucestershire (1000-1100)
D-shaped buckle, decorated in a devolved version of the Anglo-Scandinavian Ringerike style. An animal's head can be seen in the middle of the bow.

NMS-75BB29, 34mm, Haveringland, Norfolk (1000-1100)
Buckle bearing a crude interpretation of the Anglo-Scandinavian Ringerike style. Animals' heads, with typical crests, can be seen either side of the buckle bar.

SF-1623C7, 24mm, Risby, Suffolk (1000-1100)
This buckle is decorated with tendrils surrounding an animal characteristic of the Anglo-Scandinavian Urnes style.

WILT-BBDA52, 51mm, Shrewton, Wiltshire (1050-1150)
A remarkable Anglo-Scandinavian buckle and buckle plate with interlace decoration in the Urnes style. Traces of an iron pin can be seen.

Medieval

The PAS has recorded over 26,000 Medieval buckles, making them one of the most commonly found objects. Finds are widespread but concentrated in the eastern counties of England. The variety of buckles produced in the Middle Ages is overwhelming, with those of copper-alloy predominating amongst metal-detector finds. Buckles were used on many types of straps (leather and textile), not just belts, and their sizes vary significantly. Most Medieval buckles seem to be of single loop type and were attached to a plate, to which the strap was riveted.

IOW-FE5D98, 24mm, Godshill, Isle of Wight (1350-1650)
Simple double-looped buckles were used through much of the Middle Ages into the Post Medieval period, and as such are hard to date.

DRESS FITTINGS

IOW-432DD4, 23mm, Newport, Isle of Wight (1250-1450)
Typical of many Medieval buckles is a v-shaped lip on the frame, which served as a rest for the pin.

LEIC-A7A485, 40mm, Beeby, Leicestershire (1250-1400)
Some Medieval buckles had integral plates, such as this one with holes for the rivets so it can be fixed to a strap, perhaps a spur leather.

KENT-29C558, 42mm, Little Chart, Kent (1250-1400)
An interesting feature of this buckle is the roller on the frame, which would have eased the threading of the strap through the frame. This might suggest the strap was textile.

WMID-8939F9, 34mm, Sudborough, Northamptonshire (1350-1400)
Buckle with a plate formed from a single sheet of metal folded around the strap bar. Some buckles had a supporting frame within the plate, but others (like this) lack this feature. This D-shaped buckle frame is cast, but the pin is formed from a small triangular metal sheet.

BH-46E5F7, 33mm, Baldock, Hertfordshire (1200-1300)
Medieval buckle plates lend themselves to be decorated, as on this example showing a relief-moulded bird.

LANCUM-5C5EE5, 52mm, Sleaford, Lincolnshire (1150-1350)
The open-work on the plate of this Medieval buckle bears a remarkable resemblance to some Roman finds recorded by the PAS (see HAMP-6636CF) which has led to some confusion in identification.

LON-FEF449, 37mm, Southwark, London (1400-50)
Lead buckles are not common outside London, where finds from the Thames foreshore are well preserved. This example retains its iron pin, and some of the leather of the strap (hidden within the plate).

57

DRESS FITTINGS

Buckle on a belt in a Medieval painting. The loose end is secured by threading it through the belt. (Image: Michael Lewis)

Post Medieval

During the Post Medieval period it became fashionable (and more practical) to hold the strap in place by threading it through a secondary loop on the buckle: in the Middle Ages the strap was often threaded under the belt, and then left to hang – hence a greater need for strap ends (see below). We therefore see double-loop buckle frames becoming more common; on these types, buckle-plates become superfluous. Buckles on shoes, hats, knee-breeches and neck-stocks, as well as on straps and belts were commonly used at this time. The PAS has recorded 16,000 Post Medieval buckles.

BUC-C67E63, 58mm, Quainton, Buckinghamshire (1550-1650)
While it can be difficult to tell the difference between Late Medieval and Post Medieval double loop buckles those with mouldings, as seen here, are usually Post Medieval.

WMID-9CC53C, 35mm, Queensway, Northamptonshire (1620-80)
Sub-rectangular and trapezoidal buckle frames are a favoured form during the Post Medieval period.

SUR-D30C03, 50mm, Shottesbrooke, Berkshire (1550-1650)
Sometimes decoration can be quite elaborate, such as the use of floral motifs and fleur-de-lys on this cast buckle.

SOM-26B57A, 28mm, Crewkerne, Somerset (1660-1720)
A chape on the end of this buckle's copper alloy pin allowed it to be removed and swapped between shoes, a useful consideration with a silver buckle.

58

DRESS FITTINGS

BUCKLE CLASPS

Buckle clasps are intriguing and were relatively common in the Medieval period with over 600 examples being recorded by the PAS. They functioned in a similar way to buckles, but instead of having a pin they have a folding closure (the clasp) to secure the belt or strap in place. On all examples, the buckle frame is rectangular to accommodate the clasp.

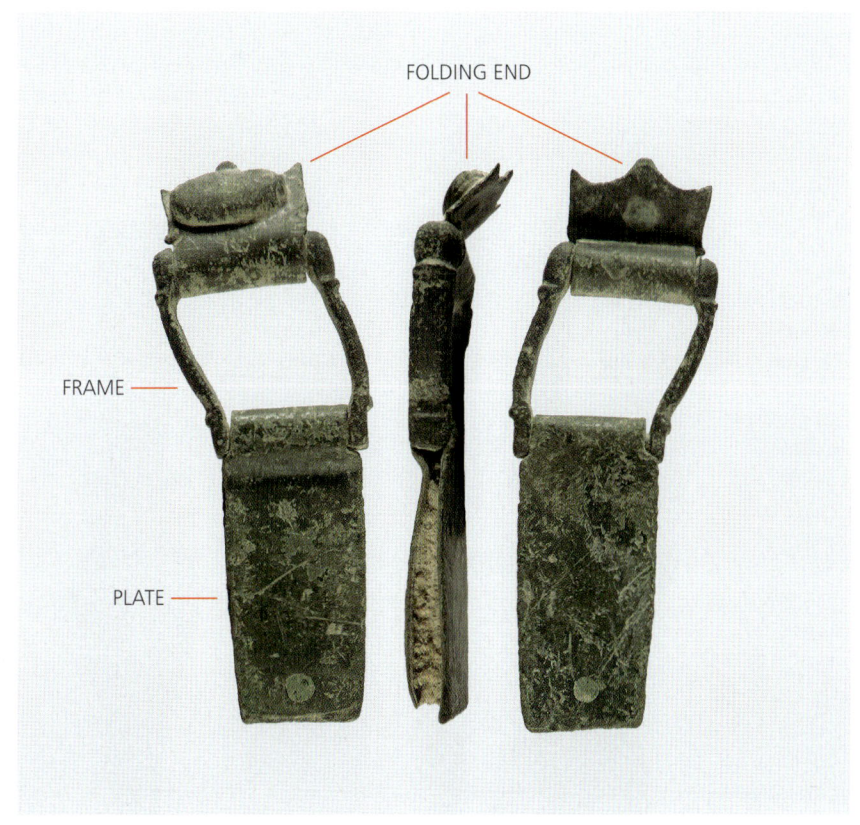

SUSS-C963BB, 39mm, Chichester area, West Sussex (1300-1450)
This buckle clasp contains a whitish textile between its plates. It is apparent that the clasp mechanism would be particularly suitable for gripping textile belts and straps.

WILT-CDD28B, 30mm, Marlborough, Wiltshire (1300-1400)
This is presumed to be the frame of a buckle clasp, though since the clasp mechanism does not survive, this could actually be a frame for a buckle proper (that is, one having a pin rather than clasp). Needless to say, this artefact type is not entirely understood!

KENT-CF9AD8, 38mm, Ringwould with Kingdown, Kent (1350-1400)
Many buckle clasps have anthropomorphic decoration, in this case a king's head, a popular Medieval motif.

DRESS FITTINGS

STRAP ENDS

Strap ends, as their name suggests, adorned the ends of belts and straps. Although many are ornate, others are simple, their purpose being primarily functional – to protect the end of the strap to which they were fitted: a leather or textile belt with a strap end will not fray or be easily damaged. Also, since straps often hung loose, the weight of the strap end helped the belt to hang. Throughout history the styles of strap ends varied considerably, and were made of an array of materials, such as bone and antler, as well as metal. Strap ends are common, with almost 10,000 of them recorded on the PAS database.

Roman

Almost 400 Roman strap ends have been recorded by the PAS. As it is likely that they were worn with the buckles discussed above, they were probably military.

NMS-A286F4, 46mm, Snetterton, Norfolk (43-100)
Strap end from a Roman soldier's 'apron' – the studded leather straps suspended from a soldier's belt. It was probably originally inlaid with niello, a black silver sulphide, and was worn as a mark of distinction rather than for protection.

SF-E271D7, 41mm, Foulden, Norfolk (325-400)
A Late Roman 'amphora-shaped' strap end. These get their name from their shape, their side loops resembling the handles on a wine amphora although the resemblance is probably coincidental.

DENO-912E87, 42mm, Harmston, Lincolnshire (325-400)
Late Roman heart-shaped strap end, which is a variant of the amphora type. The strap was fitted into a slot in the upper end and secured by the single rivet.

DOR-E880D5, 84mm, Puddletown, Dorset (250-400)
The tip of this Late Roman strap end is bifurcated like a finger nail cleaner (see page 107). It is not known if this was a decorative feature or was intended for practical use.

DRESS FITTINGS

Early Medieval

The earliest Early Medieval strap ends tend to be plain and made from folded sheet metal, making them difficult to date unless found in a grave. Middle and Late Anglo-Saxon strap ends are distinctive and fairly common, with more than 3,300 of them being recorded with the PAS. Most finds come from eastern England but the area of the Anglo-Saxon kingdom of Wessex, in the central south west, has also yielded large numbers of strap ends. Middle and Late Anglo-Saxon strap ends were usually decorated. Whilst this can be crude, many have fine, delicate, designs. In the Late Anglo-Saxon period, strap ends show foreign influences with Viking and Carolingian designs being employed.

WILT-066815, 41mm, Cumnor. Oxfordshire (820-920)
Not all Middle Anglo-Saxon strap ends were well made. The animal decoration on this example is simplified but can be seen; the beast is crouching with its head shown in the top right hand corner of the rectangular panel.

WILT-88A4AB, 67mm, Thetford, Norfolk (800-900)
Middle Anglo-Saxon silver strap end with intricate animal interlace, emphasised with great effect by the use of black niello inlay. As with all strap ends its upper part is split for the insertion of the strap which was secured by two rivets.

LANCUM-8FC83C, 42mm, Ivinghoe, Buckinghamshire (820-920)
This Middle Anglo-Saxon strap end bears crude geometric decoration. It is interesting to see that the animal's head (usually shown on the ends of these strap ends), is represented, but is only just recognisable. A stain on the underside probably represents a missing hook, once soldered into place.

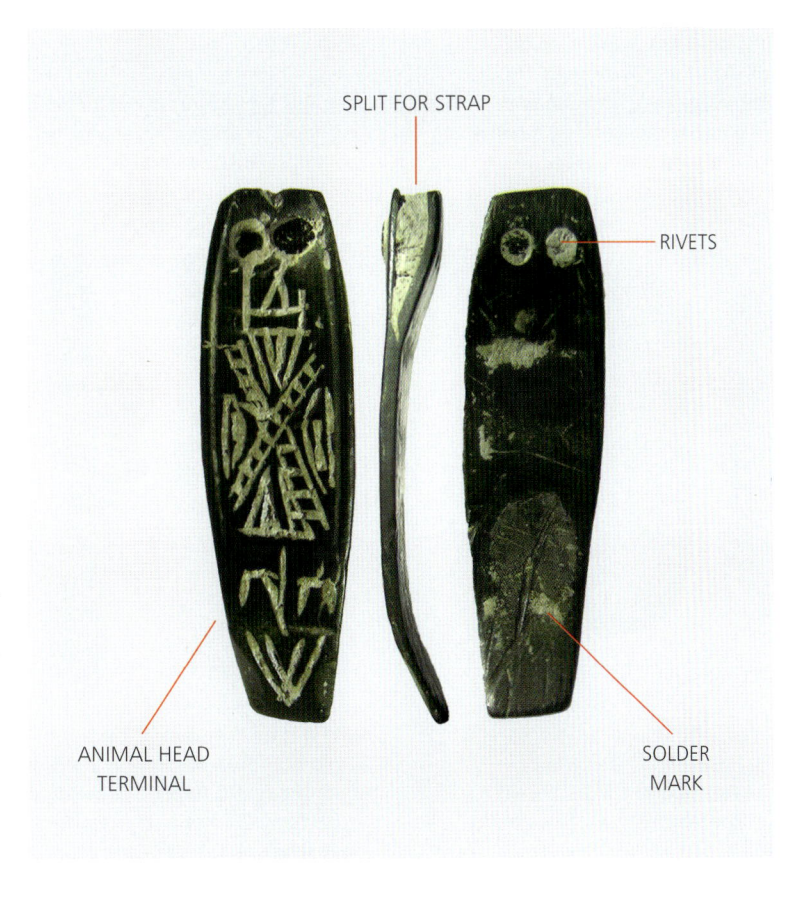

SPLIT FOR STRAP
RIVETS
ANIMAL HEAD TERMINAL
SOLDER MARK

DRESS FITTINGS

LEIC-53D3E4, 28mm, Belton in Rutland, Rutland (820-920)
Silver strap end bearing Trewhiddle style decoration, which, although named after a find from near St Austell, Cornwall, is widespread, with examples from Scotland. At the top is an animal's head, below which tendrils surround its body. V-shaped notches on the edges of the animal's body are common in the Trewhiddle style. The black niello inlay is missing but deeply scratched keying for it can be seen. The animal head terminal is missing but the palmette (in the half-round panel at the top) survives.

FAKL-5B3421, 42mm, Pocklington area, East Yorkshire (820-920)
Middle Anglo-Saxon strap end with a typical Trewhiddle style animal. This is crouching and looking left, its feet and toes are clearly shown. At the top of the strap end is the palmette motif often seen on these strap ends.

NMS-393CA2, 59mm, Congham, Norfolk (900-1000)
Tongue-shaped strap end decorated with the chain interlace characteristic of the Viking Borre style. This strap end bears traces of a white metal coating and, interestingly, the fitting on its back shows that it had a second life, having been converted into a brooch.

LVPL-537933, 32mm, South Cave, East Yorkshire (900-1100)
Viking Age strap end decorated with two longitudinal ribs. This type occurs in northern Europe and Scandinavia but oddly, in Britain finds come from two separate zones: around the Irish Sea and in north eastern England.

BERK-C7CD6C, 47mm, Stoke Lyne, Oxfordshire (900-1100)
Anglo-Scandinavian lead-alloy strap end, with decoration that consists of a Borre style animal's head and a devolved ring-chain motif (see above: NMS-393CA2). Lead strap ends, like lead brooches, are a feature of the Late Anglo-Saxon period.

WILT-B18A63, 49mm, Hankerton, Wiltshire (1000-1100)
Anglo-Scandinavian strap end decorated in the Urnes style. The ring is gripped in an animal's jaws and another animal's head can be seen, bottom right, looking downwards. Unusually, this strap end is double sided.

DRESS FITTINGS

SOM-F33A5F, 51mm, Charminster, Dorset (930-1100)
Strap end decorated in the Late Anglo-Saxon Winchester style. This consists of stylised acanthus leaves as seen on manuscripts attributed to Winchester, although the style actually draws on Carolingian art as seen on some of the imported strap ends (see below: ESS-BE9A25).

DENO-6BEFD3, 45mm, Farnsfield, Nottinghamshire (900-1100)
Unusually, this Late Anglo-Saxon Winchester style strap end is decorated on both faces.

SWYOR-B557B2, 38mm, Saxton, North Yorkshire (850-1100)
The net-like interlace and roundels on both faces of this strap end are typically Irish. Some of these strap ends have small holes through the tip of the animal's nose which might be associated with their use on book straps. Like other Irish objects of the period they are likely to have been imported into England by the Vikings.

SUR-996B96, 60mm, Chipstead, Surrey (950-1100)
This strap end shows a devolved version of the Winchester style. In contrast to the small, Middle Anglo-Saxon, strap ends, those of the Late Anglo-Saxon period tend to be broad and tongue shaped.

ESS-BE9A25, 32mm, Glemsford, Suffolk (800-900)
This silver strap end is of a type made in the Carolingian Empire, which covered much of western Europe during the 9th century. Carolingian art influenced the Vikings who interpreted it in their own way. These objects show contacts across the North Sea during the Early Medieval period.

DRESS FITTINGS

HAMP-9E6A09, 28mm, Buriton, Hampshire (800-900)
Strap end bearing a highly devolved version of Carolingian acanthus leaf decoration.

NMS-C179C1, 39mm, Tharston, Norfolk (800-900)
This strap end also bears devolved acanthus decoration. The use of a separate plate to accommodate the end of the strap is typical of Carolingian strap ends.

Medieval and Post Medieval

The PAS has recorded almost 6,000 Medieval strap ends. These can be set alongside the 27,000 Medieval buckles, suggesting that most belts were not fitted with strap ends. The Scheme is more selective in recording Post Medieval material, but nonetheless a further 136 examples of these later strap ends have been recorded.

YORYM-8295D8, 58mm, Welton, East Yorkshire (1150-1450)
This three-part composite strap end consists of a forked spacer (hidden in image) and two sub-rectangular, narrowing, plates. Typically Medieval in both form and decoration, it also has an open-work quatrefoil (on its plate) and a cruciform terminal.

YORYM-4141EA, 49mm, Ellerker, East Yorkshire (1150-1450)
Forked insert from the centre of a Medieval strap end where it would have been sandwiched between two pieces of sheet metal.

HAMP-2093B1, 50mm, Enham Alamein, Hampshire (1250-1450)
Elaborately decorated, the designer of this object has increased capacity for embellishment by expanding it with a central, openwork, roundel.

NLM-43D6BA, 23mm, South Ferriby, Lincolnshire (1350-1400)
Medieval 'pendant loop' – these were attached to straps and belts allowing objects to be suspended.

DRESS FITTINGS

IOW-B04F1C, 30mm, Arreton Isle of Wight (1270-1450)
Of simple form, this strap end consists of two metal plates riveted together, between which survive the remains of a textile strap.

WMID-E13EA5, 24mm, Sherburn, North Yorkshire (1350-1450)
Simple strap end with a cusped top and small terminal projection. Within it is a forked spacer as YORYM-4141EA on page 64.

This Medieval painting shows an elaborate belt, with floriate fittings and a pointed strap end. The colours used suggest the metal is intended to be silver or pewter (Image: Michael Lewis).

65

DRESS FITTINGS

BH-AA7B47, 42mm, Royston, Hertfordshire (1300-1400)
This Medieval strap end was made from two thin sheet metal plates, separated by a forked spacer. It was held together by a rivet at each end.

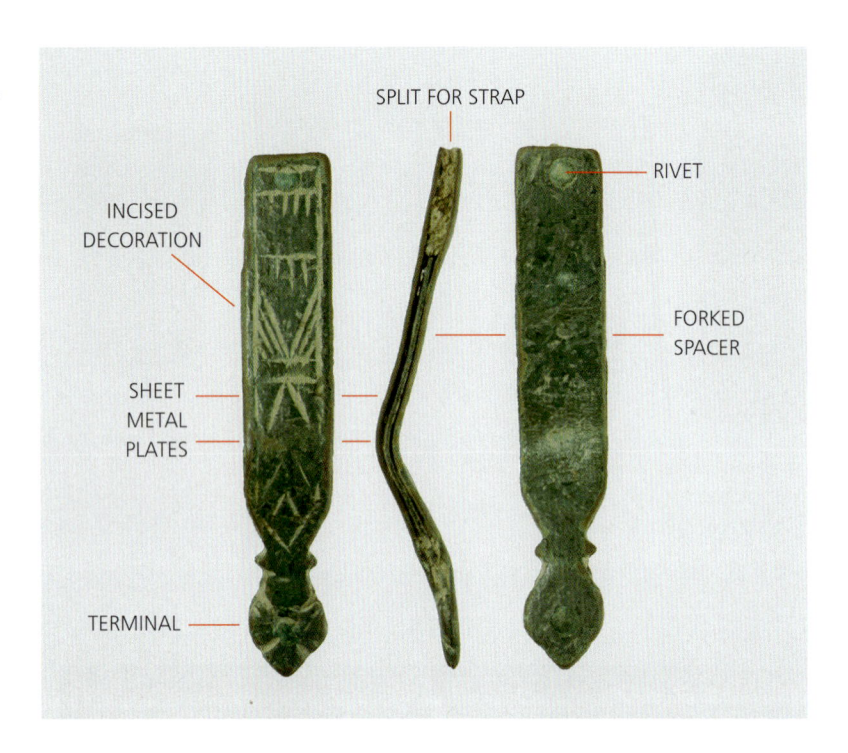

INCISED DECORATION
SPLIT FOR STRAP
RIVET
SHEET METAL PLATES
FORKED SPACER
TERMINAL

NMS-DE1602, 18mm, Oxborough, Norfolk (1300-1400)
Decorated with a scallop shell motif, this strap end has a solid bar mount (on its display side) and three rivets, of which two have surviving roves (on the back); presumably the bar and roves are for better securing the strap end to a belt or strap.

LON-331FB2, 42mm, City of London (1450-1600)
Cast in lead, this intriguing Late or Post Medieval strap end shows an openwork eagle, with outstretched wings, between two scrolls. The reverse is undecorated.

WILT-CEF689, 50mm, Marlborough, Wiltshire (1350-1450)
Strap ends with inscriptions are not as common as might be expected. This, with a D-shaped projecting buckle, has the religious legend *ihs*, an abbreviation for Jesus.

NMS-8F6F3C, 23mm Salle, Norfolk (1625-75)
Enamel is used to great effect on this highly decorative Post Medieval strap end. Its design is broadly cruciform, embellished with C-shape scrolls.

DRESS FITTINGS

BUTTONS

There are 6,400 buttons on the PAS database, of which over 5,000 are Post Medieval and more than 800 Medieval. Buttons date back to prehistoric times, with examples made from jet being found in Early Bronze Age graves. Over some considerable periods of time buttons were not used, as they were not useful on some types of clothing: they are appropriate for use with leather, furs and fine textiles, but with the open weave textiles used over much of the past, pins and brooches are more practical. Buttons were not used in the Roman period; the button and loop fasteners of this time were really a type of toggle. It also seems that buttons were not used during the Early Medieval period, when their role was fulfilled by brooches and pins, but they re-appeared in the Middle Ages. Later, buttons were not only functional objects, but used much like badges, to denote allegiance and belonging. During the Post Medieval period buttons were used on an epic scale, with garments bearing them in close-packed rows; an 18th century suicide note bemoans the stress caused by "all this buttoning and unbuttoning".

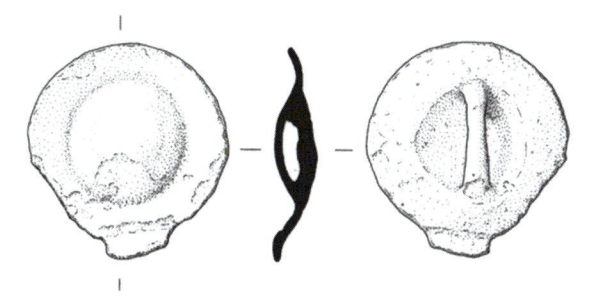

NMS-160212, 36mm, Great Ellingham, Norfolk (110-800 BC)
Simple button with a transverse bar across its back. Similar buttons, found in Bronze Age hoards, allow it to be dated.

LVPL-095C33, 13mm, Eccleshall, Staffordshire (43-300)
Buttons like this have been found on Roman sites. Their design seems to have been based on that of the button and loop toggle fasteners of the period.

YORYM-79EC41, 17mm, Langtoft, East Yorkshire (1150-1700)
This button, with its rectangular loop is hard to date. Its design shows a moulded-relief quatrefoil embellished with enamel.

LON-E92322, 30mm, Shadwell, City of London (1300-1700)
Cast lead-alloy Medieval button consisting of a large central boss surrounded by eight smaller ones. The casting scar can be seen on the reverse.

WMID-185494, 12mm, Fazeley, Staffordshire (1400-1550)
Buttons like this, with biconvex head and rounded loop were designed to be cast in one piece and are common finds.

SUR-91E807, 14mm, Stratfield Saye, Hampshire (1400-1600)
Cast in one piece, the loop on this lead button was drilled though the lug. It is decorated with a cinquefoil at its centre surrounded by three concentric rings of raised pellets.

DRESS FITTINGS

SUR-96C6B8, 15mm, Coombe Bissett, Wiltshire (1400-1600)
Heart-shaped button with central trough and linear decoration. Its integral loop is rectangular with a drilled hole.

BH-4C6874, 16mm, Hyde, Bedfordshire (1450-1650)
This looped pyramidal button was cast in one piece and has a drilled hole. The long shank is typical of many of these buttons, and may reflect the thickness of the cloth through which it was passed, for example, on a padded doublet. The long shank would have also been helpful when buttoning a stiff cloth.

WMID-C2E4D4, 27mm, Rugby, Warwickshire (1475-1525)
Depicted on this button is St Barbara, with a gospel book and martyr's palm. She is shown with her symbol, the tower in which she was imprisoned. Its inscription helpfully reads SANCTA BARBARA.

BH-636BA2, 10mm, Effingham, Surrey (1650-1700)
Many Post Medieval buttons have pressed designs, such as this silver example showing the crowned head of a maiden.

SWYOR-030587, 33mm, Cattal, North Yorkshire (1600-1800)
Button in the form of a seven-petalled flower with each lobe forming a small flower head of its own; these have four cells of alternating blue and white enamelled petals arranged around a central raised boss.

SUR-0FE9EA, 28mm, Hurley, Berkshire (1801-30)
Military button of the 51st Regiment of Foot. It has on its reverse the name of its maker, I M Gowan of Gerrard St, London. Although less than 300 years old (the date range for PAS finds) military buckles, like this can be informative and are often recorded by the PAS.

DRESS FITTINGS

BUTTON AND LOOP FASTENERS

These would have acted as toggles to hold a cloak or some other garment in place. First occurring in the Iron Age, they became common in the Roman period, with over 550 examples recorded on the PAS database. While button and loop fasteners are widespread, there is a major concentration of them in Yorkshire which might be seen as their place of origin. Many of them bear Iron Age (Celtic) decoration, again suggesting a native, rather than Roman, origin.

SUR-6D49C3, 42mm, Nettlebed, Oxfordshire (70 BC-AD 50)
While not actually button and loop fasteners, these 'studded rings' seem to have acted in a similar way; the stud being passed through a hole in a leather strap. They have been found in Iron Age graves in association with swords and may have formed part of a baldric from which the weapon was suspended.

SOM-BF7D5F, 29mm, Misterton, Somerset (50-150)
The red enamel inlay on this button and loop fastener shows the survival of Celtic decoration in the Roman period.

BH-992B56, 29mm, Shipton under Wychwood, Oxfordshire (50-150)
Simple button and loop fasteners of this form appear to be an early type as they are found on 1st and 2nd century sites.

LEIC-8B810E, 35mm, Branston area, Lincolnshire (50-150)
The moulded decoration on this Roman button and loop fastener would not be out of place on any piece of Iron Age metalwork.

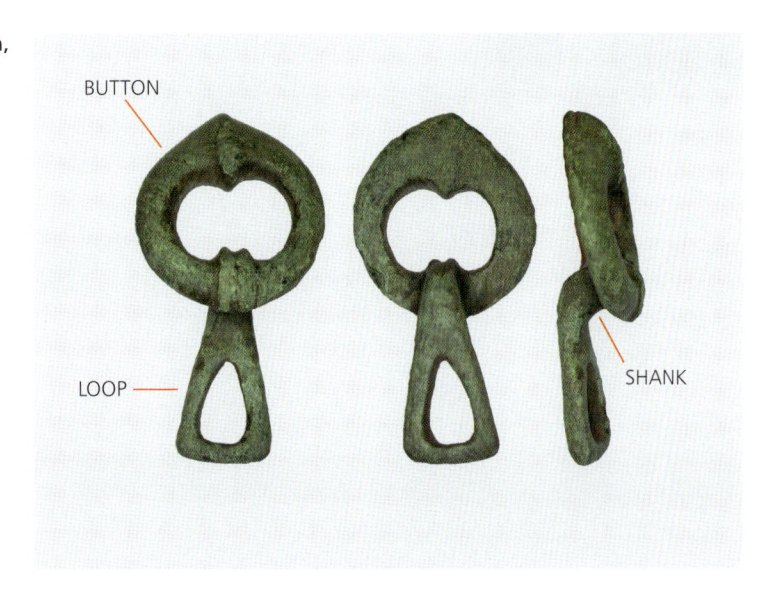

69

DRESS FITTINGS

NLM-0AEC15, 31mm, Barrow on Humber, North Lincolnshire (50-150)
The use of a 'petal-boss' in the decoration of a Roman button and loop fastener shows the survival of a Celtic motif.

SWYOR-CAD8F3, 32mm, Plompton, North Yorkshire (50-150)
Despite its simple form, dated finds suggest that this button and loop dates from the 2nd century.

YORYM-65D7F2, 26mm, Langtoft, East Yorkshire (50-150)
It is impossible to know if objects like this are Late Iron Age or early Roman in date; the Roman Conquest gives us our first solidly dated sites and we perhaps over emphasise this later period when dating finds.

TOGGLES

The PAS has recorded over 420 toggles, of which 280 are assigned an Iron Age date and over 90 are Roman. Toggles are widespread but, like the button and loop fasteners, they are most common in Yorkshire and down into Lincolnshire. It is possible that the toggles recorded by the PAS represent a fraction of those produced, most of which were probably made from bone or wood.

ESS-1E286B, 37mm, Stansfield Mountfitchet, Essex (300 BC-AD 100)
This toggle represents a development of the simple bar toggle as it is fitted with a loop for attaching it to a cord or garment.

YORYM-BB9C93, 18mm, North Cave, East Yorkshire (100 BC-AD 100)
This dumb-bell shaped toggle is difficult to date as the type spans the centuries both before and after the Roman conquest.

SF-C982A5, 23mm, Worlingworth, Suffolk (200 BC-AD 100)
The barrel-shaped toggle represents a further variant which shares the same, Late Iron Age/Early Roman, date range.

DRESS FITTINGS

CUFFLINKS

During the 17th century it became fashionable for gentlemen to wear garments with buttoned cuffs and, in view of need for laundering, these 'cufflinks' needed to be readily removed and became an item of masculine jewellery. Cufflinks consisted of two buttons joined by a wire loop, threaded through button holes on the cuffs. Many cufflinks were made of silver, with pressed decoration. There are over 650 cufflinks on the PAS database of which over 500 are made of silver.

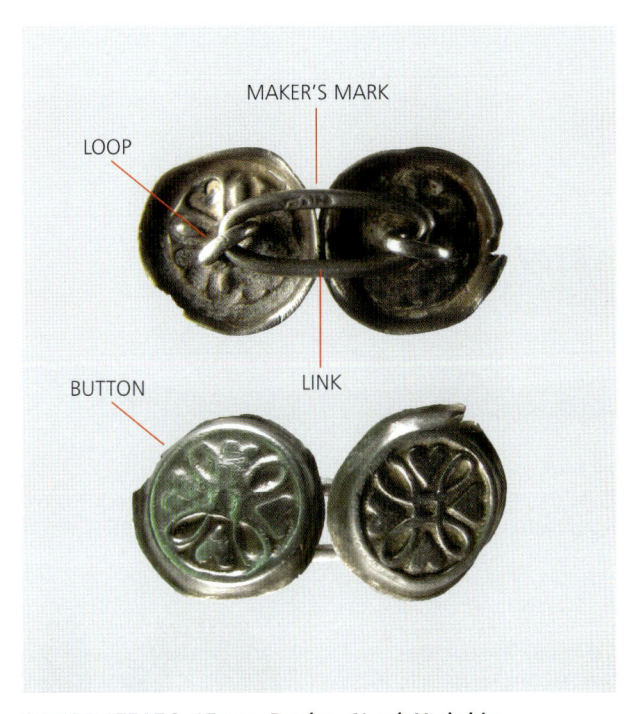

SWYOR-1EEA7C, 17mm, Barden, North Yorkshire (1600-1700)
The design on this silver cufflink is a quatrefoil of four loops, with a heart between each arm. Maker's marks were usually placed on the loop linking the two buttons.

ESS-7168A5, 14mm, Brentwood, Essex (1650-1700)
Another common cufflink type (perhaps used as a collar stud) is formed of two button discs joined by a bar. This example has a crown and heart motif associated with the marriage of Charles II to Catherine of Braganza (1662).

IOW-00AD9D, 15mm, Brighstone, Isle of Wight (1700-1800)
A floral motif embellishes this pair of cufflinks, which have the maker's mark TD on the wire loop that joins them.

DRESS FITTINGS

PINS

Pins are common finds with over 5,600 of them on the PAS database dating from the 14th century BC to recent times. Their function is often unknown, as they were used both to secure clothing and hair. Pins played an important role in display – they were often decorated and could be elaborate.

The copper-alloy pins shown here only represent a small sample of what was made and used. In some periods bone pins were common, of which there are over 160 on the PAS database, their style sometimes following that seen in metal. Iron pins are known but seldom survive outside excavated sites. Composite pins, with metal shanks and glass heads, were used in the Middle Anglo-Saxon period. These small objects were sometimes made in precious metals: over 400 silver pins have been recorded with the PAS of which 200 are Post Medieval and over a hundred Early Medieval.

Prehistoric

GLO-439E61, 170mm, Portbury, Somerset (1400-1250 BC)
Middle Bronze Age 'Picardy pin'. As the name suggests these are a Continental type, although a small number have been found in Britain. Over 60 Bronze Age pins, of various types, have been recorded by the PAS. Most come from a band stretching from Norfolk across to Oxfordshire.

BUC-7C4708, 52mm, Haversham area, Buckinghamshire (1500-1200 BC)
Quoit headed pins of this type are found in hoards of the Middle Bronze Age 'Ornament Horizon' and help give this period its name.

DOR-514CD7, 114, Gussage St. Michael, Dorset (300 BC-50 AD)
This Iron Age ring-headed pin has a typical bent shank through which is a small rivet that perhaps held a decorative element.

YORYM-0205E5, 48mm, Cawton, North Yorkshire (300 BC-50 AD)
Iron Age 'swan's neck' pin with enamel inlay. Although much of its shank is missing this remains a graceful object.

LANCUM-5ECCE3, 115mm, Leyburn, North Yorkshire (800-300 BC)
This early Iron Age swan's neck pin has a head bearing simple notched decoration.

72

DRESS FITTINGS

Roman

NLM-7B625D, 36mm, Roxby cum Risby, North Lincolnshire (75-150)
This elegant Roman pin, with multiple mouldings around its head, is probably early in date.

WILT-84A9C2, 29mm, The Deverills, Wiltshire (50-400)
This pin could be mistaken for Early Medieval but the absence of a collar around its shank points to a Roman date.

SF-501254, 28mm, Great Barton, Suffolk (50-400)
The lack of a collar and its thick, tapering, shank indicates a Roman date for this pin.

BERK-24BC62, 60mm Kingston Bagpuize with Southmoor, Oxfordshire (150-300)
The double curve on the shank of this pin represents a feature seen on Iron Age swan's neck pins but is unusual on Roman examples. It may relate to the way in which this pin was used, allowing it to grip the cloth.

LON-BDA9D5, 71mm, City of London (50-100)
While very stylised, the hair-style on this bone pin suggests a date in the second half of the 1st century when high, false, curls were fashionable.

NMS-80C104, 92mm, Feltwell, Norfolk (50-100)
The head of this elegant pin shows a hand holding an object, which could be an egg, a pomegranate or an apple, all of which carried symbolic meanings.

YORYM-276641, 34mm, Wigginton, North Yorkshire (100-400)
Head of a Roman pin representing a sitting bird. While this pin-head has been dated to the Roman period, a later date is possible; other bird-headed pins appear Early Medieval.

NLM-F24D77, 58mm, South Ferriby, North Lincolnshire (43-100)
Although we cannot be certain, the strange shape of the head of this Roman pin has been interpreted as representing a military standard.

DRESS FITTINGS

WMID-1DF801, 104mm, Doverdale, Worcestershire (280-500)
This pin is zoomorphic although its animal's head design is difficult to interpret. The type appeared in the late Roman period but continued into Early Medieval times. Similar terminals were used on penannular brooches. annular brooches. An enlarged detail of the distinctive head appears between the two views.

Early Medieval

YORYM-0D6D93, 23mm, Skirpenbeck, East Yorkshire (800-80)
Early Medieval pin with a faceted globular head marked with incised dots. Although crude, it is still possible to see the diagnostic collar beneath the head. Such Anglo-Saxon pins are relatively common finds with over 2,000 of them appearing on the PAS database. They are strikingly common in Norfolk, Lincolnshire and East Yorkshire, suggesting that this may reflect particular styles of dress in these areas.

LANCUM-657D57, 38mm, Gisburn, Lancashire (700-800)
Disc-headed pin decorated with simplified interlace, a form typical of the 8th century. The hole, at one edge, suggests that this pin formed part of a triple or double pin set. The back of the pin head is tin plated.

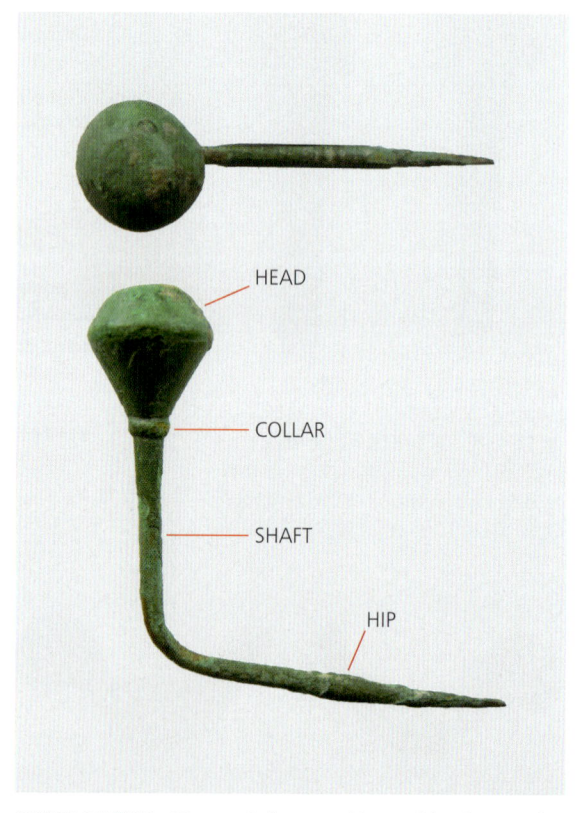

HAMP-0CF728, 40mm, Soberton, Hampshire (800-80)
This biconical headed pin shows many of the features of an Early Medieval pin. Below the head is a collar and the shank is 'hipped' with a slight swelling on its lower part. The grooves around the shank might have helped hold the pin in place. Many of these pins are, like this example, bent, which might be an original feature. It is important that finders do not alter archaeological objects, for example by straightening them.

DRESS FITTINGS

WILT-019B91, 26mm, The Deverills, Wiltshire (800-80)
Another of the common form of Middle Anglo-Saxon pin, the massed ring and dot decoration adds interest to its faceted head.

SWYOR-77388A, 48mm, Folkton, North Yorkshire (900-1100)
'Kite-headed' pin of a type that originated in Ireland and was brought into England by the Vikings.

SOM-50B5A1, 34mm, Alvediston, Wiltshire (720-820)
'Racquet-headed' pin with a crude, incised, decoration based on more elaborate examples. There is a small collar between the head and shank.

BH-34AE6D, 25mm, Heydon, Cambridgeshire (720-1000)
'Writhen-headed' pin of Middle Anglo-Saxon date.

NCL-3DE1D1, 36mm, near Middleton on the Wolds, East Yorkshire (720-820)
Gilt pin head with interlace decoration. Both gilding and interlace are typical of the 8th century.

NMGW-E8F8A8, 163mm, Port Eynon, Swansea (875-1000)
This pin is strikingly different from the others described here; it is an Irish ring-headed pin and was probably imported by the Vikings.

WILT-C4F039, 42mm, Liddington, Wiltshire (700-850)
A central linking element from a triple or double pin set, this plate would have been set between two disc-headed pins. The workmanship on this object is rather poor, showing that not all craftsmen were highly accomplished.

DRESS FITTINGS

LVPL-5A9738, 55mm, Selby area, North Yorkshire (600-700)
Double spiral-headed pin, of a type that lacks a collar, probably reflecting an early date.

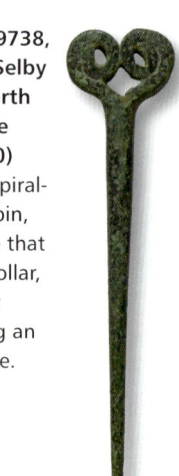

LEIC-C2E6D7, 28mm, Granby, Nottinghamshire (750-850)
Silver-gilt pin head decorated with two pairs of facing birds, their heads turned back over their bodies. They are surrounded by interlace; all typical features of the 8th century. A pin would have been riveted to the disc through the two holes and the linking piece attached via the single hole.

SWYOR-3DEE70, 43mm, Wragby, Lincolnshire (750-850)
Central section of a triple pin set made from gilt copper-alloy; a tour de force of animal interlace.

Medieval

PUBLIC-3A4600, 56mm, City of London (1300-1400)
The octagonal prism head on this Medieval pin has been soldered onto the shaft.

SWYOR-2268B6, 73mm, Horncastle area, Lincolnshire (1350-1450)
The grooved appearance of this cylindrical pin head has been formed by winding wire around the shaft.

SF-5BE675, 22mm, Bury St Edmunds area, Suffolk (1200-1300)
The head of this silver pin is a cube, with its corners cut off. Each of the five larger faces is decorated with a cross motif.

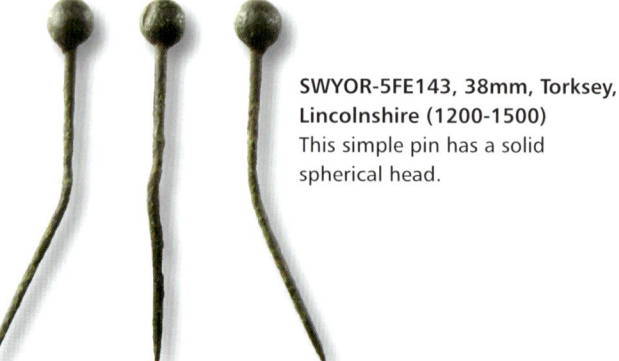

SWYOR-5FE143, 38mm, Torksey, Lincolnshire (1200-1500)
This simple pin has a solid spherical head.

DRESS FITTINGS

Late/Post Medieval

PUBLIC-B28696, 12-15mm, Greenwich, London (1400-1600)
Selection of pins from the Thames foreshore, showing variety in size and decoration of pins used, although all have wound, wire heads. These are very common finds.

SOM-D59551, 35mm, Lopen, Somerset (1500-1600)
Formed of two silver hemispheres soldered together, the head of this pin has been decorated with bosses, knops and filigree, and then heavily gilded.

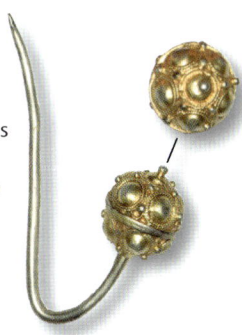

SOM-EFB851, 45mm, Alvediston, Wiltshire (1500-1600)
This extraordinary pin has its head made from two dished jettons (see page 278) soldered together; the jettons are of Nuremberg type.

KENT-029402, 72mm, Cambridgeshire (1500-1600)
This intriguing pin is formed from rolled sheet metal, and has a head formed of two scrolls. Superficially, it resembles some Early Medieval pins (see LVPL-5A9738 opposite).

HOOKED TAGS AND DRESS HOOKS

These objects usually consist of a small metal plate with holes at the top (presumably to sew them into place) and a hooked projection at the other end. They were used in both the Anglo-Saxon (c.600-1050) and Post Medieval periods (c.1500-1700), but not, as far as we know, during the Middle Ages. The Anglo-Saxon examples, referred to as hooked tags, are usually made from flat sheet metal. Most are copper-alloy, but silver examples are also known. They are decorated with various designs with many having simple stamped motifs, but others bear fine, incised decoration embellished with niello inlay. Post Medieval dress hooks were cast, and their form and design can vary considerably. These objects are common, with almost 1,000 hooked tags and over 4,000 dress hooks being recorded on the PAS database, but their function is less clear. Anglo-Saxon hooked tags have been found in graves, placed just below the knee suggesting that they supported stockings. Post Medieval dress hooks probably had a similar function (acting a bit like buttons) though they are rarely depicted in art, suggesting that they were mostly hidden beneath clothing, perhaps (again) holding stockings in place. That said, some are very elaborate, suggesting they were designed to be seen.

Early Medieval

PUBLIC-07A6DD, 22mm, Old Romney, Kent (900-1100)
Finds from excavations suggest that most of these simple, circular, hooked tags were of Late Anglo-Saxon date.

WMID-2DA711, 20mm, Norbury, Shropshire (1016-1035)
Made from a coin of Cnut this hooked tag is relatively well dated, and therefore is important.

DRESS FITTINGS

DOR-9E4B58, 38mm, Near Blandford, Dorset (820-920)
Silver hooked tag with Middle Anglo-Saxon Trewhiddle style decoration.

LON-585A83, 36mm, Thaxted, Essex (820-920)
The use of silver with niello inlay suggests a Middle Anglo-Saxon date for this hooked tag.

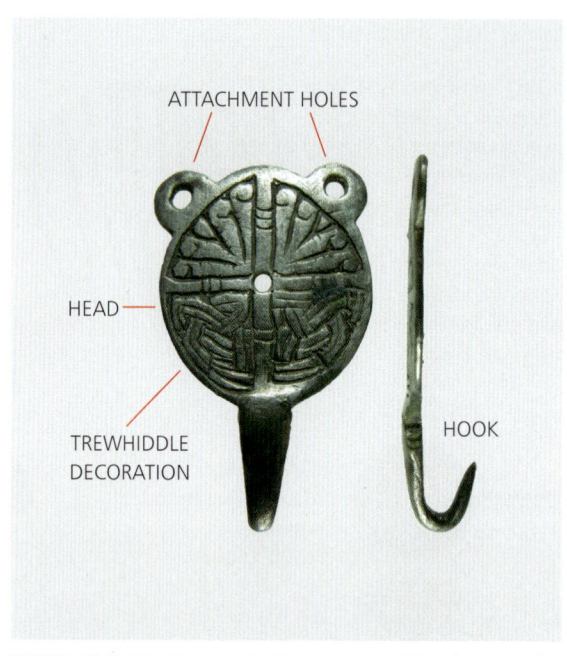

ATTACHMENT HOLES
HEAD
TREWHIDDLE DECORATION
HOOK

HAMP-0B4001, 33mm, Andover, Hampshire (820-920)
Middle Anglo-Saxon silver hooked tag with incised Trewhiddle style interlace and plumes. It shows that not all circular hooked tags can be assumed to be late in date.

Post Medieval

LEIC-CC8A32, 28mm, near Henley in Arden, Warwickshire (1500-1600)
This ornate Post Medieval silver dress hook consists of several parts soldered together and then gilded. It is strikingly different in form from the Early Medieval hooked tags.

SOM-C4CC5F, 30mm, Milbourne Port, Somerset (1500-1600)
Early form of dress hook still retaining traces of gilding. It is thought that hooks of this type were attached to cord rather than directly to the garment.

HAMP-136E66, 32mm, Twyford, Hampshire (1500-1600)
The rope-like decoration of this dress hook is formed of an openwork trefoil knot, known as a Hungerford knot. This is a very common type of dress hook.

DRESS FITTINGS

SF-86EAB3, 24mm, Great Glemham, Suffolk (1500-1600)
Rectangular dress hooks, like this one, were probably imitating more elaborate silver-gilt examples.

SWYOR-0C5ACD, 33mm, North Cave, East Yorkshire (1500-1600)
The design on this dress hook is uncertain but probably floral. Its condition is unstable, and it is unlikely that it would have survived much longer in the plough soil.

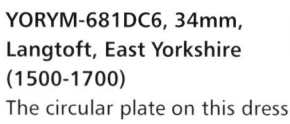

YORYM-681DC6, 34mm, Langtoft, East Yorkshire (1500-1700)
The circular plate on this dress hook bears an open-work design probably featuring a cross.

YORYM-49BDAC, 24mm, Cundall with Leckby, North Yorkshire (1600-1700)
The trefoil form of this silver dress hook is a common precious-metal type. It is partly gilt and decorated with twisted filigree wire and granulated pellets, typical of the 17th century.

SUSS-68E280, 34mm, Warnham area, West Sussex (1650-1700)
This object is in fact a clasp, which would have been joined to a fitting of similar form, but hooked.

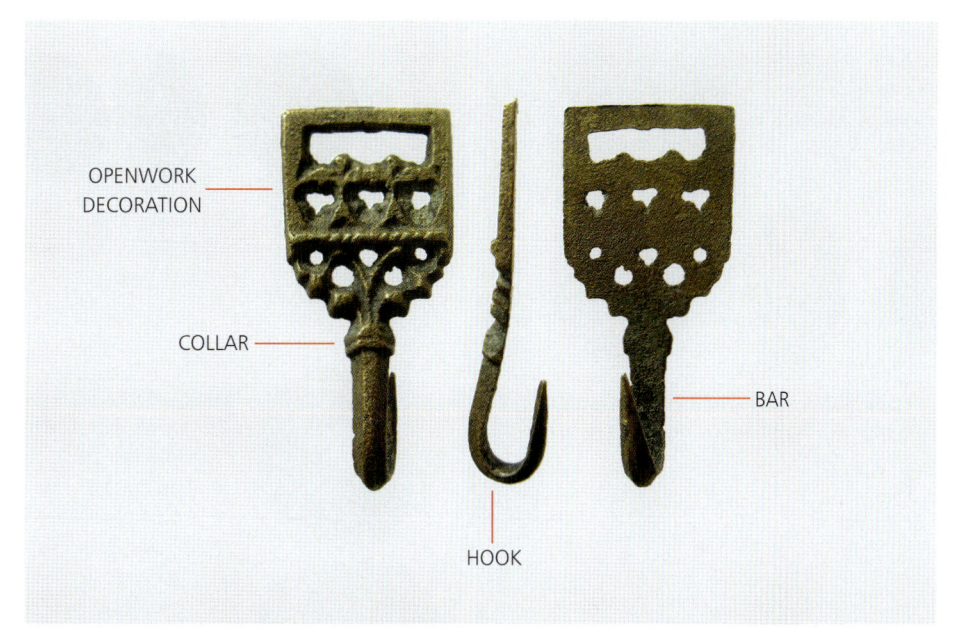

LON-70CFCD, 33mm, City of London (1500-1600)
The intricate openwork decoration of this dress hook shows that base-metal examples followed the decoration used on silver examples.

79

DRESS FITTINGS

BEADS

While the PAS has recorded over 1,400 beads, this fails to reflect how common they were in the past; since most of them were made of glass (not metal) they are likely to be under-represented on the PAS database. Beads were commonly used from the Iron Age onwards. This can present problems in dating them as some types of bead were used over a long period of time; dark blue, annular beads, for example, were commonly used from c.800 BC through to recent times. Some beads are distinctive and can be dated with some confidence, such as whorl decorated Iron Age beads and Early Anglo-Saxon 'traffic light' beads. There is evidence for the manufacture of glass beads in Britain throughout the past, but this was probably based on re-melting imported glass. Not all beads were made from glass – amber was used in the Early Bronze Age and continued to be utilised over the centuries. In more recent times, beads were made in a great variety of forms, and during the slave trade were exported to Africa where they were highly prized.

GLO-46CA05, 10mm, Newent, Gloucestershire (1500-1100 BC)
This bead can be dated by comparison with finds from Middle Bronze Age hoards. As is often the case, it is hollow, to economise on the use of precious metal.

KENT-0F91BC, 16mm, City of London (43-200)
Glass 'melon' beads of this type occurred in the Iron Age and are also found in Early Anglo-Saxon graves, but are most common on Roman sites. The decoration could be easily impressed while the glass was still soft.

NMS-277381, 16mm, Binham, Norfolk (100 BC-200 AD)
Blue glass bead inlaid with 'eye' motifs are thought to be of Roman date.

ESS-33CCA3, 27mm, Ramsey with Parkeston, Essex (800 BC-AD 100)
Iron Age glass beads can be distinctive as shown by this fine example. The decoration was formed by trailing white glass onto still-soft blue glass and pressing it into the surface.

NLM-4E2672, 7mm, Northorpe, Lincolnshire (50-400)
Blue glass beads were made over a long period of time; this biconical bead is probably Roman.

NMS-8C0278, 26mm, Postwick with Witton Norfolk (43-200)
Roman glass 'melon' bead, of a type also found in Anglo-Saxon graves.

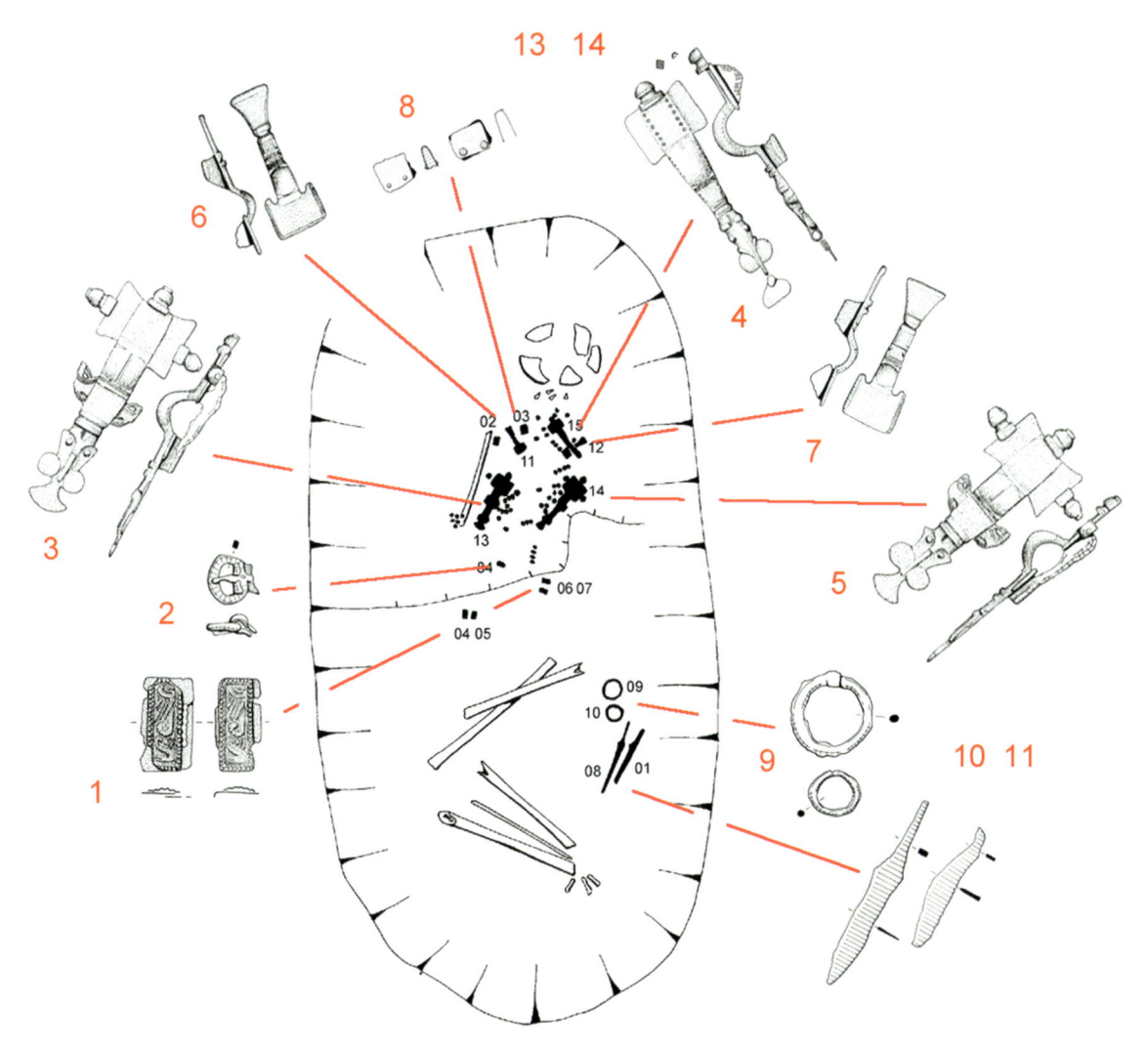

A magnificent collection of plain and polychrome glass beads found in a woman's grave at the Cleatham, North Lincolnshire, Anglo-Saxon cemetery. The beads had tumbled when their cord had decayed and their original order was lost. Bone was poorly preserved at Cleatham, but this grave shows how the grave goods were worn. Two pairs of sleeve clasps (1) were at the wrists and there was a small buckle (2) on the line of the high, female, waist. Unusually, the grave contained three cruciform brooches (3, 4 and 5) which may not have been positioned as worn in life. There were also two small long brooches (6 and 7) set on the shoulders to secure the woman's gown. The position of the two strap ends (8) suggests that they may have been grave-side offerings rather than grave goods. The two rings (10 and 11) may have been associated with a bag containing a knife and a fire-steel (10 and 11). (Plan and image: Kevin Leahy)

DRESS FITTINGS

WAW-0A0A84, 14mm, Hagley, Worcestershire (50-700)
Finds from the same area suggest that this amber bead is of Roman date, but the material was used during the Early Bronze Age and in the early part of the Early Medieval period.

LIN-0E61E1, 13mm, Sleaford area, Lincolnshire (480-580)
Early Medieval 'traffic light' glass bead, named from their red/yellow/green colours. Detailed research allows them to be dated.

NLM-599405, 19mm, Crowle, North Lincolnshire (400-700)
Dark blue glass beads are impossible to date unless they come from an archaeological context, such as a grave.

KENT-7009B3, 16mm, North Downs, Kent (625-670)
Biconical bead made from wound gold wire. These are found in the graves of high status Anglo-Saxon women.

NMGW-624CD3, 16mm, Cherington, Gloucestershire (400-600)
Amber beads become more common in the later 6th century replacing blue glass beads. Irregular-shaped examples like this are found in Anglo-Saxon graves.

SOM-4B0603, 21mm, Evercreech, Somerset (450-550)
Polychrome glass beads patterned with red dots and crosses have been found in large numbers in Early Anglo-Saxon graves.

KENT-2F2024, 25mm, Great Chart with Singleton, Kent
This interesting copper alloy object might be a pinhead rather than a bead. It is constructed of a cube with its corners cut off to form pyramidal faces. It is difficult to date with any confidence.

LON-7686A2, 35mm, Tower Hamlets, London (1500-1950)
Glass 'trade' beads were used in European dealings with Africa to acquire gold, ivory and slaves. Glass was uncommon in Africa, hence these items had a local value as currency.

SF-172C00, 8mm, Eye area, Suffolk (1450-1700)
This openwork cylinder could have been a mount for a cane or parasol, but its small size points to it being a bead or a spacer from a necklace.

DRESS FITTINGS

LACE TAGS

Lace tags, also known as aglets, protected the ends of laces, much as we have plastic coverings on shoelace ends today. During the Medieval and Post Medieval periods, laces, known as points, were used to tie a wide variety of garments as an alternative to buttons. Many lace tags are of simple form, but some are extremely decorative. There are over 300 lace tags on the PAS database of which over 180 are Medieval and 140 Post Medieval.

KENT-5D4C95, 18mm, Eastling, Kent (1200-1300)
Although this object looks like a pin, it could be a Medieval lace tag. The transverse rivet holes support this interpretation.

LON-0D052B, 15mm, Greenwich, London (1500-1560)
This elaborate Post Medieval lace tag is formed of a gold cylinder decorated with filigree.

LON-BAD2C1, 43mm, Castle Baynard, City of London (1500-1650)
Made of a simple rolled sheet of copper-alloy, this lace tag has an intricate raised lattice and floral design. Decorating sheet metal by stamping in this way is a Post Medieval technique.

SUR-91CC76, 35mm, Artington, Surrey (1600-1800)
Easy to produce, this lace tag is made of a triangular piece of sheet metal. It has small holes at its open end to enable it to be fixed to a textile lace.

BH-B5CA87, 11mm, Boughton under Blean, Kent (1625-48)
This lace tag can be dated as it is made of a silver penny of Charles I. A small piece of white textile held within the folds shows its role.

DRESS FITTINGS

SLEEVE CLASPS

This is a group of dress fittings worn by Anglo-Saxon women to secure the cuffs of their sleeves. They are Anglian, not being worn in the areas of southern England settled by Saxons – a pattern of use confirmed by the 600 sleeve clasps recorded by the PAS. Sleeve clasps were not used during the early years of the Anglo-Saxon settlement of England, being introduced from southern Scandinavia around AD 470. In Scandinavia, they were worn by both men and women, with men using them on their trouser legs, so the name 'sleeve clasp' is somewhat inappropriate.

NMS-758CA5, 39mm, Oxborough, Norfolk (470-570)
Stiffening bar from a sleeve clasp. This would have been soldered to a clasp like NMS-BAC147 below.

NMS-BAC147, 29mm, Oxborough, Norfolk (500-550)
Many sleeve clasps were made in two parts, with a flat plate onto which was soldered a stiffening bar. This often became detached and, as on this example, is represented by traces of solder.

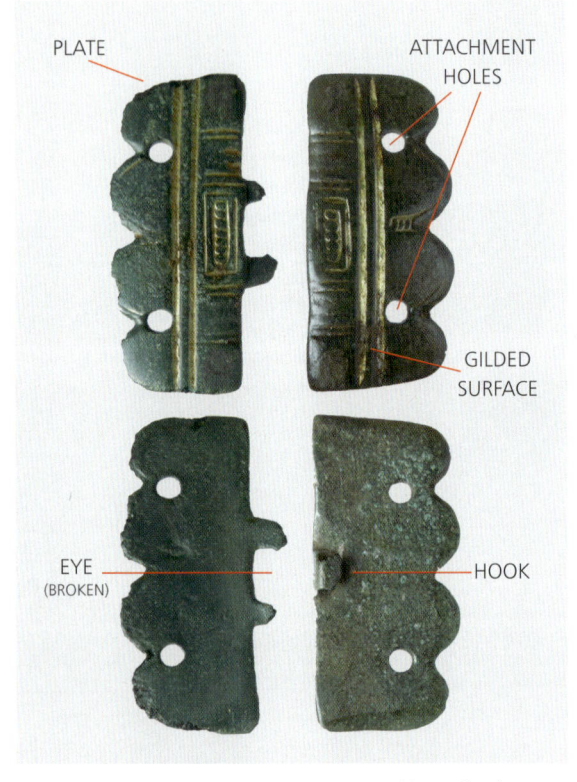

FAKL-4F5333 & FAKL-4F31B8, 38mm, Skirpenbeck, East Yorkshire (470-550)
Sleeve clasps were worn in sets of four, a pair on each wrist. They formed a hook and eye, the hook, seen on back of the clasp on the bottom right, engaging with an eye (now broken) on the other half.

LVPL-D7B1D8, 31mm, Scopwick, Lincolnshire (500-550)
Some sleeve clasps were ornate. This example is decorated in Anglo-Saxon Style I animal art, showing a central mask flanked by two eagles' heads.

NMS-4B5F35, 32mm, Fincham, Norfolk (470-550)
This sleeve clasp was cast in one piece, its underside hollowed to reduce the weight. It would have been sewn to the garment through the three loops.

NMS-BA7985, 32mm, Oxborough, Norfolk (470-550)
Simple sleeve clasp cut from sheet metal and bearing stamped decoration.

DRESS FITTINGS

GIRDLE HANGERS

Almost 300 girdle hangers have been recorded by the PAS. These are found in the areas of eastern and northern England settled by Angles. In graves, they are found at the waist and appear to have been suspended from the belt. They probably represented keys marking a woman's status as mistress of her household. Some of the simpler girdle hangers could have been used as keys but the more elaborate types must have been symbolic.

NLM-369137, 48mm, Binbrook, Lincolnshire (500-570)
Terminal from an Early Anglo-Saxon girdle hanger. It is decorated with rows of stamped impressions, and the upper junction of the sides and stem could represent animals' heads.

LIN-1E2097, 132mm, Folkingham, Lincolnshire (500-570)
Fragments of a complete, decorated girdle hanger. It is difficult to see how this complex object could have functioned as a key, so it is perhaps symbolic of one.

FAKL-508584, 157mm, Bridlington, East Yorkshire (500-570)
Girdle hangers were often worn in pairs, this example bears traces of rust staining and probably lay next to an iron knife in the grave.

85

Chapter 3
Ornaments

DRESS PENDANTS

Human beings have always had a desire to adorn themselves; suitably perforated animals' teeth have been found in late Palaeolithic graves. While some pendants may have been decorative, many (perhaps the majority) were amulets, intended to provide protection or show allegiance to a cause. Many Early Medieval pendants bear decoration which is incomprehensible to us. Perhaps this was always the case – a hidden animal preserves its power. During the Middle Ages religious imagery is popular on pendants, some containing relics, others showing depictions of saints or with biblically inspired inscriptions. After the Reformation the variety of motifs expands, with some highlighting political alliance (such as to the Crown) or being used to remember deceased loved ones.

SUSS-CB3674, 30mm, Chichester area, West Sussex (1300-1100 BC)
Bronze Age pendant made from wound gold wire. This was a single find, but a similar one was found in the Burton (Wrexham) Hoard providing a Bronze Age date.

SWYOR-3C6D73, 49mm, Saundby, Nottinghamshire (50 BC-AD 200)
In the archaeological literature, objects like this are referred to as 'danglers', a sure sign that their function is unknown. Their decoration, however, leaves no doubt about their Late Iron Age to early Roman date.

LIN-EDDE63, 35mm, Sudbrooke, Lincolnshire (43-250)
The phallus was an important protective symbol in the Roman world, symbolising masculine strength, vigour and fertility. Such symbols appeared everywhere and were considered guards against the evil-eye.

LIN-9FC476, 32mm, North Kesteven, Lincolnshire (43-400)
Pendant decorated with two horses' heads. This object is clearly Roman and seems to have been a pendant, but its meaning is unknown to us.

ORNAMENTS

IOW-05E330, 17mm Isle of Wight (600-670)
Early Medieval gold pendant set with a glass gem. Its shape and the form of its loop are typical of these pendants. They are found in the graves of Anglo-Saxon women and date from the time when England was being converted to Christianity.

LEIC-437467, 27mm, Shepshed, Leicestershire (600-70)
Gold pendant set with what is assumed to be a garnet. It was found in the plough soil, but objects found near it suggest that it came from the grave of a rich Anglo-Saxon woman.

SOMDOR-1440D6, 36mm, Dorchester, Dorset (600-70)
Gilt copper-alloy axe-shaped pendant decorated with animal interlace. There is a possible C-shaped head just to the right of the centre, and beasts' tails and feet are shown elsewhere. The obscurity of the decoration is probably deliberate. This object may have been worn by a person, but it could have been fixed to horse trappings.

DOR-1B7E81, 24mm, Charminster, Dorset (600-80)
Early Medieval filigree gold and garnet pendant. Associated finds (two silver crescents, a blue glass bead and the remains of a bone comb) suggest that it came from a disturbed Anglo-Saxon grave.

NMS-98E733, 24mm, North Elmham, Norfolk (582-602)
Pendant made from a Merovingian copy of a gold solidus of the Byzantine Emperor Maurice Tiberius (r.582-602). The obverse and reverse of the coin do not match: they were copied from two different coins. The suspension loop is typically Early Medieval.

IOW-125794, 22mm, near Shalfleet, Isle of Wight (500-50)
Bracteates were brought into England from Scandinavia during the 5th and 6th centuries. This gold 'D' bracteate shows a characteristic interlaced animal; its head is beneath the loop. More than 20 bracteates have been reported to the PAS as Treasure.

87

ORNAMENTS

FAKL-500088, 29mm, Bridlington, East Yorkshire (520-50)
Bracteate pendants were made from thin sheet metal where the back bears the negative of the face. The design on this silver 'C' bracteate was based on late Roman coins. This example shows a horseman, his large head facing right, below which is a highly stylised horse.

HAMP3426, 18mm, Wargrave, Berkshire (470-570)
Scutiform means shield shaped. These small silver pendants are found in the graves of Anglo-Saxon women. Some of them have miniature handles on their backs showing that they were intended to represent shields, guarding and protecting the wearer.

LIN-D3E540, 19mm, Spilsby area, Lincolnshire (850-950)
While Christians wore crosses, the Vikings, not to be out-done, started to wear silver representations of Thor's hammer.

SF9305, 40mm, Wickham Market, Suffolk (850-900)
Silver Valkyrie pendant showing a woman carrying a shield with a sword in her right hand. Pendants like this are found in Scandinavia and parts of England settled by the Vikings.

YORYM-FF8193, 28mm, Boroughbridge, North Yorkshire (1200-1400)
Cross-shaped pendants evoking divine help are more common that might be expected. This silver example has the letters AGLA, thought to derive from the initial letters of the Hebrew phrase 'Atta gibor le'olam Adonai' (you are mighty forever, O Lord). During the Middle Ages these words were considered to offer protection against fever and ill-health.

SF-153D94, 30mm, Bromeswell, Suffolk (1100-1700)
Simple cross-shaped pendants, like this one made of lead, are difficult to date.

ORNAMENTS

SWYOR-5DC01E, 33mm, Kirton-in-Lindsey, North Lincolnshire (1400-1550)
Related to pilgrims' badges (see below) this Medieval pendant evokes St Margaret of Antioch, who is likely to have been venerated at Ketsby, Lincolnshire. The village is now deserted, and its church gone, but it was dedicated to St Margaret and may have acquired a relic of the saint.

HAMP-CDC99B, 25mm, Buriton, Hampshire (1669-1800)
Religious pendants remained popular in the Post Medieval period, particularly from the late 17th century. This commemorates Maria Maddalena de' Pazzi (1566-1607), an Italian Carmelite nun canonised in 1669.

IOW-3B50B4, 19mm, Freshwater, Isle of Wight (1600-1700)
Love gifts, such as this silver heart-shaped pendant, became popular. This example is inscribed 'accept of this'.

SOM-DDF682, 18mm, Croscombe, Somerset (1750-1800)
This pendant of gold and rock-crystal contains black textile embroidered in gold thread with the letters AH. It was made in memory of a deceased loved one.

BADGES

From about the 14th century, badges became popular with pilgrims visiting holy sites. These not only denoted that the individual wearing it had undertaken a passage of pilgrimage to a particular shrine, but such badges were also treasured for their efficacious powers; Medieval people believed that an object touched upon a holy relic acquired some of the properties associated with the saint, helping to protect and cure the wearer. In time, badges were also worn to show political allegiance, to comment on matters of the world or simply for their aesthetic qualities. The term 'badge' is used for over 1,000 objects on the PAS database of which almost 800 are Medieval and 180 Post Medieval. Most (635) are lead, followed by 300 copper-alloy and 80 silver examples.

LON-4FC379, 38mm, Dowgate, City of London (1450-1500)
The Virgin and child was a popular motif in the Middle Ages. Rather than a pin, this lead badge has stitching holes.

89

ORNAMENTS

NMGW-DB8D66, 41mm, Swansea Bay, Swansea (1400-1550)
Badges of St Thomas (Becket) of Canterbury are amongst the most popular pilgrim souvenirs in Europe, such was the impact of this saint's martyrdom in 1170. This lead badge represents the bust reliquary at Canterbury that contained part of St Thomas' skull.

PUBLIC-364487, 73mm, City of London (1300-1400)
This intricate openwork badge probably shows St Thomas' martyrdom in Canterbury cathedral.

SF-739782, 25mm, Alderton, Suffolk (1400-1500)
Badge of St Roche of Montpellier, who was evoked by those fearing the plague, showing him dressed as a pilgrim. Beside Roche can be seen a small dog which, according to legend, soothed the saint's plague sores by licking them.

SUR-6DA5CB, 40mm, Clanfield, Oxfordshire (1400-1550)
Openwork badges are popular pilgrim signs in the Middle Ages. This lead badge shows a bird – perhaps a dove, representing the Holy Spirit – surrounded by the first words of the Ave Maria prayer. This badge is probably of generic religious type, rather than being associated with a particular shrine.

SUR-FFF175, 25mm, Ipsden, Oxfordshire (1400-1550)
Depicted on this badge is the scene of the Annunciation, when the angel Gabriel 'announces' to Mary that she will bear the God Child (Christ). Between the two figures is a lily, a symbol of Mary's purity.

LANCUM-619B37, 25mm, Appleby, Cumbria (1400-1525)
St George was a popular royal saint. Badges of his cult, such as this showing him killing the dragon, are often made of silver.

90

ORNAMENTS

SUR-10BCA4, 22mm, Stanford Dingley, Berkshire (1200-1500)
This lead badge seems to imitate a coin. There was a fashion for mounting coins as brooches in the Late Anglo-Saxon and early Norman periods (see WILT-C94353, page 48) and this perforated disc may belong to that tradition.

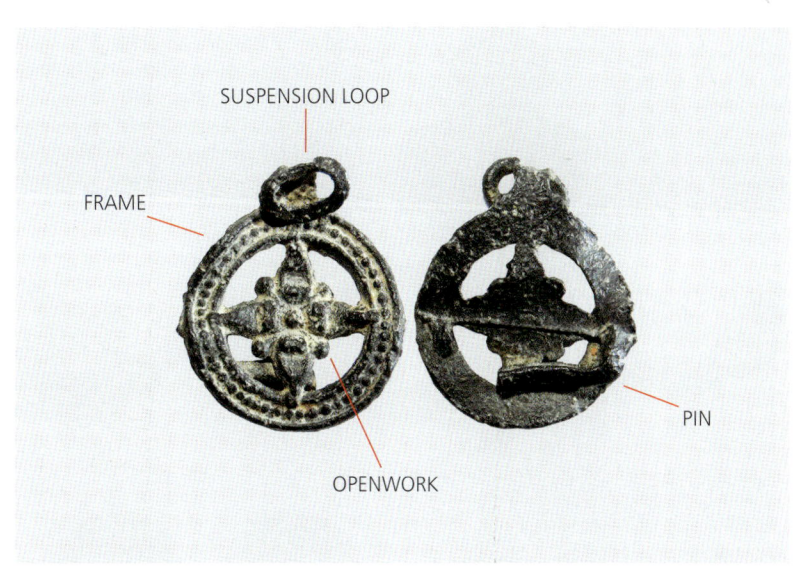

PUBLIC-2E6AF6, 15mm, Tower Hamlets, London (1375-1425)
Known as a 'hanging eye' badge, this lead example allowed for the suspension of amulets, sometimes religious in nature. On the reverse of this badge is an integrally cast pin.

Labels: SUSPENSION LOOP, FRAME, OPENWORK, PIN

IOW-B72041, 15mm, Arreton, Isle of Wight (1475-1550)
The S-shaped pin of this silver-gilt badge, suggests it is a Post Medieval cap badge; the pin would have passed though the brim and into the crown of the cap, and be used to model its appearance.

YORYM-1716A4, 36mm, Stillingfleet, North Yorkshire (1470-85)
The boar emblem was associated with Richard III (r. 1483-5) and such badges were given to his followers. This example is silver-gilt, and is much like one found near Bosworth, where, in 1485 Richard was killed in battle.

LON-39F433, 60mm, Southwark, London (1656)
Badges were produced for Freemen of the City of London. On the face of this lead badge are the arms of the City of London, and on its back the words 'FOR ANTHONY CREED A FREEMAN 1656'.

ORNAMENTS

LANCUM-CD0D37, 66mm, Kirkham, Lancashire (1910-35)
Military cap badges are common detector finds. This example, for the Royal Artillery, has a slider attachment.

LANCUM-935317, 39mm, Longtown, Cumbria (1937)
Badges of gollies were popular throughout much of the 20th century, from their first production in 1928. They were acquired by collecting labels from jars of Robertson's preserves. This example dates from 1937 and commemorates the Coronation of King George VI.

FINGER RINGS

Finger rings have been worn throughout time, from at least the Bronze Age. They became particularly common during the Roman period, with over 8,500 of them being recorded with the PAS. Not only are rings personal adornments, they also had an important social role. They could show allegiance to a particular god or, in Christian times, saint. They could act as amulets, guarding against evil and show political allegiances. In both the Roman and Medieval periods sumptuary laws regulated who could wear certain metals and with what stone settings. Rings were used to denote status, such as senior ecclesiastics, ambassadors and secular rulers, or the status of a married woman. Rings were often given as gifts; Early Medieval kings were renowned as the 'givers of rings'. During the Post Medieval period, finger rings are commonly used as love gifts, including as marriage rings. Rings could bear seals, act as keys, or commemorate the dead.

SOM-36B525, 29mm, Axbridge, Somerset (1400-1150 BC)
While impossible to date precisely, rings like this have been found in Middle Bronze Age hoards belonging to the 'Ornament Horizon'.

SWYOR-50CC3C, 15mm, Epworth, North Lincolnshire (200 BC-AD 200)
Simple rings have been attributed to the Iron Age but, as the adjacent find shows, they have also been found in Bronze Age hoards. Similar finger rings are found in Early Anglo-Saxon graves, making dating difficult.

ORNAMENTS

DENO-D7631D, 23mm, Loddon, Norfolk (100-200)
Roman silver ring set with an intaglio, a gem engraved with a motif which could be applied to a wax seal on a document. The motif shown appears to be an ear of wheat, perhaps associated with the goddess Ceres.

GLO-8C3E10, 21mm, Brent Knoll, Somerset (200-325)
A particularly elegant example of a Roman 'keeled' silver finger ring. This is a common type of Roman ring.

NCL-D1B498, 27mm, Revesby, Lincolnshire (50 BC-AD 100)
This Roman silver ring is of a simple form but contains a fine intaglio showing the Roman god Bacchus and a satyr; these companions of Bacchus were half-man and half goat, constantly drunk, and spent their time chasing nymphs.

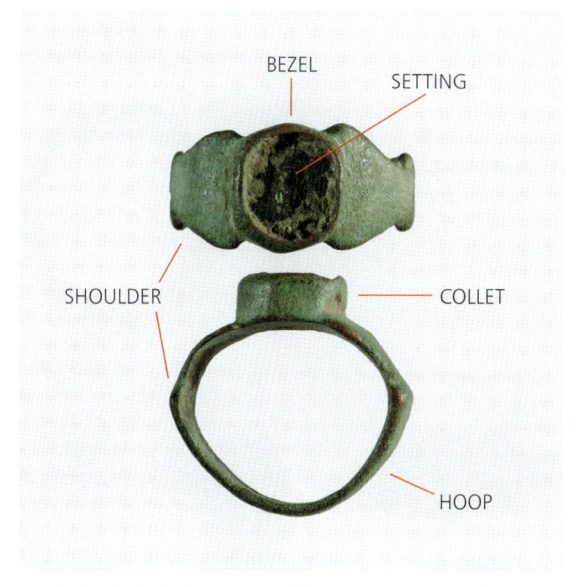

YORYM-F21E77, 21mm, Bridlington, East Yorkshire (200-300)
The narrow shoulders either side of the bezel are a feature often seen on Roman rings. The bezel would have originally contained a glass gem or intaglio.

HAMP-EC91E2, 22mm, Tangley, Hampshire (300-400)
Now damaged, this filigree gold ring with its blue intaglio setting represents the highest quality of Roman finger rings.

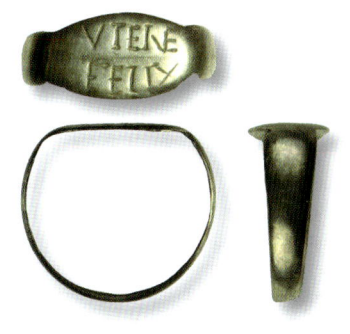

DOR-8F5E8E, 20mm, Gussage St. Michael, Dorset (43-400)
Roman silver finger ring inscribed VTERE FELIX (use with luck), hopefully bringing the wearer good fortune.

93

ORNAMENTS

SWYOR-D86B87 24mm, Walkeringham, Nottinghamshire (43-300)
The letters TOT on this Roman silver ring are thought to refer to the Celtic god Totatis. Most of these rings have been found in Lincolnshire and they are likely to represent a local cult.

DOR-8FF913, 20mm, Gussage St. Michael, Dorset (200-400)
Roman finger ring on which is a key for a slide lock, a good way of keeping a key safe and literally to hand.

WILT-9D4288, 23mm, Brixton Deverill, Wiltshire (500-650)
Silver slip-knot rings like this are found in Early Anglo-Saxon graves, sometimes linked to form necklaces. They were also used in the Roman period and so an Anglo-Saxon date cannot be assumed.

HAMP-C25EF3, 24mm, Ropely, Hampshire (820-920)
Middle Anglo-Saxon silver finger ring decorated with a Trewhiddle style animal, as seen on strap ends of the period (see page 62).

FAKL-6C1815, 23mm, West Acre, Norfolk (850-950)
Gold ring decorated with granulation and cloisonné enamel inlay. The inlay appears to be linked to that seen on some Late Anglo-Saxon brooches (see page 47).

IOW-3AA603, 26mm, Calbourne, Isle of Wight (850-1000)
These twisted rings are often attributed to the Viking Age, although some might date to other periods.

ESS-9CB5B8, 24mm, Tendring district, Essex (850-1000)
Viking gold ring with heavy stamped decoration.

NCL-90DD85, 25mm, Wood Enderby, Lincolnshire (850-1000)
The use of heavily stamped decoration, such as on this silver finger ring, is a feature of Viking jewellery.

94

ORNAMENTS

BH-D15C9F, 25mm, Little Munden, Hertfordshire (900-1000)
Gold ring decorated with filigree wire and balls of granulated gold. Rings of this type are Late Anglo-Saxon.

NMGW-3D1996, 19mm, Llancarfan, Vale of Glamorgan (1100-1200)
Geometric motifs and black niello are used to striking effect on this silver finger ring.

NMS-8EADF3, 25mm, Burgh St Peter, Norfolk (1200-1300)
Stirrup-shaped finger rings were popular in the Middle Ages. This gold ring is set with a blue stone.

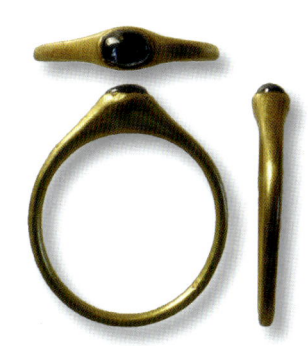

CAM-A8B768, 25mm, Huntingdon area, Cambridgeshire (1200-1400)
During the Middle Ages, gem stones were often polished, but not cut, for display in finger rings; as on this gold ring with a raised bezel, offering a setting for a polished blue stone.

IOW-0723C2, 25mm, Shorwell, Isle of Wight (1300-1400)
Schematic flower motifs, such as on this silver-gilt finger ring, were common. Of interest, this ring has its loop inscribed with +IESVS NAZAR+ (Jesus of Nazareth) in Lombardic script.

BH-EAE7D3, 27mm, Croxley Green, Hertfordshire (1350-1500)
The bezel of this finger ring serves as a seal matrix, with a reversed letter S; presumably denoting the name of its owner.

ORNAMENTS

DENO-508A9A, 21mm, East Bridgford, Nottinghamshire (1400-1550)
Some Medieval rings bear depictions of saints, as on this gold iconographic finger ring showing St Christopher. Its inscription reads *loyalte* with each letter in its own oval panel and embellished with leaves. Enamel inlay would have made this a startling object.

WMID-11E732, 19mm, Tamworth, Staffordshire (1400-1600)
Simple gold finger ring with the 'Black Letter' inscription *tout mon + ceur* (all my heart); each word is separated by a petalled leaf. Its original enamel inlay is represented only by the rough keying that held it in place. Black Letter is a style of writing which appears to consist of rows of vertical lines; it is elegant but can be difficult to read.

BH-04DFE9, 20mm, Bampton, Oxfordshire (1600-1700)
Gold signet rings, such as this, were owned by aristocrats. It has not been possible to ascertain the family that once owned this ring, as it lacks the colours needed to identify the heraldic arms.

SWYOR-0C5A58, 22mm, Hatfield, South Yorkshire (1400-1600)
Finger rings with two clasped hands, known as *fede* rings, became especially popular during the 15th century when they were given as symbols of love, marriage or betrothal. Their name is taken from the Italian *le mani in fede* (hands in faith).

HAMP-174CF2, 27mm, Ringwood, Hampshire (1600-1700).
This gilded Post Medieval finger ring has an oval bezel that would probably have been used by a merchant to make his mark; in this case TE.

YORYM-C9C446, 18mm, Monk Fryston, North Yorkshire (1750-1900)
Silver finger ring in the form of a buckled belt; a type that seems to have been a popular love gift.

ORNAMENTS

BRACELETS AND ARM RINGS

The PAS has recorded more than 2,300 bracelets and arm rings (armlets). They first appeared during the Bronze Age, from which we have almost 70 examples recorded on the database, and continued to be used throughout the Iron Age, also with 70 examples. Most of the bracelets on the PAS database are Roman with over 2,000 examples: they were very popular and there are many distinctive types. The Anglo-Saxons seem to have made little use of bracelets and armrings, unlike the Vikings, who produced some stunning examples in gold and silver. Bracelets were rarely used during Medieval times but re-appeared in more modern times. We do not know why fashions should change in the way that they did. Bracelets had some symbolic importance – Roman soldiers were awarded bracelets for gallantry, and Early Medieval sources make constant reference to kings being 'givers' of rings, which might be reflected in the armlets found in Viking hoards.

**BERK-A5FFE5, 98mm, Windsor, Berkshire
(1300-1100 BC)**
Middle Bronze Age gold bracelet encircled by four smaller gold rings, a practice that has been seen on other bracelets and torcs.

**SUR-590F5D, 87mm, Hurstbourne Priors, Hampshire
(1300-1000 BC)**
Cast bronze bracelet with incised geometric decoration. It was found in a hoard that also contained two other bracelets, part of a twisted torc, a spiral ring, a palstave axe and a socketed hammer. Bracelets like these are a northern French type and will have been imported.

**NMS-A71FB2, 31mm, Griston, Norfolk
(1000-700 BC)**
This terminal from a Bronze Age bracelet, can be paralleled by examples found in gold hoards.

**HAMP-5E48D1, 70mm, Soberton, Hampshire
(1150-750 BC)**
Late Bronze Age gold bracelet; its expanded terminals are typical of the type.

ORNAMENTS

BH-FA1F96, 49mm, Watlington, Oxfordshire (200 BC-AD 43)
Beaded bracelets of this form were used from the end of the Bronze Age into the Iron Age.

HAMP-93A632, 37mm, Bishops Waltham, Hampshire (800 BC-AD 50)
Finds from excavations show that this bracelet type started in the Late Bronze Age and may have survived until the Roman Conquest.

YORYM-620A34, 43mm, Bainton, East Yorkshire (100-400)
Fragment of a Roman glass bracelet, a type mainly found in northern Britain. This example consists of a D-sectioned ring with lines of coloured glass applied to its outer edge. There are 16 glass bracelets on the PAS database.

LON-43EA71, 41mm, Much Hadham, Hertfordshire (50-100)
An object does not need to be complete or beautiful to be important. This bracelet fragment bears decoration like that seen on 1st century Roman military metalwork, suggesting that it was part of an *armilla*, a bracelet awarded to a Roman soldier for a feat of arms.

SF-D1A307, 33mm, Bury St Edmunds area, Suffolk (200-400)
Fragment of a bracelet of a type found in Late Roman graves. The decoration was file-cut and the ring and dot motifs applied with a drill.

ORNAMENTS

PUBLIC-5B8028, 103mm, Codicot area, Hertfordshire (50-250)
Roman 'snake head' bracelet, named from the form of its terminals. This was a popular type and may have been in use longer that the suggested date.

SF-3082A5, 59mm, Ilketshall, Suffolk (1600-1900)
This Post Medieval bracelet is in the form of a bit from a horse's bridle. In its centre is a thistle or tulip motif.

WMID-22DE66, 60mm, Ilam, Staffordshire (1500-1950)
These bracelets are a lot later than their looks would suggest. Known as '*manillas*', and made from copper or brass, they were introduced into West Africa by the Portuguese during the 1490s. While commonly linked to the slave trade they were generally used as money in West Africa as late as the 1940s. Manillas come in a range of sizes and forms with each local tribe having a favoured type.

ORNAMENTS

TORCS

The word torc comes from the Latin torqueo, to twist, which aptly describes many of them – although some neck-rings, while described as torcs, were not twisted. There are 100 torcs on the PAS database, of which more than 60 have been assigned to the Iron Age, almost 30 to the Bronze Age and 7 Roman, although it can be difficult to distinguish between Iron Age and Roman torcs. The majority of the torcs (53) are copper-alloy while 42 are gold, most being represented only by fragments. With the exception of the Leekfrith torcs (WMID-FD08, page 17) all of the torcs recorded by the PAS are stray finds and lack an archaeological context, which stands in contrast to the finds from Snettisham, Norfolk, where excavations revealed at least 12 pits containing 180 gold torcs, together with silver and copper-alloy torcs. One can only wonder why this material was consigned to the ground.

CAM-E5D871, 427mm, East Cambridgeshire (1300-1100 BC)
This Middle Bronze Age gold torc is an astonishing object. Uncoiled it would have a length of 1,265mm with the terminals (shown in more detail in the centre) adding a further 108 mm at each end. It has a cross-shaped section which, when spirally twisted, gives a superb effect. As no torcs have been found in graves, it is not known how they were used; they may have been worn by chieftains, priests, wooden statues or just admired for their beauty.

ORNAMENTS

DENO-4B33B7, 179mm, Newark, Nottinghamshire (250-50 BC)
Iron Age torc made from electrum (an alloy of 67% gold, 32% silver, 1% copper). It is made up of eight 'ropes' each formed from around four twisted wires. These ropes were fixed into the two hollow terminals. These have lovely, swirling, decoration typical of La Tène early Celtic art.

SWYOR-E0B0B4, 108mm, Babworth, Nottinghamshire (100 BC-AD 200)
Not all torcs were made from gold – this 'beaded' torc is copper-alloy. The ends of a curved bar would have been fitted into the two sockets.

ORNAMENTS

EAR RINGS

Considering their size, and the fact that they are easily lost, it is surprising that the PAS has only recorded 116 ear rings, most of which (86) are Roman. Of the remainder, most are Post Medieval or Modern in date. No Medieval ear rings have been recorded. Many of the ear rings are plain and the identifications and dating must be viewed with some circumspection.

BERK-0D1A05, 46mm, Cholsey area, Oxfordshire (2400-2200 BC)
Late Neolithic to Early Bronze Age 'basket shaped' gold ear ring. The oval part of this object was originally curved across its width to form a 'basket'. Found to either side of the head in graves, they were ear rings or perhaps hair ornaments.

BH-16AE53, 32mm, Stagsden, Bedfordshire (50-150)
Roman lunulate gold earring decorated with filigree wire. Ear rings like this have been found in graves showing their function and, as there seems to be no way of removing it from the ear, it must have been worn permanently.

BH-A08638, 21mm, Stanstead Abbots, Hertfordshire (50-300)
'Slip-knot' type silver ear ring. While difficult to date with certainty there are good Roman parallels for this simple object.

NARC-2D3482, 36mm, Shepton Mallet, Somerset (100-200)
This Roman ear ring was secured with a hook and ring arrangement. The combination of different elements like the green glass bead and filigree cylinders is characteristic of high class Roman ear rings. It is unlikely that this object was made in Britain, it was probably an import from the eastern Mediterranean.

ORNAMENTS

BODKINS

These were used by women to keep their hair in place, especially when it was worn as a knot. Essentially, bodkins are long blunt needles, many found being made of silver, but would have also been formed of bone and wood. It is possible that they were also used to insert the crossing laces which secured women's bodices in the 17th century, the slot for ribbon, the hole for cord. The PAS has recorded over 220 bodkins, most of which are Post Medieval.

SUR-997F8C, 64mm, Whitchurch, Buckinghamshire (1600-1700)
As is typical, this silver bodkin has a long rectangular eye. It also has a circular hole in the terminal, and an engraved letter E.

NMS-032A66, 142mm, Pulham Market, Norfolk (1600-1700)
This silver bodkin has a decorative terminal with engraved geometric design. It is also stamped with the maker's mark G (within a shield) and the owner's initials MC.

STAFF TERMINALS

CAM-64F318, 46mm, West Wratting, Cambridgeshire (1050-1200)
Staff terminals are a feature of the early part of the Medieval period. Many are openwork, like this ball-shaped example and, while we can be fairly confident of their date, their role and function is unknown.

BERK-2B1D3E, 53mm, Kingstone Bagpuize with Southmoor, (1050-1200)
Another common form of Medieval staff terminal. There are 83 of these intriguing objects on the PAS database.

Chapter 4
Personal Care

COMBS

Combs have been used throughout history, but they rarely survive archaeologically as most were made of organic materials such as bone, antler, horn, ivory or wood. There are a few exceptions, which include a fine Iron Age example, shown below, which might have been used for combing the manes and tails of horses; recent mane combs are made of metal. Combs once formed part of Christian ritual, and fine ivory examples have been found, for example in the grave of St Cuthbert (died 687). Many bone and antler combs have been found in Anglo-Saxon graves and cremation urns, showing concern over personal appearance. Anglo-Saxon combs were composite, being made up from separate strips of antler into which the teeth were cut, held together by side plates, secured by tiny metal rivets. Medieval and Post Medieval combs demonstrate variety in form and craftsmanship and are hard to distinguish from one another, especially if found outside an archaeological context.

WAW-250340, 53mm, Tanworth in Arden, Warwickshire (25-75)
Copper-alloy Iron Age comb decorated in Celtic style using a 'matting-like' background similar to that on contemporary mirrors. It is strikingly similar to a modern horse mane comb.

LON-A5C847, 45mm, City of London (1200-1500)
Ivory Medieval comb noteworthy for its small size; it may have belonged to a child or it may have been a beard or moustache comb. The fine teeth would have been useful in the continuous battle against nits.

CAM-4580E4, 72mm, Ellington Thorpe area, Cambridgeshire (1500-1800)
Wooden combs are rare finds. This example was found in the foundations of a house dating to the early 17th century. These combs would have once been very common.

PERSONAL CARE

TWEEZERS

The PAS has recorded over 700 pairs of tweezers, 366 of which have been assigned a Roman date and 244 dated to the Early Medieval period although it is often difficult to distinguish between tweezers made in these two periods. Most were used for cosmetic purposes and probably had a depilatory function. Many have been found in contexts dating to the Early Anglo-Saxon period, including cremation urns, where we also see miniature 'votive' tweezers. Like combs, they must have been considered important to be so frequently included with burials. From the Middle Ages tweezers, or tweezer-like objects, seem to have had a range of alternative uses. Often this role is not readily apparent, though tweezers are clearly very useful when undertaking delicate tasks where the use of fingers alone proves too cumbersome.

YORYM-3D23D1, 53mm, Millington, East Yorkshire (50-400)
These plain tweezers are difficult to date, a Roman or an Early Medieval date being equally possible.

SUR-AD2DBE, 57mm, Bradfield, Berkshire (50-400)
Pair of elaborate tweezers, lacking nips but perhaps representing a Roman sword.

LEIC-007995, 55mm, Grimston, Leicestershire (50-400)
These tweezers were made from a strip of sheet metal folded to shape. Other finds from the site suggest a Roman date.

BM-1F8675, 74mm, Piercebridge, County Durham (50-400)
While resembling tweezers, this finely made iron object is more likely to be a pair of surgical forceps.

YORYM-D20E36, 69mm, Levisham, North Yorkshire (450-850)
During the Middle Anglo-Saxon period tweezers tended to have broader nips, as seen on this example, than were used in the Roman and Early Anglo-Saxon periods.

105

PERSONAL CARE

CAM-649201, 48mm, Milton Keynes area, Buckinghamshire (1100-1500)
Constructed from a single metal strip, the mid-point on these Medieval tweezers has been formed to create a suspension loop. A slide ring has been added over both arms making it possible to lock them in position.

SWYOR-272F62, 44mm, Exton area, Rutland (1200-1500)
The large rectangular terminals of this pair of tweezers suggested to the recorder they had an alternative use, perhaps to hold the pages of a Medieval book. Given the tendency of parchment to curve this is possible.

NMS-9D2111, 73mm, North Lopham, Norfolk (1600-1700)
These 'tweezers' were probably crimpers, for closing and securing pastry joins, as when making pies.

EAR SCOOPS

Before the advent of the cotton wool bud, ear scoops were invaluable for cleansing ears, removing the build-up of wax deposits. It is also possible that they were used for extracting perfume from bottles. Around 70 of them have been recorded with the PAS, half of which are Roman, the others spread over later periods. Many ear scoops were included in toilet sets, along with tweezers and finger nail cleaners.

BH-77EC94, 45mm, Farnham, Essex (50-200)
A typical Roman ear scoop. At one end is a tiny cup, at the other was a loop to allow it to be suspended as part of a toilet set.

PERSONAL CARE

LIN-CFABA7, 46mm, Apley, Lincolnshire (50-400)
Elegant Roman ear scoop with delicate mouldings. The spoon element is quite large and this may have been primarily used for ointments.

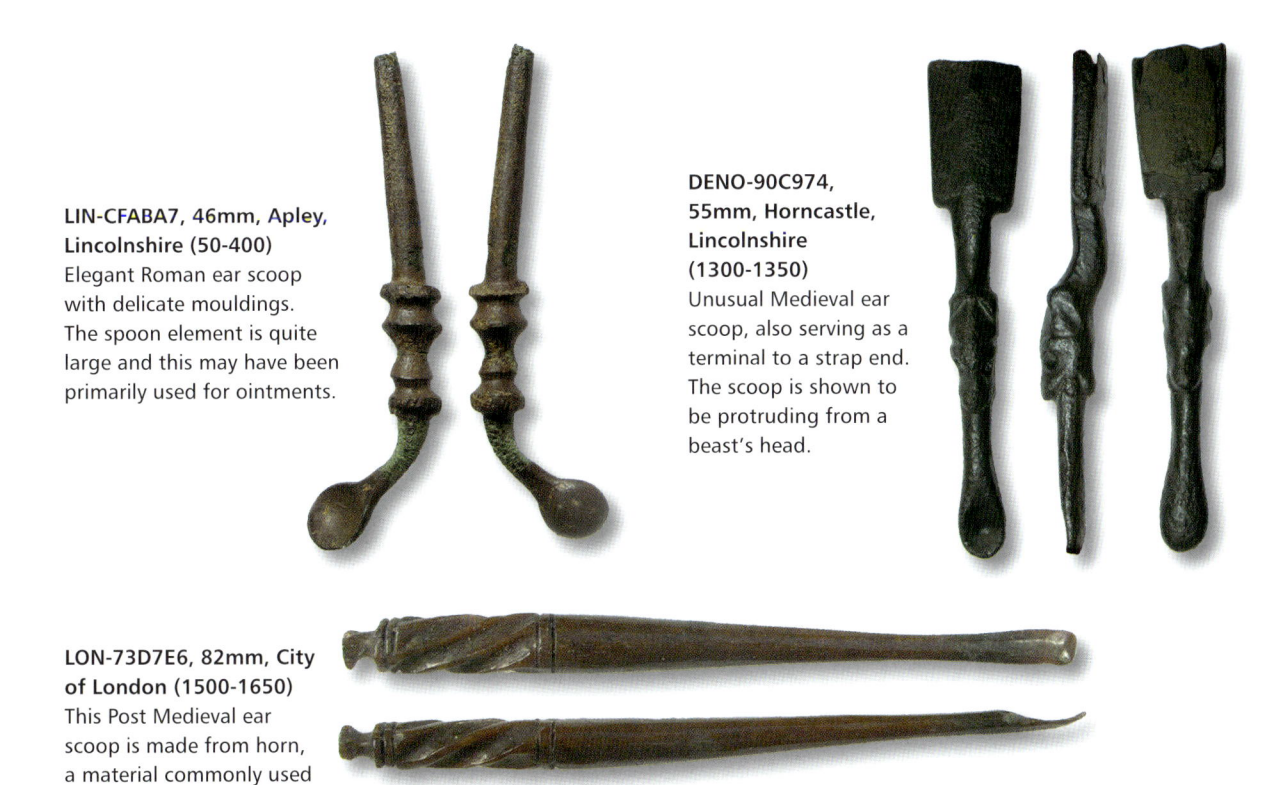

DENO-90C974, 55mm, Horncastle, Lincolnshire (1300-1350)
Unusual Medieval ear scoop, also serving as a terminal to a strap end. The scoop is shown to be protruding from a beast's head.

LON-73D7E6, 82mm, City of London (1500-1650)
This Post Medieval ear scoop is made from horn, a material commonly used in the past, but which seldom survives.

NAIL CLEANERS

Nail cleaners represent part of the massive increase in small metal objects that occurred following the Roman Conquest as new object types were first used; toilet implements, for example, became common. Over 550 examples have been recorded, almost all of which have been assigned to the Roman period. Not surprisingly, these objects are found throughout Roman Britain.

DOR-DCFD4A, 52mm, Berwick St John, Wiltshire (50-400)
The split end is a feature common to Romano-British nail cleaners; elsewhere in the Roman Empire, simple spike nail cleaners were used.

YORYM-05DCE8, 53mm, Wetwang, East Yorkshire (50-200)
The finish and style of these tweezers is typical of Roman metalwork.

DOR-DBB5C1, 42mm, Gussage St Michael, Dorset (50-200)
Not all nail clearers were elaborate. This example was simply cut from sheet metal.

107

PERSONAL CARE

COSMETIC MORTARS

These are likely to have been used for grinding small quantities of powders. Roman women wore makeup and these little grinders would have been useful in turning coloured stones into usable powders. They may also have been used in the preparation of medicines – eye ointment, for example, was provided in the form of small briquettes which were ground for use. Almost 400 cosmetic mortars have been recorded by the PAS along with 200 of the pestles that were used with them.

WAW-64685C, 76mm, Shudy Camps, Cambridgeshire (100 BC-AD 200)
Bulls' heads appear on Late Iron Age metalwork but continued to be used into the Roman period. If not Iron Age, this mortar at least follows a native tradition of decoration.

SUR-D37C15, 65mm, Whitchurch, Hampshire (100 BC-AD 200)
Cosmetic mortars are curved with a deep groove along one face and were fitted with loops.

SOM-8CAF0C, 55mm, Pitney, Somerset (100 BC-AD 200)
This object is the counterpart of a cosmetic mortar. It has a similar claw-like shape but lacks a groove. It was the pestle which was rubbed up and down in the groove to grind powders.

PERSONAL CARE

RAZORS

Although the first razors appear in the Early Bronze Age, flint razors may have been used earlier in prehistory. In addition to its cosmetic role, shaving may have been carried out for reasons of hygiene (evicting lice) or as part of a ritual as a sign of mourning. Of more than 100 razors recorded by the PAS, 53 are from the Bronze Age and 40 are Roman. It is likely that the use of iron has led to Roman razors being under-represented, as this metal is normally discriminated out by detectorists. Finds from Early Medieval burials show that the Anglo-Saxons shaved but, as the razors were made from iron they, again, are unlikely to be found.

SUR-D8D06E, 90mm, Bampton, Oxfordshire (1800-1400 BC)
Early Bronze Age leaf-shaped razor. The edges have been hammered to work-harden them and to make them thinner to produce a sharp edge.

LANCUM-220D90, 94mm, Milnthorpe, Cumbria (800-500 BC)
Razors of this form date from the Late Bronze Age into the Early Iron Age. The design is of Continental origin.

NLM-9EFC35, 47mm, Wickenby, Lincolnshire (200-400)
This Roman razor originally had an iron blade which is now represented by a rust stain.

PERSONAL CARE

MIRRORS

Nowadays we are surrounded by mirrors, but in ancient times one's own reflection was less regularly seen, and rarely seen as clearly as now. The main purpose of mirrors was as a cosmetic tool, though during the Middle Ages they were also a love gift full of meaning; mirrors (like the hopeful gift giver) would enter the lady's bedchamber and see her close in the flesh! They also had a religious use; a mirror could be opened at a saint's shrine to capture the 'radiant grace' which would be re-emitted when needed. The PAS has recorded over 60 mirrors in addition to which there are 200 finds of copper-alloy Medieval mirror cases.

DOR-F12EF3, 302mm, Chesil, Dorset (80 BC-AD 50)
This bronze mirror was found with glass and stone beads, two brooches, a spiral copper alloy bracelet, a pair of tweezers and a coin of the Roman Republic dated to 83-82 BC. As a group it is clear that they came from a grave. Mirrors represent a pinnacle of Iron Age art. Their backs, as on this example, were decorated with swirling, curved designs epitomising Celtic design.

PERSONAL CARE

YORYM-F1D606, 37mm, Welton, East Yorkshire (80 BC-AD 50)
Handle fragment from a Late Iron Age mirror.

NMGW-23D631, 98mm, Smannell, Hampshire (50-100)
To get a reflective surface the Romans used 'speculum', a high tin, copper alloy. Polished, this would reflect like glass but, unfortunately, it was brittle and would break easily. Roman mirrors are, for reasons not understood, strongly concentrated in East Anglia.

LANCUM-9E1E16, 81mm, Wroughton, Wiltshire (50-400)
Roman mirror handle, the mirror disc being inserted into the slot.

111

PERSONAL CARE

WILT-3CA276, 44mm, Silchester, Hampshire (1300-1450)
Medieval mirror cases can be elaborately decorated. Riveted through each side of this example are 11 projections, which may have been collets for gem settings. Around them are six square panels, the remnants of fixing for applied sheet metal plates.

BH-D9A5B1, 47mm, Buckland, Hertfordshire (1300-1450)
Medieval mirror cases were made in two identical parts, hinged to allow them to be opened. The lugs at the bottom enabled the case to be secured with thread or wire. Within the case would be fixed a piece of silvered glass which acted as a mirror. Such mirror cases are widespread throughout the country.

NARC-CC3D05, 42mm, unknown, Oxfordshire (1200-1400)
The designs found on lead mirror cases are often much more decorative than on those made of copper-alloy, reflecting the ease with which lead alloys can be cast.

PERSONAL CARE

CHATELAINES

Chatelaines allowed for the easy carrying of multiple cosmetic implements (tweezers, finger nail cleaner and ear scoop) as shown above. In the absence of pockets, they were attached to a belt, or to the clothing, to ensure that these small objects were to hand and not lost. Chatelaines could, however, themselves be lost; there are over 65 of them on the PAS database, of which 27 are Roman and 17 Medieval. Roman chatelaines were often inlaid with enamel but during the Middle Ages their decoration became more conservative and most share the same, rather complex, functional form. Chatelaines again became common during the 19th century when a range of tools were suspended on chains from women's belts.

NCL-B79326, 47mm, Warkworth, Northumberland (50-200)
Roman chatelaine inlaid with enamel, which now appears white having lost its colour over the centuries. The toilet implements were suspended from a bar between the two lower lugs.

SUR-042BE0, 40mm, Fritwell, Oxfordshire (100-200)
Fine enamel-decorated Roman chatelaine brooch; its pin and pin fittings can be seen on the back, and beneath it are the two lugs that held the bar for the toilet implements.

LEIC-8572C4, 93mm, Narborough, Leicestershire (100-200)
This chatelaine still retains one of its three toilet implements. Roman chatelaines are thinly spread across England but there are small groupings, such as in East Yorkshire.

HAMP-235970, 47mm, Micheldever, Hampshire (600-700)
Early Medieval chatelaine of Continental type. It has been shown upside down so the animal decoration can be seen; the two animals are shown in profile, facing each other, their conjoined V-shaped jaws meeting at the top to form a lozenge-shaped panel. Either side of this, one eye of each beast can be seen, their front and back legs touching on the centre line.

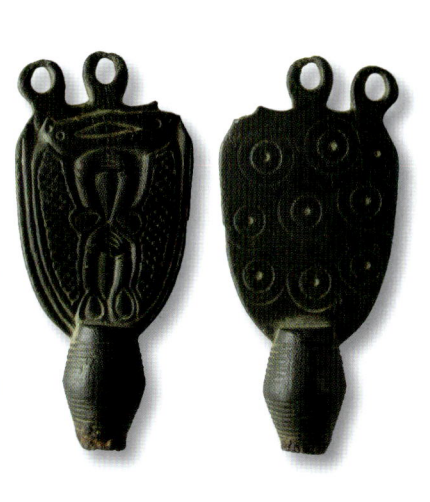

113

PERSONAL CARE

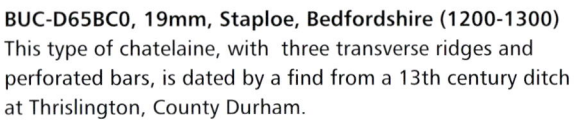

BUC-D65BC0, 19mm, Staploe, Bedfordshire (1200-1300)
This type of chatelaine, with three transverse ridges and perforated bars, is dated by a find from a 13th century ditch at Thrislington, County Durham.

LON-794E32, 234mm, City of London (1650-1700)
Like many Post Medieval objects, this chatelaine takes advantage of the availability of drawn copper-alloy wire.

DENTAL IMPLEMENTS

Dentures (perhaps surprisingly) are not uncommon metal-detected finds with 25 being recorded, 14 of them made of gold. Gold dental plates start around AD 1800 and go out of fashion around the 1930s when materials such as Vulcanite (a hardened rubber) start being used. The amount of gold in the alloy is usually just enough to give the metal a yellow appearance. How they were lost is a mystery! The novel ways in which human beings have tried to maintain a full set of teeth are fascinating, and sometimes surprising. Occasionally, the teeth of the dead were pushed into the gums, or teeth were transplanted from a living donor, paid to make the sacrifice. Later generations, however, have preferred artificial substitutes.

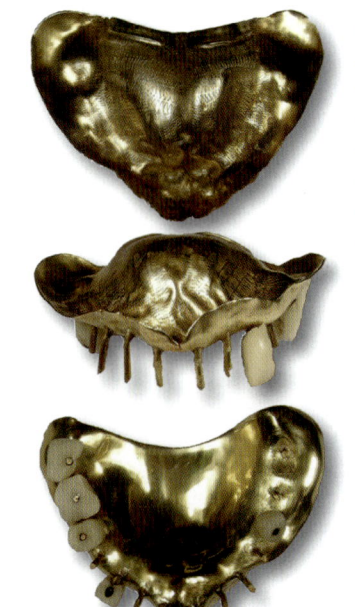

LANCUM-3DE363, 68mm, Carnforth, Cumbria (1838-1920)
These dentures are made from gold, with porcelain teeth set onto posts soldered onto the base plate.

PERSONAL CARE

WMID-BC8AC7, 53mm, Barrow, Shropshire (1800-1930)
While the teeth are missing, this lower dental plate retains an accurate representation of the wearer's gum and loops that secured it to surviving teeth.

LVPL-85A4D6, 51mm, Kellington, North Yorkshire (1890-1930)
Swaging blocks, such as this, were used to make dentures. An impression was taken from the jaw and from it a copper-alloy casting was made. The soft gold was then hammered over the casting to copy the shape of the jaw.

HAMP-3FDE76, 85mm, Westminster, London (1900-1914)
Pewter tray for taking dental impressions from which false teeth would be made. The tray is stamped 'C. ASH & Sons ENGLAND' who were Briton's leading supplier of dental appliances and false teeth.

WIG CURLERS

During the 17th and 18th centuries the wearing of periwigs (wigs) became common, and they adorned the heads of both men and women. When not in use, wigs were kept on a stand, with wig curlers being used to help keep the curls in place. There are 15 wig curlers on the PAS database and, like many of the objects included here, they are easy to recognise once you know what they are!

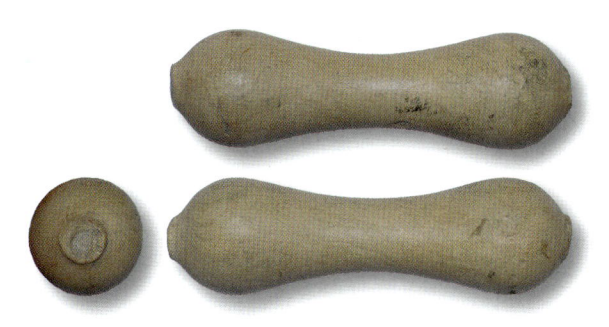

PUBLIC-78CD8E, 62mm, Southwark, London (1650-1800)
Wig curlers were often made from the same clay sources used for pipes, and there is evidence of manufacturers making both wig curlers and pipes.

Chapter 5
Religion and Belief

AMPULLAE

The tradition of pilgrims collecting holy water from sacred sites is a long one. At first this was probably taken away in ceramic vessels, but by the Middle Ages these vessels (*ampullae*) were made of lead. They had small handles so they could be hung on a leather or textile string around the neck. Such holy water might be drunk, rubbed onto the skin, or sprinkled around, to unleash mystical properties believed to protect and cure. The PAS has recorded over 1,600 *ampullae*, which are widespread across the country. They are often found on fields where they had perhaps been applied to an ailing crop.

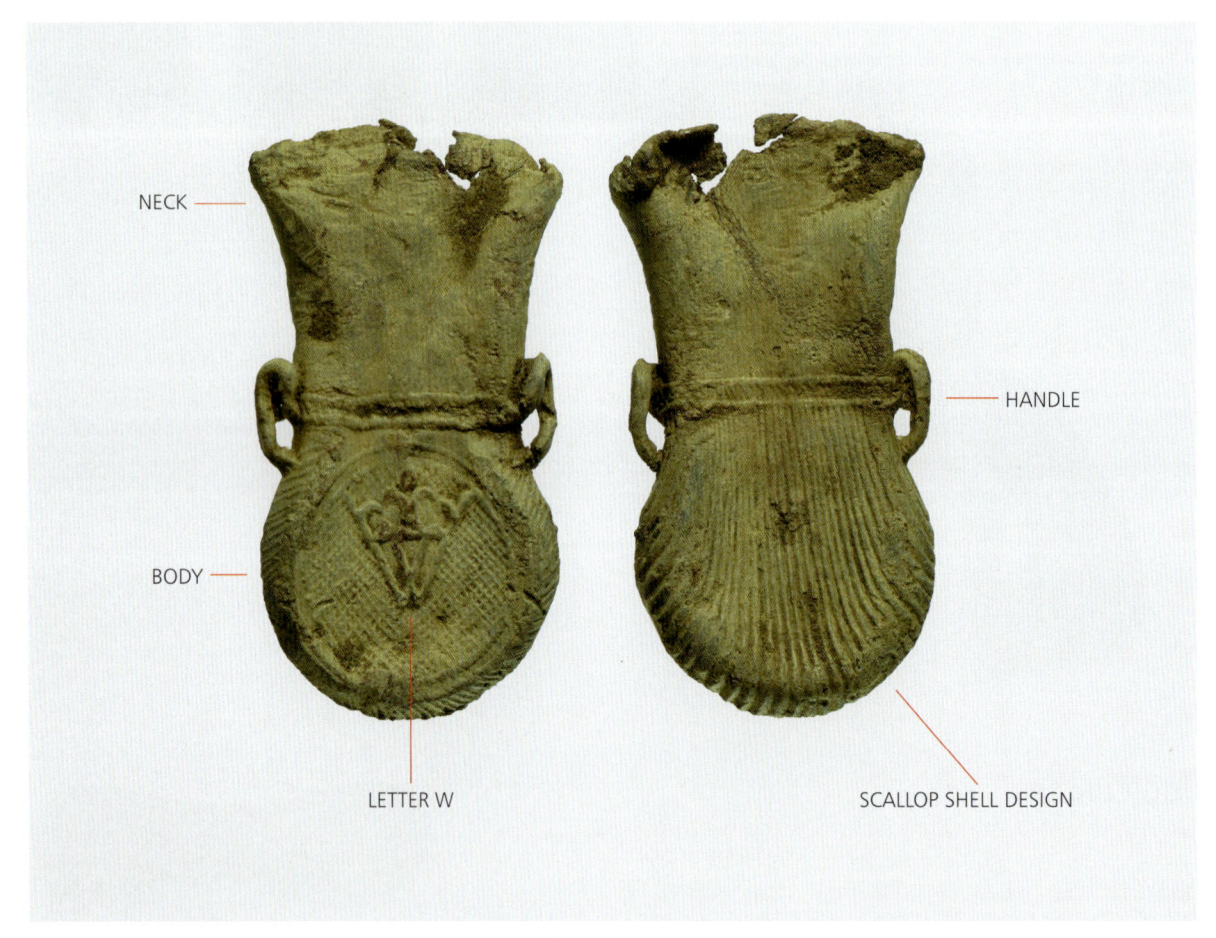

SF-B28208, 56mm, Bressingham, Norfolk (1150-1350)
Many *ampullae* bear a letter W, believed to represent the important pilgrimage site of Walsingham, Norfolk, where a 'replica' of the House of the Annunciation had been constructed. This housed a statue of the Virgin and child, which became a focus of religious devotion throughout the Middle Ages. It is also possible the letter actually reads 'V V' for '*Virgo Virginum*' – Virgin of virgins (for the Virgin Mary), a common apotropaic symbol offering protection.

RELIGION AND BELIEF

LIN-BA47C6, 54mm, Stainton by Langworth, Lincolnshire (1300-1500)
Ampullae of barrel form are uncommon, this lead example is decorated with shields.

IOW-A1FF86, 51mm, Northwood, Isle of Wight (1300-1500)
Appearing on this lead *ampulla* is a stylised scallop shell motif. Such shells were associated with pilgrimage in general, but with the cult of St James 'the Great' at Santiago de Compostela in northern Spain, in particular.

LIN-C5FADF, 44mm, Hogsthorpe, Lincolnshire (1330-1530)
This lead *ampulla* has a fancy flared body. The meaning of its chevron design is not clear.

BULLAE

Seals, known as 'bullae' were attached to papal 'bulls', documents issued in the name of the pope by the papal curia (and other authorities). Confusingly, both the documents and seals share the same plural 'bullae'. It is the seal, always made of lead, that is found by metal detector users. The documents to which these seals were attached were normally edicts (proclamations) or indulgences, remitting the penalties of sin, and grants of land or rights. Their design was remarkably conservative, showing the profiles of Saints Peter and Paul on one side and the name of the pope on the other. They are, for something issued by one of the most sophisticated organisations in Europe, surprisingly crude. It is likely that many of those found were discarded during the mid-16th century Reformation. Over 400 *bullae* have been recorded, widespread across the country.

KENT-01AD9F, 40mm, Denton with Wootton, Kent (719-816)
Extraordinarily early in date, this *bulla* was issued in the name of Pope Leo III. He crowned Charlemagne as Holy Roman Emperor on Christmas Day AD 800. These early *bullae* do not have the pictorial imagery found on later papal seals.

RELIGION AND BELIEF

BH-256B91, 27mm, Baldock, Hertfordshire (1277-80)
Papal *bullae* were sometimes reused, and this of Pope Nicholas III was probably re-worked to be a weight. It is notable that whoever re-purposed the object did so preserving much of the image and legend upon it.

WILT-5D31FF, 39mm, Teffont, Wiltshire (1410-25)
This is a well preserved seal of the antipope Pope John XXIII. At this time the Church was divided, with rival popes holding power, one of whom, John XXIII, was supported by the English crown. It shows, as is typical, the faces of St Peter and St Paul on one side (and their abbreviations – SPE SPA), and the name of the pope on the other.

SOM-FBA501, 42mm, Cheddon Fitzpaine, Somerset (1461-71)
This *bulla* shows an elaborate image of Paul II with his cardinals and his flock. Paul was the only pope to use this design, which was likely to have been politically motivated.

BH-8F07F3, 38mm, Farnham, Essex (1503-12)
Bullae issued by the Order of the Hospital of St John of Jerusalem are occasionally found. This one is in the name of its Master, Amaury d' Amboise. At the time this seal was made, the Order had a large number of estates in England.

FIGURINES

There is a strong and ancient European tradition of making representations of gods and, in later times, saints. These were used for personal devotion but also embellished liturgical items, such as reliquaries and processional crosses. Figures of saints were popular in the Middle Ages and represent the intense piety of an age when religion represented the very foundation of people's lives. Following the Reformation, much religious art was rejected and, thanks to the printing press, it was replaced (in part) by personal study of newly available religious works, including English translations of the Bible. In the Post Medieval period many ornaments were owned for purely aesthetic purposes, such as to furnish the home, though religious figurines remained common. The PAS has recorded over 1,100 figurines, of which almost 600 are Roman,

SF-2492B7, 31mm, Fen Ditton, Cambridgeshire (100 BC-AD 200).
Ducks are a common emblem in the Iron Age, though it is strange to us that this warrior society was so interested in these birds which seem to lack something of the gravitas later achieved by the eagle.

widespread throughout the country. Over 200 Post Medieval figurines have been recorded and almost 180 Medieval.

RELIGION AND BELIEF

LIN-CEB738, 37mm, Great Sturton, Lincolnshire (1-100)
The boar, an animal of great ferocity, was a popular emblem in the Iron Age appearing on the coins of the Corieltauvi, the tribe whose lands included what is now Lincolnshire.

BERK-F1499B, 78mm, Beckley, Oxfordshire (50-200)
Statuette of the Roman god Mercury, shown wearing a silver torc, in his hand is a purse, one of Mercury's symbols. His missing left hand probably held the caduceus, a snake-entwined staff, another of his other attributes.

WILT-5A8A35, 78mm, Salisbury, Wiltshire (50-400)
Powerful statuette of a leopard, an animal sacred to Bacchus. Unusually, the base of this Roman statuette survives.

RELIGION AND BELIEF

LVPL-1F8252, 59mm, Kirton in Lindsey, North Lincolnshire (50-400)
Statuette of the Roman goddess Minerva, wearing her characteristic helmet. Although corroded, this bronze preserves its Classical elegance.

HAMP-378231, 34mm, Andover, Hampshire (100-300)
This figurine represents a bound captive. Its function is unknown but it appears to have been a fitting of some sort. Eight of these bound captive, or slave, mounts have been recorded by the PAS. Outside Britain, they are only found along the Empire's Rhine-Danube frontier.

ESS-998F26, 155mm, Colchester Essex (50-400)
Pipe-clay statuette of a Roman goddess. As she is fully dressed, and matronly, she is likely to represent Juno, the wife of Jupiter. These pipe-clay statuettes were cast in moulds and must have been made in large numbers.

RELIGION AND BELIEF

BH-ED9F44, 63mm, Baldock, Hertfordshire (50-200)
Statuette of a goddess wearing a helmet and armour. A hole through one hand would have held a spear, and in the other arm she holds a cornucopia, a horn of plenty. These devices show that the figure represents both Minerva and Fortuna.

LEIC-9F3451, 55mm, Bosworth, Leicestershire (50-400)
Figurine of an eagle, probably from a Roman priest's sceptre.

ESS-E6F9E3, 80mm, Thorrington, Essex (50-300)
Figure of Priapus, the Roman god of fertility and protection. Priapus is shown with an erect phallus and bunches of grapes reflecting his mother, Aphrodite, the goddess of love, and his father the wine god, Dionysus.

RELIGION AND BELIEF

FAKL-20CB45, 66mm, Silkstone, West Yorkshire (50-300)
Crude lead figures like this present a problem for archaeologists trying to date them. It is likely that they are Roman and represented Priapus, a rustic god popular in the countryside. This is one of the better crafted lead figures of Priapus.

NLM-A243C8, 52mm, Caistor, Lincolnshire (500-600)
Most early Anglo-Saxon art consists of highly stylised animals and faces, but we see a small number of human figures. It is likely that some of these represent gods but it is usually impossible to identify them. The hollow back of this figure is filled with lead suggesting that it was a mount of some kind.

IOW-00EB11, 60mm, Calbourne, Isle of Wight (1250-1450)
Figurines of the Virgin and Child were popular in the Middle Ages and are often considered to be fittings from precentors' staffs or croziers, but they also may have been used as devotional aids at the home.

RELIGION AND BELIEF

WILT-3E4001, 84mm, The Deverills, Wiltshire (1450-1530)
Gilt figure of St John the Evangelist from a processional cross. It would have been set below and to one side of the crucifix with a figure of the Virgin on the other side.

IOW-F54117, 28mm, Arreton, Isle of Wight (1700-1950)
Seated figure of the Buddha. From the Post Medieval period onward, increasing contacts with the rest of the world brought a wide range of religious figures into the country; Buddhist and Hindu items are most popular.

CRUCIFIXES AND CROSSES

The crucifix and cross are the two most recognisable of all Christian emblems, symbolising both the physical and spiritual suffering of Jesus Christ. The two are often confused. A crucifix bears the figure of Christ, while a cross is plain. It is no surprise, therefore, that the PAS has recorded 125 crucifixes, with the cross being commonly represented on other items making them difficult to quantify.

LIN-75FD54, 40mm, Newball, Lincolnshire (600-700)
The arms of this gold cross are set below the centre line of the upright, which is not how the cross is usually shown. If, however, the wearer inverted it, by raising it up to her face, it would appear correct.

RELIGION AND BELIEF

YORYM214, 53mm, Holderness, East Yorkshire (620-660)
Gold pectoral cross set with cloisonné garnets. The stones are poorly shaped but were laid on pieces of waffle-patterned gold foil to make them glitter. The foil in turn was set on a bed of calcium carbonate to level the cells. The central, circular, stone has an annular groove cut into its face which was probably inlaid with gold.

DENO-89E427, 29mm, Newark area, Nottinghamshire (500-670)
Small pendant cross with filigree decoration and set with cabochon, pebble-shaped, garnets. Like most gold objects this cross is hollow. Gold is highly valuable but easy to shape and solder, which leads to the economical use of hollow, box-like structures, when using the metal.

BH-0D0F26, 50mm, Therfield, Hertfordshire (1150-1300)
Limoges cross terminals nearly always depict a symbol of one of the four evangelists, this one appearing to show a winged bull, representing St Luke. The bull's small head can be seen in the middle of the central ring. Originally inlaid with coloured enamel this would have been a striking object.

IOW-32DA02, 62mm, Niton and Whitwell, Isle of Wight (1250-1300)
This figurine of the suffering Christ parallels one found beneath an early 14th century floor at Carmarthen Greyfriars, Carmarthenshire.

RELIGION AND BELIEF

LVPL-97D3FA, 35mm, Cwm, Denbighshire (1300-1400)
This crucifix has Christ on the display side, with Mary and Child on the reverse. As a pendant of simple form, it would have been an object for personal devotion.

WILT-8A17A9, 31mm, Kingston Deverill, Wiltshire (1100-1550)
Simple lead crosses, such as this, are hard to date. The purpose of the four pellets attached to it is unknown.

NLM-018DB7, 56mm, Roxby cum Risby, North Lincolnshire (1850-1900)
A huge variety of crucifixes were produced in the Post Medieval period. This figure of Christ was originally set on a panel of inlay, perhaps ivory.

RELIGION AND BELIEF

RELIQUARIES

The veneration of relics formed an important part of the Christian Church from its earliest beginnings. The PAS has not yet recorded an Early Medieval reliquary, although it is possible that the hollow pendant crosses described above may have contained relics. Likewise, some of the Irish mounts brought into England by the Vikings may have been removed from reliquaries or shrines. The cult of relics was an important feature of the Middle Ages. Relics were not only the bones of saints (1st class relics) but also personal items and objects associated with their life on earth (2nd class). Secondary relics (3rd class) were produced by placing a piece of cloth onto an actual relic or dipping it into water poured over a relic. It was believed these items held spiritual properties that could bring protection and cures to those who touched them. Faith in relics was a rational response to a world that people could neither control nor understand, their potency being assured by miracles. Every Christian altar was required to hold relics, and relics were also the focus of pilgrimage, besides personal devotion. Relics were avidly collected by the aristocracy who needed fine containers (reliquaries) in which to keep and display them. These varied from magnificent shrines to personal items kept close to the believer. The PAS has recorded 18 reliquaries most of which were in the form of small personal pendants, and many other items that probably came from shrines that held relics.

DUR-6A4CE7, 22mm, Durham area, County Durham (1100-1300)
This roundel, worked in coloured enamels at Limoges, probably decorated a Medieval reliquary.

GLO-296B71, 52mm, Long Newton, Gloucestershire (1180-1230)
Figure of an angel from a Medieval reliquary, carefully modelled, the angel has been gilded and has blue glass eyes.

HESH-ABC735, 88mm, Radstock, Somerset (1150-1300)
Limoges-produced enamels are often found by metal detectorists, such as this mount from a reliquary casket or chasse. It is decorated with a wave pattern set against enamel inlay traces which, together with gilding, survive.

RELIGION AND BELIEF

LANCUM-10A482, 52mm, Longtown, Cumbria (1150-1300)
Many Limoges produced reliquaries are decorated with figure mounts, such as this saint, probably an Evangelist, with a gospel book. Originally this figure would have been decorated with brightly coloured enamelling, and had blue glass eyes.

BH-DE1292, 29mm, Darcorum, Hertfordshire (1450-1525)
This gold object is probably a back-plate from a personal reliquary. It is engraved with a seated image of God the Father holding aloft the crucified Christ. Above his head is a dove representing the Holy Spirit. Traces of the original enamel inlay can be seen.

SWYOR-4BFBAD, 32mm, Barwick in Elmet, West Yorkshire (1600-1700)
This silver reliquary pendant is believed to have been made for recusants (those following Catholicism once it had been outlawed) living in Yorkshire. It has on it an inscription evoking both Christ (*ihs*) and the Virgin Mary (MRA).

SWYOR-7346E4, 43mm, Skellow, South Yorkshire (1500-1800)
Upon this cross-shaped gold reliquary pendant is the phrase IN HOC SIGNO VINCES (under this sign you shall conquer), associated with the story of the conversion to Christianity of the Roman emperor Constantine the Great (r. 306-37).

127

RELIGION AND BELIEF

STATUES

Statues (full-sized or large figures) are not common finds and, when discovered, are usually incomplete. From the Roman period we have fragments from the breaking up of full-size bronze figures. These fragments are important, as they show that cities of Roman Britain were not behind other parts of the Empire in having their civic monuments. Finds of statues from later periods are much less frequently found, though some Medieval finds might be fittings from fine wooden monuments destroyed at the Reformation. The PAS has recorded 69 fragments of statues, although some of these records actually refer to statuettes.

LIN-C6AFB3, 115mm, Carholme, Lincolnshire (50-150)
The size of this finger shows that the statue from which it came was more than life size. It was found near to the Roman city of *Lindum Colonia* (Lincoln), one of the most successful cities in Roman Britain. Other fragments of bronze statues are known from Lincoln and the surrounding area; during the 19th century the leg of a life-sized horse was found in the city and in 2010 fragments of a further life-sized horse were found at North Carlton, north of Lincoln (LIN-31B698).

YORYM-08CBC4, 81mm, Brompton on Swale, North Yorkshire (100-400)
Finely cast ear from a Roman bronze statue. This fragment may have been preserved for ritual reasons.

128

RELIGION AND BELIEF

ESS-010D50, 180mm, Risworth, North Yorkshire (50-100)
Stone heads are not uncommon finds in Britain. While they are often described as 'Celtic', there is no evidence for them being pre-Roman and many of them could be much later. This example, however, is thought be of Roman date.

NARC-D112F1, 19mm, Potterspury, Northamptonshire (50-400)
Eye from a Roman bronze statue. Other finds suggest that the eyes from statues were often kept, perhaps for ritual purposes, as in the case of the ear also described on the previous page.

YORYM-5936A7, 131mm, near Arncliffe, North Yorkshire (1450-1600)
Statues in Medieval churches were often decorated and adorned. The lily embellishments on this crown resembles that seen on Medieval coins, though its inscription is illegible. It probably originally adorned a life-sized wooden figure of the Virgin.

RELIGION AND BELIEF

MONUMENTAL BRASSES

Rubbing of a late 14th century memorial brass to members of the Redford family, St. Mary's church, Broughton, Lincolnshire. This fine monument shows details of both the armour and the feminine dress fashionable at the time (Image: Kevin Leahy).

Tombs not only provided a resting place for the deceased, but also ensured the dead were remembered and prayed for by the living. Medieval people believed in purgatory, a place between Heaven and Hell, where the dead suffered but could progress to Heaven through the good works of those on earth, which included praying for their souls. Many monumental brasses were melted down at the Reformation, or taken away later, leaving on the stone slab just the hollow into which they had been set. The PAS has recorded over 90 fragments of monumental brasses; these are widespread but there is a strong concentration in Norfolk which is the county with the greatest number of Medieval churches.

RELIGION AND BELIEF

SF-71BFE4, 62mm, Cockfield, Suffolk (1427)
This fragment of a monumental brass is inscribed in Gothic letters with C XX VII which, when complete, must have been M CCCC XX VII, and hence it can be precisely dated to 1427. The fragment shows signs of reuse, perhaps as a gnomon for a sundial, which has ensured its survival.

FAKL-31AF67, 64mm, Keyham, Leicestershire (1520-50)
The depiction of two women on this memorial brass fragment is beautifully executed and of great charm. The figures can be dated by the style of their headdresses. The women could be the supplicant (mourning) daughters of the deceased. Marks on the back of the plate show the traces of an earlier monument; the brass being turned over and a new monument added onto its plain back, a not infrequent practice.

VOTIVE MODELS AND MINIATURE OBJECTS

Miniature objects have been found on shrine sites, showing that they had deep, symbolic, significance. It is often impossible to know to which god a model was dedicated or what it meant. Some were probably offerings made by devotees visiting a shrine, while others represented a request being made to the god. Over 300 Roman miniatures have been recorded, scattered across the country but there appears to be a concentration in Wiltshire.

GLO-0817D7, 15mm, Cotswolds, Gloucestershire (50-200)
This lead model represents a type of axe-hammer used during the Roman period but, interestingly, it represents only the axe-head rather than the complete object.

RELIGION AND BELIEF

YORYM-7505A8, 21mm, Rowley, East Yorkshire (800 BC-AD 400)
Model in the form of a Late Bronze Age socketed axe. These have been found in Iron Age contexts but most date from the Roman period, 600 years after socketed axes were in use.

DOR-638AE5, 27mm, Micheldever, Hampshire (500 BC-AD 400)
Model wheels like this have been found in Late Bronze Age and early Iron Age contexts.

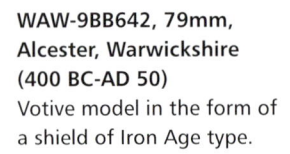

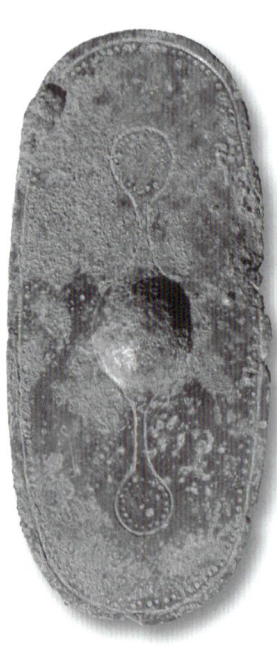

WAW-9BB642, 79mm, Alcester, Warwickshire (400 BC-AD 50)
Votive model in the form of a shield of Iron Age type.

LEIC-7B9381, 73mm, Frisby on the Wreake, Leicestershire (50-200)
Votive models of weapons are particularly common. This model is in the form of a Roman military sword, a *gladius*.

NMS-8F67CD, 36mm, Bolnhurst with Keysoe, Bedfordshire (50-200)
Common form of Roman votive axe, which includes its haft.

SUR-1AC0D5, 80mm Guildford, Surrey (50-400)
These Roman miniature shovels may have been associated with the fire used on altars.

RELIGION AND BELIEF

SUR-EB17F7, 43mm, Reigate, Surrey (50-400)
Roman votive model of a hammer, linked perhaps to Vulcan or some otherwise unknown Celtic god.

BH-2A3485, 32mm, Fowlmere, Cambridgeshire (150-300)
Finely cast model axe, complete with a haft. It is not known to which Roman, or Romano-Celtic, gods these axes were dedicated.

SWYOR-C78757, 46mm, Stamford, Lincolnshire (200-400)
Leg from a Roman ritual stand. This would have been one of four legs on a miniature stool or stand and, with its original enamel inlay, it would have been a striking object. Finds of similar objects on temple sites confirm its ritual function.

NARC-E42213, 32mm, Wadenhoe, Northamptonshire (250-400)
Roman votive stand, originally made in three tiers, two of which survive. The use of these small objects is not known; suggested functions include candle stand or incense holders.

LIN-E7E358, 68mm, Hunstanton, Norfolk (1960-2008)
Stone depiction of the Hindu God, Ganesha, clearly recognisable from his elephant head. This is one of a number of Hindu objects found in the intertidal zone along the Lincolnshire and Norfolk coasts probably representing ritual deposition.

Chapter 6
Literacy and Learning

It is difficult to know how many people were literate in the past. Even before the arrival of the Romans, names, written using the Latin alphabet, appeared on Iron Age coins, although it is unlikely many people could read them. The Roman Empire was based on writing and the population must have been expected to read monumental inscriptions and the propaganda on coins. Documents, written on strips of wood, occasionally survive, but PAS records of seal boxes, once attached to Roman correspondence, suggest writing was not uncommon. The early Anglo-Saxons used the runic alphabet and the few inscriptions that survive imply literacy, at least in some sections of society. With the introduction of Christianity in the late 6th century, large numbers of books were written and copied, some of which are artistic masterpieces. While religious texts predominate, books on other topics, including science, were written. Other than on coins, little Early Medieval writing has been recorded by the PAS, although finds of styli show that writing was fairly widespread. The printing press first appeared in England in 1476 leading to a massive increase in the availability of books, and although most of them failed to survive, fittings from their bindings show just how many of them were produced. The PAS has recorded almost 700 Medieval book fittings and more than 1,100 Post Medieval examples.

BOOK FITTINGS

Book clasps came about due to the natural tendency of parchment to curve, making it necessary to clamp the books shut to keep the pages flat. Many later books were in soft covers, made from satin or velvet, so clasps helped keep them in place. Strong fittings were useful in libraries as they allowed books to be chained to the shelves.

A Medieval statue of an Evangelist from St Mary's Abbey, York, showing a book fitted with a clasp (1088-1140). (Image: Kevin Leahy)

LITERACY AND LEARNING

Medieval painting showing a late Medieval book and its fittings. (Image: Michael Lewis)

NMS-F85129, 26mm, West Acre, Norfolk (1175-1215)
One element of a two-part Medieval book clasp, with the other being joined by the spindle bar. Through the animal-headed terminal is a hole, by which a cord would have been threaded and used to fasten the book closed.

IOW-7D75B7, 54mm, Godshill, Isle of Wight (1300-1400)
This inscribed clasp functioned much like a strap end, but secured a book strap. The socketed end would have held one end of the book strap, with the hole on its underside fitted over a peg on the book cover. The ring at the end of the clasp may have taken a cord, probably to make it easier to pull the clasp on and off the peg.

LITERACY AND LEARNING

LVPL-878076, 41mm, Whitegate and Marton, Cheshire (1100-1400)
The dome on the front of this clasp would have protected the leather book cover and kept it off damp surfaces.

GLO-5B1D88, 42mm, Cotswolds, Gloucestershire (1400-1500)
This Medieval clasp, which like the others was fitted onto a strap, has striking geometric patterns. Its zoomorphic terminal is pierced near the mouth for a cord.

LVPL-85D9A9, 43mm, Washingborough, Lincolnshire (1500-1700)
During the Post Medieval period clasps were riveted to the book cover, as in this case. Its hook (here incomplete) would have connected to an eyelet attached to the clasping mechanism on the book's opposing cover.

HAMP-4EF407, 27mm, Fareham, Hampshire (1600-1700)
This hooked fitting is probably from a three-part book clasp. It would have passed over the closed pages of the book linking two mounts on the covers. It was hinged at one end, the end bears a hook allowing it to be released.

LITERACY AND LEARNING

SEAL MATRICES

Seals were the way in which people in the past could verify the authenticity of documents and ensure that their contents remained confidential during transit, much like signatures, passwords or pin-numbers do today. As might be expected, the seals of the highest echelons of society were larger and more ornate than those used by the majority. It is apparent that by the Middle Ages, large numbers of people needed to 'sign' legal documents. Seals survive on many manuscripts in archives, but it is the devices used to make them (seal matrices) that are found by metal detectorists. Over 5,000 Medieval matrices and almost 1,000 Post Medieval examples have been recorded with the PAS. They have been found all over England, but with a high density in East Anglia. Such objects are casting a new light on Medieval society; poor quality lead seal matrices are likely to have been used by peasants who, interestingly, must have been involved in property transactions. Many seals bear the names of women, showing that they also had property rights.

LON-9D59FA, 11mm, Southwark, London (50-200)
Engraved with a figure of the goddess Fortuna, this Roman carnelian intaglio would have fitted into a finger ring, making it a convenient way of sealing documents.

LON-CF9D8B, 14mm, City of London (50-400)
Roman intaglio seal matrix, engraved with a lively scene of a dog chasing a hare.

SF-BE7CB0, 55mm, Hampshire area (900-1000)
Gilt copper-alloy seal matrix decorated in the Late Anglo-Saxon Winchester style; the animals and the acanthus leaf motifs being typical of this decoration. On the face is the figure of a man, resembling depictions on contemporary coins. The inscription reads +SIGILLVM ÆLFRICVS (the seal [of] Ælfric).

BERK-FDCFD2, 54mm, Little Bedwyn, Wiltshire (1160-1258)
This important Medieval seal matrix was made for a knight identified as Fulk (III) FitzWarin, a Marcher lord who rebelled against King John and was subsequently outlawed. In 1202, Fulk and his followers took refuge at Stanley Abbey, not far from the findspot.

LITERACY AND LEARNING

LIN-268456, 28mm, Gosberton, Lincolnshire (1200-1300)
A significant number of Medieval matrices bearing the names of women have been recorded with the PAS, such as this lead example of 'Christian, daughter of Peter'. These matrices shed important light on the role of women in the Middle Ages, showing that they were engaged in commercial transactions.

SUR-8A3643, 36mm, West Clandon, Surrey (1200-1300)
The PAS has recorded around 60 unfinished seal matrices suggesting that they were being cut locally. On this example a start has been made on setting out the design.

LEIC-BB7846, 28mm, Langar cum Barnstone, Nottinghamshire (1250-1300)
Ecclesiastical seal matrices, such as this one of Brother Robert Remund, are relatively common finds. Brother Robert took as his symbol a Tau cross (shown inverted here), which is commonly associated with the Franciscan Order.

Found near to a minor Medieval port on the Humber these seal matrices point to a wide-spread need to authenticate documents.

138

LITERACY AND LEARNING

HAMP-4E0317, 40mm, Wherwell, Hampshire (1300-1400)
Foreign seals are found in England. This silver example belonged to Peter of Barastre, an ecclesiastic from a commune near Arras in northern France. It depicts an image of St Peter, the owner's name-Saint.

IOW-6A58A8, 16mm, Chillerton and Gatcombe, Isle of Wight (1300-1400)
The motif on this 'off the peg' Medieval seal matrix is interesting. It has ihs (for Jesus) at the centre of a star and, in its angles, letters: IhS/N A S AR (joined) E N (Jesus of Nazareth).

BH-034FA3, 20mm, Wycombe, Buckinghamshire (1300-1400)
Some seal matrices were not made for specific individuals, but had standard designs bought 'off the peg'. This example has the popular motif of a squirrel eating a nut, surrounded by the legend 'I crack nuts', which is thought to be a euphemism for sexual prowess.

FAKL-B5F763, 23mm, Scotter, Lincolnshire (1600-1700)
Personal arms (heraldic crests) are common on many Post Medieval seal matrices. However, it is often not possible to associate these arms with particular families since they lack the colours (tinctures) needed for identification.

SF-DADC4B, 27mm, Hemingstone, Suffolk (1600-1700)
Presumably used by individuals of modest wealth are Post Medieval seal matrices with initials (as opposed to those with crests or more elaborate motifs). These vary significantly in quality, and include examples that are simply made, such as this inscribed NP.

KENT-D8D25B, 27mm, Nonington, Kent (1714-1850)
The gold handle is more impressive than the glass 'stone' used on this seal matrix. The stone is a neo-classical copy, although some Medieval seal matrices reuse actual Roman intaglios.

LITERACY AND LEARNING

SEAL BOXES

These were used to enclose and protect a wax seal. By opening its lid, it was possible to check the document's authenticity and authority without opening the document. It also showed if it was permitted to be sent via the Roman Imperial post system. The PAS has recorded almost 400 Roman seal boxes with a distribution widely scattered across England.

NLM-20F1C9, 30mm, Misterton, Nottinghamshire (100-200)
Roman seal boxes were made in two parts, linked by a hinge. The lower part had holes in its base through which the wax protruded, holding it in place. The lid was decorated with enamel inlay.

SWYOR-9CC75B, 25mm, Ackworth, West Yorkshire (100-300)
This seal box bears Celtic style decoration showing the fusion of cultures in Roman Britain.

SF-4729B0, 30mm, Gedgrave, Suffolk (100-300)
The rectangular notches in the sides of this seal box held the cord that encircled the document; its ends being secured by the wax seal.

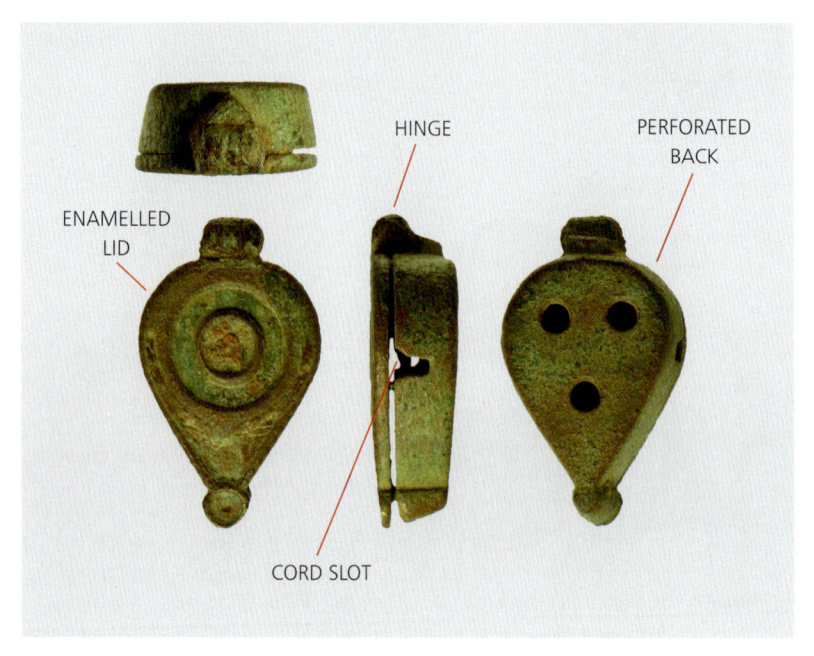

ENAMELLED LID — HINGE — PERFORATED BACK — CORD SLOT

140

LITERACY AND LEARNING

WRITING IMPLEMENTS

The PAS has recorded around 170 styli on its database. They can be tricky items to identify, as it can be difficult to distinguish between styli and large pins, particularly if they are found broken. There are also many lead styli on the PAS database, which could be better described as pencils. Of the styli, 82 were deemed to be Roman, 37 Early Medieval and 42 Medieval, although it is important to note that, in many cases, styli are impossible to date. They were used in conjunction with a wax covered tablet, the pointed end being used to scratch through the wax revealing the wood beneath. The flat end was used as an eraser to smooth over any mistakes. Parchment was expensive and waxed tablets were a cheap and flexible alternative. During the Middle Ages it is likely that more people could read than we might think. Writing, however, was a separate skill; many people could read, but not write.

DOR-A0F03A, 70mm, Winfrith Newburgh, Dorset (50-400)
Probable Roman stylus, with its flat end forming a useful eraser.

WILT-14E437, 80mm, Salisbury, Wiltshire (50-400)
This plain stylus is difficult to date. It is probably Roman but an Early Medieval date cannot be ruled out.

LIN-365092, 64mm, East Lindsey, Lincolnshire (720-850)

LIN-D1E975, 80mm, near Louth, Lincolnshire (700-800)
Both these styli came from a site which has produced other Middle Anglo-Saxon finds and they can therefore be dated by association.

BERK-67C6B2, 48mm, West Hanney, Oxfordshire (1180-1220)
Romanesque in style, this is a possible stylus handle in the form of a winged beast; the head end probably formed the terminal, rather than the point.

LITERACY AND LEARNING

DUR-E10B17, 100mm, Walworth, County Durham (1200-1700)
This simple lead stylus is hard to date. Its design is no different from the iPad pencil, showing it to be of intuitive form. Although pencils now contain graphite we still speak of pencil 'lead', harking back to a time when lead was actually used to make a mark.

LON-8BC7C4, 105mm, Southwark, London (1200-1600)
It is thought that the lanceolate nib of this Medieval pen would help retain ink for writing. Its handle is reminiscent of that found on late Medieval cutlery suggesting a date in that period. Maintaining the correct ink flow must have presented some problems for the scribe.

NMGW-72BE5A, 42mm, Pembrokeshire (1600-1800)
Post Medieval lead inkwells are not easily dated, but the style of the lettering on the base of this example, NT and perhaps NJ, although unclear, proves helpful.

WAX SPATULAE

A wax spatula was used to spread beeswax over the recessed area of a wooden writing tablet before using a stylus to write on it. Spatulae were also used to clear used tablets before they were reused. Over 80 spatulae have been recorded, most of which were Roman.

NLM-9E4586, 54mm, Binbrook, Lincolnshire (100-250)
Handle from a Roman wax spatula. These are often in the form of a bust of Minerva, the goddess of wisdom and therefore appropriate for a tool associated with writing.

LITERACY AND LEARNING

WILT-9ECD01, 164mm, Highworth, Wiltshire (100-250)
Unusually, this fine wax spatula still retains part of its original iron blade. It too has a handle in the form of the goddess Minerva.

PARCHMENT PRICKERS

Writing on vellum needed particular tools, not only to write with, but also to prepare the vellum for writing. One of these tools was a pricker, used to mark the lines onto which the script was written. These are uncommon and are hard to distinguish from some other find types.

PUBLIC-5D9B16, 79mm, City of London (1270-1500)
This object shows the changes that can occur in our knowledge of an object type with the discovery of new finds. When first found these objects were considered to be Roman, but it has become clear that they are Medieval in date. For many years they were described as parchment prickers, used in the setting out of pages before writing. More recently, Continental finds have shown them to be associated with wax writing tablets (which were not marked out) and therefore they have been described as styli.

LITERACY AND LEARNING

AESTELS

Aestels have been the subject of some discussion. The Old English word *'aestel'* can mean guide, index or pointer. When King Alfred the Great (r. 871-899) sent each diocese in his kingdom a copy of Pope Gregory the Great's book *Pastoral Care* he included, with each one, an *aestel*. It is thought that these were pointers for following the text while reading. The objects we describe as *aestels* are made of gold; those distributed by Alfred were described as being worth '50 gold *mancuses*' (a skilled worker would earn about 12 *mancuses* a year). Our *aestels* are fitted with sockets that could have held a bone or ivory pointer. Eleven *aestels*, none of them alike, have been recorded by the PAS. Their distribution is widely scattered across England.

SF-3ABEB9, 31mm, Drinkstone, Suffolk (850-900)
Gold object decorated with filigree and granulation, with a setting on top containing a small glass gem. As with most other possible *aestels* this example has a domed top and a flat underside. The socket would have held a bone or ivory pointer.

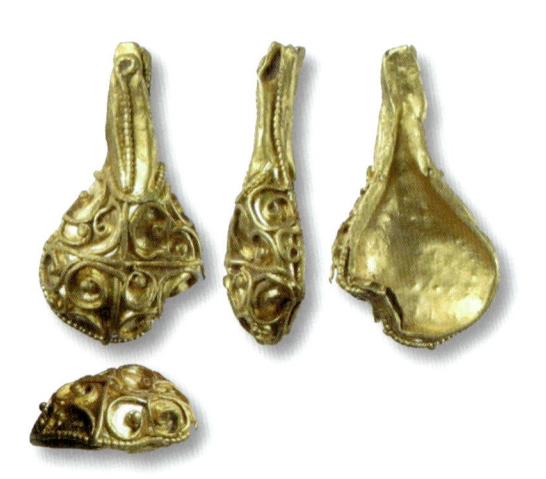

SWYOR-69C958, 27mm, York, North Yorkshire (800-900)
Now crushed, this filigree gold object has the same form and socket seen on other *aestels*.

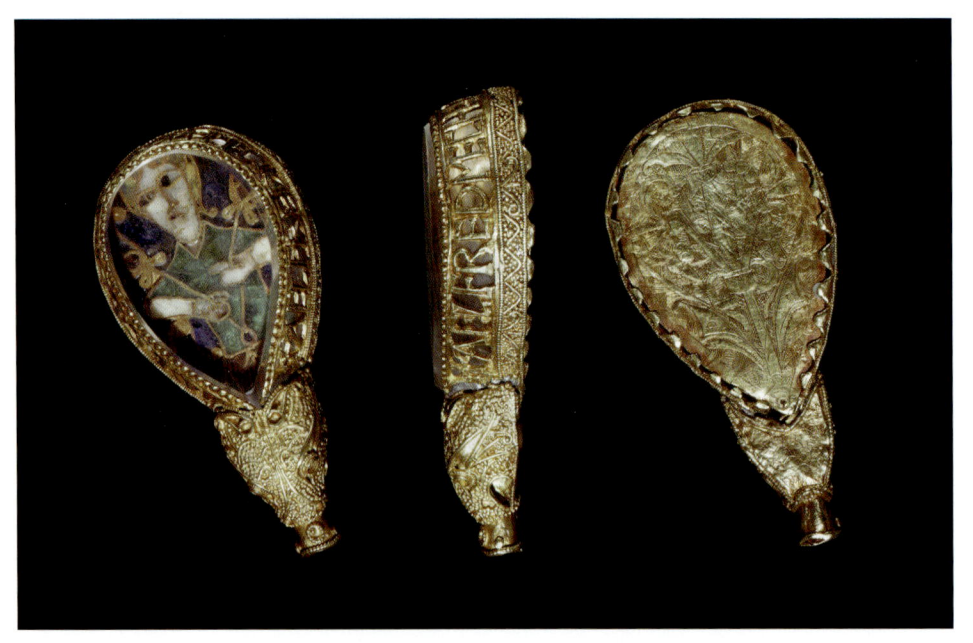

The Alfred Jewel is one of the great icons of British archaeology. Made from gold and set with an enamelled figure beneath a rock crystal, it bears the inscription + Aelfred mec heht gewyrcan 'Alfred ordered me to be made'. The Jewel was found in 1693 at North Petherton, Somerset, it dates to 871-99. (Image © Ashmolean Museum, University of Oxford, AN1836 p.135.371)

LITERACY AND LEARNING

INSCRIBED OBJECTS

Most of the inscriptions recorded by the PAS are on coins, and objects such as seal matrices, papal *bullae* and monumental brasses (see pages 118 and 130-131). However a small amount of text has been recorded that appears to have been purely documentary and not part of an object.

DUR-C3E4FE, 59mm, Lanchester area, County Durham (150)
Roman military diploma, marking the honourable discharge of a Celtic soldier from the Roman military. It originally consisted of two bronze sheets, about A5 in size, bound together with wire loops and was issued to a man named Velvotigernus during the reign of the emperor Antoninus Pius on the 13th day before the Kalends of December (i.e. 19 November, AD150). It records that the sailor, the son of local tribal chieftain Magiotigernus (tigernus is thought to mean king or master) had completed his service of 26 years in the Roman Navy, serving with the Classis Germanica (the fleet in Germany). Diplomas are important as they describe the recipient's origins, career and the administration at the time.

SF-BA1337, 90mm, Lidgate, Suffolk, (50-400)
A Roman 'curse tablet' consisting of a strip of lead, folded when found, on which has been scratched the Latin inscription: [A]NVLI QVI PERIERVNT/ IS MVLI[]R IS BARO SI INGEN/ VS SI[] SERVS ('The rings which have been lost, whether woman or man, whether free or slave......'). This is a common formula calling for retribution for someone who had stolen rings to be punished, whatever their status.

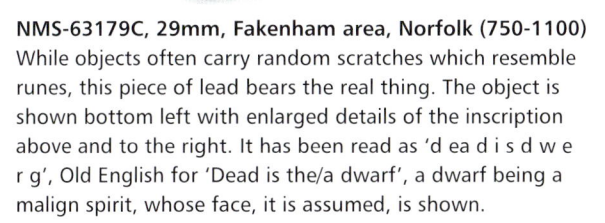

NMS-63179C, 29mm, Fakenham area, Norfolk (750-1100)
While objects often carry random scratches which resemble runes, this piece of lead bears the real thing. The object is shown bottom left with enlarged details of the inscription above and to the right. It has been read as 'd ea d i s d w e r g', Old English for 'Dead is the/a dwarf', a dwarf being a malign spirit, whose face, it is assumed, is shown.

NLM-93E575, 21mm, Blyborough, Lincolnshire (50-1900)
Rolled sheets of lead have been described as Roman curse tablets but, unless an inscription can be seen, they are better interpreted as lead weights or off-cuts.

145

LITERACY AND LEARNING

SUNDIALS

Until recent times, sundials were the only way of setting a clock. They have been used since ancient times and Medieval scratch, or Mass, dials can be seen on the south walls of many churches. The portable sundial, also known as the Aquitaine or perforated ring dial, was perfected in the late 16th century, and was a convenient way of checking the time. They are not uncommon detector finds, with 137 examples on the PAS database, although few are complete.

NMS-196DE7, 245mm, Hopton on Sea, Norfolk (1300-1500)
Medieval scratch sundial cut onto a stone which would have originally been built into the south wall of a church.

LON-84ADD8, 32mm, City of London (1580-1620)
Carved from animal bone, only one half of this portable sundial now survives. Not surprisingly, only the daylight hours are marked on it.

IOW-EA5F72, 12mm, Brading, Isle of Wight (1660-1700)
Ring sundials, such as this, are formed of two parts; a ring and a sliding collar pierced with a hole. The collar allowed the sundial to be set for the time of the year, the months being abbreviated to their first letter. When suspended, sunlight would shine through onto the hour markers on the inner ring.

LITERACY AND LEARNING

BM-A5C5A1, 75mm, Lawshall, Suffolk (1652)
This sundial, of conventional form, but missing its gnomon, was found within the earth floor of a thatched house. It is thought it may have been made as a memento of a solar eclipse on 29 March 1652, the year to which it is dated.

Scratch sundial on the wall of a barn near Kenilworth Abbey, Warwickshire. Daylight was divided into 12 hours, the length of which varied throughout the year. These dials allowed the canonical hours to be kept.
(Image: Kevin Leahy)

Chapter 7
Domestic Life

HOUSEHOLD AND FURNISHINGS

LOCKS AND KEYS

Most ancient locks are represented only by their keys, but these still show how the mechanism worked. Locks came in two basic forms, one involving a sliding bolt, the other a hasp that had to be freed before it could be released. It is easy to secure a bolt from the inside, but things are more difficult if the bolt is to be operated from outside. The simplest form is the slide lock, which was operated using the keys of the type represented by girdle hangers (page 85) which reached through the door engaging and sliding the bolt. More complex variations, involving the key raising pins to release the bolt, are represented by the Roman and Early Medieval keys shown below. In a rotary lock, represented by many Medieval and Post Medieval keys, a series of shaped 'wards' stop the key from rotating and moving the bolt. The other basic form of key used in antiquity was a padlock in which one end of the U-shaped hasp was fitted with barbs. These sprang out when the hasp was pushed into the body of lock preventing it from being withdrawn. To open the padlock a key was pushed into a hole opposite to the hasp; this was shaped to fit around the barbs and compress them so that the hasp could be withdrawn and the lock opened. Over 3,400 keys have been recorded with the PAS of which 2,335 are Medieval and 542 are Roman.

LEIC-1C4B92, 41mm, Peckleton, Leicestershire (50-400)
In a Roman lock a group of vertical pins slipped into holes in the bolt, so that it could not be moved. The pegs on the bit of a key, like this, fitted into these pins from beneath, allowing them to be raised and the bolt slid aside.

SWYOR-F1D5D6, 115mm, Winthorpe, Nottinghamshire (50-400)
Handle, in the form of a lion, from a fine and elaborate Roman key. The bit and shank of the key were made from iron and have not survived.

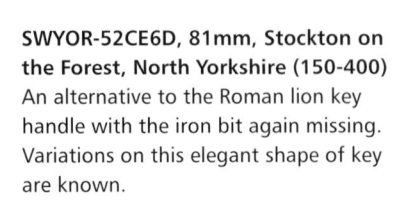

SWYOR-52CE6D, 81mm, Stockton on the Forest, North Yorkshire (150-400)
An alternative to the Roman lion key handle with the iron bit again missing. Variations on this elegant shape of key are known.

DOMESTIC LIFE

LANCUM-50C0B8, 28mm, Chipping, Lancashire (200-400)
Roman finger ring on which is the bit for a key. The clefts in the bit suggest that it fitted a lock of some complexity.

LIN-A542BE, 79mm, East Lindsey, Lincolnshire (710-850)
Typical form of Anglo-Saxon key. This reached into the lock, with the holes in the flat plate fitting around security posts and the two prongs raising a spring to release the bolt.

DOR-FAB445, 53mm, Burleston, Dorset (1000-1100)
The discovery of keys like this on Anglo-Saxon sites confirms their dating. The two prongs raised a spring so that the bolt could be moved.

LANCUM-B3B2F7, 87mm, Austwick, North Yorkshire (850-1350)
This key was used to open a form of Anglo-Saxon or Medieval barrel padlock. It was pushed into the end of the barrel compressing the barbed springs to release the hasp.

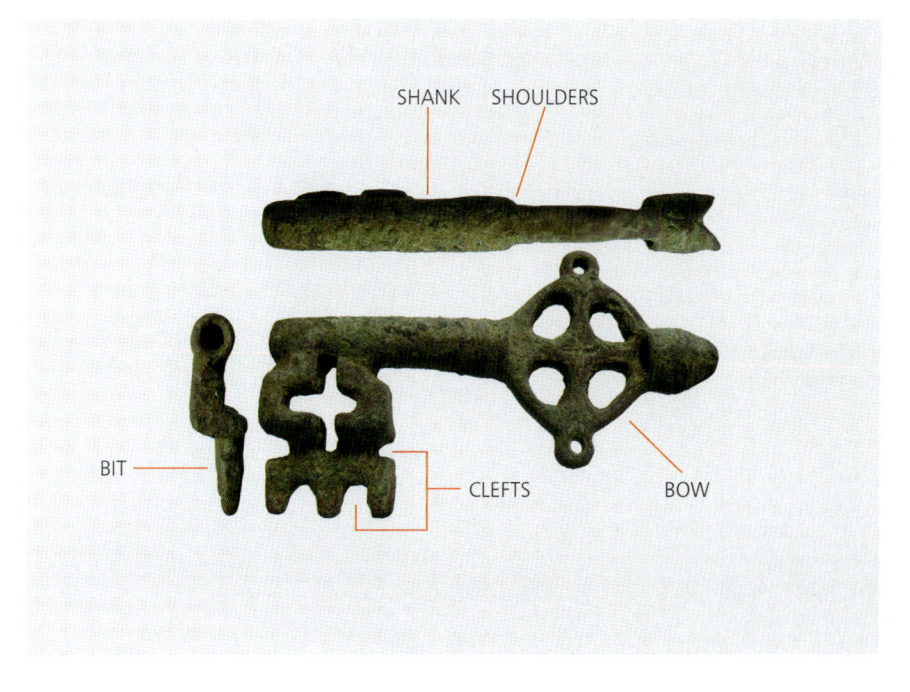

WAW-E49DD4, 68mm, Morton Bagot, Warwickshire (1300-1500)
This elaborate Medieval key is for a locking mechanism where the key would be rotated to open the lock. The clefts in the complex bit would have fitted around wards so that it could be turned. The edge of the key moved the bolt.

SHANK   SHOULDERS

BIT   CLEFTS   BOW

149

DOMESTIC LIFE

PUBLIC-1EE7C5, 56mm, East Yorkshire (50-400)
The shaped pegs on the key fitted into the holes in this bolt from a Roman lock, allowing them to be raised and the bolt moved.

LEIC-E85044, 67mm, Boxworth, Cambridgeshire (50-400)
These Roman finials have been described as lock-pins or handles. Their function is, however, unclear.

NMS-B14138, 37mm, Scole, Norfolk (1200-1400)
Complex key for a boxed rotary lock. The spike on the end of the shank would have ensured that the key was properly positioned.

BERK-841F58, 134mm, Haddenham area, Buckinghamshire (1270-1400)
On this iron rotary key the bit is formed of three elements with clefts cut to fit around complex wards in the lock mechanism.

PADLOCKS

Almost 500 padlocks have been recorded by the PAS of which 14 are Roman, 400 Medieval and 81 Post Medieval. It is perhaps surprising, given these are functional objects, that some padlocks are in the form of rather charming animals and human heads.

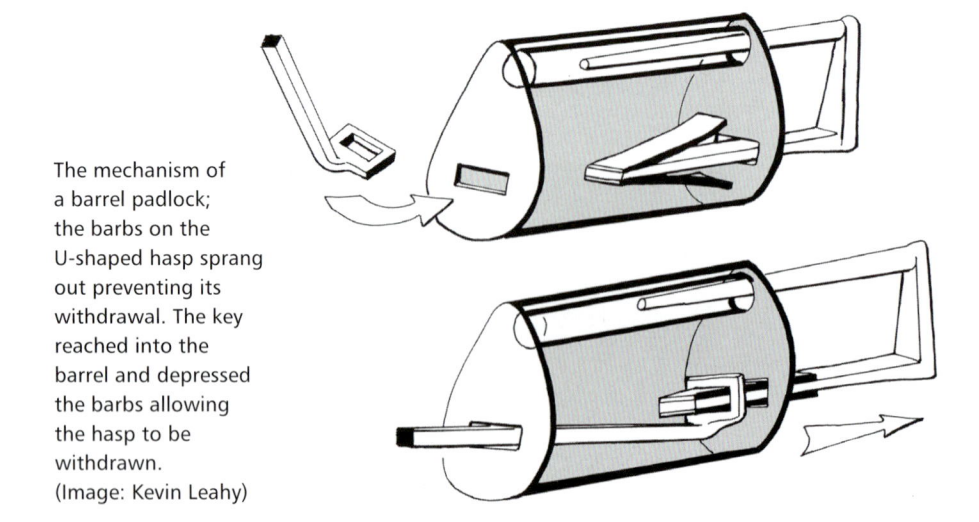

The mechanism of a barrel padlock; the barbs on the U-shaped hasp sprang out preventing its withdrawal. The key reached into the barrel and depressed the barbs allowing the hasp to be withdrawn.
(Image: Kevin Leahy)

150

DOMESTIC LIFE

SUR-302076, 34mm, Bix and Assendon, Oxfordshire (50-400)
Roman padlock case in the form of a woman's head. Unlike the other padlocks this example does not appear to have used the barbed hasp principle (see previous page).

YORYM-BA035A, 42mm, Pickering, North Yorkshire (1100-1500)
Padlocks in the shape of animals were commonly used in the Middle Ages. This example is in the form of a horse, complete with saddle. One arm of the U-shaped hasp was inserted into the horse's nose, the other into its chest. To open the lock the key was pushed into the three holes in the horse's behind.

SOM-6AE232, 29mm, Frampton area, Dorset (1100-1600)
This barb-spring padlock is complete, although its internal iron mechanism has corroded, fusing the individual elements of the object together. The hasp was inserted into the body from its right-hand side, an extended prong going through a hole in a post to the left. The key-hole, obscured by rust, is visible at the other end.

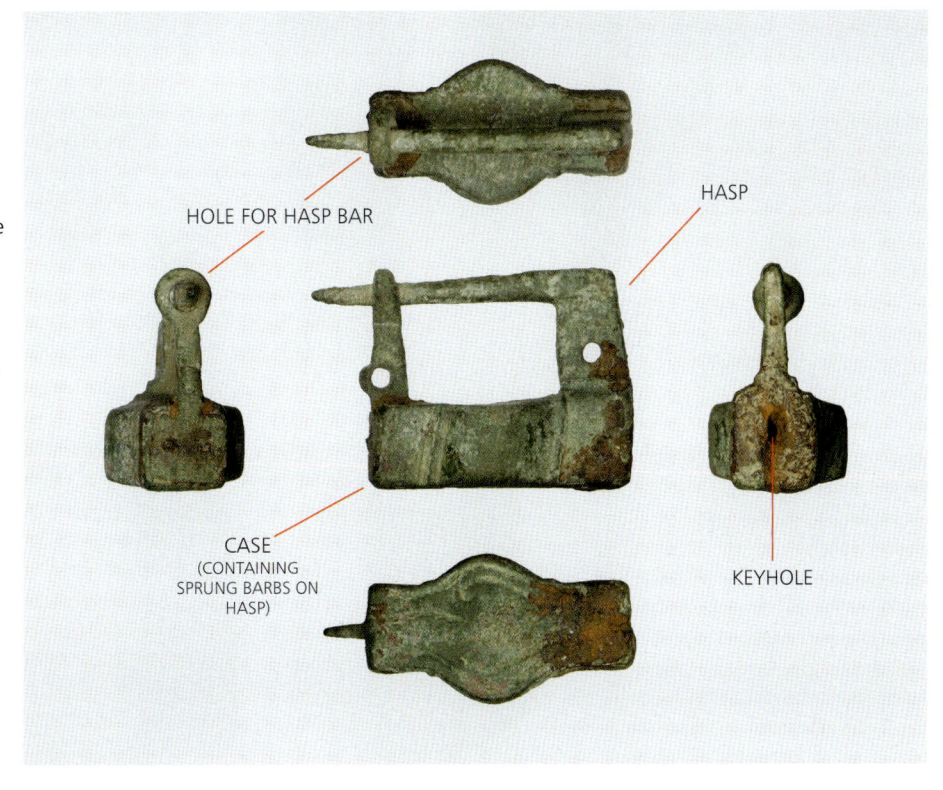

HOLE FOR HASP BAR

HASP

CASE (CONTAINING SPRUNG BARBS ON HASP)

KEYHOLE

DOMESTIC LIFE

NCL-BCC144, 40mm, Revesby, Lincolnshire (1230-1450)
On this Medieval padlock a pin on the body fitted over a loop on the now missing hasp. The holes for the complex key can be clearly seen.

SF-315EA8, 31mm, Herringswell, Suffolk (1050-1500)
This is the spring mechanism from a barb-spring padlock; the barbed-springs would have fitted into the barrel, and the pointed arm into a cylindrical receptacle above.

SF-E41A06, 110mm, Rusbrooke with Rougham, Suffolk (1500-1800)
Although heavily corroded, the triangular form of this iron Post Medieval padlock is clear to see. It employed a rotary key as used on a modern lock.

DENO-213196, 28mm, Barnby in the Willows, Nottinghamshire (1500-1850)
This padlock shows what was to become their modern form: a hasp, now missing, engaged into two holes in its top. Corrosion around these holes show that the hidden mechanism was made from iron. The keyhole is hidden by a sliding cover.

152

DOMESTIC LIFE

DECORATIVE FITTINGS

The terms 'fitting' and 'mount' are often used when we are unsure of an object's function. Usually it is not known to what these fittings were attached; they could have been from a piece of furniture, a building or a vehicle. Most 'fittings' have no recognisable function and could just be adornments. Others carry the figures of gods, and therefore may have provided comfort to their owners, as well as fulfilling the important role of showing the owner's good taste and wealth, which was needed to commission high grade works.

SUR-488165, 84mm, Reigate area, Surrey (50-100)
Elegant and highly classical mount depicting Attys, consort of Cybele, who is often shown as a shepherd. This fitting probably came from the leg of a table and is similar to one found at Pompeii.

KENT-BD4034, 36mm, Chilham, Kent (100-200)
Hollow mount in the form of the head of Bacchus, the Roman god of, among other things, wine. It would have been highly appropriate in a Roman *triclinium* (dining room).

SWYOR-1016E4, 43mm, Darrington, West Yorkshire (50-400)
Foot from the leg of a Roman tripod-vessel decorated with a lion's head. While this object appears genuine, caution is called for when dealing with classical objects like this as they were much copied in the 18th century.

153

DOMESTIC LIFE

NMS-9E7647, 41mm, Great Witchingham, Norfolk (1100-1200)
It is not certain what this object is, but it is probably some sort of Medieval furniture fitting, such as a hasp; its square aperture is likely to have fitted over a stud or loop riveted to a door or lid. Furniture, as we understand it, was not much used before the Late Medieval period and was mainly restricted to chests, benches and trestle tables.

NMS-C523C2, 26mm, Foulsham, Norfolk (1200-1300)
The form of this object suggests it helped strengthen the edge of a small casket or box. One of its pointed-oval terminals still retains the rivet that originally secured it in place

SUSS-D16C52, 34mm, near Arundel, West Sussex (1500-1800)
Small mount in the form of a six petalled flower of Post Medieval date. It was fixed in place through its central aperture and could have been used in many ways.

IOW-C2FE99, 43mm, Newport, Isle of Wight (1660-1710)
Drop-handle, from a drawer fitting, which has a rectangular suspension loop. It curves out to assist finger-grip when in use.

HAMP-BBB344, 45mm, Cheriton, Hampshire (1700-1900)
Furniture fittings, such as this were probably drop-handles, but an alternative use, as a door escutcheon for masking a keyhole, has also been proposed. The hole shows signs of wear.

DOMESTIC LIFE

FIRE STEELS AND STRIKE-A-LIGHTS

Fire steels were used to generate a spark from a 'strike-a-light' – a piece of flint or pyrites. The spark was directed into a tinder box containing a dry, flammable material such as charred linen and a flame kindled. There are six iron fire steels on the PAS and 13 pieces of flint that may have been used as strike-a-lights. Almost all those recorded with the PAS are of Post Medieval date.

LON-6357F6, 79mm, City of London (1600-1700)
Iron fire steels, such as this example, sometimes had a rectangular striking bar. The curving arms provided grip for the person using the tool to make fire and protected the knuckles during the violent process of striking a spark from a flint.

FAKL-EAFCF3, 59mm, Harthill with Woodhall, South Yorkshire (400 BC-AD 1700)
While they are impossible to date, the battered areas on this flint and the traces of iron staining suggest that it was used as a strike-a-light although contact with a plough can leave iron stain on flint.

LON-71B542, 64mm, City of London (1600-1700)
In this example of a fire steel the tool has a curved handle for the person using it to grip.

CANDLESTICKS AND CANDLE HOLDERS

The importance of candles prior to the existence of electric lighting is easy to underestimate but, in the not too distant past, many activities were rendered difficult, or impossible, when the sun went down. Roman pottery lamps, common elsewhere in the Empire, are rare in Britain, probably due to the high cost of imported olive oil. In the Medieval period much use was made of cresset lamps, small pottery bowls filled with fat and a floating wick. Only four of these have been recorded by the PAS.

Away from the fireside and in church, light was provided by candles and their cheaper alternative, rush lights – the pith from a reed dipped in fat. Candles are represented in the PAS record by their holders; more than 260 have been recorded with the PAS of which 165 are dated to the Medieval period. However, as it can be difficult to distinguish between a candle

NMS-CFEEE3, 41mm, Salthouse, Norfolk (1300-1400)
Candle holders can be difficult to date. The holes through the octagonal socket on this example resemble a gothic window, suggesting a Medieval date.

holder of the late Medieval and the early Post Medieval periods this figure should be treated with some caution.

DOMESTIC LIFE

WILT-21F000, 124mm, The Deverills, Wiltshire (1300-1400)
Relatively few folding candle holders survive. This example is spiked so that it could be thrust into a wooden beam to provide light anywhere in the house.

KENT-28DF24, 68mm, Mersham, Kent (1350-1400)
With its tripod base, this candle holder was intended for use at the table.

LANCUM-662926, 68mm, Driffield, East Yorkshire (1300-1400)
Candle holder with a complicated structure, allowing its height to be adjusted. It is made from sheet metal, rather than being cast.

WILT-BE3B82, 110mm, Dinton, Wiltshire (1475-1700)
The shaft of this candle holder has a baluster shape, a form which was used on Post-Medieval furniture.

NARC-6F6352, 53mm, Norton, Northamptonshire (1250-1400)
While we see masterpieces of Medieval metalwork not everything was great art; although crude, the dog forming the base of this candle holder has a certain charm.

156

DOMESTIC LIFE

SWYOR-C2C5EE, 137mm, Hawkswick, North Yorkshire (1450-1600)
Unusually complete candle holder. Its base is hollow, and crafted much like a bell. It is of a style that overlaps the Middle Ages and Post Medieval periods. It is thought the broad lip served as a drip tray for candle wax. Beeswax candles were expensive but gave a good light and a sweet smell. Tallow, made from rendered animal fat, was used by most people; it was cheap, but foul smelling.

LON-B55847, 103mm, Tower Hamlets, London (1500-1800)
This urn-shaped candle holder has, at its base, a threaded screw suggesting that it dates from the Georgian period.

DOMESTIC LIFE

HAMP-917D56, 90mm, Winchester, Hampshire (1650-1750)
Post Medieval candle wick trimmer. These acted like a pair of scissors with a cutting edge on the lid of the box; the handle has been lost. The box caught the trimmings so that they did not fall onto the table cloth. Until the invention of the self-trimming wick (which turned to the side to be burnt away), candles had to be constantly tended.

YORYM-19CA39, 61mm, Burythorpe, North Yorkshire (1600-1800)
Post Medieval candle-snuffer of familiar form.

DOMESTIC LIFE

LAMP HANGERS

Light from above was provided by lamps hanging from ceilings, normally suspended from a beam. These would have been suspended quite low, often above tables, so the rising heat from the lamp did not cause fire, and also to take full advantage of the dim light that they provided. Their use would have allowed table surfaces to be clear and reduce the risk of knocking over freestanding candles. More than 90 lamp hangers have been recorded, six of which were attributed to the Roman period, the rest being Medieval.

BM-272101, 61mm, Piercebridge, County Durham (50-300)
This lamp hanger is plain in form but parallels from excavations in Italy show it to be Roman. The intricate chain is cleverly formed by threading figure of eight-shaped links through each other.

DOR-8E1C9B, 42mm, Gussage St Michael, Dorset (50-400)
These objects have been identified as a Roman lamp-hangers but, while this identification is probably correct, some doubt remains. Hopefully, one will be found with a lamp, confirming their function.

SUR-217AC4, 33mm, Goring, Oxfordshire (1100-1300)
It is not certain how this pyramidal openwork object functioned, but it is reasonable to think it was the suspension for a Medieval lamp; the chains for the lamp itself would have hung from the holes at the base of the object.

BH-2469D7, 32mm, Heydon, Cambridgeshire (1350-1450)
Less elaborate than the example on the left, but the same in function. It was suspended by the single, central ring and the lamp held by the four rings below it.

159

DOMESTIC LIFE

FOOD AND DRINK

CAULDRONS

Cauldrons were important as they allowed food to be cooked by boiling. They could be made larger than pottery vessels and therefore large quantities of food could be prepared at the same time, allowing communal eating and feasting. On a smaller scale, a cauldron of food could be kept cooking over the fire, with vegetables, grain and meat (if available) constantly added. This 'pottage' was the staple food for many centuries. Most cooking was carried out using ceramic vessels and, while pottery is recorded by the PAS, most of what we see is in the form of small fragments which are difficult to identify. The majority of the 400 or so cauldron fragments recorded on the PAS database are Medieval or Post Medieval in date, their legs being particularly common finds.

SF-832744, 139mm, Saxlingham Green, Norfolk (1200-700 BC)
This find represents one of the two handles from a Bronze Age cauldron, the thin sheet metal body not having survived. These fine cauldrons represent the feasting that formed part of aristocratic life during later prehistory.

Late Bronze Age cauldron from the West of Scotland, made by riveting together thin sheet metal plates. (Image: from Catalogue of the National Museum of Antiquities of Scotland, Edinburgh, 1892)

DOMESTIC LIFE

LANCUM-60BED6, 290mm, Grassington, North Yorkshire (800-900)
Early Medieval sheet metal cauldron together with the remains of its iron handle. This would have been a valuable object and we can only wonder as to why it was buried on a settlement site.

DOMESTIC LIFE

GAT-0FE28F, 345mm, Llanengan, Gwynedd (1300-1500)
Cauldrons could be cast whole or made of metal plates riveted together. This cauldron was cast in one piece – a vertical joint line between the two halves of the mould is clear to see. There is evidence that it was repaired, such was the importance of these objects in the Medieval household.

DOMESTIC LIFE

SUSS-F7103D, 83mm, Funtington, West Sussex (1300-1500)
Cauldron or skillet legs are common metal detector finds and show the growing use of metal cooking vessels in the Post Medieval period. This example is in the form of a human foot.

LON-6458E1, 135mm, Custom House area, London (1500-1700)
This cauldron has moulded decoration and was found complete. Black, oily, deposits on, and within it, suggest that it was used, not for foodstuffs, but in some industrial or craft process, reminding us that cauldrons could have multiple uses.

DOMESTIC LIFE

HANGING BOWLS

This term is the name given to a group of Early Medieval bowls which have three suspension hooks around their rims. On most of them, the hooks were attached using decorated mounts (escutcheons) and many of them have elaborate discs in their centres. These are mystery objects; although they are purely late Celtic in style most of them are found in Anglo-Saxon graves where their decoration is quite unlike the disjointed animals favoured by the Anglo-Saxons. We have no idea why this should be the case and do not know what these fine bowls were used for, either by the post-Roman Celtic population or the Anglo-Saxons. The PAS has recorded almost 130 hanging bowls and bowl fragments, mostly from Norfolk and Lincolnshire but also with a strong concentration in the West Midlands.

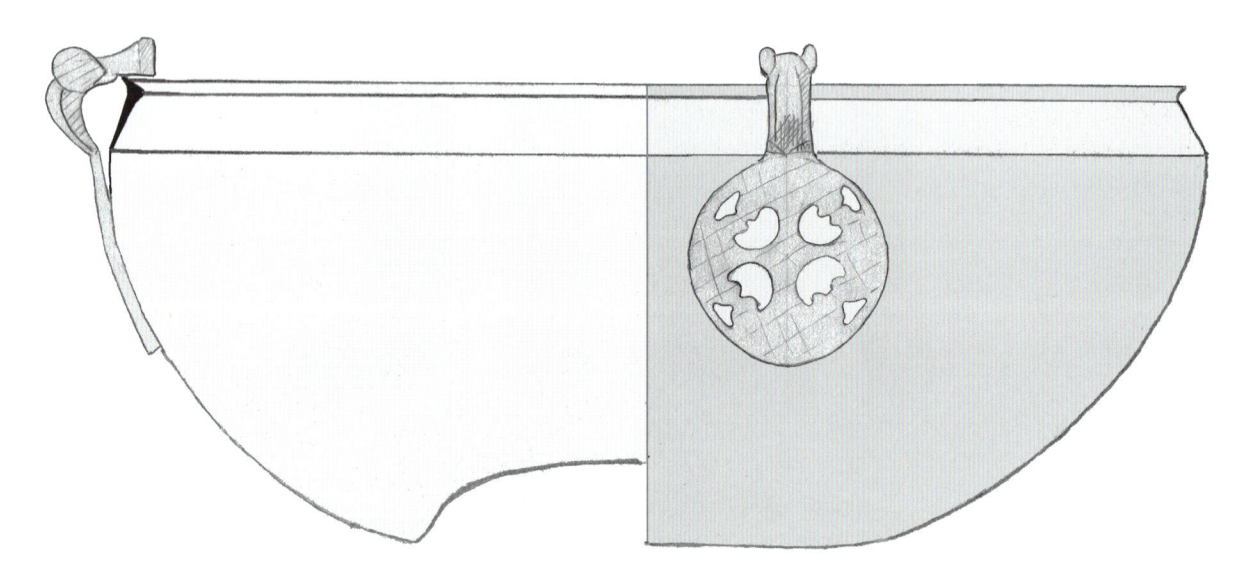

Hanging bowl, 270mm, Norfolk, (400-600) recorded by Kevin Leahy in 1991, prior to the start of the PAS. (Image: Kevin Leahy)

SUSS-F9E7AA, 50mm, Patching, West Sussex (600-700)
The Celtic inspiration of the decoration on this fine hanging bowl mount would not be out of place on any Iron Age object; it is interesting to consider how this art survived through the Roman period. The use of enamel is also Celtic and stretches back into the Iron Age.

NMS-DFAC75, 45mm, Caistor St Edmund, Norfolk (600-700)
Contrary to what is commonly thought, Celtic decoration was not interlace but consisted of whirling spirals, as seen on this hanging bowl mount. This example is inlaid with red and yellow enamel.

DOMESTIC LIFE

WILT-6925E4, 45mm, Stratford Toney, Wiltshire (600-700)
A Celtic metal worker copied the interlace on this hanging bowl mount from Anglo-Saxon art.

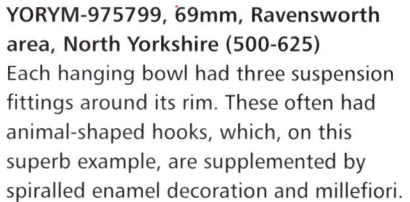

YORYM-975799, 69mm, Ravensworth area, North Yorkshire (500-625)
Each hanging bowl had three suspension fittings around its rim. These often had animal-shaped hooks, which, on this superb example, are supplemented by spiralled enamel decoration and millefiori.

PANS AND SKILLETS

These were shallow cooking vessels and were probably used like frying pans. Some of them, however, are excessively fine and must have been used at the table rather than in the kitchen. During the Post Medieval period many skillets were made from pottery. The PAS has recorded 80 skillets and six pans.

NLM-9B1FA0, 71mm, Market Rasen, Lincolnshire (250-400)
Distinctive handle fragment from a Roman patera. Some of these bear a manufacturer's stamp mark or the name of their owner.

SWYOR-05A592, 52mm, Stockton on the Forest, North Yorkshire (50-300)
Patera handles often bear enamel decoration suggesting that they were used during eating rather than for cooking.

DOMESTIC LIFE

WMID-3FE965, 90mm, Staffordshire Moorlands, Staffordshire (100-200)
This pan lists some of the forts along Hadrian's Wall. The closely related Rudge Cup also lists forts, and beneath its rim is a line suggesting the crenulations along the top of a wall; this is our only evidence that Hadrian's Wall was crenelated. The enamel decoration on the Moorlands pan is strongly inspired by Celtic art.

YORYM-20B68C, 96mm, Eastrington, East Yorkshire (50-150)
This enamel decorated bowl does not bear a long inscription as seen on other examples, but down the handle are the words VTERE FELIX meaning 'use in happiness'. The letters retain alternating blue and red enamel.

BERK-5105C9, 300mm, Long Compton, Warwickshire (550-670)
This long-handled skillet was found in the grave of an Anglo-Saxon woman. Objects like these have been found in Roman contexts but the Anglo-Saxon examples, like this one, tend to be shallower and rounder, with flat rims like those on hanging bowls.

DOMESTIC LIFE

IOW-0D5540, 349mm, Shalfleet Isle of Wight (600-800)
The presence of the cross on this Anglo-Saxon skillet suggests that it had a religious use, perhaps in baptism.

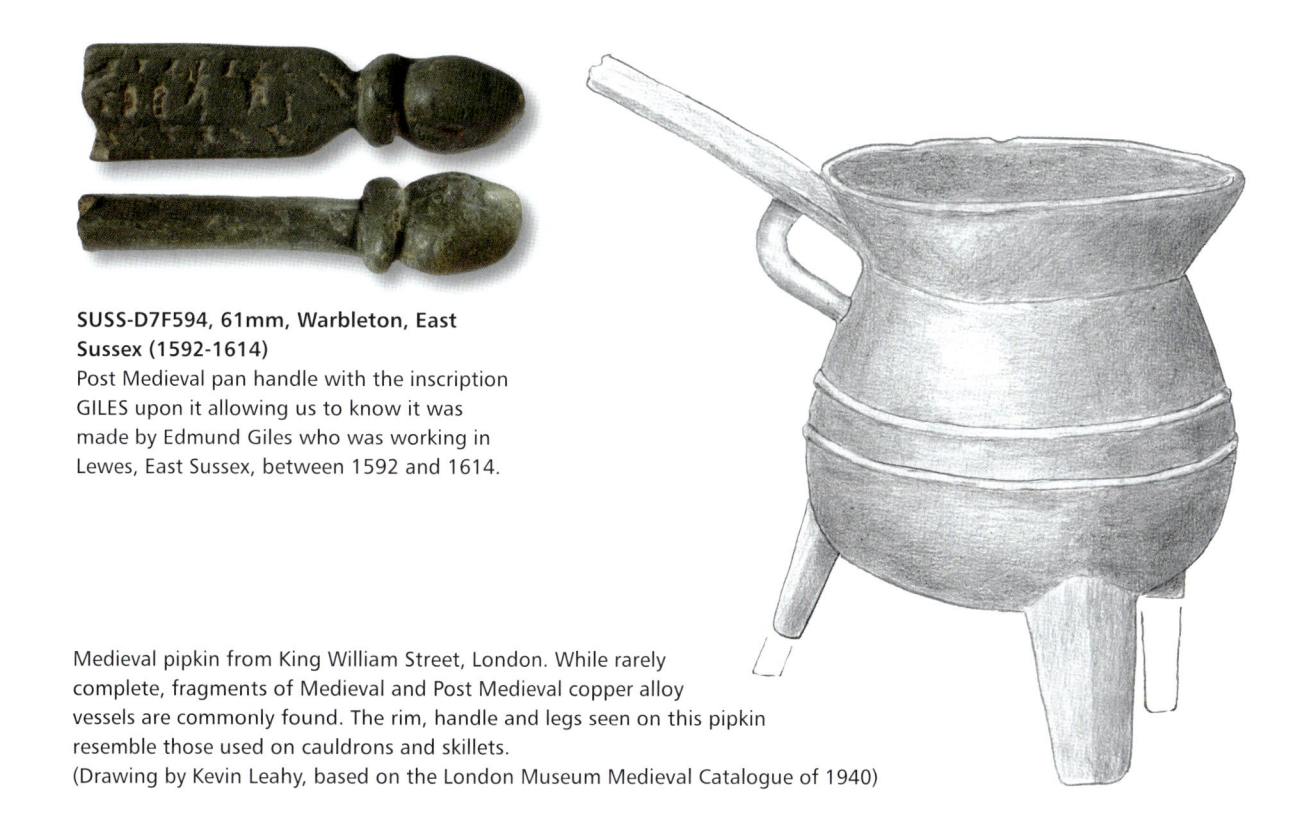

SUSS-D7F594, 61mm, Warbleton, East Sussex (1592-1614)
Post Medieval pan handle with the inscription GILES upon it allowing us to know it was made by Edmund Giles who was working in Lewes, East Sussex, between 1592 and 1614.

Medieval pipkin from King William Street, London. While rarely complete, fragments of Medieval and Post Medieval copper alloy vessels are commonly found. The rim, handle and legs seen on this pipkin resemble those used on cauldrons and skillets.
(Drawing by Kevin Leahy, based on the London Museum Medieval Catalogue of 1940)

DOMESTIC LIFE

NARC-3775C7, 135mm, Northamptonshire area (1475-1550)
Shallow, flat-based vessels are known as skillets. This example has been likened to one found on the Mary Rose (lost in 1545). The two surviving legs have been shortened due to fire degradation, showing the pan was much used.

BUCKETS

A bucket is a vessel with a single, transverse handle across its open top and, while we might see them as purely practical objects, in the past they sometimes had a much deeper significance. Some were decorated and may have been used for serving high volume drinks, like ale, at feasts. Metal fittings survive from wooden buckets, built using staves, like barrels, but sheet metal buckets are also known. Miniature wooden buckets are found in Anglo-Saxon graves. Over 100 buckets have been recorded with the PAS of which 42 are Early Medieval, 30 Roman and 21 Iron Age. Early Medieval bucket fragments are particularly common in Norfolk, and Roman buckets seem to be a feature of the West Midlands.

SF-9E1B87, 61mm, Icklingham, Suffolk (50 BC-AD 200)
Bucket handles in the form of bulls' heads were popular in the Iron Age but continued to be used into the Roman period. Their use must have carried some, now forgotten, symbolic meaning.

168

DOMESTIC LIFE

PUBLIC-749A73, 54mm, Usk, Monmouthshire (50-200)
These objects are understood to be reinforcing plates from the bases of Roman sheet metal buckets. Without them the thin metal would quickly wear through.

SF-E6A847, 47mm, mid Suffolk (500-600)
Handle mount from an Early Medieval wooden bucket. There would have been one of these mounts on each side of the bucket with a ring for the handle at the top of the vertical bar. The mount bears characteristic Anglo-Saxon stamp decoration and the two side loops both end in stylised birds' heads.

EWERS AND WINE JUGS

Ewers were large jugs made for carrying water to the table. During the Middle Ages it became common for the upper echelons of society to wash their hands at the table. The process even became ceremonial, as part of the move towards a more genteel society. This is reflected in other ways also; life was less communal with the upper classes sleeping in individual rooms rather than bedding down in the great hall. More than 120 ewer fragments have been recorded with the PAS, most of which were assigned a Medieval date.

SWYOR-E54DB2, 127mm, Appleby, North Lincolnshire (50-300)
The handle from a Roman wine jug of astonishing sophistication. The lion's head is superbly modelled, its eyes inlaid with silver. This object was probably imported from Italy, examples like it having been found at Pompeii and Herculaneum. The wine jug represented the epitome of civilised life, using the appropriate vessel to consume an imported luxury drink.

DOMESTIC LIFE

The kitchen at Gainsborough Old Hall, Lincolnshire showing the great fire-places and ovens in which bread and pies were baked. A louvre in the roof allowed the escape of smoke. As a fire precaution the kitchen was separate from the main building, the food being passed through the screens passage to the great hall. (Image: Kevin Leahy)

DOMESTIC LIFE

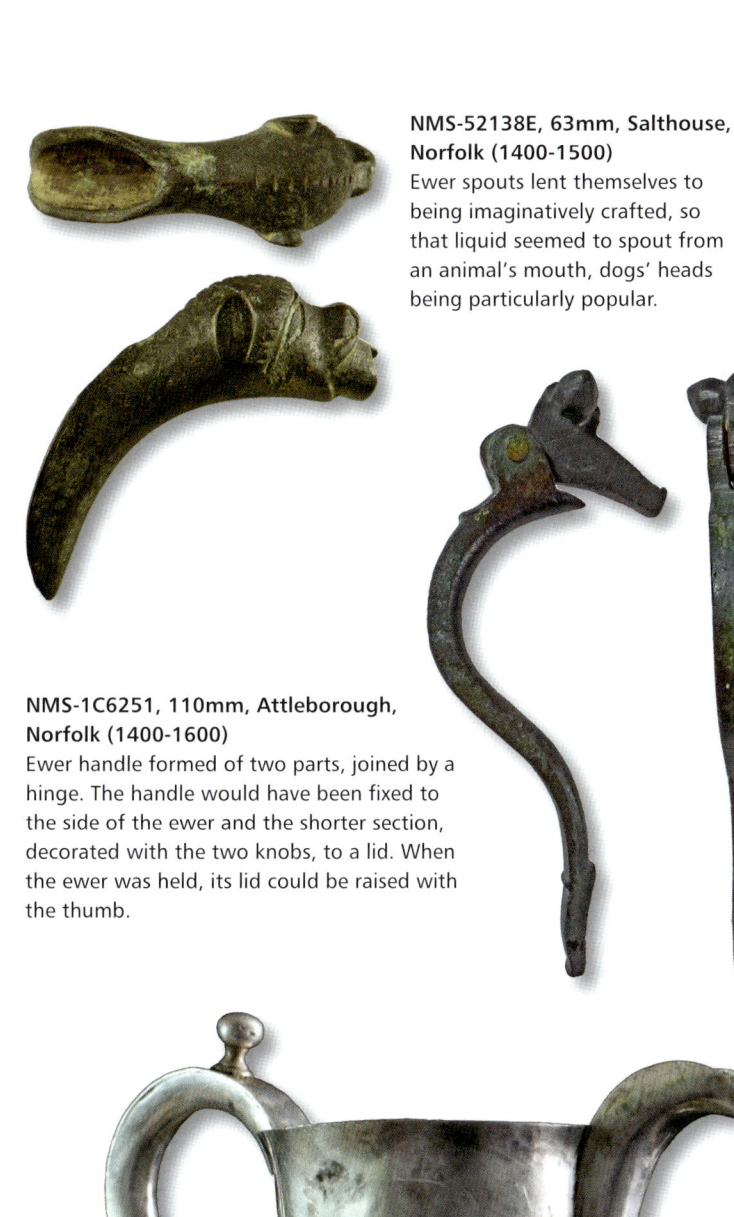

NMS-52138E, 63mm, Salthouse, Norfolk (1400-1500)
Ewer spouts lent themselves to being imaginatively crafted, so that liquid seemed to spout from an animal's mouth, dogs' heads being particularly popular.

NMS-1C6251, 110mm, Attleborough, Norfolk (1400-1600)
Ewer handle formed of two parts, joined by a hinge. The handle would have been fixed to the side of the ewer and the shorter section, decorated with the two knobs, to a lid. When the ewer was held, its lid could be raised with the thumb.

NMS-772B2B, 102mm, Somerton, Norfolk (1300-1500)
On this spout can be seen a decorative openwork bridge. This would have been joined to the vessel itself, providing the spout with additional support; it obviously failed!

DOR-D03CB6, 293mm, Kingston Russell, Dorset (1635-6)
This silver ewer was probably concealed during the English Civil War. On it is a 'hall mark' which allowed it to be precisely dated.

171

DOMESTIC LIFE

MORTARS

Certain foodstuffs and medicines had to be ground down to be used. This work was made easier using a pestle and mortar. The PAS has recorded 69 mortars of which 26 are Medieval, 23 Roman and 12 Post Medieval. The material most commonly used was stone (with 37 examples), followed by pottery (12) and copper-alloy (10).

LON-490B54, 180mm, City of London (50-200)
Fragment of a Roman pottery *mortarium* made in Verulamium (St Albans) white ware. These large bowls were used in the preparation of food, and while it is heavily worn, the interior of this example still bears some of the hard grits used to prolong its life. Once a sauce had been made it was poured out using the spout.

DOMESTIC LIFE

DENO-47D631, 118mm, Newark on Trent, Nottinghamshire (1300-1700)
In use, the stone mortar was set into a block of wood, the four lugs preventing it from moving. One of these has also been shaped to serve as a spout for pouring the contents.

NLM-EA5F73, 88mm, Gainsborough, Lincolnshire (1649-60)
Fragment of a mortar bearing the crest of the Commonwealth, when Parliament ruled without a king. It is possible that, following the Restoration of the monarchy in 1660, this expression of loyalty to Cromwell and his republicans became a dangerous embarrassment, and the object was discarded.

DOMESTIC LIFE

KNIVES

The knife is probably the most important tool made by man – almost 4,000 examples have been recorded on the PAS database to date, of which 2,200 are copper-alloy, almost 1,000 made of flint and 420 are iron. This figure is deceptive; the low number of iron knife blades is due to their poor survival in the ground, and the copper-alloy 'knives' are often only represented by the fittings from lost iron blades. Knives have always been multipurpose tools, used for preparing and eating food, and cutting and carving as part of craftwork. It is likely that the same knife was used for all of these tasks, with specialist tools developing according to specific needs and the status of the owner.

FAKL-A20791, 83mm, Kettlethorpe, Lincolnshire (4000-2700 BC)
The flint used to make this Neolithic knife is in no way inferior to steel, having a hard, razor sharp edge ideally suited to cutting meat. Over 900 flint knives have been recorded by the PAS.

CORN-729D30, 100mm, Brantham, Suffolk (2700-1700 BC)
In the late Neolithic period, some knives were made with carefully polished edges. It is not known why this was done as polishing would not have produced a sharper edge than simple flaking.

IOW-5539A2, 45mm, Northwood, Isle of Wight (2700-1600 BC)
Plano-convex, or 'slug', knife bearing the all-over flaking often employed in later prehistory. Examples of these highly useful knives are found in Early Bronze Age graves.

DOMESTIC LIFE

LANCUM-3BEC10, 111mm, Morecambe Bay, Lancashire (2450-2150 BC)
The copper knife marks the introduction of metal working into Britain. The new material must have been used for reasons of prestige, as pure, unalloyed, copper is soft, weak and greatly inferior to flint. The PAS has recorded almost 300 Bronze Age knives, half of which were flint, the rest copper-alloy.

NCL-F3D0E3, 145mm, Driffield, East Yorkshire (1000-800 BC)
This Late Bronze Age knife is deceptive. Despite its simple shape it has a complex, carefully worked section. Hammering the edges would have both sharpened and work-hardened them.

GLO-5E5633, 102mm, Portishead, Somerset (1100-800 BC)
The curved blade of this socketed knife is an original feature and other, similar knives are known. They may have been used in woodworking and would have been useful in hollowing out a wooden bowl.

SUR-5680D4, 104mm, Whitchurch, Warwickshire (950-750 BC)
Socketed bronze knife or dagger; such examples show it can be difficult to distinguish between tools and weapons.

DOR-CA6972, 31mm, East Knoyle, Wiltshire (50 BC-AD 50)
The difficulty of distinguishing between knives and daggers is made still more complicated by small objects like this which might have come from a razor which has lost its iron blade. Parallels suggest that it is either late Iron Age or very early Roman. The PAS has recorded only 14 Iron Age knives, most of which were represented by their copper-alloy fittings.

DOMESTIC LIFE

LIN-536F87, 64mm, Syston, Lincolnshire (50-400)
Several Roman erotic knife handles have been recorded by the PAS. These tend to show three people engaged in sexual activity, but this example is odd, even by the standards of such objects. In the centre, a woman, leans against the back of a small man or boy, her legs held under the arms of a second man. His genitalia are clearly shown, but oddly, he seems about to engage the small man on the left, rather than the woman. If this wasn't strange enough, the smaller figure holds, in his arms, a severed human head, its facial features can be seen. No doubt this was all deeply significant, if mystifying to us today.

DENO-AEBF93, 72mm, Ossington, Nottinghamshire (50-200)
This Roman folding knife and spoon set would have been ideal for al fresco dining. The iron knife blade would have been safely lodged in the groove and the spoon bowl would have swivelled at the other end, next to the lion's head.

SF-CA2A74, 63mm, Wickham Skeith, Suffolk (50-400)
Folding knife, retaining part of its iron blade. It is modelled in the form of a panther with one leg. It, and others like it, bear a remarkable resemblance to some Roman carved table legs.

HAMP-8C8E54, 57mm, Alresford, Hampshire (50-400)
Roman folding knife handle in the form of a hound chasing a hare: a common motif in Roman art. Over 400 Roman knives have been recorded with the PAS, 75% of which are represented only by their copper-alloy fittings.

DOMESTIC LIFE

FAKL-E7ADEA, 112mm, North Kesteven, Lincolnshire (450-670)
Iron knives can be very difficult to date, but this well-preserved example came from an Anglo-Saxon cemetery site. This knife is 'whittle-tanged', that is to say that the tang consists of a spike which was pushed into one-piece handle.

KENT-8A4D03, 96mm, Bexley, London (1300-1500)
Over 700 Medieval knives have been recorded, of which over three quarters are represented by copper-alloy fittings. Not surprisingly these are spread across the whole of the country but are densest in the areas of highest population levels in eastern England. A rare survival is this wooden knife handle from the London foreshore, although it has lost its iron blade. These scale-handled knives are a type that became common in the Late Medieval and Post-Medieval periods.

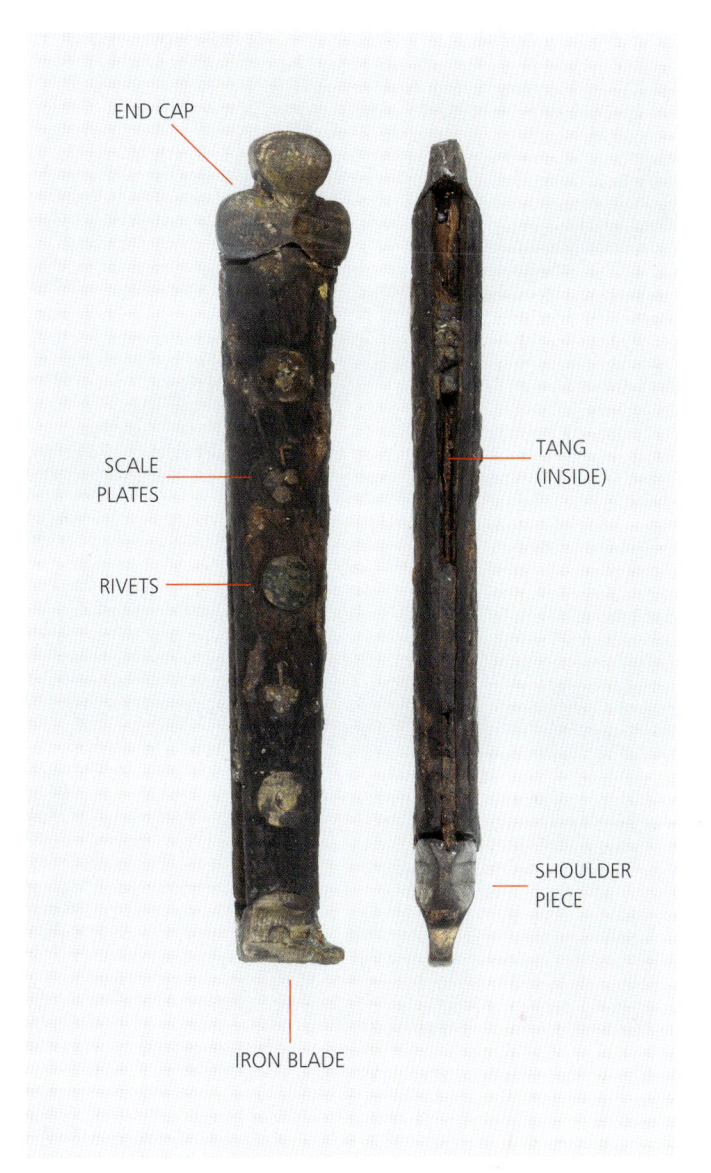

END CAP
SCALE PLATES
RIVETS
TANG (INSIDE)
SHOULDER PIECE
IRON BLADE

LVPL-5DCED4, 89mm, Strubby with Woodthorpe, Lincolnshire (1450-1550)
Late Medieval or Post Medieval knife handle, with silvered or tinned scales forming the handle. These are finely embellished with an array of inscribed linear patterning, adding to its aesthetic appeal.

DOMESTIC LIFE

LON-E1AD95, 18mm, Westminster, London (1450-1500)
Beautifully decorated composite knife hilt with floral motifs. Within the copper-alloy hilt is part of its iron tang.

LON-61ECBA, 191mm, City of London (1450-1600)
Unusually complete knife with iron blade, and ivory handle. While late in date it still employs an old style, spiked, whittle-tang.

HAMP-C93E3B, 29mm, Cheriton, Hampshire (1500-1600)
Anthropomorphic end cap from a knife handle in the form of a female bust, wearing a high, flat-backed, hat, which helps to date the object. The figure's facial features are clear, but simply executed. Decorative knife caps were a feature of this period and occur in many forms, horses' hooves being particularly popular.

DOR-6D6F65, 15mm, Stoke Wake, Dorset (1500-1600)
A further example of a decorated end cap formed of two opposing beasts' heads. On this example, both heads have rounded, beak-like snouts and open mouths divided by a zig-zag pattern.

DOMESTIC LIFE

WHETSTONES

Whetstones or honestones were an important accompaniment to knives, as it was vital to keep blades sharp by applying them on such stones. It is often possible to recognise whetstones by the way in which the stone has been worn by constant use. Some stones were better than others and were therefore traded over long distances. 300 whetstones have been recorded by the PAS but, in most cases, it is not possible to assign them to a particular period.

FASAM-F55282, 43mm, Gosberton, Lincolnshire (50-400)
This whetstone can be dated because it bears the Latin inscription [M?]ΛNDΛCVS MATTΛVI, which probably translates as 'Mandacus(?), son of Mattavus'. This is possibly a Celtic/British name and patronym. Similar grooved stones were used in recent times by pinners, to point pins.

LIN-3D5C6E, 241mm, East Lindsey, Lincolnshire (500-1100)
Finely made perforated whetstone found on a Middle Anglo-Saxon site and dated by its association.

NLM-E1ED34, 74mm, near Caistor, Lincolnshire (800-900)
Even without the perforation the characteristic signs of wear on this object show it to have been a whetstone.

YORYM-4399F2, 120mm, Yapham, East Yorkshire (700-1100)
The tough stone from which this whetstone was made was imported from Scandinavia, and was one of the many hones imported by the Vikings.

DOMESTIC LIFE

SPOONS

Forks were little used before the Post Medieval period, so people ate using knives, spoons and fingers. Spoons are relatively common finds, although most were made from wood, bone or horn which have not survived. The PAS has recorded over 2,800 spoons, of which 618 are Roman, 14 Early Medieval, 327 Medieval and over 1,700 Post Medieval, reflecting a move to metal spoons with the onset of a more polite society. Not all spoons were used for eating; they were also used for stirring and measuring, some having a ritual function.

HESH-9A4B83, 111mm, Nesscliffe area, Shropshire (300 BC-AD 100)
These Iron Age spoons are of a well-known type of which 25 examples are known, all but one from Britain or Ireland. They are often found in pairs, one marked with a cross, the other with a hole through it (damaged on this example). Their use is unknown, but may it well have been ritual.

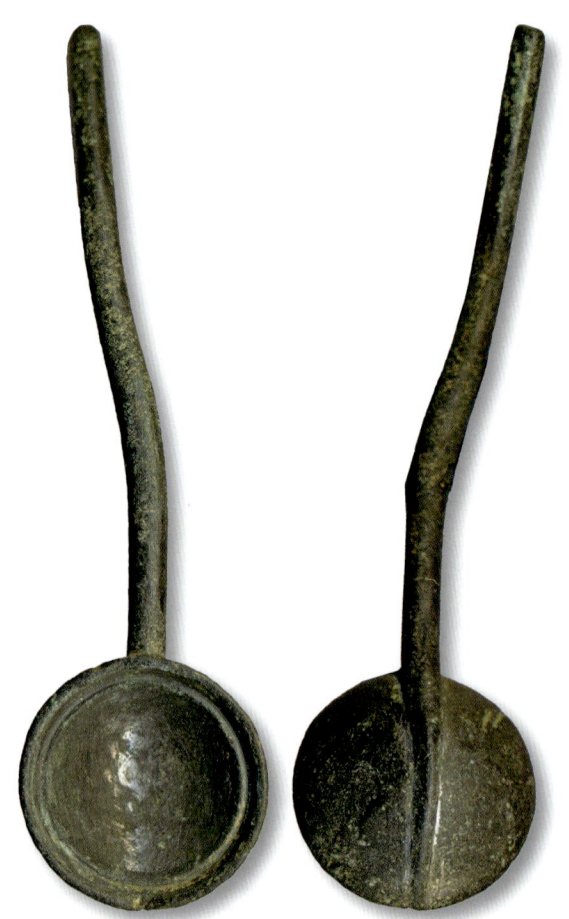

DOR-63E644, 73mm, Micheldever, Hampshire (50-200)
Tin-plated Roman spoon with a round bowl which, at 7mm, is comparatively deep. The handle is incomplete.

180

DOMESTIC LIFE

IOW-6A25B6, 146mm, Yarmouth, Isle of Wight (200-400)
Roman spoon, originally tinned to make it look like silver. The off-set bowl is a feature seen on many Roman spoons.

SUSS-FCA787, 153mm, Arlington, East Sussex (1400-1500)
Large silver spoon of Medieval date with what seems to be the remnants of a maker's mark, and an acorn-shaped terminal. Marks on one side of the bowl suggested to the recorder that the owner was right-handed.

NLM-A04255, 46mm, Ulceby, Lincolnshire (1400-1500)
Handle of a silver Medieval spoon with a finely executed figure of the Virgin and Child. Given the popularity of this motif amongst the laity there is no suggestion that this was necessarily made for ecclesiastical use.

DOMESTIC LIFE

NMGW-05E56D, 113mm, Coity Castle, Bridgend (1400-1600)
Staining between the mouldings on this spoon's handle suggest suggests the presence of an organic material (such as bone, wood or leather), and file marks on its terminal point to it having originally been longer. These are all part of the spoon's history or 'object biography'.

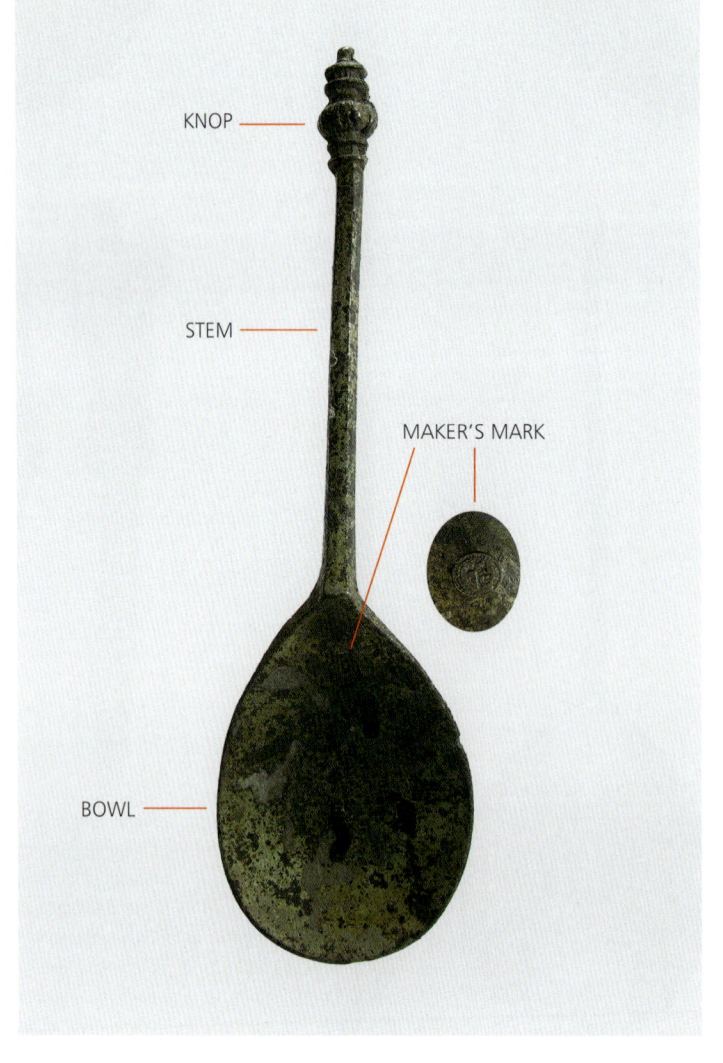

LON-948F05, 163mm, City of London (1500-1600)
Pewter or lead alloy spoon with a variation of the popular 'writhen' knop. It is stamped with the maker's mark TP; like silver Hall Marks, pewterer's marks can sometimes be dated.

KNOP
STEM
MAKER'S MARK
BOWL

182

DOMESTIC LIFE

LVPL-EFA49A, 131mm, St Asaph, Denbighshire (1600-1900)
This spoon has a tiny bowl and a very long handle. Its function is unknown but it may have been used for getting preserves out of a jar.

SUR-7A7AF6, 140mm, Merrow, Surrey (1620-1670)
This simply shaped spoon resembles the so-called Puritan spoons of the middle of the 17th century.

IOW-84497C, 36mm, Niton and Whitwell, Isle of Wight (1775-1945)
These objects are not uncommon and can be incorrectly identified. While they look like tiny spoons, they are part of the feed mechanism from a seed drill; a number of them were attached to the edge of a revolving disc, their bowls measuring out the right amount of seed.

183

DOMESTIC LIFE

CHAFING DISHES

These were used to keep food hot, once brought to the table, although it is likely that some food was actually cooked in the chafing dish. They were made of both metal and pottery, and would have held burning charcoal or other combustible material. Found from the Middle Ages onwards, it is likely their use is much older. Fragments of 250 metal chafing dishes have been recorded with the PAS although most of them are represented only by distinctive fragments. Ceramic chafing dishes are also known, seven of which appear on the PAS database.

WILT-120692, 170mm, Longbridge Deverill, Wiltshire (1600-1800)
Although made of pottery this find shows how a chafing dish worked. Fuel, probably charcoal, was placed in the dish, the holes through it allowing an air supply. This example has an integral handle but handles from metal chafing dishes are common finds.

KENT-7B6924, 61mm, Eastchurch, Kent (1400-1600)
T-shaped handles might have been used on other items besides chafing dishes, but this is their most likely function.

SUSS-4F2667, 53mm, Horsted Keynes, West Sussex (1450-1550)
All that survives of this Medieval chafing dish is its handle, formed of an inverted heart-shape. The heavy lug, by which the handle was attached to the dish, is typical; with the end of the projecting boss expanded to hold it in place.

PUBLIC-9E5051, 60mm, Ivinghoe, Buckinghamshire (1500-1650)
Swivelling arm from a chafing dish, the man's head was one of three, attached to the side of dish. The arms were swivelled around the heads and across the open top on the chafing dish, the bowl containing the food resting on them.

SUR-B93613, 64mm, Nether Wallop, Hampshire (1500-1650)
Detail of a swivelling arm from a chafing dish tripod support.

DOMESTIC LIFE

TAPS

Controlling the movement of water has been a great human achievement, allowing habitation (and things to grow) in areas otherwise impossible. A well-laid drain probably says more for civilisation that any statue. The humble tap is nowadays less appreciated, but itself was a great invention allowing the flow of water to be reduced or stopped, and liquids to be recovered from large containers, such as barrels and ceramic cisterns. Over 300 taps and tap keys have been recorded with the PAS, all of which date to the Medieval or Post Medieval periods.

SF-130CB2, 58mm, Akenham, Suffolk (1400-1600)
The modernist angular forms of the polygonal spigot and rectangular spout on this tap belie its age. The top of the handle is missing, the spike, projecting from the top of the spout held the handle of a bucket being filled.

SOM-901263, 54mm, Misterton, Somerset (1400-1700)
Cockerels commonly appear on the keys of barrel taps, perhaps a play on the word 'cock – stopcock'. By turning the tap by 90 degrees the transverse hole could be moved to open or close the tap.

KENT-21ED9B, 77mm, Wingham, Kent (1440-1700)
Tap for a barrel that combines the motif of a beast for a spout and the chicken, or cock, for its key.

DOMESTIC LIFE

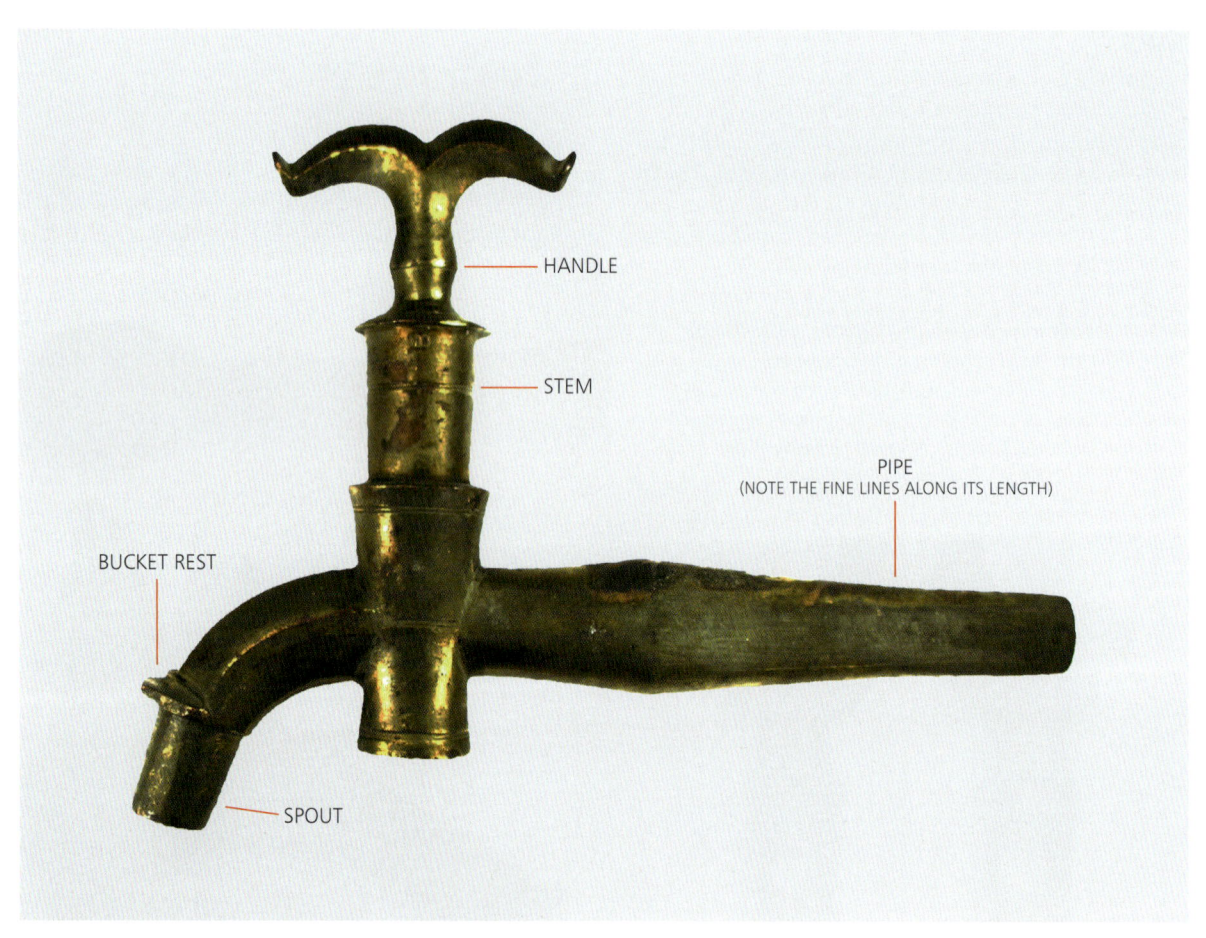

LON-81C758, 163mm, City of London (1600-1750)
Although starting to look like a modern tap this Post Medieval example from London still retains features from its Medieval forebears. Its bifurcated key resembles those seen on Medieval taps.

DENO-E09322, 88mm, Callow, Derbyshire (1200-1400)
This magnificent Medieval tap was probably used in a monastic *lavatorium*, where the monks washed. It is likely to have been an import from the Low Countries.

DOMESTIC LIFE

TANKARDS

Of the 84 tankards recorded by the PAS, 54 are copper-alloy, 4 pottery, 12 lead-alloy or pewter and one wooden. Tankards were known in the Iron Age but were made from wood, using the same stave construction as was employed on barrels; only their metal fittings normally survive. The PAS has recorded 28 Iron Age tankards and 10 Roman examples, although it can be difficult to distinguish between them. The Anglo-Saxons used both pottery and glass drinking vessels, but they are not often found. There are only three Medieval tankards in the PAS dataset, which probably reflects the fact that most people are likely to have been using wooden or horn cups. The end of the Middle Ages saw the sudden appearance of pottery vessels. In the Post Medieval period pewter became commonly used, especially for vessels used to drink beer; the high lead content of some alloys was later viewed as problematic, since it is poisonous.

NMS-8E40B7, 51mm, Lingwood and Burlingham, Norfolk (100 BC-100 AD)
This finely-enamelled handle is all that survives of a Late Iron Age tankard.

SWYOR-BEC04D, 29mm, Thirsk, North Yorkshire (100 BC-100 AD)
This strange looking fragment came from the handle of a Late Iron Age or Early Roman tankard.

NMGW-03EEE8, 46mm, Pentyrch, Cardiff (50-100)
Only a fragment of this tankard survives, but this shows it to have been an accomplished piece of Celtic decoration, probably made in the years following the Roman Conquest.

DOMESTIC LIFE

LON-AAED92, 220mm, Tower Hamlets, London (1500-1700)
Wooden objects were common in the past but seldom survive, making this Post Medieval tankard a remarkable find. It is of stave construction, with its wooden parts held together by two iron bands; the handle being integrally carved from one of the staves. On the base of the vessel are carved, quite primitively, the letters RH.

DOMESTIC LIFE

LON-D2F634, 110mm, Southwark, London (1650-1750)
Pewter vessel decorated with an anchor, engraved with the inscription 'H Butcher Goldern' and 'Park St Southwark'. The capacity mark, a crowned WR for William III, is found near the rim, close to the handle. On the top of the handle itself are the owner's initials, HF B.

SWYOR-F96201, 33mm, Tickhill, South Yorkshire (1650-1750)
All that survives of this tankard is its thumb-rest. It would have been fixed at the top of the handle and worked like a lever, so when pulled, the lid of the tankard would have opened.

189

DOMESTIC LIFE

PASTIMES AND ENTERTAINMENT

TOYS

Playthings reveal how children lived in the past and provide a view of their world. We cannot assume that all miniature objects were toys; as we have seen, many of them may have had a religious or votive role (see pages 132-133) but others must have been for play. In the past, children were expected to help in the work of their community – feeding animals, weeding, bird scaring and caring for younger siblings, but there was still time for playing. Throughout time, children have replicated the work and actions of their elders though play. Dolls help young girls imitate the role of the mother, miniature utensils show household management. Boy's toys include weaponry, items associated with hunting and transport. Toys are often objects that simulate, but simplify, adult play, such as dice, shy, and board pieces. Many toys were simply made or reused items, which, through children's own creativity took on new, imagined, roles. The finds recorded with the PAS show that toys were being industrially produced from about the 17th century and, of the 1,600 toys recorded by the PAS, over 1,300 are Post Medieval in date. These represent household equipment, guns and figures. Most were made from lead alloys, the use of which would be viewed with horror today.

YORYM-FE7E01, 45mm, Brandsby-cum-Stearsby, Lincolnshire (1400-1600)
Based on the form of contemporary vessels this Medieval lead jug is decorated with simple incised lines.

YORYM-4769D5, 37mm, Stockton-on-the-Forest, North Yorkshire (1400-1800)
This set of three conjoined cups seem to have been based on a 'fuddling cup' - the full sized cups were filled with liquid and the challenge was to drink without getting soaked. This small version imitated larger examples made of ceramic.

BH-C38D1C, 89mm, Redbourn, Hertfordshire (1600-1700)
Miniature toy firearms are common Post Medieval finds, this one being in the form of a musket. Its fishtail shaped butt is typical of English muskets of the 17th century.

190

DOMESTIC LIFE

YORYM-FB9929, 35mm, Filey, North Yorkshire (1600-1800)
Toy cannon are common detector finds, although not often found complete as the gun carriage was usually wooden. Many were designed to fire shot with gunpowder, and date from a time when a child could buy a halfpenny worth of gun powder with ease.

IOW-A3C45E, 35mm, Shorwell, Isle of Wight (1600-1800)
Whirly-gig or buzz-wheels are intriguing toys, as in the case of this lead example. A thread passed through their two central holes allowing them to be spun, first clockwise and then anti-clockwise, their momentum re-twisting the two threads for the return. As they revolved the serrated edges of the disc made a buzzing sound. They could be quite dangerous when in the wrong hands, and it must be assumed some children used them to harm others!

IOW-9F69C2, 34mm, Shorwell, Isle of Wight (1700-1800)
'Shies' were very popular, most children finding it fun to knock down figures with stones. Often they were made in the form of cockerels, but less usually found are those of other birds, such as this owl made of lead. They are a version of a cruel adult sport where the target was a tethered live bird.

LANCUM-5727FE, 53mm, Nateby, Cumbria (1600-1800)
Horn books are unusual finds and imitate 'books' made of horn in a wooden frame, often used for teaching the alphabet or Lord's prayer. How these, much smaller, lead objects were used is unclear. They might have simply been children's toys.

LIN-16BF84, 37mm, Londonthorpe and Harrowby Without, Lincolnshire (1660-85)
This example of a 'horn book' is made from lead alloy and bears a depiction of Charles II. The alphabet upon it misses out the letters J and V, as is common at this time, but it is noteworthy that the letter N is reversed.

DOMESTIC LIFE

LON-67D29E, 43mm, Greenwich, London (1700-1800)
The minute detail on the clothing worn by the man on this figurine allows it to be dated. The horse's harness is shown in useful, and convincing, detail.

LON-60302A, 51mm, City of London (1600-1800)
The openwork frame on this lead mirror is particularly ornate, and a remarkable survival. Many lead toys recorded with the PAS are from the Thames foreshore, where the anaerobic (airless) conditions of the river mud help maintain preservation.

NCL-DB1E00, 93mm, Healeyfield, County Durham (1550-1600)
Crudely made flat lead dolls are relatively common finds. Their basic features being marked out with delineation and some raised areas.

LON-88796E, 32mm, Wandsworth, London (1600-1800)
This lead toy plate bears a cartouche on its rim containing a maker's mark, which was a stipulation of the Worshipful Company of Pewterers, though not commonly found on toys at this time.

NLM-60ED23, 30mm, Market Rasen, Lincolnshire (1400-1800)
Many toys found in the countryside are made of copper-alloy as lead toys are unlikely to survive in the plough-soil. This small cauldron emulates those used for cooking (see pages 162-163). Pincushions were sometimes contained in miniature cauldrons which might explain their use.

DOMESTIC LIFE

GAMING PIECES AND DICE

Games of skill and chance are deeply rooted in the human mind, but all that survives of many board games are playing pieces and dice. Occasionally we see a grid for games, like nine men's morris, scratched onto a surface, but only one of these has been recorded by the PAS. There are over 500 gaming pieces on the PAS database, of which 159 were dated to the Early Medieval period being, in the main, made of lead. The PAS has also recorded 103 Roman gaming pieces, 99 of Medieval date and 91 Post Medieval examples. There are also 33 gaming chips recorded, most of which are Post Medieval and five chess pieces, of which three are Medieval.

LANCUM-4EBF20, 160mm, Ulverston, Cumbria (50-1700)
A stone onto which has been scratched a grid for playing the game known as 'Nine Men's Morris'. This game was known to the Romans but was also very popular in the Middle Ages.

NLM-7ABE36, 12mm, Swinhope, Lincolnshire (900-1050)
Lead cones like this are thought to have been gaming pieces, perhaps in *Hnefatafl*, a tactical board game popular with both the Vikings and Anglo-Saxons.

LON-55F862, 29mm, Southwark, London (1150-1350)
Made from bone, this gaming piece is thought to be a king from a Medieval chess set. The crown-shape is represented by the triangular cut to the top, a feature that can be traced back to the pieces used in India where the game originated.

WILT-50D9A9, 29mm, Lacock, Wiltshire (50-250)
Disc made from a piece of Roman pottery which may have been a gaming piece. Alternatively, it could have been used as a counter for calculations. Pebbles were also used in this way; our word 'calculate' comes from the Latin *calx*, a small stone.

SF-735931, 18mm, near Bury St Edmunds, Suffolk (850-1100)
Early Medieval lead gaming pieces are found in many forms, of which this is a rather elaborate example.

DOMESTIC LIFE

GLO-AB74A4, 19mm, Tortworth, Gloucestershire (1300-1700)
It is not known in what game this Medieval lead object was used. It is interesting that it has a hole through its middle, but whether this is integral to its use as a gaming piece is not clear; it may have been used as a method of stringing the pieces together.

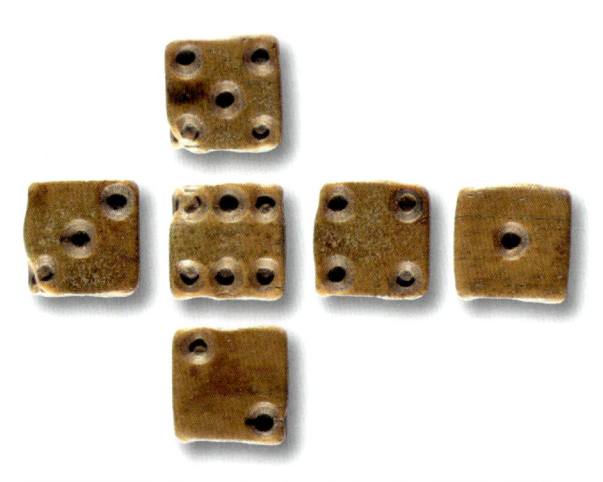

PUBLIC-6103A1, 9mm, City of London (100-1450)
Dice are hard to date and this finely made bone, or ivory, example from the Thames must be assigned to a wide time band.

LON-3E8E62, 12mm, Southwark, London (1500-1700)
The opposing sides of this bone Post Medieval die add up to 7; so 1 is opposite 6, 2, opposite 5, and 3 opposite 4. Irregular arrangements are most common from the 13th to the 16th century but are also found on Roman dice.

LVPL-A37F16, 49mm, Winwick, Lancashire (1700-1800)
Domino piece made of bone or antler, with part of the carved areas still filled with a black inset, thought to be burnt ivory. Although the game has a long history it was not until the 18th century that it was commonly played in Europe.

WMID-39E73E, 25mm, Churchstoke, Powys (1850-1900)
Some gaming pieces imitated coins, such as this example drawing inspiration from a half-guinea of George III (r.1760-1820). To avoid falling foul of counterfeiting laws of the Victorian period, many such pieces replicate earlier coinage, as in this case. These imitation spade guineas were last made between the two World Wars, when they were sold for two shillings and sixpence for a hundred. They are not rare.

NLM-202662, 19mm, Messingham, North Lincolnshire (1850-1950)
Glazed pottery playing piece used in a game, known, in some areas, as jacks, or five stones; the aim of which was to toss the jacks and then catch them on the back of the hand.

DOMESTIC LIFE

PIPES

The first mention of smoking in England appears in William Harrison's Great Chronologie which notes, for the year 1573 'the use of an Indian herbe called tobaco' (sic). It soon became very popular and was long thought to have health benefits, though an early sceptic was King James I, who said of tobacco smoking that it was a 'custome lothesome to the eye, hateful to the nose, harmful to the brain, dangerous to the lungs, and in the black and stinking fume thereof, nearest resembling the horrible stygian smoke of the pit that is bottomless'. There is little point in enumerating the pipe fragments recorded by the PAS; these are so common as to be ubiquitous.

LON-FD1184, 179mm, Southwark, London (1580-1610)
An extraordinary and extremely rare survival is this half of a wooden mould for making clay pipes. The form of the pipe, its tiny bowl being almost in line with the stem, is very early, making this the earliest known wooden pipe mould.

SWYOR-326DE9, 44mm, Heptonstall, West Yorkshire (1660-1680)
The only decoration on this pipe bowl is a simple line of rouletting close to its rim. When tobacco was most expensive the bowls of pipes are noticeably smaller, therefore needing less tobacco. Early pipes tended to have larger holes through their stems and were less hard-fired.

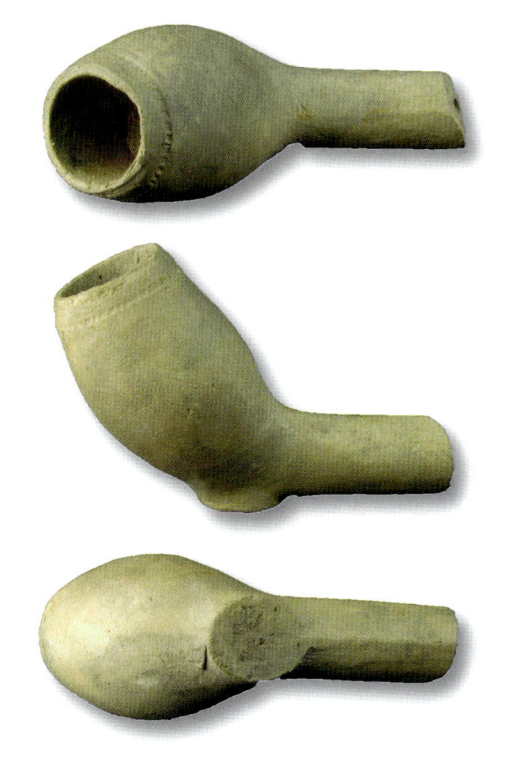

DOMESTIC LIFE

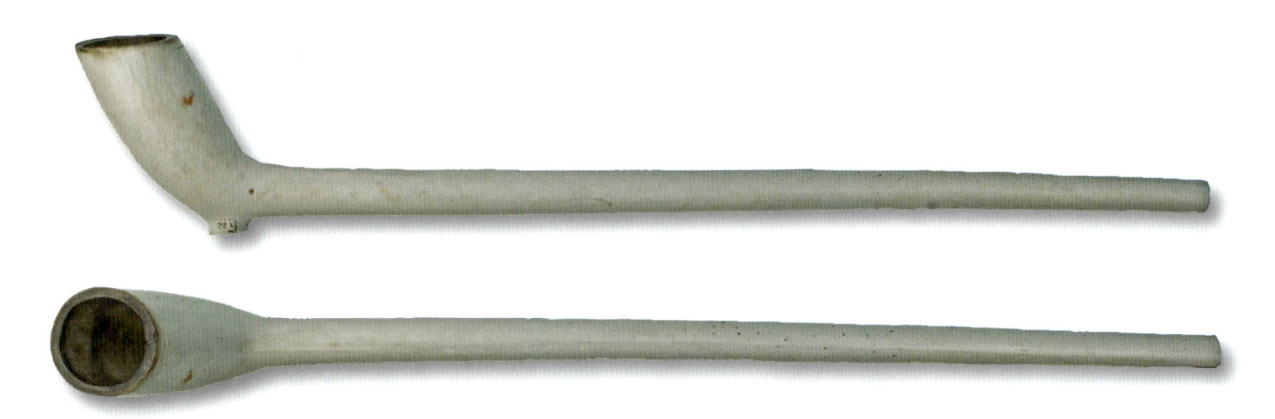

KENT-462DE2, 209mm, Millwall, London (1600-1700)
Clay pipes are normally found incomplete, as most of those now discovered were probably discarded when broken. This example bears the maker's mark P, on one side of its projecting spur, and an anchor, on the other. The changing shapes of clay pipes means that they can be used to help date the sites on which they are found.

LVPL-D03967, 38mm, Handbridge, Cheshire (1860-1910)
In the 19th century clay pipes reflected political and social change. They were made to represent popular heroes of the time and social and religious groups, such as the Freemasons. Following the influx of Irish migrants to England, especially following the potato famine of the 1840s, some pipes were designed with Irish folk in mind. This example bears a shamrock and Irish harp, and may have been produced in Chester.

PIPE TAMPERS

These were used to firm down tobacco within the pipe bowl. They show great diversity in their designs, which comment on popular culture and the thinking of those frequenting smoking houses. The PAS has recorded 375 pipe tampers, many of which are risqué, reflecting the masculine environment in which they were used.

DENO-0C6CC4, 40mm, Wingerworth, Derbyshire (1700-1900)
Originally gilded this pipe tamper has an interesting design in the form of the Lincoln Imp, a Medieval carving in Lincoln cathedral, which is one of the emblems of the city.

DOMESTIC LIFE

WMID-B907D3, 59mm, Harlaston, Staffordshire (1700-1850)
Pipe tamper, showing a hand holding a pipe, which is more instructive than first seems; two fingers above the stem, two below and the thumb near the tip, are shown balancing the pipe.

WILT-FE9706, 67mm, Warminster, Wiltshire (1700-1900)
Scenes of a couple having intercourse and lewdly positioned women were popular on pipe tampers. This bawdy content was perhaps inspired by a classical tale, or just old fashioned smut.

MUSICAL INSTRUMENTS

Musical instruments are rare finds, apart from 'jews harps' which are commonly found by detectorists with 436 records. There are only 28 other musical instrument parts on the database, most being Post Medieval in date and consisting of the metal fittings from wooden instruments.

LON-58D1C9, 153mm, Southwark, London (1100-1300)
This simply made Medieval whistle or flute is made from a sheep or goat's tibia. There is evidence of a cork-like material at the flared end, probably forming a 'fipple' which channelled the air, thus enabling the instrument to function.

DOMESTIC LIFE

BH-8B5B02, 70mm, Caddington and Slip End, Bedfordshire (1700-1800)
Known as jews harps (not 'jaws harps'), or jews trumps, these simple instruments are used by peoples throughout the world and form an important element in traditional music. They are played by plucking a central bar (reed) whilst the harp was held in the teeth. As in this case, only the harp frame, not the iron reed, usually survives.

SUR-6A5811, 34mm, West Clandon, Surrey (1700-1830)
Most musical instruments were made from wood and little survives of them. Metal keys from woodwind instruments are occasionally found by detectorists, of which this example is likely to have come from a clarinet or oboe. The shape of the key helps date it.

BELLS

Bells have fulfilled many roles through time. They were used in music, in worship, and also in clocks; the word 'clock' actually comes from the Medieval Latin word clocca (bell). Crotal, or rumbler, bells, on the other hand, were used to keep animals (and children) under supervision. The PAS has recorded over 3,400 bells, or bell related items, of which most (2,500) are Post Medieval, 670 Medieval and almost 200 Roman.

NMS-B8B8AC, 25mm, Brinton, Norfolk (50-400)
The function of this small Roman bell is unknown. It could have been used on an animal, but a religious use is also possible.

WILT-99FB4B, 46mm, The Deverills, Wiltshire (800-1100)
Copper plated iron bells dating from the Early Medieval period have been associated with Irish missionaries. Examples found in hoards of tools suggest that they were used by tradesmen, perhaps to announce their presence.

198

DOMESTIC LIFE

SF-ECD886, 29mm, Beyton, Suffolk (750-1100)
These small hexagonal bells are found on Viking sites and may have been used to indicate the whereabouts of children.

WAW-058F84, 40mm, Welford on Avon, Warwickshire (1200-1400)
During the Medieval period small sheet metal bells, like this, were attached to clothing, perhaps as an adjunct to dancing.

SWYOR-2E1806, 24mm, Scotter, Lincolnshire (1200-1400)
Two small Medieval bells, once attached to an animal's harness or to clothing. Some may have been used on the jesses attached to the legs of hunting hawks.

YORYM-749FFC, 52mm, Burstwick, East Yorkshire (1200-1400)

HAMP-5ED289, 38mm, Winterbourne Stoke, Wiltshire (1650-1850)
Cast copper-alloy crotals, like this example, are very common Post Medieval finds. It seems that they were attached to the harness of animals, and were used over a long period of time.

199

Chapter 8
Tools and Manufacture

AXES

These are amongst the earliest and most useful of tools, used in all stages of woodworking, from felling trees to the fine dressing of wooden objects. They were also highly effective weapons. In total, the PAS has recorded over 4,700 axes, of which around 1,600 are flint or stone, almost 2,500 copper or bronze, and 127 iron. In addition to their practical role, axes have always had symbolic meanings, being found in ritual contexts and on ceremonial sites. The rock used to make stone axes was transported over long distances, even when local material would have served just as well: people wanted axes that came from special places. The shapes of bronze axes were carved onto monuments, as at Stonehenge, and axes dominate Bronze Age hoards. In the Roman period, we see votive models of axes being made and found on the sites of shrines. Medieval and Post Medieval axes are predominately working tools, not weapons.

Stone and Flint

Stone and flint polished axes were introduced into Britain in the Neolithic period. Extensive work has been carried out on them, which has allowed many axes to be traced back to the sites where the rock was quarried. Less work has been done on flint axes, although elaborate Neolithic mines have been excavated where flint was extracted from deep in the chalk in which it occurs, such as Grimes Graves, Norfolk. The PAS has recorded over 500 stone axes and almost 1,100 flint axes.

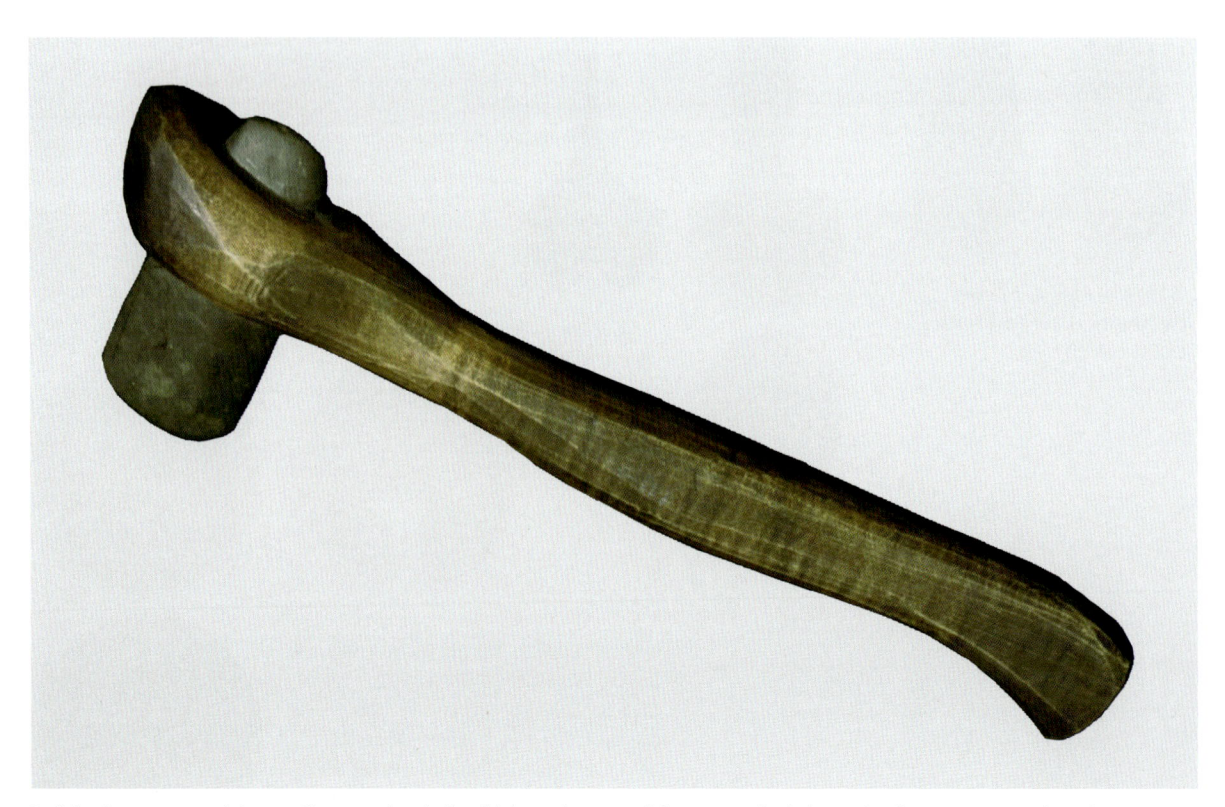

Polished stone axe with a replica wooden haft which copies a surviving example. It is a mistake to presume that these carefully finished implements would not have had hafts made with equal care. (Image: Kevin Leahy)

TOOLS AND MANUFACTURE

SF-2899A7, 118mm, Wetherden, Suffolk (500,000 - 180,000 BP)
Lower Palaeolithic, Acheulean handaxe; these are also referred to as 'bifaces', which describes the way that they were made, by removing flakes from both faces. It is unlikely that these objects were ever hafted, hence the term handaxe is used. The PAS has recorded almost 330 handaxes from an area south of an imaginary line between the rivers Humber and Severn, which was not scoured during the last Ice Age.

SUR-85BDCC, 92mm, Shiplake, Oxfordshire (500,000 - 180,000 BP)
Another Acheulean handaxe, which has been carefully made and is symmetrical. It shows aesthetic taste existed so long ago. These implements were made by Homo heidelbergensis, beings that existed before Homo sapiens sapiens, the genus of human to which we belong.

WMID-8583D7, 96mm, Fazeley, Staffordshire (500,000 - 180,000 BP)
Not all Lower Palaeolithic handaxes were made from flint. This example is quartzite, which has led to a cruder finish. Around 180,000 years ago an Ice Age put an end to human occupation in Britain, covering the country with a massive layer of ice.

TOOLS AND MANUFACTURE

KENT5277, 92mm, Kennington, Kent (60,000-40,000 BP)
This Bout Coupé handaxe has a distinctive shield shape and thin section. It dates from the Middle Palaeolithic when rising temperatures allowed people and animals to move back into Britain. Only five such handaxes have been recorded by the PAS. They are important finds as they were associated with Neanderthals and show the presence of these people in Britain.

LON-440D70, 185mm, Wandsworth, London (9000-4000 BC)
Rising temperatures after the last Ice Age led to the spread of woodland and Mesolithic tranchet axes were a response to this change. They get their name from the tranchet technique used to sharpen them, in which large flakes were removed from both sides of the cutting edge. The PAS has recorded over a 100 tranchet axes, mainly from the south and east of England.

TOOLS AND MANUFACTURE

FAKL-04D403, 141mm, Iford, East Sussex (3300-2200 BC)
While resembling a tranchet axe, these flaked implements are more finely worked and lack the lozenge-shaped section. They were a later development.

DENO-A41483, 274mm, Scarrington, Nottinghamshire (4000-2200 BC)
Polished axes were a feature of the Neolithic period. This example was made, not from flint, but from an igneous rock, which was flaked to shape and then polished.

203

TOOLS AND MANUFACTURE

NLM-0DBF37, 151mm, Broughton, Brigg, North Lincolnshire (2700-2350 BC)
Only the cutting edge of this flint axe is polished, a feature of Late Neolithic axes. Flint axes are often considered separately from those made from other stones as, until recently, it was impossible to say from where they came. Most of the flint axes recorded by the PAS are concentrated in the lowland zones of England where chalk and flint are found.

BERK-8CD431, 132mm, Witney, Oxfordshire (4000-2300 BC)
This axe was made from a rock which, unlike flint, could not be flaked. It was shaped by pecking and grinding before being polished.

TOOLS AND MANUFACTURE

LANCUM-4F71B1, 181mm, Langdale, Cumbria (3500-2350 BC)
Great Langdale was one of the main sources of stone axes. The volcanic tuff found there can be flaked to shape before being polished; this find represents an intermediate stage: flaked but not polished, it is an 'axehead roughout'. Axes made from this stone are found around Langdale but, surprisingly, there is a second concentration across the other side of England in East Yorkshire and northern Lincolnshire.

View of the stone axe 'factory' at Great Langdale, Cumbria. The light-coloured bands consist of waste chips from the manufacture of axes. (Image: Kevin Leahy)

TOOLS AND MANUFACTURE

Bronze Axes

While bronze axes represented a technological breakthrough, they were no great improvement on stone; in fact, it is likely that flint and stone continued to be used well into the metal age. The first metal axes were made of pure copper which was soft and weak. The addition of tin to the copper formed bronze, an alloy with greatly improved properties. Bronze axes develop through time, starting with simple flat axes, to which side flanges were then added to secure them in their hafts. The addition of transverse stop ridges led to the palstave axe which was, in turn, superseded by the cup-like socketed axe. The complexities of the terminology used to record these finds makes it difficult to produce detailed figures from the data collected, but in general terms around 370 Early Bronze Age axes have been recorded by the PAS, 600 Middle Bronze Age examples, and more that 1,200 axes of the Late Bronze Age.

NMS-7AA906, 142mm, Marham, Norfolk (2350-1800 BC)
This simple Early Bronze Age flat axehead is one of the earliest forms of metal axe found in England. Its cutting edge has been hammered to sharpen and work-harden it.

LVPL-613611, 120mm, Fangfoss, East Yorkshire (2150-1650 BC)
Developed form of Early Bronze Age flat axe. Its edges have been hammered to raise the flanges, which help stop the blade twisting in its haft.

TOOLS AND MANUFACTURE

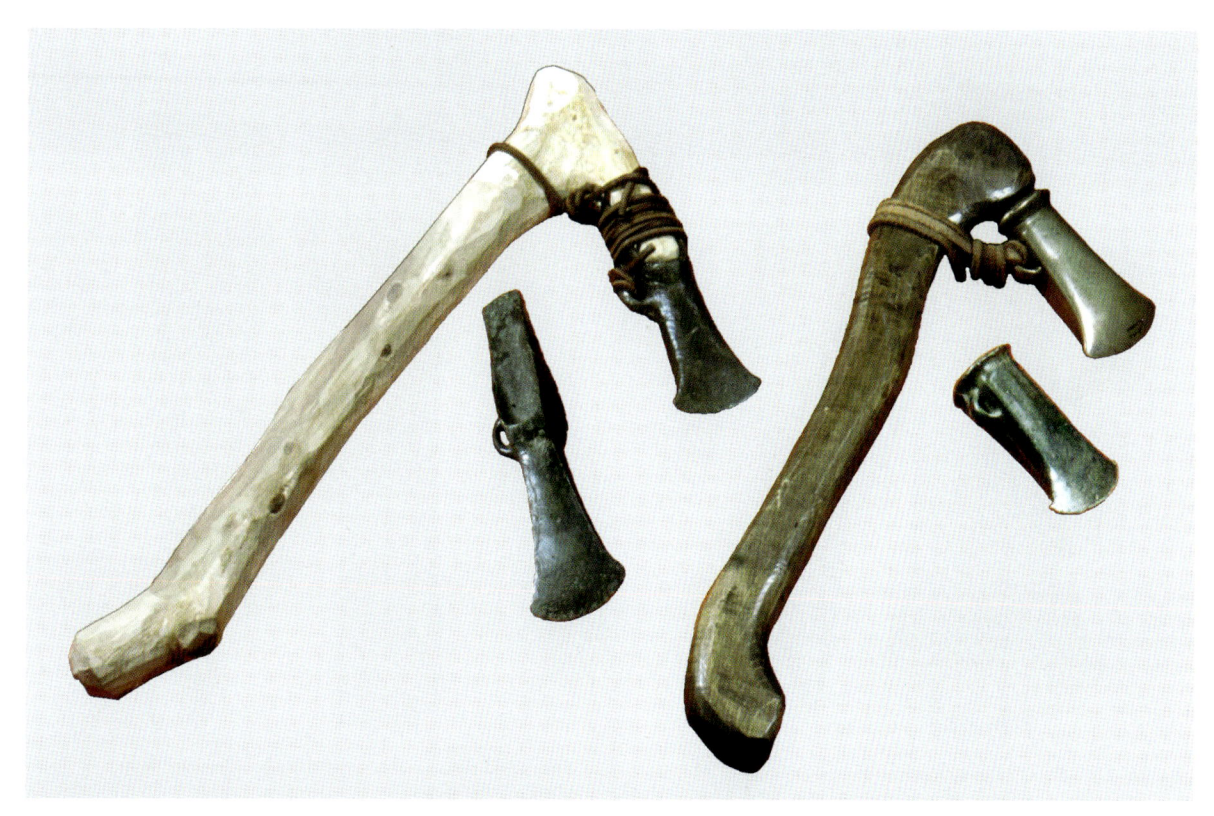

HAMP-B0D6B5, 158mm, Stowe, Buckinghamshire (1500-1150 BC)
Like the developed flat axes, Middle Bronze Age palstaves had side flanges to stabilise them, but they were also fitted with a transverse stop ridge to prevent the axe from being driven back and splitting the haft.

Bronze axes with replica hafts. Flat axes were probably hafted in much the same way as their stone forebears, but the addition of flanges called for the use of hafts with an elbow. Socketed axe hafts had a wooden projection which went into the axe's socket. Bindings were used to keep these axes in place. (Image: Kevin Leahy)

TOOLS AND MANUFACTURE

FLANGE — SEPTUM

LOOP

STOP RIDGE

BLADE

HAMMERED CUTTING EDGE

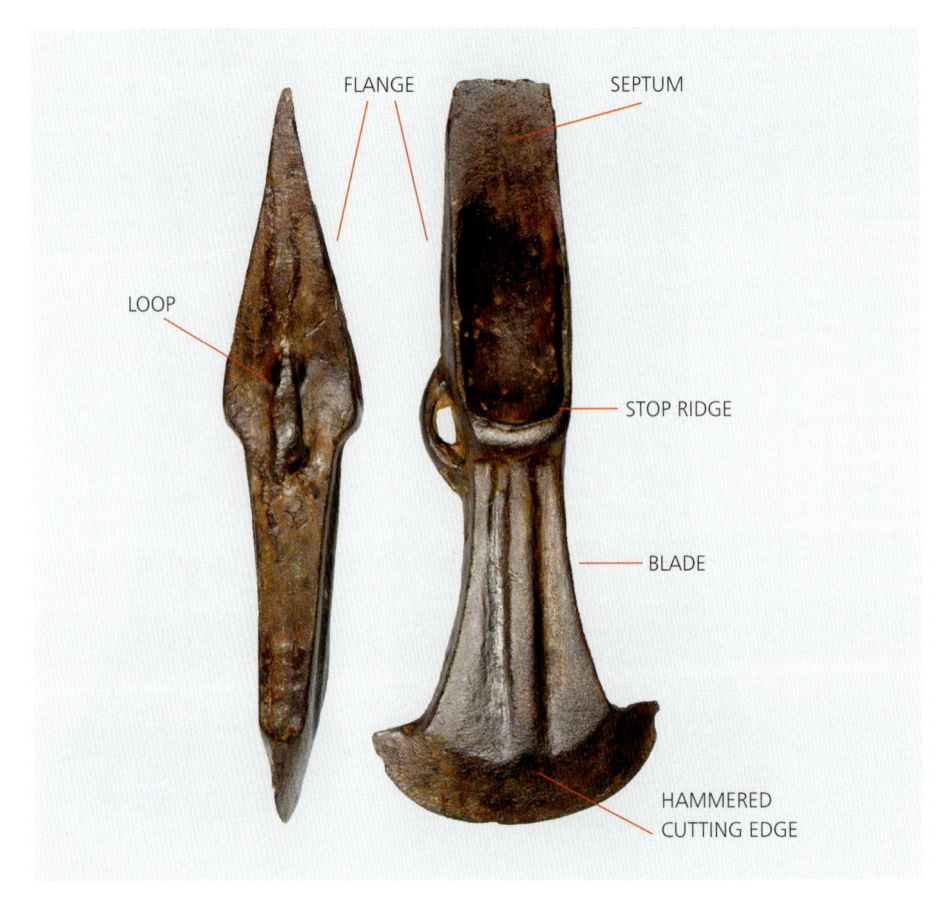

CORN-7DBCCC, 153mm, Cuckney, Nottinghamshire (1400-1125 BC) This developed Middle Bronze Age palstave axe was fitted with a side loop to secure the axe to its haft.

NMGW-759FC0, 141mm, Conwy (1150-950 BC)
A feature of this late palstave is its very deep stop ridge. It dates from the time when changes in metal work were heralding the start of the Late Bronze Age.

WILT-C4C954, 120mm, Marlborough, Wiltshire (1400-1150 BC)
While most socketed axes date from the Late Bronze Age, a few, like this long, slender example, are of Middle Bronze Age date.

208

TOOLS AND MANUFACTURE

WILT-739705, 84mm, Tilshead, Wiltshire (1000-700 BC)
This short stubby axe is of a type seen as dating from the very end of the Bronze Age into the Iron Age.

FAKL-FB5DF6, 124mm, Cadney, North Lincolnshire (800-700 BC)
Fine socketed axe of Sompting type. These axes mark the end of the Bronze Age and probably continued to be made after the introduction of iron working.

NMGW-718725, 86mm, Glyn Tarell, Powys (1000-800 BC)
Finds of socketed axes are widespread but there are concentrations in East Anglia, southern England and South Wales. Short, blocky socketed axes, like this one, are common in south-east Wales leading to them being known as the 'South Wales type'.

TOOLS AND MANUFACTURE

HESH-07CD71, 107mm, Ellesmere, Shropshire (1000-700 BC)
Elegant faceted axes like this are found throughout Eastern England but with a concentration in East and West Yorkshire.

LANCUM-0033B8, 81mm, Quernmoor, Lancashire (1000-800 BC)
Marked with three distinctive parallel ribs on each face, this axe is of Yorkshire type, found in Northern England. Unusually it is one of the few examples that shows any signs of wear. It is shorter than usual, and the angle of its cutting edge has been changed.

Iron Axes

The properties of iron meant that a new technology had to be adopted. While bronze is easily cast, iron was wrought, being worked by hammering and fire welding to shape and to join pieces together. Early attempts to copy bronze objects in iron caused problems and eventually new forms were adopted taking advantage of the new material. Iron axes are problematic; they changed little after their initial development and, with the exception of a few distinctive types, most cannot be dated. Iron corrodes badly and objects are often in poor condition when found, again making dating difficult. When first introduced, iron was inferior to bronze, being soft and weak, but was more readily available. The addition of carbon to iron to produce steel resulted in a harder and tougher material.

NMS-FF5E45, 90mm, Narborough, Norfolk (800-600 BC)
Early iron axes copied bronze socketed axes, which presented great problems to the smiths who made them. While it is easy to cast a socketed axe, forming it from wrought iron meant a lot of forging and fire welding. Soon, the shaft-hole axe head was developed and is the form still used. This was easier to make and took full advantage of the properties of the new material.

TOOLS AND MANUFACTURE

WMID-2C2FB2, 155mm, Ilam, Staffordshire (600 BC-AD 1700)
The wide date range for this implement shows the difficulty of dating iron axes and, indeed, many iron objects. This axehead could be Roman but it might equally be Medieval.

LANCUM-085845, 155mm, Lea Green, North Yorkshire (700-1200)
T-shaped axes are a distinctive Early Medieval type that appears to have come into use in the 7th century and lasted into the Medieval period.

This illustration from a Late Anglo-Saxon manuscript shows Noah using a T-shaped axe to trim timbers for the Ark. (Image: Michael Lewis)

TOOLS AND MANUFACTURE

HESH-66CF45, 176mm, Bitterley, Shropshire (1000-1500)
Axes with drooping, bearded blades are generally dated to the Early Medieval and Medieval periods. This example has an off-set blade showing it to have been a side-axe used to make flat surfaces.

BH-E23E57, 178mm, Potters Bar Furzefield, Hertfordshire (1300-1500)
The form of this Medieval iron broad axe, which is still attached to part of its mineralised wooden haft, suggests it is a woodworking tool, though this would not preclude its use in battle.

LON-0DC7C3, 234mm, City of London (1600-1700)
This axe is probably Post Medieval. It appears to be formed of an iron plate, which essentially wraps around the shaft. Its design might be simple, but it would have been an effective tool.

TOOLS AND MANUFACTURE

ADZES

This tool resembles an axe but its blade has a cutting edge set at 90 degrees to the haft. Adzes were used not as felling or chopping tools but to produce flat surfaces on timbers. As with axes, iron adzes are difficult to date, leading to them being under represented in the PAS database, with only 12 examples compared with 85 flint, 16 stone and 9 bronze adzes.

FAKL-ADD3FF, 195mm, Iford, East Sussex (9000-4000 BC)
The asymmetric way in which this Mesolithic flint tool was sharpened shows it to have been an adze.

KENT-90CE46, 114mm, Manston, Kent (3500-2100 BC)
More finely flaked than the Mesolithic tranchet adze shown above, this Neolithic flint adze is strikingly asymmetric.

213

TOOLS AND MANUFACTURE

LANCUM-64B7A7, 110mm, Gisburn, Lancashire (1500-1150 BC)
Palstave-adzes are unusual objects but the PAS has recorded eight of them from across the Midlands.

HESH-69A2A6, 110mm, Ellesmere, Shropshire (1550-1750)
This adze is undatable. Parallels for it exist in excavation reports but similar adzes can be seen in 19th century tool makers' catalogues.

AXE HAMMERS

The function of these massive stone implements is not known. They are unwieldy and often poorly shaped. While their form seems to follow that of Early Bronze Age battle axes (see page 335), none has ever been found in a grave. They would have been effective if an opponent was to be hit with one, but it would have been dangerous to face a more nimbly armed enemy while wielding an axe hammer. The PAS has recorded 18 axe hammers, widespread across central and northern Britain.

LANCUM-35CCF6, 225mm, Greysouthen, Cumbria (2500-1500 BC)
This Early Bronze Age axe hammer is crude and graceless and cannot be seen as a prestigious object.

TOOLS AND MANUFACTURE

HESH-191F76, 207mm, Cleobury Mortimer, Shropshire (2500-1500 BC)
This carefully worked Early Bronze Age axe hammer was made from a granular stone and was shaped by pecking and grinding.

PERFORATED IMPLEMENTS

This term is used for stone objects which are perforated, but there is little else that links them. Their size and shape is as varied as the rocks from which they were made. Their date range is also uncertain; they have been found in contexts dating from the Mesolithic to the Bronze Age. Their function is equally vague; they have been described as mace heads, net weights, digging stick weights or even bolas weights. This amorphous class of object type contains 73 records.

WILT-6FD4E9, 48mm, Grittleton, Wiltshire (9000-1600 BC)
This perforated implement was made by chipping a hole through a natural quartzite cobble. This is a very hard stone and it would have been difficult to make the hole; a softer material would have presented far fewer problems and, for many purposes, would have been equally satisfactory.

215

TOOLS AND MANUFACTURE

SWYOR-D4ABF7, 137mm, Bridlington, East Yorkshire (9000-1600 BC)
Cushion-shaped perforated implement. The material from which it was made is similar to those used to make Neolithic axes, suggesting that it is of similar date.

LON-8DC9F7, 148mm, Hammersmith and Fulham, London (2900-2100 BC)
This striking object may have started out as a polished stone axe and then later been perforated. The use of figured stones is a feature of some perforated implements.

TOOLS AND MANUFACTURE

FLINT WORKING AND TOOLS

In the long span of human history, most of the materials that surround us are recent inventions; metal only appearing in Britain around 2,500 BC and plastics in the late 19th century. All that survives for the greater part of the past are pieces of flint and stone. These seemingly simple items are likely to represent what were sophisticated peoples. The length of time over which flint was used, coupled with its near indestructability, means that worked flint can be found almost everywhere; the PAS has recorded more than 80,000 worked flints. While arrowheads are easily recognised, the flakes and chips that represent the waste from flint working are more difficult and, although very common, are under-represented on the PAS database. Caution is needed when mapping finds of worked flint as the records often reflect where field-walking has been carried out, rather than areas of prehistoric activity.

STRIKING PLATFORM

FLAKE SCARS

'CONCHOIDAL' RIPPLE MARKS

CORTEX

SWYOR-CAAACC, 35mm, Sykehouse, South Yorkshire (6500-4000 BC)
Flint implements were made by removing flakes from a lump of flint known as a core, as shown above. These flakes could then be carefully worked to the required shape and finish. Scars on the sides of this core mark where flakes have been removed. The 'conchoidal' ripple marks seen on the scars are typical of humanly worked flints.

TOOLS AND MANUFACTURE

DOR-595C3B, Donhead St Mary, Wiltshire (9000-3700 BC)
The manufacture of flint implements produces large quantities of waste known as debitage. Groups of flint flakes, like this, show that flint working was being carried out and that there was activity on the site during prehistory.

Flint Implements

The great advantage of flint is that it is easily worked and gives a very hard, razor-sharp edge. Flint was used to produce a wide range of implements, some of which are shown below. Some worked flints, such as arrowheads, can be dated, or at least assigned to periods of the past. Others present greater problems. A feature of flint implements is the presence of 'retouch', careful flaking to produce the required shape, which can be seen on the items illustrated here.

IOW-2C1195, 40mm, Brighstone, Isle of Wight (3500-800 BC)
Scrapers are the most common type of Prehistoric flint implement found. They can be recognised by the steep, scaled flaking around one or more sides. While some scrapers can be assigned to a period, many are difficult to date.

TOOLS AND MANUFACTURE

FAKL-54BF08, 20mm, Silpho, North Yorkshire (4000-1400 BC)
It is not clear what all flint scrapers were used for, although the preparation of animal skins seems likely. After scraping, the skins would have been preserved by smoking, and made pliable by the application of animal fat or brains.

SWYOR-0240F7, 31mm, Ripponden, West Yorkshire (3300-1000 BC)
This button or thumbnail scraper bears large areas of invasive retouch, allowing it to be dated to the Late Neolithic or Bronze Age periods.

FAKL-E28BA7, 117mm, Iford, East Sussex (9000-1400 BC)
Rod-like implements, such as this example, are known as 'fabricators'. It has been suggested that they were used to carry out the fine flaking of flints, but a bone point would have been more suitable. Another possibility is that they were used with iron pyrites to make fire, but there is no supporting evidence for this. As well as having an unknown function, fabricators were in use over a long period of time making dating difficult.

FAKL-555264, 66mm, Iford, East Sussex (9000-500 BC)
Flint cobble with battered faces, showing that it has been used as a hammer stone. These are impossible to date as even today a stone can make a useful tool.

219

TOOLS AND MANUFACTURE

DUR-C32B35, 21mm, Broomhaugh and Riding, Northumberland (9000-3300 BC)
This Prehistoric flint implement appears crude, but in fact the row of notches down one side shows it has been carefully fashioned. The use of these denticulate (toothed) implements is not known.

DENTICULATE RETOUCH

FAKL-7CD2A4, 63mm, Iford, East Sussex (9000-3300 BC)
Serrated implements resemble denticulated tools, but the teeth are much more finely worked. Such tools could have been used as small saws.

DENTICULATE RETOUCH

RETOUCH (PRESSURE FLAKING)

PUBLIC-C8395E, 50mm, Utterby, Lincolnshire (9000-4000 BC)
Spikes can occur on naturally broken flints, but in this case the point has been fashioned by careful, 'pressure flaking' to form a useful awl.

220

TOOLS AND MANUFACTURE

SF-ADFBC6, 106mm, Mildenhall, Suffolk (3500-2500 BC)
Flint chisel, or small axe of Neolithic date. It is not certain how objects like these were used.

METAL TOOLS

Metal slowly took over from flint and stone, although it is probably fair to say that the flint workers' finest creations came after the introduction of metals (see page 320). Bronze tools are immediately recognisable and are generally well preserved, while iron suffers badly from the ravages of time. Our knowledge of the dating of tools comes from metalwork in hoards and excavation finds, where they occured with objects that have an established chronology; for example, the hoard from Marlborough (page 223) dated tools that could not otherwise be recognised as Roman.

BH-8196E7, 54mm, Nether Wallop, Hampshire (2350-800 BC)
Simple tools, like this awl, are difficult to date, but it is likely to be Bronze Age.

KENT-2A2156, 77mm, Barham, Kent (1000-700 BC)
Apart from being made from bronze this morticing chisel is indistinguishable from its modern counterpart.

TOOLS AND MANUFACTURE

Found by a digger driver, subsequent to the excavation of the Anglo-Saxon settlement at Flixborough, North Lincolnshire, this tool hoard contained axes, adzes, spoon bits and draw knives; everything needed to build a house or a ship. The hoard was found within two lead vats, which is a feature shared with other tool hoards. (Image: Kevin Leahy)

WILT-5D7742, 90mm, Stockbridge, Hampshire (1150-800 BC)
Its rounded cutting edge and the presence of flash left from the casting process show that this chisel was never finished. It is unlikely that it ever received a wood, or bone handle.

WMID-E1B777, 64mm, Swinfen and Packington, Staffordshire (1150-800 BC)
This object represents a common type of Late Bronze Age socketed chisel. When looking at such tools it is worth thinking about what they were used for: they must reflect a sophisticated woodworking tradition which has otherwise failed to survive.

TOOLS AND MANUFACTURE

WILT-0E9BA9, 168mm, 160mm, Marlborough, Wiltshire (50-400)
This iron chisel, or ring punch, was found in a hoard of Roman tools, allowing it to be dated. Found by itself we would never have guessed that it was Roman. It is likely to have been used to make holes in leather or wood.

DENO-886907, 140mm, Horncastle, Lincolnshire (50-400)
These Roman dividers were set using a small wedge which, when tapped into place, would have prevented the arms from moving. Screw threads, as used to set modern dividers, were known to the Romans but were not common.

NMS-C3A962, 70mm, Spixworth, Norfolk (1000-1550)
The form and size of this one-piece Medieval awl suggests it was for leatherworking.

LON-50F201, 95mm, Tower Hamlets, London (1200-1400)
Spoon augers were used for boring holes in wood. Originally, the leaf-shaped tang would have fitted into a transverse wooden handle (like the top of a T), the cutting edge being on the semi-circular section to the right.

223

TOOLS AND MANUFACTURE

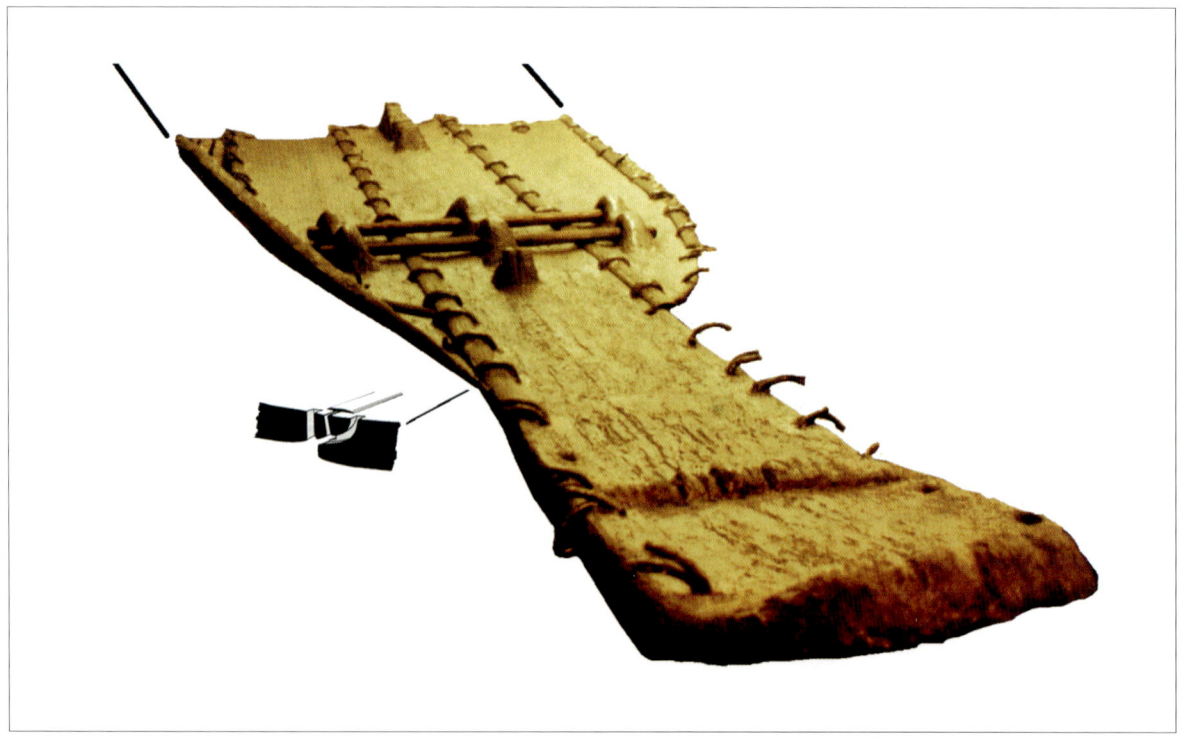

LON-4261F3, 167mm, City of London (1600-1700)
The DG stamp on the face of this Post Medieval iron chisel may have been the mark of its maker or owner.

LON-FF4D35, 197mm, City of London (1600-1850)
This tool is a caulking iron, used to hammer tow into the joints between a boat's planks. It was found in the river Thames.

One of the complex plank built boats from North Ferriby on the Humber Estuary. The massive planks were carved from solid oak leaving the heavy cleats standing proud. Rods passed under the cleats kept the planks in line. The planks were sewn together with withies which went through complex joints carved into the edges of the planks. These boats have been dated to c. 2000 to 1700 BC and show a remarkable level of woodworking skill. (Image: Kevin Leahy)

TOOLS AND MANUFACTURE

METALWORKING TOOLS

With so much metalwork being recorded with the PAS it is surprising how few metalworking tools have been found. Perhaps metalworkers found it too easy to put their worn out or broken tools back in the melting pot. The few pieces we have must serve to represent what were common objects. There are 102 hammers on the PAS database, of which 39 are Bronze Age and 25 Post Medieval. Six Bronze Age anvils have been recorded which, again, stand for the many that failed to survive. A small number of metal and stone moulds appear on the database, but most moulds were made from clay which was broken up and disintegrated after use. Every object tells a fascinating story; starting from the raw materials from which it was made, its manufacture, through to how it was used and finally discarded. Tools form a vital part of this story.

YORYM-ABCCE1, 55mm, Ellerton, East Yorkshire (1100-800 BC)
Bronze Age hammer which is clearly a variant on the socketed axe design; a useful and practical tool.

KENT-0278AC, 61mm, Elham, Kent (1600-800 BC)
The spike on this Bronze Age anvil would have been set into a block of wood to give stability and to absorb the shock of hammer blows.

PUBLIC-B21001, 100mm, Dorset (1500-1100 BC)
This bronze anvil was cleverly designed to provide a range of surfaces on which to work. The perforation would have been used when holes were being punched through sheet metal.

BUC-E32496, 60mm, Fleet Marston, Buckinghamshire (1000-800 BC)
Set into a block of wood this Bronze Age tool could have been used as a stake anvil, or, if fitted into a handle, it would have made a useful raising hammer.

TOOLS AND MANUFACTURE

SF-0276F4, 149mm, Bradfield St Clare, Suffolk (50-400)
Parallels point to this being a Roman iron hammer; comparable to the votive model on page 133.

NMS-757094, 74mm, Grimston, Norfolk (1400-1700)
Tools like this claw hammer can be found in any modern joiner's tool bag, the claw (now incomplete) being used to pull out nails. The design and decoration however, show this hammer is not modern.

LANCUM-730AB5, 57mm, Langham, Essex (1500-1900)
Although tiny, this Post Medieval hammer would have been useful for driving in panel pins or for small-scale metalworking, such as that which would have been carried out by a clockmaker or jeweller.

LVPL-115F71, 90mm, Dutton, Cheshire (1700-1900)
This miniature Post Medieval anvil has the same form as a full-sized blacksmith's anvil. While small, it could have been used for precision metalworking as practised by a jeweller or clock-maker.

NCL-D31196, 49mm, Wilksby, Lincolnshire (50-1800)
This undated object appears to be a stake anvil, and was probably designed to be portable. For use, the stake would have been hammered into the ground or wood. Anvils like this were used by mowers to tap out dents on the blades of their scythes, but this object seems too small for that role.

226

TOOLS AND MANUFACTURE

DIE STAMPS

These are important as they represent a method of mass producing decoration; once a die is made, it is possible to produce hundreds of thin sheet metal reproductions. The manufacture of sheet metal itself, however, presented problems for the craft-worker: before the introduction of the rolling mill, during the 16th century, sheet metal had to be made by hand, starting with an ingot which was hammered down to the required thinness. Dies were used in the *Pressblech* technique, in which a piece of foil was laid over the die and was itself then covered over with a sheet of lead. The back of the lead was hammered, transferring the decoration from the die to the foil. 36 *Pressblech* die stamps have been recorded by the PAS making an important addition to our knowledge of Early Medieval metalworking.

DUR-3C5813, 46mm, Thwing, East Yorkshire (570-700)
Anglo-Saxon die for making foil mounts decorated with two eagles' heads (pointing upwards at the top) and an interlaced snake (the head is at the bottom).

YORYM-D6E0A2, 28mm, North Duffield, North Yorkshire (570-700)
Remarkably, this piece of lead, probably used when making a foil from the die from Thwing (also shown here), was found 65km away.

NLM-468D41, 56mm, Fen Drayton, Cambridgeshire (570-700)
Anglo-Saxon die for making foils decorated with the figure of a warrior wearing a wolf-skin, its face covering his head. This figure appears on foil mounts used on the helmet found at Sutton Hoo, suggesting that it could have been made in England, not Sweden as was originally thought.

NLM-690F57, 42mm, Swinhope, Lincolnshire (870-970)
The object is a die for making filigree pendants of the Viking Hiddensee-Rügen type. The discovery of it suggests that sophisticated Viking jewellery was being made in England.

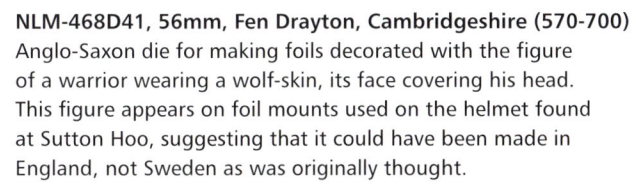

NMS-25CDD3, 32mm, South Norfolk (450-650)
This die was used for making Early Medieval bracteates, like those shown on pages 87-88. Unlike *Pressblech* dies, which bear positive (raised) images, *bracteates* are made from negative dies. Evidence for the manufacture of bracteates in England is important, as they originated in northern Europe.

TOOLS AND MANUFACTURE

HAMP-8A5E03, 44mm, Hursley, Hampshire (1300-1500)
Medieval matrix plate, engraved with a fleur-de-lys and a human face within a wreath. The engraved motifs could be transferred to sheet metal by covering the sheet metal with a cushioned pad which was then hammered.

KENT-3355EE, 56mm, Margate, Kent (1725-1850)
Upon this chisel-like binding stamp or finishing tool is the word 'poems'. The object relates to the hand stamping of gilded lettering on the spines of Georgian and Victorian books.

SWYOR-5A0422, 18mm, Tickhill, South Yorkshire (1800-1930)
Printer's block bearing a monogram consisting of the letters I E and M. It is likely the holes would have been used to secure the block in place rather than it being clamped into a printer's galley.

MOULDS

Used for the casting of metals, moulds offer important information about past technology. Most were made of clay and, unless recovered during an excavation, fail to survive, but we have some permanent moulds made from bronze and stone. These are sophisticated and, in modern terminology, would be described as gravity die casting. During the Bronze Age, people were

SF-2D55E2, 167mm, Hempnall, Norfolk (1400-1100 BC)
Both halves of a two-part mould for casting bronze palstaves. The view on the left shows the back of one half. In the centre, the two halves are shown placed together as they would have been during use. On the right, are the inner faces of the two half-moulds with, at the top, the basin into which the molten metal was poured. While casting bronze into a bronze mould might sound tricky there is no danger of the axe and mould fusing together; the incoming metal was cooled too quickly for this to occur.

TOOLS AND MANUFACTURE

clearly producing large numbers of identical axes. Most stone moulds come from the west of the country, where suitable stone is found, with metal moulds being found in the east.

In order to make a clay mould a pattern is required. This has the same shape as the required casting but is usually made from another material, such as wood, which is easily carved and shaped. In most cases moulds are made in two parts which can be separated for the removal of the pattern, and closed and sealed for the casting of the molten metal. The exception is the lost wax process, where the pattern is made from wax and the mould built around it. The wax is then melted, and runs out of the one-piece mould. The hollow interiors of objects such as socketed axes, spear heads and statues were formed using clay cores, which were placed in the moulds, leaving a gap between the core and the inside of the mould into which the metal flowed. The PAS has recorded 133 moulds, 62 of which are Post Medieval, 28 Medieval, 17 Roman, seven Iron Age and seven Bronze Age. Most (46) are copper-alloy with 25 stone moulds also being recorded.

SF-839555, 153mm, Sutton, Suffolk (1150-800 BC)
One half of a two-part bronze mould for casting socketed axes. The hollow interior of the axe was formed by a clay core that was secured between the two halves, above the mould cavity. The line around the mould is a tongue and groove arrangement sealing the joint and allowing the two halves to be aligned.

INGATE CHANNEL
SHOULDERS HOLDING CORE
MOULD CAVITY
ALIGNMENT SEAL

CORN-031000, 99mm, St Keverne, Cornwall (1000-800 BC)
Part of one half of a stone mould for casting socketed axes. The groove next to the cutting edge is a vent to allow air to escape during the casting process. Near the centre of the cutting edge is a copper-alloy dowel that ensured that the two halves were aligned. Stone moulds needed heating before use to ensure that they were not shattered by thermal shock and the molten metal did not solidify too quickly.

TOOLS AND MANUFACTURE

FASAM-90AC74, 42mm, City of London (193-235)
One half of a clay mould for casting fake Roman coins. At the top is a casting funnel, either side of which are holes into which projections on the other part would have fitted, ensuring an accurate alignment. It is not possible to identify the coins being made.

BH-95F015, 75mm, Standon, Hertfordshire (50 BC-AD 50)
Part of a mould used in the manufacture of Iron Age coins. It is likely that the metals forming the alloy were placed in the small recesses and the tray then heated so that they fused, forming pellets of the right weight and alloy composition.

NMS-E99B33, 50mm, Brancaster, Norfolk (50-100)
One half of a copper-alloy mould for casting Roman brooches of Dolphin type (see page 34). This half of the mould contained the underside of the brooch, with the curved lower part of the head, and its central hook and a long groove for the catch plate.

SWYOR-B40A88, 79mm, East Yorkshire (500-550)
Early Medieval casting technology was based on clay moulds, although some use was made of stone moulds for casting ingots. It has been suggested that lead cruciform brooches, like this example, were patterns on which clay moulds were formed; the decorative details then being added by carving the soft clay.

TOOLS AND MANUFACTURE

SF-B22470, 37mm, Clare, Suffolk (1200-1400)
It is not clear whether this is a stamp or a mould, but the design suggests it is for an object of Medieval date. If it was a stamp, which seems mostly likely, it could have been used for making thin metal appliqué plates or for decorating leather.

LVPL-35AD66, 28mm, Washingborough, Lincolnshire (1300-1400)
Although seal matrices are common finds, moulds for them are rare discoveries. This example is part of the mould for a seal-matrix handle, the rest of the matrix being formed by a further two parts set below it. The high quality of the mould has led to the view it was made by a goldsmith.

LON-E0BD25, 58mm, City of London (1500-1700)
This Post Medieval stone mould was used for casting lead tokens, embellished with the arms of the Worshipful Company of Carpenters. Four tokens would have been cast simultaneously.

NMGW-5BEBA4, 45mm, Wenvoe, Vale of Glamorgan (1600-1800)
Hinged mould for casting lead shot. The shot made in this mould would have been only 5 to 6mm in diameter and therefore too small for most guns. An alternative suggestion is that it was shot for toy guns (see pages 190-191). One of the mould's two handles is missing.

TOOLS AND MANUFACTURE

INGOTS

Metal was distributed in the form of ingots before being melted and cast into moulds or hammered out to produce sheet metal. Some types of ingot can be assigned to particular periods of time and broadly dated. Of the 663 ingots recorded by the PAS, 278 are copper-alloy, 181 silver, 103 gold and 54 lead.

SUR-599873. 148mm, Brockham, Surrey (1200-700 BC)
Plano-convex (dish-shaped) ingot of Late Bronze Age type. These ingots are usually represented only by fragments.

SF4728, 40mm, Wantisden, Suffolk (1000-700 BC)
This late Bronze Age ribbed plate looks as if the molten metal was cast on a planked surface, the metal running into the grooves. This sort of 'ingot' is important having, so far, only been identified in three Late Bronze Age hoards.

SOM-23F798, 522mm, Westbury, Somerset (164-189)
Roman lead ingot with the Imperial inscription IMP DVOR AVG ANTONINI ET VERI ARMENIACORVM, allowing it to be dated to the period when Marcus Aurelius and Lucius Verus ruled as co-emperors (AD 161-9). Its weight is an impressive 19.3 kg (62 lb).

232

TOOLS AND MANUFACTURE

BH-7253E7, 52mm, Manuden, Essex (800-1100)
Finger-shaped silver ingots are found in Viking period hoards and represent the Vikings' bullion economy, based, not on coins, but on silver objects, ingots and scrap.

SWYOR-55BBB2, 26mm, Spofforth, North Yorkshire (800-950)
Many Viking hoards contain fragments of jewellery which have been cut up as bullion. This piece comes from an arm-ring of Permian type. These probably originated in northern Russia but are found throughout Britain, Ireland and Scandinavia.

CASTING WASTE

The PAS has recorded 780 pieces of casting waste. These include in-gates, through which the metal was poured into the mould – they were cut off the solid casting and usually went straight back into the melting pot. However, sometimes they survived, and can be dated by analogy with the moulds. There are also pieces of spillage; droplets of metal, spilt during the casting process. Most waste is from the casting of copper-alloy (accounting for 611 finds), followed by lead (118), silver (17) and gold (12).

NMGW-0F0ECA, 30mm, Wenvoe, Vale of Glamorgan (1600-800 BC)
Casting gate of probably Bronze Age date, together with the funnel through which the molten metal was poured into the mould. The top of the casting gate has the typical cauliflower surface caused by escaping gasses during the casting process.

IOW-CE75F0, 30mm, Calbourne, Isle of Wight (1400-700 BC)
This casting gate is of the sort that would have been produced using a bronze mould for casting an axe, such as that shown on page 229; the flow of metal dividing to pass either side of the clay core and into the mould.

233

TOOLS AND MANUFACTURE

TEXTILE WORKING

Clothing is a fundamental need and, in the past, involved considerable labour. With the exception of spindle whorls, the PAS has recorded little direct evidence for textile working. Like cloth itself, many of the tools involved in making textiles were subject to decay, being made of wood. Loom weights were used to keep the warp (vertical) threads under gentle tension during weaving, but were not used on all loom types. Tools are found that were used to push the weft (horizontal) threads up into place on a loom, however many of these pin-beaters were made of bone, limiting their survival and discovery. The making up of clothing is represented by small numbers of needles, thimbles and scissors. Further evidence of textile working is provided by lead cloth seals (shown on page 281).

SPINDLE WHORLS

Spinning was a time-consuming job with women spending many hours making yarn using drop spindles, now represented by whorls. A flick of the fingers set a spindle revolving, kept turning by the whorl's momentum while the woman paid out fibre to form the yarn. Once the spindle had reached her feet she wound the yarn around it and started again. The PAS has recorded over 5,700 spindle whorls most of which (3,400) are Medieval. 5,400 of the whorls are made from lead, reflecting the good response that this metal gives on a metal detector as we know that other materials were also used. While Medieval spindle whorls are widspread, they are most common in the Midlands and north, across into Cheshire.

PUBLIC-DD674B, 36mm, Driffield, East Yorkshire (50-250)
Pottery spindle whorls can be difficult to date, but this one was made from a sherd of Roman samian ware, a very distinct pottery type.

LIN-D92A22, 26mm, Saltfleetby, Lincolnshire (1000-1100)
Scratched on to this Early Medieval lead spindle whorl is an inscription in Norse runes. The text seems to make reference to obscure gods, suggesting the survival of paganism in an area where most people where Christian.

LVPL-D90567, 35mm, Barmby Moor, East Yorkshire (1200-1500)
The radiating lines and raised dots on this biconical lead spindle whorl are typical of many Medieval whorls on the PAS database. Although the spinning wheel appeared in England by 1300, the drop spindle continued to be used.

LON-81EDE9, 30mm, City of London (1450-1550)
This Late Medieval spindle whorl is made from a green-glazed stoneware and is thought to have been imported from modern-day Belgium.

TOOLS AND MANUFACTURE

NEEDLES
These are very common objects and were much used in the past, even though the PAS has recorded fewer than 200 of them. From the proverb 'like finding a needle in a haystack' – we know they are, once lost, notoriously difficult to find.

LON-3999BB, 79mm, City of London (50-400)
This Roman bone needle can be dated by parallels with finds from excavations.

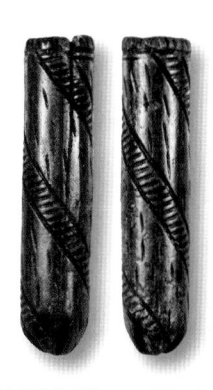

YORYM-166731, 35mm, Westow, North Yorkshire (1150-1450)
Needles were valuable and easily lost. Medieval needle cases, like this, would have been very useful in keeping them safe.

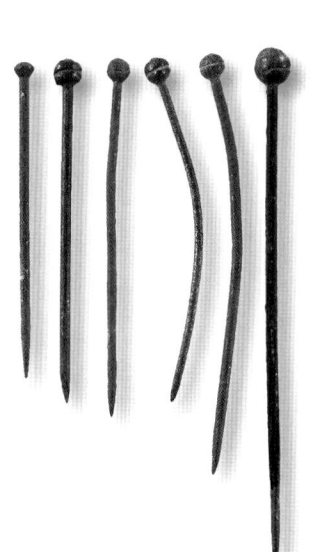

NMS-0169A5, 69mm, Barton Bendish, Norfolk (1200-1500)
The eye of this Medieval needle was made by splitting the end of the shank and re-joining the ends to form a loop.

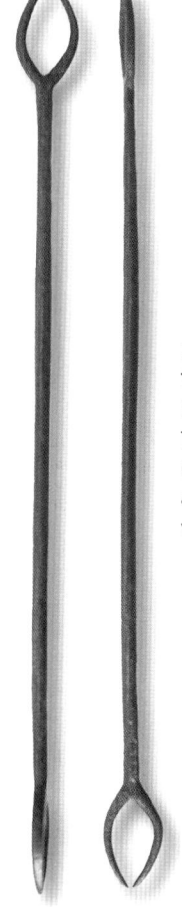

LON-B536F9, 50mm, Tower Hamlets, London (1400-1600)
Six Post Medieval pins, characterised by their wound wire heads. They can be found in large numbers on urban sites, including the London foreshore, and were probably multi-functional; being used in dress making as well as for securing garments whilst being worn.

LON-A0460A, 114mm, Tower Hamlets, London (1500-1600)
This netting needle was used for fine work, such as making and repairing women's hair nets.

TOOLS AND MANUFACTURE

THIMBLES

Though thimbles are commonly associated with sewing, their use was probably much wider, protecting fingers from a number of hazards, particularly when handling coarse materials. There are almost 4,000 thimbles on the PAS database, of which 3,400 are copper-alloy and 340 are silver. Most thimbles (2,285) have been assigned to the Medieval period, followed by those of Post Medieval date (1,567).

WMID-CE672D, 19mm, Claverley, Shropshire (1400-1550)
Thimble of a common Medieval type known as a beehive. The indentations are arranged as a spiral band and are relatively evenly spaced.

DUR-AEDD59, 18mm, Langthorpe, North Yorkshire (1450-1550)
Sometimes Medieval and Post Medieval thimbles have open tops giving the so-called ring thimble.

WILT-E0D5FE, 18mm, Collingbourne Kingston, Wiltshire (1600-1700)
Inscribed within the hearts on this Post Medieval silver thimble are the initials S and M. The thimble also has the marker's mark IR.

LOOM WEIGHTS

LEIC-B1BEA8, 69mm, Langar cum Barnstone, Nottinghamshire (400-800)
One half of an Anglo-Saxon pottery annular loom weight. These are often found on Middle Anglo-Saxon settlement sites, and seem specific to them. The vertical warp-weighted loom on which they were used was replaced in the early 10th century by a horizontal loom which did not use weights. There are 15 loomweights on the PAS database of which nine are assigned to the Early Medieval period and three each to the Bronze and Iron Ages.

PIN BEATERS

LON-1A16F3, 112mm, Wandsworth, London (700-1100)
Bone pin beaters were used on Early Medieval looms to beat the threads up into place. Constant handling and contact with the yarn has given this object a lovely, tactile polish. There are 18 pin beaters on the PAS database.

TOOLS AND MANUFACTURE

WEAVING COMBS

LON-C703F4, 128mm, Westminster, London (440-100 BC)
Bone combs, like this, have been found on Iron Age sites and have been identified as weaving combs used to push threads into place on a loom, an interpretation which might be contested. This is the only possible weaving comb on the PAS database.

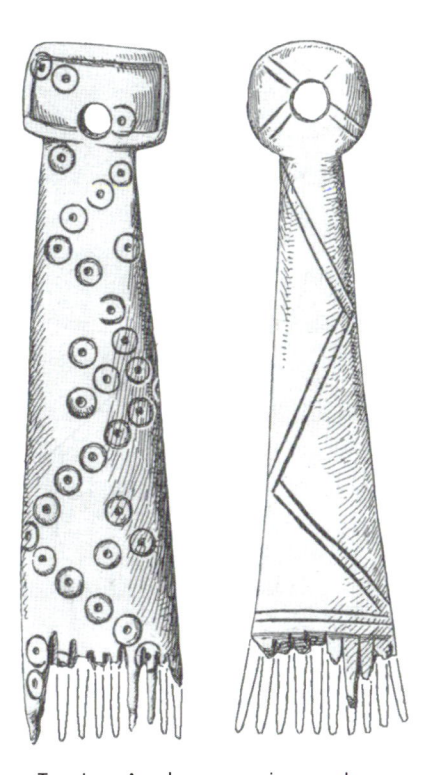

Two Iron Age bone weaving combs from Nether Wallop, Hampshire and Hasingfield Cambridgeshire. These are two more typical weaving combs of the type found in large numbers on sites where bone survives, such as the Glastonbury lake villages. (Image from the British Museum, *Guide to Early Iron Age Antiquities*, 1925, page 153)

WEAVING BATTENS

SWYOR-EB10D8, 550mm, Craven, North Yorkshire (800-900)
Anglo-Saxon weaving batten or *weaving* sword. Like pin beaters these were used to consolidate the threads during weaving. A very similar sword beater was found in the same well as York's Coppergate helmet.

TOOLS AND MANUFACTURE

SCISSORS AND SHEARS

The PAS database contains 23 pairs of shears, but they are a tricky artefact to date. There are 80 records of scissors but, in view of the fragmentary nature of many of them (they could be parts of candle-wick trimmers or grape scissors) further analysis is not possible.

LANCUM-8B35A7, 202mm, Lea Green, North Yorkshire (800-1100)
These shears are only dated by the fact they were found on an Early Medieval site.

LON-A1E3B3, 147mm, London (1400-1500)
Iron scissors rarely survive, but these of Medieval date have been preserved by the anaerobic conditions of the Thames mud.

WILT-E88E7C, 111mm, Hullavington, Wiltshire (1400-1500)
The internal projections on these Medieval shears are now misaligned, but would have created a series of oval openings, chamfered to present cutting edges.

LINEN SMOOTHERS

BERK-9BCBC7, 84mm, Chalgrove, Oxfordshire (1650-1750)
Linen smoothers were used to impart a polish on linen after laundering. While a Post Medieval date is suggested for this object, linen smoothers are known from the later part of the Early Medieval period and through the Middle Ages.

TEXTILE DRESSING

BUC-074B47, 59mm, South Stoke, Oxfordshire (1350-1700)
Harbicks were used to secure the cloth to the 'cropping board' or 'horse' during the process of shearing off the nap to produce fine fabric.

YORYM-562707, 51mm, Yapham, East Yorkshire (1600-1900)
A Post Medieval 'tenter hook'; these were used to secure wet cloth over tenter frames to control shrinkage.

TOOLS AND MANUFACTURE

AGRICULTURE

Agriculture is the basis of human life – without it we don't eat. Some evidence for early farming is clear: prehistoric field boundaries survive on Dartmoor, and Medieval ridge and furrow field systems can still be seen on fields not ploughed since the 14th century. Finds relating to farming are harder to find; farming has always been a tough business, with little to throw away.

Nonetheless, the finds that are discovered give an indication of what was once common.

PLOUGHS

Only seven PAS records for 'plough' appear on the PAS database. Until recent times most ploughs were substantially wooden and the few metal components were cared for and seldom lost.

NLM-F10454, 313mm, near Torksey, Lincolnshire (700-1100)
This is one of a group of three iron ploughshares found together. The burying of hoards of iron implements was a feature of the Anglo-Saxon period; we have a number of hoards containing tools, usually plough coulters rather than shares.

GAT-6C65C4, 495mm, Carmel, Anglesey (50-1500)
While the ploughshare passed under the soil, lifting and turning it, the coulter acted as a massive iron knife, slitting the turf allowing it to be turned. Coulters change little over time and are impossible to date unless found in an archaeological context such as a hoard or an excavation.

TOOLS AND MANUFACTURE

QUERNS

In order to make bread, women had to spend long hours grinding grain into flour with a hand quern. The Roman period brought improvements, including large, animal-powered mills, and watermills: the windmill came later, perhaps brought back by returning Crusaders. The most important element in the process of grinding flour (other than hard work) was the quern stone and later, the larger millstone. These needed to be made from hard, tough stones, some of which were widely traded. The PAS has recorded over 400 quern and millstones.

IOW-2D4B90, 285mm, Brighstone, Isle of Wight (4000-100 BC)
The Neolithic saddle quern is the earliest type known. Grain would be placed in the hollow face of the stone, and then a stone rubber would be worked back and forth. This was hard work and filled much of a woman's time in prehistory.

LVPL-0A8382, 300mm, Peover, Cheshire (100 BC-AD 400)
Iron Age rotary quern. This was set on an iron pin in middle of the flat, lower, stone, with the grain being placed in the upper hopper. Using a handle located in the side hole, the stone was rotated and flour milled.

CENTRING PIN HOLE FEED CHANNEL

GRAIN HOPPER

HANDLE HOLE

GRINDING SURFACE BENEATH

TOOLS AND MANUFACTURE

CORN-4C0E82, 530mm, Ludgvan, Cornwall (50-400)
Lower stone from a Roman rotary quern. Roman quern stones could be very large and powered by donkeys or water-wheels. They might be better described as millstones.

SOM-D9C047, 260mm, Otterhampton, Somerset (1150-1600)
This type of quern stone is known as a pot quern, because of its pot-like shape. It was used as the upper stone, its lugs served as handles for turning the stone to grind corn. These querns were in use over a long period of time from the Medieval into the Post Medieval period.

SF-7E11A7, 185mm, Great Glemham, Suffolk (1500-1900)
This quern is made of volcanic stone and would have been turned using a stick slotted into one of the three drilled holes on the upper surface. The incised radial grooves on its other side aided grinding. The type was introduced into Britain during the Post Medieval period although lava quern stones were being imported from the Eifel Mountains in Germany during the Roman and Early Medieval periods.

242

TOOLS AND MANUFACTURE

SICKLES

These small implements hardly look suitable for harvesting but, in antiquity, the practice was to take just the heads of cereals leaving the stalks behind. The PAS has recorded about 50 sickles, half of which are copper-alloy and most of the remainder flint.

BERK-C5DE66, 143mm, Aston le Walls, Northamptonshire (2700-1500 BC)
Late Neolithic-Early Bronze Age flint sickle showing signs of silica-gloss from cutting cereal stalks.

BERK-AC4A08, 141mm Kingston Bagpuize with Southmoor, Oxfordshire (1000-600 BC)
Late Bronze Age sickle. It was fixed to its wooden handle (a fragment of which survives) by a peg through the hole in its socket. The blade shows signs of hammering to harden and sharpen it.

GLO-32DD84, 116mm, Backwell, Somerset (1600-1200 BC)
The thin blade of this Middle Bronze Age sickle was supported by a stiff rib running parallel to the cutting edge.

Chapter 9
Trade and Commerce

Purse shown suspended on a belt in a Medieval painting. Note how vulnerable the purse and its contents were to theft. (Image: Michael Lewis)

PURSES

Pockets are a fairly recent addition to clothing. For centuries their role was fulfilled by purses and chatelaines, usually hung from a belt. Unlike a modern purse, early examples consisted of a cloth or leather bag suspended from the waist. They were vulnerable to the attentions of a 'cut-purse', the Medieval version of the pick-pocket. Metal purse fittings often survive, with the PAS recording more than 2,200 of them. Many small coin hoards may have originally been in simple bag-like purses. Purses were an important dress accessory, often being decorated or carrying religious inscriptions.

HAMP-23A7D7, 93mm, Wingham, Kent (500-600)
Objects like this have been found on Early Anglo-Saxon cemetery sites and may have been purse mounts, although it has also been argued that iron examples were fire steels. At one end of the bar is a stylised eagle's head.

244

TRADE AND COMMERCE

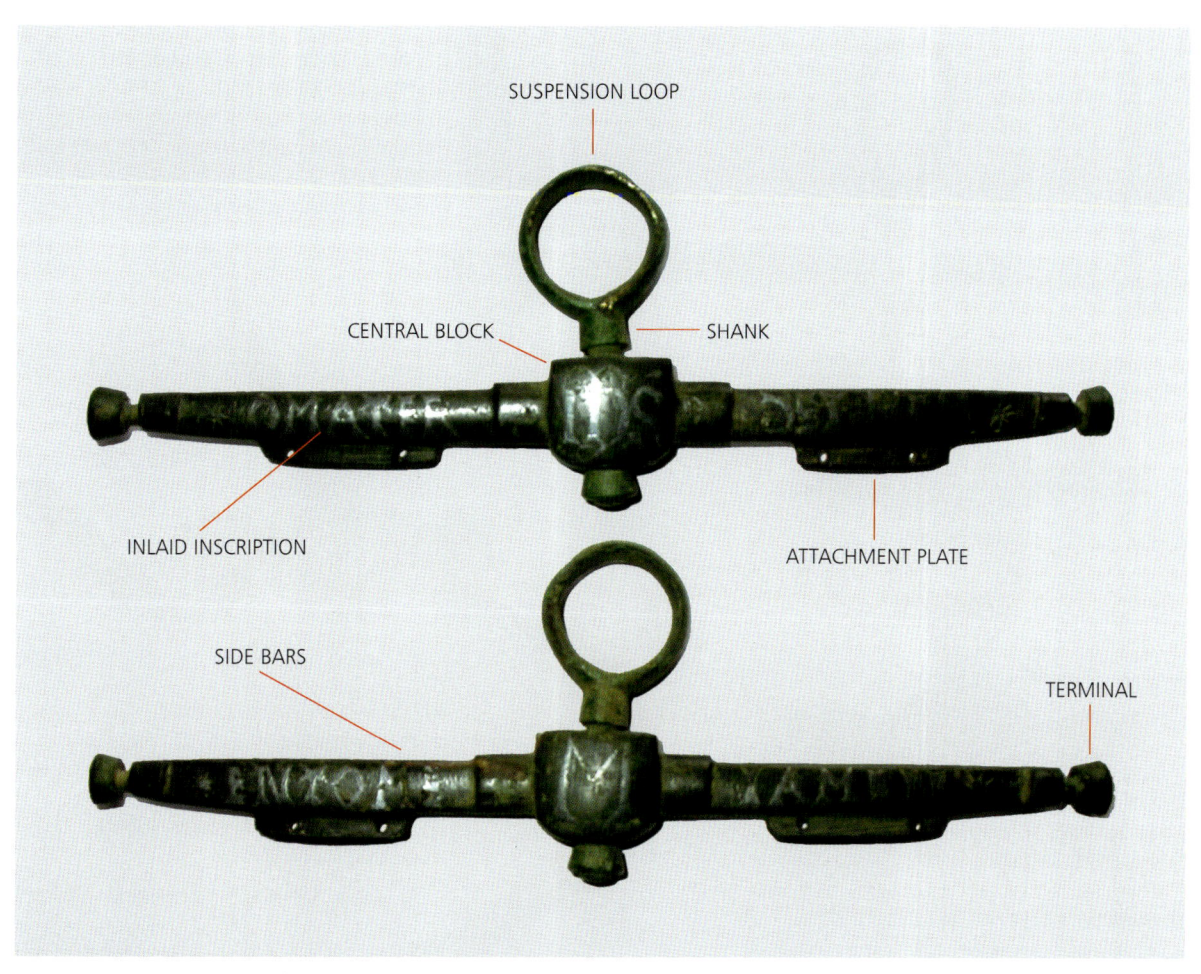

SUR-B93AC3, 174mm, Owslebury, Hampshire (1450-1500)
The inscription on this Medieval purse bar reads O MATER DEI MEMENTO MEI AMEN (O Mother of God, remember me, Amen), which is a typically pious inscription of the period.

IOW-C8DDD8, 163mm, Chale, Isle of Wight (1450-1600)
On each side of the central block of this Late or Post Medieval purse bar, is a highly stylised animal's head from which project the two side bars. The bag of the purse was attached through the holes in the lower plates.

TRADE AND COMMERCE

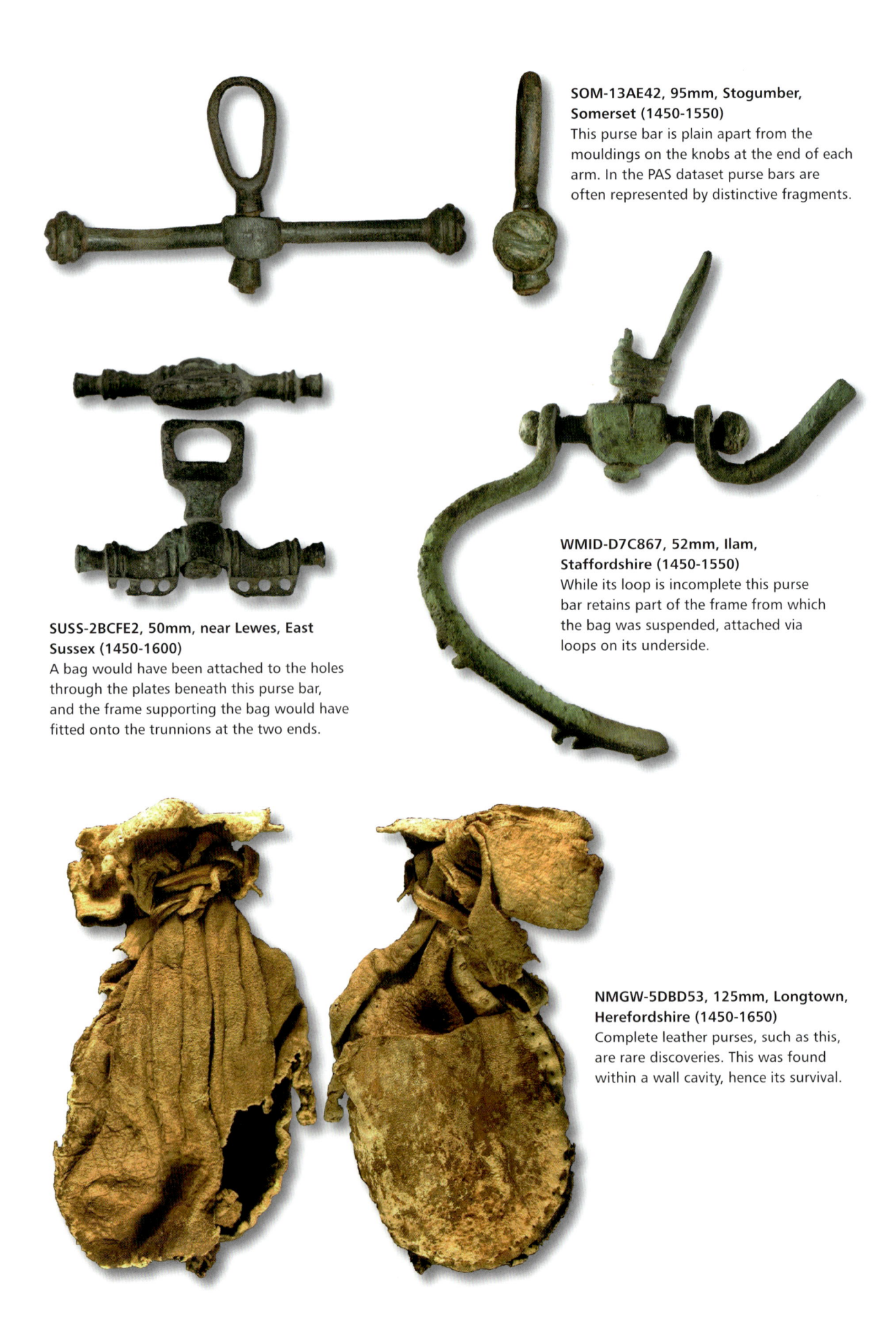

SOM-13AE42, 95mm, Stogumber, Somerset (1450-1550)
This purse bar is plain apart from the mouldings on the knobs at the end of each arm. In the PAS dataset purse bars are often represented by distinctive fragments.

SUSS-2BCFE2, 50mm, near Lewes, East Sussex (1450-1600)
A bag would have been attached to the holes through the plates beneath this purse bar, and the frame supporting the bag would have fitted onto the trunnions at the two ends.

WMID-D7C867, 52mm, Ilam, Staffordshire (1450-1550)
While its loop is incomplete this purse bar retains part of the frame from which the bag was suspended, attached via loops on its underside.

NMGW-5DBD53, 125mm, Longtown, Herefordshire (1450-1650)
Complete leather purses, such as this, are rare discoveries. This was found within a wall cavity, hence its survival.

TRADE AND COMMERCE

COINS

Coins are of enormous archaeological and historical importance. With more than 680,000 recorded by the PAS to date (2017) they are the most common find-type on the database, providing an immense data set capable of both statistical and historical analysis. In addition to individual coin finds, the PAS has, as part of the Treasure process, also recorded many coin hoards, some containing large numbers of coins. These allow us to consider the processes of hoarding in Britain, showing that factors other than safekeeping may have led people to bury hoards – some perhaps being deposited for ritual reasons.

Coins can provide crucial dating evidence for archaeological sites, although we must remember that the date of striking and the date of subsequent loss may, in some cases, have been a century or more apart. In addition, coins can offer invaluable evidence for site use, contemporary economics and trade, politics and even propaganda. Coins also serve as documents, and give highly condensed information: to this end, we have transcribed and translated many of the inscriptions of the examples below. By convention, any text lost from an inscription is shown in [square brackets] and, on Medieval coins, the use of Lombardic, as opposed to Roman, letters is shown in lower case: e.g. DnS:hYB. The terms obverse and reverse are used for the face (head) and back (tail) of a coin.

This short synopsis can do little justice to a massive topic. Countless books have been written about coins; some publications we believe to be helpful are listed at the end of this book. It is hoped that what follows will provide an overview of the changes that took place in British coinage over the past 2,200 years. Further information on any coin featured can be found on the PAS on-line database, by using its find number (eg SF-C3EDCC, a coin of the Emperor Carausius).

Iron Age Coins

Coin production began in Britain towards the end of the 2nd century BC with some of the first examples being cast rather than struck. Early issues, in gold or silver, were uninscribed, while later coins, bearing the names of rulers and places, provide the earliest evidence for writing in Britain and show the growing influence of the Roman world. The distribution of Iron Age coins indicates potential regional, or perhaps tribal, boundaries in Britain during the years prior to the Roman conquest in AD 43. Over 7,000 Iron Age coins have been recorded by the PAS, to which have been added about 37,800 coins from the Celtic Coin Index which had started recording coins in 1961.

PUBLIC-479809, 18mm, Ripple, Kent (175-100 BC)
Cast copper-alloy 'Thurrock' *potin* of the South Eastern Region/Cantiaci tribe. On the obverse is the head of Apollo. The reverse bears the letters MA above a bull, butting right. This design was originally based on coins issued by the Greek colony of Massalia (Marseille), explaining the inscription MA.

KENT-2EEAF0, 30mm, Bredgar, Kent (150-100 BC)
'Gallo-Belgic A' staters, were, as the name suggests, produced in the area of present day France and Belgium but, remarkably, this die for making them was found in Kent. Gold blanks (flans), pre-cast in moulds (like BH-95F015, page 230), were placed between a pair of dies, the upper one being struck with a hammer to apply the design

TRADE AND COMMERCE

SUSS-90E8C7, 19mm, Charlwood, Surrey (80-50 BC)
Gold *stater* of the Southern Region / Regini and Atrebates tribe, uninscribed 'Westerham' type. The highly stylised design shows a wreath, crescents and a cloak. On the reverse is a disjointed horse, facing left, with stick legs and pellets.

DENO-D9B7E3, 16mm, Belper, Derbyshire (60-30 BC)
Gold quarter *stater* of the North Eastern Region / Corieltavi tribe, 'Lindsey Scyphate' type. The obverse bears a stylised boar and, on the reverse, is an S-shaped motif with ringed pellets in each loop and a pelleted cross above. These coins are very thin and more deeply dished (*scyphate*) than other Iron Age coins. Finds of these coins are concentrated in the north eastern region of the Corieltavi (around the East Midlands).

LEIC-7F17D7, 19mm, Tutbury, Staffordshire (50-20 BC)
Gold *stater* of the North East Region / Corieltavi tribe, 'South Ferriby' type. The complex obverse design on this coin shows a wreath, a cloak, with crescents attached to a line through its centre, and a trefoil of pellets. On the reverse is the figure of a horse made up of crescents with an anchor-like face above, a star/sun between its legs and a pellet below the tail. This coin shows how far the design had changed from a Classical Greek original.

CAM-CD5F58, 19mm, Huntingdon area, Cambridgeshire (AD 8-41)
Gold *stater* of the North Thames Region / Trinovantes and Catuvellauni tribes, 'Cunobelinus Wild' type. This coin is attributed to Cunobelin, king of the Catuvellauni and Trinovantes. The obverse shows an ear of corn with CA to left and MV to right for 'Camulodunum' (Colchester). On the reverse is a horse with a branch above it and the letters CVNO for 'Cunobelin'. who was mentioned by the Roman writer Suetonius as 'King of the Britons'.

HAMP-43502B, 16mm, Froxfield, Hampshire (AD 10-40)
Gold *stater* of the Southern Region / Regini and Atrebates tribes, 'Verica Warrior' type. Attributed to Verica, king of the Atrebates in the years prior to the Roman conquest of AD 43. The legend on the obverse reads COM.F 'Commius Filius' (son of Commius) within a tablet. On the reverse is the figure of mounted warrior, holding a spear, with VIR 'Verica' behind, and REX (king) below. The accomplished design on this coin shows how the die cutter was influenced by Continental styles.

SF-A15F8C, 13mm, Hacheston, Suffolk (AD 10-40)
Silver unit of the East Anglian Region / Iceni tribe, 'Antedios Antd D-Bar' type. On the obverse is a double crescent motif on vertical wreath. The reverse bears the figure of a horse with pellet ring above, an S motif below its head, and a pellet triad below; normally shown above is an ANTD monogram. The existence of silver as well as gold coins, sometimes in half and quarter units, suggests a more sophisticated economy than might be imagined.

Roman Coins

Roman coins make up the single largest group of finds recorded through the PAS, with more than half a million examples on the database. 200,000 of the Roman coins come from hoards but the rest are single finds, removed from their archaeological context by the plough. Recording even the most poorly preserved Roman coins (aptly referred to by some finders as 'grots') has proved vital to our understanding of Roman Britain, providing new evidence for coin use and loss, the economy and trade. Thanks to the PAS, many rare or unique coin types have been recognised and almost 1,000 new archaeological sites discovered, helping to redraw the map and the history of Roman Britain.

Following the Roman Conquest in AD 43, Roman coinage circulating in Britain was based on the Augustan System which continued into the middle of the 3rd century AD. This was based on three metals with a gold *aureus* being the highest denomination, followed by a silver *denarius*, and a series of smaller base-metal (copper and brass) coins of which the *sestertius*, the *dupondius*, and the *as* are most commonly found in Britain. More than 25,000 single coins of this period have been recorded through the PAS.

Roman coins usually show the emperor, or empress, on the obverse, with their name and titles. The reverses vary tremendously, but often show a god, or personification whose support is claimed, or a piece of propaganda such as a war won or a building erected by the emperor, of which the details are given in the inscription.

BH-AB1DF8, 18mm, North Bedfordshire (79 BC)
Silver *denarius serratus* of the Roman Republic, struck by the moneyer C. Naevius Balbus. On the obverse is the head of Venus wearing a diadem, behind which are the letters S C 'senatus consulto' (by permission of the Senate). The reverse shows the abbreviated name of the moneyer C.NAE.BALB and Victory, in a *triga* (three horse chariot). Coins of the Roman Republic pre-date the Claudian invasion of Britain in AD 43 but are often found by metal-detectorists in England and Wales as they were still in circulation until the reign of Hadrian in the second century AD.

PAS-9AE984, 16mm, Water Newton, Cambridgeshire (32-31 BC)
Silver *denarius* of Mark Antony. The obverse gives Mark Antony's titles ANT.AVG.IIIVIR R.P.C and a galley, facing right. On the reverse is the inscription XVII CLASS [ICAE] (XVII legion), and a legionary eagle between two standards. These coins were struck by Antony prior to the Battle of Actium in 31 BC and honoured various Roman legions, in this case Legio XVII: CLASSICAE suggests that they were a naval unit. Because they were made of debased silver, coins of Mark Antony were not normally hoarded and stayed in circulation for over 150 years.

SUSS-10A5D3, 18mm, Chichester area, West Sussex (2 BC-AD 9)
Silver *denarius* of Augustus (31 BC-AD 140) minted in Lyon. The inscription on the obverse reads CAESAR AVGVSTVS DIVI F PATER PATRIAE with the emperor shown wearing a laurel wreath. On the reverse is C L CAESARES AVGVSTI F COS DESIG PRINC IVVENT with the figures of Gaius and Lucius standing. Their hands rest on a shield, behind which are spears and above them are sacrificial implements. Gaius and Lucius were nominated to succeed Augustus but died before him.

TRADE AND COMMERCE

Found in 2010, the Frome hoard contained 52,503 Roman coins dating from AD 251-290/1, buried in a pot after AD 291. The finder promptly reported his find to the PAS and it was excavated by archaeologists allowing its structure to be recorded. It would have been impossible, even in Roman times, to have lifted this pot with its contents in place, leading to the suggestion that it was never intended that it be recovered: it was a ritual deposit. The images show the hoard after first cleaning and during the process of recording.
(Images © Museum of Somerset, Taunton)

TRADE AND COMMERCE

BUC-1A1EFF, 20mm, Odiham, Hampshire (AD 41-42)
Gold *aureus* of Claudius I (AD 41-54) minted in Lyon. The obverse is inscribed TI CLAVD CAESAR AVG P M TR P and shows the emperor wearing a laurel wreath. The coin reverse bears the image of a triumphal arch surmounted by an equestrian statue between two trophies, its architrave inscribed DE GERMANIS. Claudius conquered Britain in AD 43, but this coin commemorates victories in German campaigns by his father Drusus.

BERK-FE5596, 33mm, Lambourn, Berkshire (AD 112-114)
Copper-alloy *sestertius* of Trajan (AD 98-117) minted in Rome. The obverse bears a fine portrait of Trajan and the inscription IMP CAES NERVAE TRAIANO AVG GER DAC P M TR P COS VI P P, giving Trajan's name and titles, and also refering to Nerva, the preceding emperor who had adopted Trajan as his successor. GER and DAC point to Trajan's victories in Germany and Dacia. The reverse has the inscription SPQR OPTIMO PRINCIPI / BASILICA VLPIA, S C, and celebrates the entrance of the newly built Basilica Ulpia, which was adorned with statues. It was located at the centre of Trajan's Forum in Rome.

NMS-0C0D8F, 25mm, Hethersett, Norfolk (AD 118)
Copper-alloy *dupondius* of Hadrian (AD 117-138) minted in Rome. Inscribed on the obverse is IMP CAESAR TRAIANVS HAD [RIANVS AVG]. The reverse reads PONT MAX TR POT COS [II] / ADVENTVS AV[G], S C (High Priest: Tribune of the People: Consul for the II? time: the Imperial Arrival: Senate Consulted). It also shows Roma, the personification of the city of Rome, seated on a piece of armour, holding a spear in her left hand, and clasping hands with Hadrian, demonstrating the link between Hadrian and Rome.

ESS-5A2744, 24mm, Colchester, Essex (AD 154-155)
Copper-alloy *as* of Antoninus Pius (AD 138-161). On the obverse is the long inscription ANTONINVS AVG PIVS P P TR P XVIII 'ANTONINVS AVG [ustus] PIVS P [ater] P [atriae] TR [ibunicia] P [otestas] XVIII, which contains much information. AVGVSTVS was a title taken by Octavian (27 BC- AD 14) and used by subsequent emperors. PATER PATRIAE means Father to the Country, and TRIBVNICIA POTESTAS XVIII showed that Antoninus Pius had been hailed as Tribune of the People for the 18th time – allowing this coin to be precisely dated. On the reverse is a figure of Britannia seated on a rock, her head propped on her right hand. The inscription on this side reads BRITANNIA CO [S IIII], S C, commemorating a victory in Britain and, COS IIII, that Pius had been Consul for the 4th time. We do not know why this coin was struck but it was issued exclusively for use in Britain.

TRADE AND COMMERCE

NCL-C43738, 18mm, Piercebridge, Darlington, County Durham (AD 147-161)
Silver *denarius* of Faustina II (AD 147-175), daughter of the Emperor Antoninus Pius and wife of his successor, Marcus Aurelius. The obverse reads FAVSTINAE AVG PII AVG FIL. On its reverse is the inscription VENVS, with figure of this goddess standing, holding an apple and a rudder. Such coins of empresses are of great interest, their elaborate hair styles being emulated by women throughout the Empire. The coin was minted in Rome.

NLM-B14741, 18mm, Roxby cum Risby, Lincolnshire (AD 200-201)
Silver *denarius* of Septimius Severus (AD 193-211), minted in Rome, with the obverse inscription SEVERVS AVG PART MAX 'Parthicus Maximus' (Great Conqueror of the Parthians). On the reverse is the legend VIRT AVGG and an image of Virtus (the personification of courage) in military dress, standing, holding Victory and a vertical spear, with a shield on the ground to the right. Severus campaigned in Britain with his sons Geta and Caracalla, and died at Eboracum (York) in AD 211.

3rd Century Roman Coins

In AD 215 a new silver coin was introduced by the emperor Caracalla (AD 198-217). This is known as a *radiate* due to the radiate crown worn by the emperor, and was probably valued at two *denarii*. *Radiates* were produced in huge quantities, particularly from the 260s onwards, dominating coin assemblages. They became increasingly debased, so that by the end of the 3rd century it was essentially a bronze (copper-alloy) coin. In this period there is also a peak in coin hoarding, leading to the discovery of massive *radiate* hoards, some containing tens of thousands of coins. *Radiates* continued to be produced until the latest issues of the Emperor Allectus (AD 293-296). There are currently over 60,000 examples on the PAS database, to which must be added the vast numbers of coins from hoards: the Frome hoard alone contained 52,503 *radiates*.

SWYOR-B92118, 22mm, Spofforth with Stockeld, North Yorkshire (AD 216)
Silver *radiate* of Caracalla (AD 198-217) minted in Rome. The obverse shows the emperor wearing a neat radiate crown with the inscription ANTONINVS PIVS AVG GERM. While titled 'Antoninus Pius' this emperor is known by his nick-name 'Caracalla' and should not to be confused with the earlier emperor. The reverse has the inscription P M TR P XVIIII COS IIII P P, telling us that Caracalla was 'Pontifex Maximus' (High Priest), Tribune of the People for the 19th time, Consul for the 4th time and 'Pater Patriae' (Father to the People). This side of the coin also shows a depiction of Sol (the sun god), standing, with his right hand raised, and holding a globe in his left.

IOW-AEBFA6, 18mm, Yarmouth, Isle of Wight (AD 260-268)
Copper-alloy *radiate* of Gallienus (AD 253-268), minted in Rome, with the obverse inscription GALLIENVS AVG. The reverse has the legend MARTI PACIFERO, (Mars the Peacemaker), showing the god Mars standing left, holding a branch in his right hand, and spear and shield in his left.

TRADE AND COMMERCE

PUBLIC-F014A5, 21mm, Beedon, West Berkshire (AD 260-268)
Base silver *radiate* of Salonina (AD 253-268), wife of Gallienus, minted in Milan. Its obverse has the inscription SALONINA AVG. Her bust is draped, and she is shown wearing a diademed 'crown'. The reverse gives the legend FECVNDITAS AVG, showing 'Fecunditas' (Fertility) standing left holding a child and reaching out to a second child. Instead of the radiate crown, seen on the coins of 3rd century emperors, the busts of empresses rest on a crescent.

LIN-02F9C0, 19mm, Great Hale, Lincolnshire (AD 271-274)
Copper-alloy *radiate* of Tetricus I, minted at the second mint of Gaul. The obverse gives the emperor's name and title IMP TETRICVS P F AVG. This coin shows the large radiate crown typical of the later coins. The reverse has the inscription LAETITIA AVG [G/N] for Laetitia (the personification of joy), standing left holding purse and anchor. Unusually for emperors of this period, Tetricus I, along with his son Tetricus II, after submitting to Aurelian in AD 274, was allowed to retire in peace, to Southern Italy.

NLM-8D5CED, 15mm, Preston, East Yorkshire (AD 275-285).
Copper-alloy Roman barbarous *radiate*, copying a coin of a 3rd century AD ruler. The obverse shows a bust dominated by a crude radiate crown. The reverse shows a standing figure with its head turned right holding a vertical sceptre in his right hand and an unidentifiable object in his left. Barbarous *radiates* were unofficial, contemporary copies, probably to fill the need for small denomination issue, and were struck in huge numbers.

WILT-C84A54, 23mm, Shrewton, Wiltshire (AD 286-93)
Copper-alloy *radiate* of Carausius (AD 286-293), produced at the 'C Mint', the location of which is uncertain. On the obverse is a formidable radiate bust and the inscription IMP C CARAVSIVS AVG. The reverse shows Pax (peace) standing holding a branch and transverse sceptre with the inscription PAX AVGGG. Carausius had declared himself emperor over a breakaway Britannic empire in AD 286 and the reverse legend relates to his attempt to appease the existing emperors Diocletian and Maximian: the three emperors shown as AVGGG and his desire for peace PAX.

HAMP-A19044, 21mm, Thruxton, Hampshire (AD 293-296)
Copper-alloy *radiate* of Allectus (AD 293-296), minted at the 'C Mint'. The obverse bears a radiate and cuirassed bust of the emperor and the inscription IMP C ALLECTVS P F AVG. On the reverse is the inscription PROVIDENTIA AVG, for 'Providentia' (the personification of forethought) standing left, holding a globe and sceptre. Allectus was Carausius' chief minister who assassinated him to become emperor in AD 293. These coins are the last of the 3rd century *radiates*.

TRADE AND COMMERCE

Late Roman Coins

Coinage reforms ordered by the emperor Diocletian (AD 284-305) between AD 294-296 led to the introduction of a copper-alloy *nummus*. These, in conjunction with a gold *solidus* and silver *siliqua*, issued first by Constantine I (AD 306-337), typified the coinage of the 4th century. *Nummi* are generally identified on the basis of the wide variety of reverse types used. They arrived in Britain in great numbers until about AD 395 after which they are scarce. The gold *solidus* and silver *siliqua* continue in use until the early 5th century, but Roman coinage largely disappears after Britain ceases to be part of the Empire during the reign of Constantine III (AD 407-411). There are currently more than 144,000 *nummi* recorded on the PAS database, 1,846 *siliquae* and 83 *solidi*.

IOW-1F8628, 20mm, Shalfleet, Isle of Wight (AD 313-314)
Copper-alloy *nummus* of Constantine I (AD 306-337), with the obverse inscription IMP CONSTANTINVS AVG. The reverse reads SOLI INVICTO COMITI (to my companion, the Invincible Sun God) showing Sol standing, with his right hand raised and holding a globe. Sol continued to appear on Constantine's coins after his conversion to Christianity. This coin was minted in London.

IOW-9E2296, 18mm, Calbourne, Isle of Wight (AD 332-333)
Copper-alloy *nummus* of the House of Constantine, minted in Trier. Its obverse reads VRBS ROMA (City of Rome) and shows a helmeted bust of Roma (the personification of Rome) left. The coin reverse shows a she-wolf suckling the twins Romulus and Remus, with two stars above. It commemorates the foundation of Rome in 753 BC.

WILT-DC35A4, 15mm, Heytesbury, Wiltshire (AD 359-360)
Clipped silver *siliqua* of Julian II (AD 355-363) of uncertain mint. Only traces of the obverse inscription survive, which would have originally read D N IVLIANV-S P F AVG 'Dominus Noster' (Our Lord), 'Julianus Pius Felix' (pious and blessed) and 'AVGustus' (Roman inscriptions did not distinguish between J and I or U and V). The reverse has the legend VOTIS/V/MVLTIS/X, within a wreath, referring to vows made by the emperor. Clipping the edges of *siliquae* to remove small quantities of silver became widespread at the end of the Roman period, probably after AD 402. This was perhaps to obtain much needed silver bullion. It was carefully done, and possibly semi-officially, so as to not damage the coins so much that they were removed from circulation. The coins found in many hoards show that heavily clipped *siliquae* remained in use for many years.

DOR-E455A2, 17mm, Wimborne area, Dorset (AD 353-361)
Contemporary copy of a copper-alloy *nummus* of Constantius II, with the obverse inscription [...]S P F AVG. The reverse depicts a soldier spearing a fallen horseman and the inscription was probably FEL TEMP REPARATIO (restoration of happy times). Contemporary copies of this coin type are numerous, with some examples measuring just a few millimetres in diameter.

TRADE AND COMMERCE

BM-8E97C8, 22mm, Cranborne Chase, Wiltshire (AD 364-367)

Gold *solidus* of Valens (AD 364-378) minted in Trier. The obverse has the legend D N VALENS P F AVG. The reverse has the inscription RESTITVTOR REI PVBLICAE (restorer of the Republic, or state) and shows the emperor standing, facing to his left, and holding a *labarum* (standard) and a globe. The bust on this coin, with its neat pearl *diadem*, is typical of late 4th century coins and is used on issues of all three metals.

YORYM-E7EA94, 24mm, Luttons, North Yorkshire (AD 364-378)

A silver *miliarensis* of the emperor Valentinian I, struck at the Trier mint. The reverse reads VIRTVS EXERCITVS, (valour of the army). The *miliarensis*, a double *siliqua*, was introduced by Constantine I when it was valued at 72 to the pound of Roman silver.

The Roman bath house at Wroxeter, Shropshire. In awe, an Anglo-Saxon poet described the Roman ruins that surrounded them as 'the work of the Giants'. (Image: Kevin Leahy)

TRADE AND COMMERCE

Early Medieval Coins

Early Medieval coins are not common finds, but the PAS has still recorded over 10,000 of them. About half come from hoards, the rest are single (chance) finds. The recording of these coins is an important factor in changing our understanding of trade, communication and the economy in Anglo-Saxon England, especially in rural locations, and the organisation of minting can be explored with greater confidence than ever before.

Following the withdrawal of the Roman legions from Britain in AD 410, coin use fell dramatically. No coins were minted in England for around 200 years. Continental coins were still imported, mostly gold *solidi* and *tremisses*, many of which were melted down for the production of jewellery. Alongside these, some imported silver *siliquae* and Byzantine copper coins have been found by metal detector users. The Merovingian *tremisses* of the late 6th and 7th centuries heralded the beginnings of renewed coin use and these were paralleled by small issues of English gold shillings. Finds of all such coins are very rare but more than 100 examples are now recorded.

ESS-10F463, 20mm, Billericay area, Essex (6th century)
Gold *solidus* produced on the continent by the Merovingians or Visigoths copying a Byzantine coin of the emperor Anastasius (r. 491-518). It is known as 'pseudo-imperial' and such coins are occasionally discovered in Britain. This example was fitted with a suspension loop allowing it be worn as a pendant.

BH-9B6B89, 10mm, Kingsey, Buckinghamshire (c. 580-670)
Gold Merovingian *tremissis* of the 'National' series struck by Angliulfus at Orléans, one of the hundreds of mints in the Merovingian territories. Finds from England represent the re-birth of coin use within the Anglo-Saxon economy of the 7th century.

WILT-DEDC91, 13mm, East Grafton, Wiltshire (650-75)
Anglo-Saxon gold shilling, also known as a *'thrymsa'*. This is of the 'clasped hands' type, and was probably minted in South-East England. It copies a Roman prototype which showed clasped hands with the inscription CONCORDIA (meaning agreement). These coins may reflect the renewed importance of Rome to the Anglo-Saxons following their conversion to Christianity after AD 597.

Middle Anglo-Saxon Coins

These date from around AD 650-850 although recent work suggests that they may have started a decade or so earlier. This period saw coins coming into more common use, with over 2,000 examples recorded on the PAS database. Most of these are silver *sceattas* of late 7th to mid-8th century date. These small coins were struck on thick flans and bear a wide variety of designs. They were probably issued by a range of people, including kings, abbots and merchants, and the many foreign coins recorded illustrate a vibrant North Sea zone of trading and interaction. By the mid 8th century *sceattas* were often debased and came to be replaced by silver pennies struck on broader, thinner, flans. Coin production was now firmly in royal hands, issued in the names of kings, although the Archbishops of Canterbury and York were also allowed to mint coins. Coins were produced by each of the main Anglo-Saxon kingdoms and reflect the power struggles of the 8th and 9th centuries and the rise of the kingdom of Mercia.

TRADE AND COMMERCE

SF-3C9416, 12mm, Woodbridge area, Suffolk (680-710)
Silver *sceat* (the singular of *sceattas*) belonging to the Primary Phase Series BX, and dating to the 680s. Like many *sceattas*, the design is imbued with Christian iconography. The bird on the reverse probably represents the Holy Spirit.

SUR-2ABC41, 11mm, Shiplake, Oxfordshire (700-10)
Silver *sceat* of the so-called 'porcupine' type (Series E), nicknamed from the obverse design which copies a Gaulish Iron-Age coin or was perhaps based on a late Roman coin. These were minted in the area of the modern Netherlands and are the most common *sceatta* type found in England. Their discovery in England reflects trade across the North Sea.

LIN-195665, 12mm, East Lindsey, Lincolnshire (737-58)
Silver *sceat* of King Eadberht of Northumbria. The obverse bears the king's name written as EOTBEREhTVS, and, on the reverse, is an animal with a long tail and a raised fore-leg. These Northumbrian coins were the first to regularly include the king's name and continued to be produced in northern England after *sceattas* were replaced by broader pennies in southern England.

SUR-9A3435, 17mm, Shottesbrook, Berkshire (765-92)
Silver penny of Offa of Mercia (r. 757-96). The obverse reads OFFA // REX. The portrait of the king is rendered in classical style wearing well-defined armour. A curled serpent above the bust was a protective symbol seen on many coins from this period and earlier. On the reverse is the name of the London moneyer +P/EN/DR/Ed.

YORYM-1463E8, 12mm, Yapham, East Yorkshire (840-4)
Copper-alloy *styca* of Æthelred II of Northumbria (first reign). The obverse reads EDILRED REX, the first D representing Ð pronounced 'th'. The reverse is inscribed MONNE, showing that it was struck by the moneyer Monne. *Stycas* are unique as a copper-alloy coinage in Anglo-Saxon England and probably owe their existence to a lack of silver in northern England during the 9th century.

DOR-EAA43D, 20mm, Tarrant Hinton, Dorset (810-5)
Silver penny of Archbishop Wulfred (r. 805-32) whose tonsured bust appears on its obverse with the inscription VVLFREDI ARCHIEPISCOPI. The reverse names the mint, DOROVERNIAE CIVTATIS (City of Canterbury), rather than the moneyer. The Archbishops of Canterbury and York were the only non-royal issuers of Anglo-Saxon coins after the mid-8th century although ecclesiastical mints reappeared in the Medieval period.

LIN-F6C6E1, 19mm, East Lindsey, Lincolnshire (822-840)
Finds of imported continental coins are important for showing trade and political contacts. This silver *denier* was issued by the Carolingian Emperor Louis the Pious (778-840). On the obverse is +HIVDOVVICVS IMP (Ludovicus Emperor). Its reverse bears XPISTIANA RELIGIO (Christian Religion) set around a temple. The PAS has recorded 28 Carolingian coins; these are widespread but with concentrations in East Anglia and on the tip of Cornwall.

257

TRADE AND COMMERCE

Late Anglo-Saxon Coins

The Late Anglo-Saxon period (AD 850-1066) was, with the Viking raids, a tumultuous time, leading to the Scandinavian conquest of much of England. After the Anglo-Saxon re-conquest, in the early 10th century, of lands taken by the Vikings, England became a unified country under the rule of the kings of Wessex. Coinage was produced throughout this period, the earlier part seeing the final Mercian issues and the coins of Wessex being joined, from the late 9th century, by Viking coinages of the 'Danelaw' in the Midlands and the North. After the reign of Æthelstan (r. 924-39), only kings issued coins. Coins dating from the late 9th century are very rare and coins remained scarce until a major reform of coinage in around 975. This established mints throughout the country and increased coin production. Coin designs were standardised and regularly replaced yielding a profit to the king. Scandinavian raiding recommenced during the reign of Æthelred II 'the Unready' (r. 978-1016) when enormous coin payments, known as 'Danegeld', were made to the Vikings. In 1016 England was conquered by the Danes under Cnut and, fifty years later, by the Normans. These incoming kings however continued to mint coins in the Anglo-Saxon style.

PUBLIC-A00281, 20mm, Tidenham, Gloucestershire (871-5)
Silver penny of King Alfred 'the Great' of Wessex (r. 871-99). The obverse is inscribed AELBRED - REX + : B for F is a usual variant on these coins. The name of the moneyer is in three lines MON | TIRVLF | ETA for 'Tirulf monetarius'. Southern English pennies from this time are very rare finds.

Found in 2007, the Vale of York hoard was lifted intact, and its contents excavated at the British Museum. Buried shortly after 927 it gives a remarkable overview of both Viking spoils and economy. It was enclosed in a silver-gilt Frankish cup dating from the mid 9th century which appears to have been wrapped in sheet lead. Within the cup were 617 silver coins, most of which were Anglo-Saxon pennies but there were 15 Arab dirhams and four Frankish deniers. The hoard also contained fragments of silver jewellery and silver ingots representing the Viking bullion economy.
(Image © The Trustees of the British Museum)

TRADE AND COMMERCE

IOW-43BDDE, 16mm, Calbourne, Isle of Wight (899-924)
Silver halfpenny of Edward the Elder using the same 'two-line type' design as many 10th century pennies, with the king's name, EADVV[ ]EARD RE around a simple cross on the obverse. The moneyer's name, VVIIIo/+++/IIARD, is written in two lines on the reverse. Round Anglo-Saxon halfpennies are very rare finds, usually a halfpenny was just that: a penny cut into halves.

DENO-984DE6, 21mm, Lusby with Winceby, Lincolnshire (900-5)
Silver penny of Cnut of Northumbria with an enigmatic inscription CVN NET TI on one side. The reverse has CNVT and REX around the arms of a cross. The Vikings had conquered Northumbria in 867, but the crosses on this coin show that by the end of the century they considered themselves to be fully-fledged Christian kings. Cut marks in its centre may be testing cuts made to make sure that it wasn't a plated copy.

DENO-07CCA4, 24mm, Aldwickle area, Northamptonshire (780)
Base silver Islamic *dirham* issued in Baghdad during the reign of Caliph al-Mahdi Billah (r. 775-85) but probably not reaching England until the late 9th century. *Dirhams* came from western and central Asia, large numbers reaching Europe through Scandinavia. Complete *dirhams* are rare, usually we only see fragments cut up for use as bullion.

SUSS-9920FE, 19mm, Eartham, West Sussex (997-1003)
Silver 'long cross' type penny of Æthelred II 'the Unready' (r. 978-1016). The obverse is inscribed AETHELRED REX and the reverse shows that it was struck by the Canterbury moneyer EADPOLD (Eadwold). Æthelred's coins are some of the most regularly found Late Anglo-Saxon issues due, in part, to the length of his reign.

GLO-1CEB74, 18mm, Pitchcombe, Gloucestershire (1017-23)
Silver penny of Cnut (r. 1016-35), the Danish Viking king who conquered England in 1016. On the obverse is the inscription CNVT RECX. Its reverse reads BRVNSTN ÐEOD, showing that it was struck by the moneyer Brunstan at Thetford; Ð being a 'th' sound.

DENO-E3DCE5, 20mm, Westborough and Dry Doddington, Lincolnshire (1066)
Silver penny of Harold II 'Godwinson', struck during the ten months of his reign. The obverse reads HAROLD REX ANGL. Unfortunately the reverse inscription PAX (peace) failed to come to pass. It was struck by the moneyer FORNA ON SNOTII (Nottingham). Harold's coins are relatively rare finds with fewer than 20 so far recorded on the PAS database.

TRADE AND COMMERCE

Medieval Coins

Medieval coins (1066-1485) are recorded in large numbers and the PAS now has over 70,000 of them on its database. Most are single finds although hoards, some very large, are known from throughout the period. It is important to record Medieval coins regardless of condition if we are to understand their use and circulation. For example, the numbers of coins found on rural sites suggests that coin use was spread throughout society. The Medieval coins recorded by the PAS show some major variations over time, particularly before 1180. Coins from the reigns of William the Conqueror (r. 1066-87) to Stephen (r. 1135-54) are considerably rarer than those from late in Henry II's reign (r. 1154-89) onwards. The early Norman coin production continued the organisation and standards of the Late Anglo-Saxon mints, but coins of Henry I (r. 1100-35) and Stephen are poorly made and often of debased silver. Important changes to the issuing of coinage began under Henry II with the introduction of the 'cross and crosslets' coinage which, between 1154-80, used the same crude design. These are known as the 'Tealby' type after the discovery of a hoard of over 6,000 of them at Tealby, Lincolnshire in 1807.

NMS-A90EAB, 21mm, Wendling, Norfolk (1080-3)
Silver penny of William I 'the Conqueror' (r. 1066-87) with a fine obverse portrait and inscription reading PILLELM REX: the wynn rune, P, was used at this time instead of W which did not exist in the Latin alphabet. The inscription EDPI ON LVNDNI on the reverse shows it was struck by the London moneyer Edwi.

GLO-B68C53, 19mm, Taynton, Gloucestershire (1073-6)
Silver penny of William I, the obverse showing the king flanked by two sceptres and the inscription PILEN REX ANGLO (William, king of the English). The reverse reads LEOFPINE ON GLEPEI (Leofwine of Gloucester). This coin was the first known example of the 'two sceptres' coin type from the Gloucester mint showing the importance of coin recording.

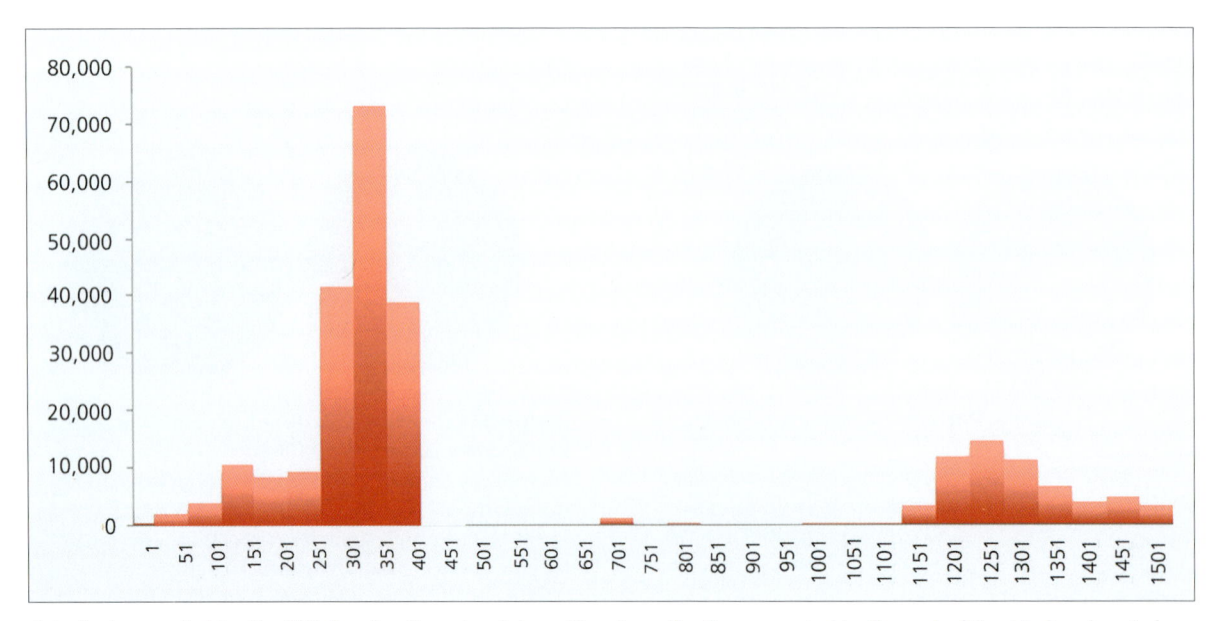

Coin finds recorded by the PAS showing the rate of deposition from the Roman period to the end of the Medieval period, the dates being divided into 50-year blocks, the vertical axis showing the number of non-hoard coins in each 50 year block The rise and fall of coin use was the result of a mass of complex historic and economic issues.
(Analysis and image: Eljas Oksanen)

TRADE AND COMMERCE

BUC-976454, 20mm, Chearsley, Buckinghamshire (1113)
Silver penny of Henry I (r. 1100-35). The obverse is inscribed HENRI REX, and the reverse BLACAMAN ON L showing that the moneyer was Blacaman of London. Henry's reign was plagued by counterfeiting and debased coins to the extent that the edges of coins were cut (snicked) before leaving the mint to show that they were not plated forgeries and to aid their acceptance. Snicking can be seen at 11 o'clock on the reverse of this coin.

SF-56ADB3, 19mm, near Bury St Edmunds, Suffolk (1135-41)
Silver penny of Stephen, with its oberse is inscribed [s]TIFNE RE[x]. The reverse inscription PVLFPINE ON L[ ] shows it to have been issued by Wulfwine of London. The turbulence of civil war – known as the Anarchy – which marked Stephen's reign resulted in coins being minted by the opposing sides and for different issuers, often poorly struck on irregular flans.

SF-9570DB, 19mm, Wordwell, Suffolk (1170-80)
Silver penny of Henry II (r. 1154-89) of 'cross-and crosslets' or 'Tealby' type. These finds represent a major recoinage and change in the organisation of minting after Stephen's chaotic reign. They are generally poorly struck on irregularly-shaped flans and often little of the inscriptions are present or legible.

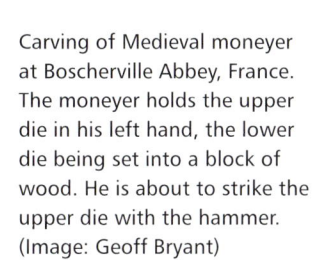

Carving of Medieval moneyer at Boscherville Abbey, France. The moneyer holds the upper die in his left hand, the lower die being set into a block of wood. He is about to strike the upper die with the hammer. (Image: Geoff Bryant)

TRADE AND COMMERCE

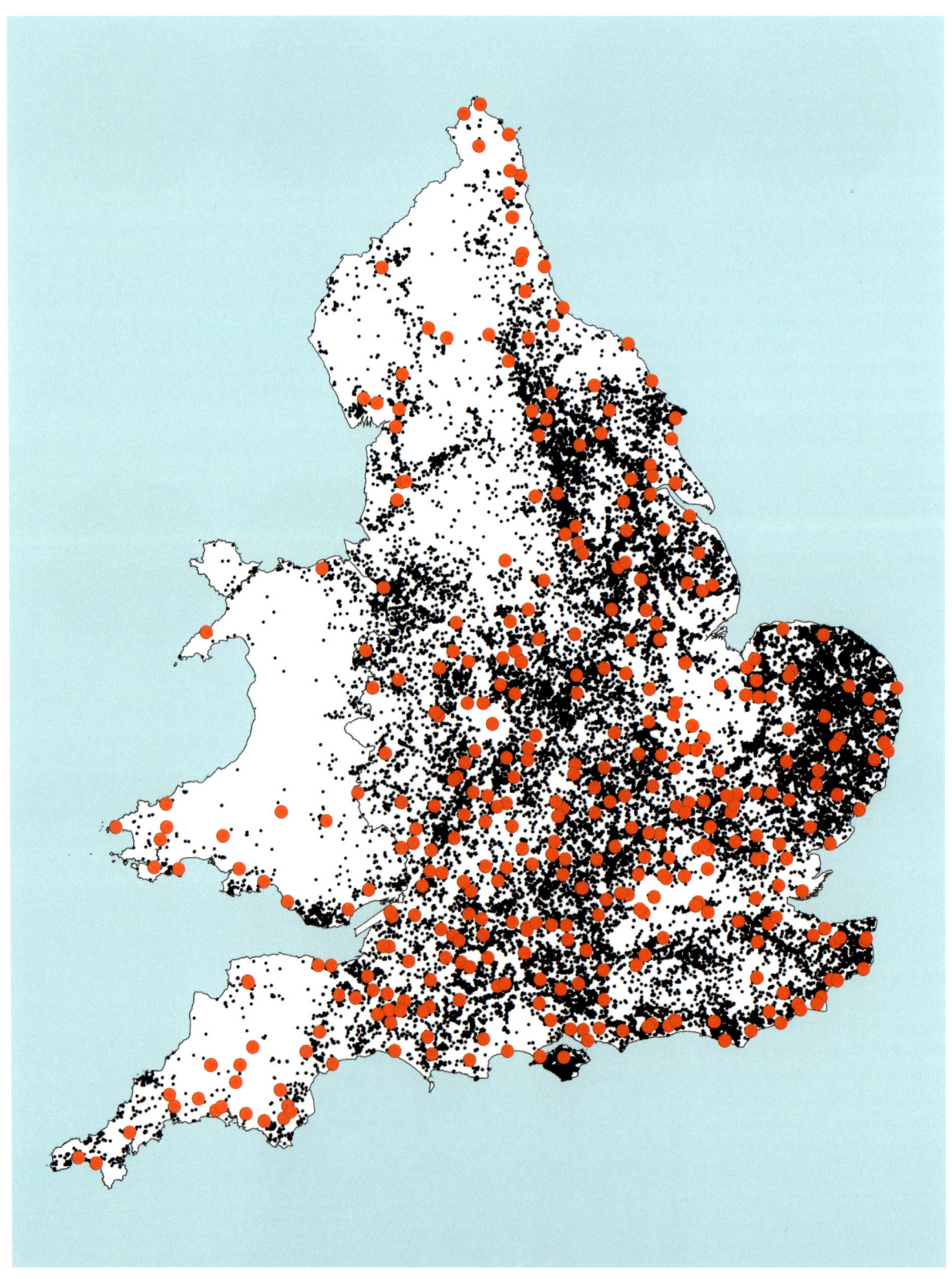

The Medieval period saw a quickening of the economy with the establishment of local markets where commerce could take place. The map shows, in red, markets known to have existed by AD 1200, set against the background of other Medieval material recorded by the PAS. (Analysis and image: Eljas Oksanen)

TRADE AND COMMERCE

The Period of 'Immobilised' Designs

Following Henry II's Tealby coinage, a series of coin issues appeared with designs that remained unchanged even when a new king came to the throne. These heralded an enormous increase in coin circulation and finds become very common. The lack of variation means that the period is dominated by just three broad groups of coins, the 'short cross' (1180-1247), 'voided long cross' (1247-79) and 'long cross' (12791489). Identifying coins within these groups involves looking for variations in the forms of letters or features such as the crown or shape of the shoulders on the bust. Identification is made harder as all 'short cross' and 'voided long cross' pennies were made in the name of Henry (regardless of who was on the throne) and the period of the long cross coinage (1279-1544) saw the throne held by five Edwards, four Henrys and two Richards! From 1279, round halfpennies and farthings were commonly issued, removing the need to cut up pennies for small change. Long based on a single denomination – the silver penny – the quickening late Medieval economy called for small change and also for higher value coins: in 1344, gold coins were introduced, and, after an unsuccessful earlier attempt, larger silver denominations appeared in 1351. Continental Europe was also an important part of the English economy and foreign coins are regularly found, especially from the Low Countries and Venice.

SOM-728CAC, 21mm, Langford Budville, Somerset (1185-9)
Silver 'short cross' penny of Henry II minted by OSBER. ON WIRIC (Osber of Worcester). Although these coins all look similar it was possible to date this example to a few years of Henry's reign based on details of portrait and lettering.

WILT-B0B14B, 18mm, Shrewton, Wiltshire (1250-6)
Silver 'long cross' penny of Henry III (r. 1216-72). Obverse reads HENRICVS REX III; the regnal number is unusual: most of the other Henrys and Edwards failed to say who they were. The inscription NICOLE ON CANT shows that this coin was struck by Nicole at Canterbury. The cross on the reverse is made up of double lines (hence 'voided long cross'). This was intended to prevent the coins from being clipped and aided in the cutting of coins into halfpennies and farthings.

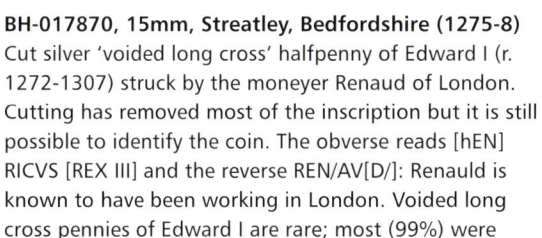

BH-017870, 15mm, Streatley, Bedfordshire (1275-8)
Cut silver 'voided long cross' halfpenny of Edward I (r. 1272-1307) struck by the moneyer Renaud of London. Cutting has removed most of the inscription but it is still possible to identify the coin. The obverse reads [hEN] RICVS [REX III] and the reverse REN/AV[D/]: Renauld is known to have been working in London. Voided long cross pennies of Edward I are rare; most (99%) were issued under Henry III.

PUBLIC-B1273B, 19mm, Elmsted, Kent (1282-9)
Silver penny of Edward I upon which the obverse reads EDW R ANGL' DNS hYB: 'EDW[ard] R[ex] ANGL[i] (king of England) DNS ('*dominus*' – lord of) HYB ('*Hiberniae*' – Ireland)'. The reverse reads CIVITAS LONDON (City of London) to show where it was minted, but the centuries-old tradition of naming the moneyer was discontinued.

TRADE AND COMMERCE

Built as part of the massive castle building campaign by Edward I, magnificent structures like this show what Edward was spending all his silver pennies on. Beaumaris was abandoned, still unfinished, in 1330 by which time it had cost £15,000. (Image: Kevin Leahy).

IOW-676306, 11mm, Arreton, Isle of Wight (1280-2)
Silver farthing of Edward I, its obverse reads +E R AN-GLIE and the reverse LON/DON/IEN/SIS (London). The re-coinage of 1279-81 saw the introduction of the first round farthings and halfpennies to be produced in substantial numbers, ending the cutting of pennies into fractions.

DOR-C188B9, 15mm, Corfe Castle, Dorset (1344-51)
Silver halfpenny of Edward III (r. 1327-77) struck at London, the obverse reading EDWARDVS REX and the reverse CIVITAS LONDON. Most of the silver coins produced at the London mint from 1347-50 were halfpennies and farthings with only small numbers of pennies.

ESS-0B7B34, 33mm, Elmstead, Essex (1363-9)
Gold noble of Edward III. The obverse reads ED/WARD:DEI:GRA :REX;ANGL:DnS:hYB:Z:AQ [T] (for Edward by God's Grace, king of England, lord of Ireland and Aquitaine). The king is shown on a ship, thought to be a reference to the English naval victory off Sluys in 1340. The inscription on the reverse is IHC:AVTEM:TRAn SIE:PER:MEDIUM:ILLORUM:IBAT (but Jesus passing through their midst went his way: from Luke 4.30, showing Christ passing, unharmed, through his enemies). Increasing European commerce, especially due to England's wool trade with Flanders, led to a need for a high value coin to supplement the penny. In 1344 the magnificent gold noble was introduced. It was rated at 80 pence or one half of a mark. The mark was a unit of account, rated at 160 pence, (two thirds of a pound: 13 shillings and 4 pence) but never actually existed as a coin in England.

264

TRADE AND COMMERCE

DEV-CD9553, 25mm, Yarcombe, Devon (1483-5)
Silver groat of Richard III (1483-5) struck at London. The obverse reads RICARD DI GRA REX AnGL Z FRAnC (Richard by God's Grace King of England and France). The reverse being inscribed POSVI DEVm ADIVTORE mEVm/CIVITAS LOnDOn (I have made God my Helper/City of London). The initial mark is the boar's head, Richard's personal badge. The groat, worth four pence, was first issued in 1279 without success and was quickly withdrawn, only becoming a regular part of the currency after 1351. The word groat comes from the French gros, meaning large.

PUBLIC-461D5E, 19mm, Wymondham, Norfolk (1279-1302)
Silver Irish penny of Edward I struck at the Dublin mint. The distinctive obverse shows the king's head set within a triangle around which is the inscription EDW R/ ANGL D/ NS HyB. The reverse is marked CIVI/TAS/DVBL/INIE, for Dublin. Small numbers of these Irish minted coins are found in England every year.

SUR-911CBA, 20mm, Effingham, Surrey (1280-6)
Silver penny of Alexander III of Scotland (r. 1249-86). The obverse reads ALEXANDER DEI GRA the inscription continuing on the reverse REX SCOTORVM (king of the Scots). While obviously influenced by English designs, Scottish coins of Alexander III show a fine profile portrait and mullets (not pellets) in the arms of the cross. They are regular finds in England.

IOW-79A7D9, 19mm, Ventnor, Isle of Wight (1290-1304)
Silver continental sterling imitation issued by John II of Avesnes, Count of Hainaut and Holland, and minted at Mons (modern day Belgium). The obverse reads IOHS COMES HANONIE and the reverse MON/ETA/MON/TES. These coins are referred to as 'crockards', as the portrait shows a crocket of flowers not a crown. Copying of English sterling coins was common across northern Europe and although these coins looked like sterling (English) pennies they often contained less silver and were banned from circulation in England.

SWYOR-EBD4A2, 27mm, North Cave, East Yorkshire (1469-77)
Silver double *patard* of Charles the Bold, minted in Flanders. On the obverse is the inscription + KAROLVS : DEI : GRA : [DVX] : BVRG : CO : FLA', giving Charles' name and his titles. The reverse bears the legend + SIT : NOMEN : DOMINI : BENEDICTVM (Blessed be the Name of the Lord). In 1469, England and Burgundy agreed a treaty which made each other's currency legal tender in the other country. In England, double *patards* are, with almost 100 examples, the most common foreign type; they were equivalent to the English groat.

TRADE AND COMMERCE

Post Medieval Coins

There are over 45,000 Post Medieval coins (1485-1660) on the PAS database, helping to show the high level of coin circulation in England and Wales. The influence of the Renaissance is clear, with the full-face portraits of the Medieval period being replaced by life-like profile and three-quarters facing portraits. New coin types appeared, such as the sovereign (rated at a pound), the *testoon* (shilling), the sixpence, and such oddities as the three-farthing coin. The early part of the period saw continual debasement of the silver, and this was only remedied under Elizabeth I (r. 1558-1603). Some experiments were made with machine struck (milled) coins, but these only became established later. Gold and silver still formed the basis of the coinage in circulation, but there was some use of copper alloy coins from the reign of James I (r. 1603-25). The transition between Post Medieval and Early Modern coins is hazy but 1660 seems a good point to make the division.

LANCUM-BFCEF5, 26mm, Grindleton, Lancashire (1507-9)
Silver groat of Henry VII (r. 1485-1509) bearing a fine portrait. The obverse is inscribed hENRIC VII DI GRA REX ANGLIE (Henry VII by the Grace of God King of England) usefully giving a regnal number. The reverse shows the Royal Arms and the inscription POSVI DEV ADIVTOREM MEV (I have made God my helper). This inscription was found on coins from Edward III until Elizabeth I.

SUR-2CAC3E, 15mm, Hascombe, Surrey (1526-9)
Silver 'sovereign' penny of Henry VIII. The obverse shows the seated king, the inscription reading HDG ROSA SINE SPINA for 'H[enry] D[ei] G[racia] ROSA SINE SPINA (Rose without a thorn) – in retrospect a somewhat ill-fitting motto. The reverse is CIVITAS LONDON, showing the coin to be one of the many minted in London. The seated king design was a simplified version of that used on gold sovereigns which first appeared on coins of Henry VII.

FAKL-616A24, 26mm, Brompton, North Yorkshire (1490-1504)
Gold angel of Henry VIII (r. 1509-47). These coins get their name from the obverse which bears a figure of the Archangel St Michael, spearing a dragon (representing Satan). Around the angel is the inscription HENRIC' VIII' DI GRA REX AGN Z FRA, giving the king's name and titles. The reverse inscription reads PER' CRUCE' TVA' NOS XPE/REDET (By Thy Cross save us, O Christ, our Redeemer) showing Henry's piety. These coins were used as 'touch pieces' given to people during a ceremony where the monarch gave a healing touch to people suffering from the 'king's evil', scrofula, a swelling of the lymph nodes in the neck caused by tuberculosis. The ritual continued until quite late – in 1712 Queen Anne touched the infant Samuel Johnson for the 'kings evil'.

HAMP-36335E, 25mm, Penton Grafton, Hampshire (1547-51)
Silver groat of Edward VI. The coins issued in the first few years of Edward's short reign continued to use the portrait and name of Henry VIII and were as debased as Henry's later coins. Henry was nick-named 'old copper nose', as the copper on these coins quickly showed through the silver.

TRADE AND COMMERCE

DENO-AF6123, 27mm, Long Whatton and Diseworth, Leicestershire (1551-3)
Silver sixpence of Edward VI. The youth of the boy king, Edward VI, can clearly be seen in this portrait. This coin was struck in Edward's own name EDWARD VI D G AGL [FRA] Z HIB [RE] X with the reverse POSVI / DEV A/ DIVTO[R]/E MEV (I have made God my Helper). Edward, the only legitimate and surviving son of Henry VIII, died aged 15. While this coin can be dated only from the initial mark (a tun – a barrel = 1551-1553) Edward's reign saw the first use of dates on English coins. The denomination, VI (six pence) is given at the side of Edward's bust.

BM-527056, 24mm, Hoxne, Suffolk (1554-8)
Silver groat of Mary and Philip. The obverse only shows a portrait of Mary, although the inscription PHILIP ET MARIA D G REX ET REGINA (Philip and Mary, by the grace of God king and queen) also includes her husband, King Philip II of Spain. This coin was found as part of a small hoard.

LEIC-2A7F53, 34mm, Ashby de la Zouch, Leicestershire (1560-1)
Silver shilling of Elizabeth I (r. 1558-1603), dated by the cross-crosslet initial mark placed before both inscriptions. The legend on the obverse reads ELIZABETH.D.G.ANG.FRA. EI.HIB.REGINA and the reverse POSVI DEV.ADIVTOREM. MEV (see above). After the debasement of the coinage during the preceding reigns, Elizabeth's reign saw the restoration of the coinage's silver content.

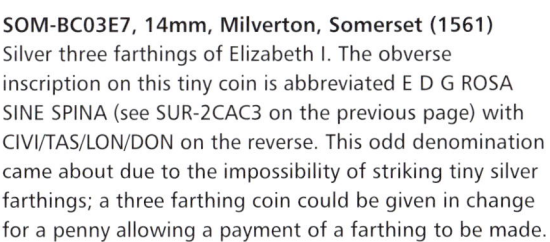

SOM-BC03E7, 14mm, Milverton, Somerset (1561)
Silver three farthings of Elizabeth I. The obverse inscription on this tiny coin is abbreviated E D G ROSA SINE SPINA (see SUR-2CAC3 on the previous page) with CIVI/TAS/LON/DON on the reverse. This odd denomination came about due to the impossibility of striking tiny silver farthings; a three farthing coin could be given in change for a penny allowing a payment of a farthing to be made.

PUBLIC-716991, 27mm, West Hanney, Oxfordshire (1622)
Silver sixpence of James I (r. 1603-25), who was also James VI of Scotland. His accession sees a change to the Royal Arms on the reverse, adding the Scottish lion rampant. This coin makes a strong political point emphasising the unity of the two kingdoms. On the obverse the inscription IACOBUS D G MAG BRIT FRA ET HIB REX (also claiming France) shows James to be King of Great Britain - MAG BRIT, not just of England and Scotland. The point is reinforced by the reverse inscription QUAE DEUS CONIUNXIT NEMO SEPARET (What God has joined together let no man put asunder).

TRADE AND COMMERCE

SUR-8C62F1, 31mm, Horley, Surrey (1634-5)
Silver shilling of Charles I (r. 1625-49) struck at the Tower of London while still under the control of the King (1625-42). The obverse reads CAROLVS D'G' MA BR FR' ET HI' REX and the reverse is CHRISTO AVSPICE REGNO (I reign under the Auspices of Christ). The coin is dated by its initial mark, a bell. The denomination is given by the XII (12 pence, equalling one shilling) behind the king's head. These coins were struck in low relief and are vulnerable to wear, but this example is well preserved.

NMS-047468, 33mm, Morley, Norfolk (1652)
Shilling of the Commonwealth. For the first time this coin has an inscription in English: THE COMMONWEALTH OF ENGLAND and GOD WITH VS.

IOW-33BA73, 12mm, Brighstone, Isle of Wight (1501-21)
Silver *soldino* of Doge Leonardo Loredan of Venice. The obverse shows the Doge, kneeling to receive the banner from St Mark, the patron saint of Venice, the inscription reading LE•LAV•DVX•S•M•V• for 'LEonardo LAVrdan DVX' (Duke Leonardo Loredan) 'San Marcus Veniti' (Saint Mark, Venice). The reverse shows a figure of Christ holding a cross with the inscription LAVS•TIBI•SOLI• (Thee alone be praised). These coins were imported into England by Venetian traders, and are known as 'Galley halfpennies' after the ships that brought them. They contained less silver than English halfpennies so their use was suppressed by the government. They are relatively common finds in England with 940 of them (650 Medieval and 290 Post Medieval) on the PAS database.

WILT-61453C, 14mm, Hannington, Wiltshire (1636-44)
Copper-alloy rose farthing of Charles I. The inscription is spread over the two faces with the king's name and title, CAROLVS D G MAG BRI, on the obverse continuing, with FRAN ET HIB REX, on the reverse. In response to a severe lack of small denomination coins, the first base-metal farthings appeared in 1613 under James I and were tinned to make them look like silver. They were worth only a fraction of their face value and were thus viewed with justified suspicion.

SUR-49F24D, 16mm, Highmoor, Oxfordshire (1649-60)
Silver halfgroat of the Commonwealth of England (under Oliver Cromwell) shows a radical change to centuries of royal coinage, here showing the shield of England on one side and the arms of England and Ireland on the other. There was no inscription, only the 'II' gives the denomination of two pence. The conjoined shields looked like a pair of breeches and, mockingly, these coins were referred to as 'breeches money'.

DENO-789371, Millthorpe, Derbyshire (1558-1649)
Hoard of clippings from coins of Elizabeth I (1558-1603), James I (1603-25) and Charles I (1625-49). While 'clipping' the trimming of the edges of silver coins was an old established practice, it became particularly common with break-down of order during the Civil War (1642-51).

268

TRADE AND COMMERCE

Early Modern Coins

The PAS is selective in recording more recent finds. Therefore, many more early modern coins (1660-1820) have been found than appear on the PAS's database, which includes only 5,000 coins of this period. Several features mark early modern coins, in particular the use of machinery to strike milled coins and the failure of the government to issue enough coins to allow commerce to take place. This led to people issuing their own money in the form of tokens (see pages 279-280).

BH-3DE557, 11mm, Berkhampstead, Hertfordshire (1675)
Silver penny of Charles II (r. 1660-85) upon which the obverse inscription reads CAROLVS II DEI GRATIA (Charles II, by the Grace of God) and the reverse MAG BR FRA ET HIB REX 16-75 (giving his titles, also claiming France and Ireland, and the coin's date). The grained edge of milled coins was a measure to counter the age-old problems of clipping.

SUR-46340D, 23mm, Tower Hamlets, London (1672)
Milled copper-alloy farthing of Charles II. The obverse inscription is CAROLVS [A] CAROLO, linking Charles to his father, Charles I. On the reverse is BRITANNIA 1672. Britannia had appeared on Roman coins of both Hadrian and Antoninus Pius, but she only reappears on copper coins during the reign of Charles II, continuing on regular coinage until 2008 when she ceased to be used on the 50 pence piece. The model for Britannia on coins of Charles II was Frances Stewart, later Duchess of Richmond, who was much favoured by the King.

WILT-2525F3, 26mm, Marden, Wiltshire (1685)
Silver shilling of James II. The obverse reads IACOBVS II•DEI•GRATIA and the reverse 1685•MAG•BR FRA ET HIB REX. Coins of this period are uncommon as the government was failing to issue enough to fulfil the needs of commerce.

FAKL-974C1E, 26mm, Langtoft, East Yorkshire (1689)
Copper-alloy Irish shilling of James II (1685-88 in England, 1685-91 in Ireland). The inscription on the obverse reads IACOBVS II DEI GRATIA and the reverse shows a crown over-lying crossed sceptres, above XII (12 pence), below r/9 (representing the month of November when this coin was struck: at that time, the year began in March), with J//R (for Jacobus rex – King James) flanking. The reverse inscription is 1689 MAG BR FRA ET HIB REX. This coin formed part of an emergency coinage issued by James in Ireland between 1689 and 1690 which is known as 'gun money', since the coins were said to have been made from old cannon. Unusually, they were dated to the month, James promising to redeem them in order of date. After James fled in 1688 these coins continued to circulate at reduced value, this shilling becoming a farthing.

TRADE AND COMMERCE

HAMP-428EC6, 28mm, Duncton, West Sussex (1694)
Copper-alloy halfpenny of William III and Mary II (r. 1688-94) showing them side by side. The obverse inscription is GVLIELMVS•ET•MARIA•: the spelling of William is due to the lack of the letter W in Latin. The reverse inscription is BRITANNIA whose figure is shown. Both William and Mary were grandchildren of Charles I and heirs to the crown but, as a married couple, they reigned jointly until Mary's death in 1694.

SUSS-BBE4A0, 25mm, Near Icklesham, East Sussex (1709)
Silver shilling of Anne (r. 1702-14). The obverse reads ANNA.DEI.GRATIA, continuing on the reverse with MAG BRI FR ET HIB REG 1709, giving Anne's title and date of minting. Anne's reign saw the Act of Union in 1707, bringing Scotland and England together in a formal union. There was also a change to the royal arms on the coinage, now showing the Scottish and English lions within a single shield divided by a vertical line.

PUBLIC-B903A4, 23mm, East Guldeford, East Sussex (1719)
Large copper farthing of George I (r. 1714-27), the inscription on the obverse reads GEORGIVS REX and the reverse continues use of the image of Britannia.

COIN WEIGHTS

At a time when coins were of irregular shape it was important to check that the weight was correct to safeguard against forgeries and coins that had been clipped. The easiest way of doing this was to use a simple balance to compare the weight of a coin with a standard weight owned by the merchant. These weights are not uncommon finds, there are almost 3,000 of them on the PAS database, of which about 1,000 are Medieval and 1,900 Post Medieval in date. They are usually small and dumpy and normally bear a design based on that seen on the actual coin.

DOR-FC7CD8, 17mm, Stalbridge, Dorset (1400-1600)
This coin weight was made for weighing gold angels (see page 266), a Late Medieval to Post Medieval coin which varied in value during the reigns of different monarchs. As is usual, the coin weight bears a design reflecting that of the coin being checked.

BH-0E9E26, 18mm, Uttlesford, Essex (1461-1500)
This coin weight is for a gold *ryal*. The *ryal* was produced from the reigns of Edward IV to Elizabeth I (1461-1600) and was equivalent to 10 shillings. It has upon it a ship, as found on the coin.

TRADE AND COMMERCE

HAMP-5FDA02, 21mm, Twyford, Hampshire (1463-1550)
Coin weight bearing the image of a ship showing it to be for a gold noble. Hexagonal coin weights, like this, have been classified as Anglo-French.

BH-773DB1, 16mm, Royston, Cambridgeshire (1585-1621)
This is a Continental weight made for an English silver crown. The obverse has the image of a crowned rose, with the letters E and C either side. On the reverse is the personal coat of arms of Lenaart van den Gheere (III or IV) of Amsterdam, which helps date it.

ESS-687282, 20mm, Langham, Norfolk (1694-1702)
Coin weight for a guinea of William III (1694-1702), the reverse shows a laureate bust of William with the inscription GUIELMVS III DEI GRACIA. On the reverse are crossed swords behind a crown with the inscription 1/GUINEA/W. Unusually, this does not represent the reverse of a real gold guinea.

TUMBRELS

A tumbrel or trebuchet was a two-part folding balance used for checking the weight of coins during the Medieval period. It had two arms, pivoting in the middle, allowing the balance to be opened into a cross shape to be used, or folded flat for storage. There are 58 tumbrels on the PAS database.

LIN-2857B5, 80mm, Spilsby area, Lincolnshire (1200-1500)
Complete tumbrel showing how they were constructed. The word 'tumbrel' comes from a type of cart, which, like these balances, tipped. The term 'trebuchet' is also used; this was a catapult with a pivoting arm.

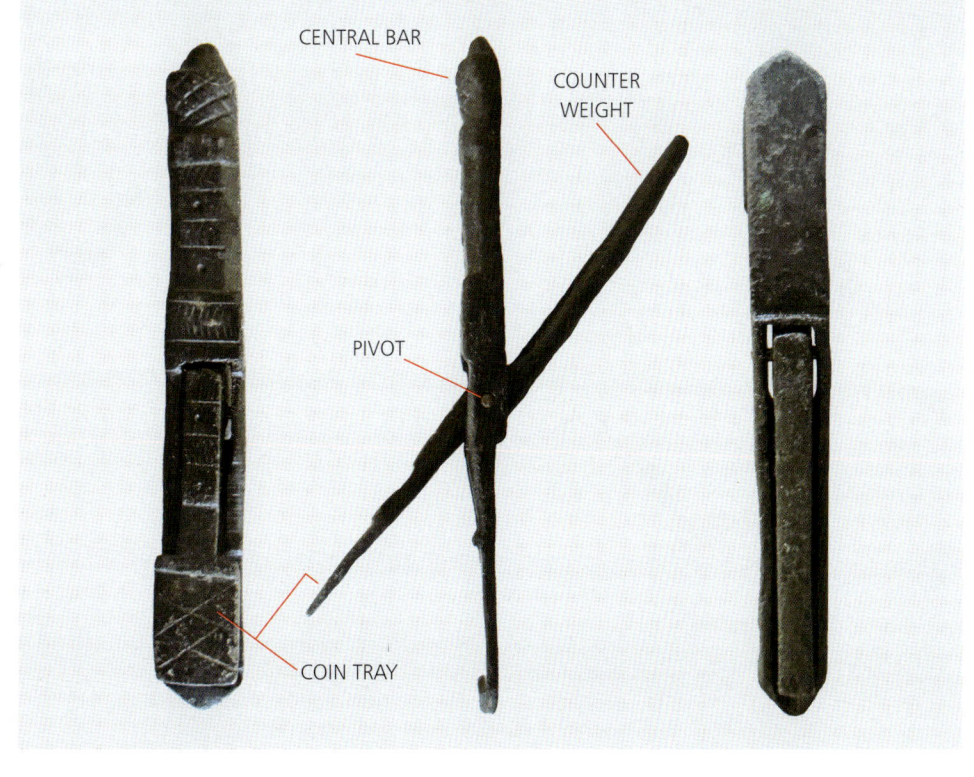

271

TRADE AND COMMERCE

BALANCES

Unlike a tumbrel, which could only check that a coin had a set weight, a scale could weigh quantities, so that the right amount of gold, silver or spice was measured out. This called for the use of standardised weights, the masses (weights) of which were known. There were two forms of scale, the balance, on which the arms were of equal length and the steelyard where one arm was much longer than the other and the weight slid along a gradated bar. The PAS has recorded over 200 scales, 134 of which are Medieval, 34 Post Medieval and 22 Roman.

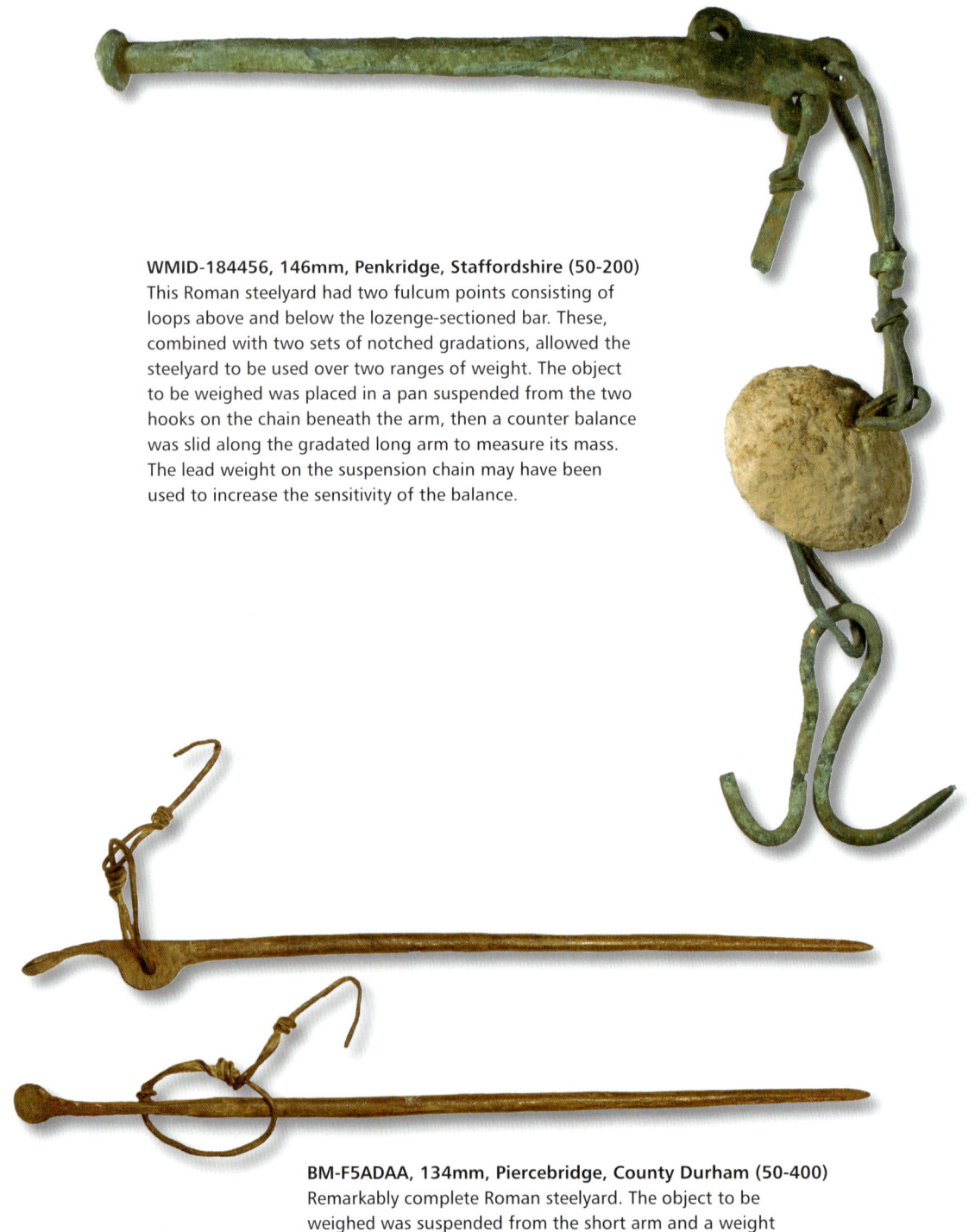

WMID-184456, 146mm, Penkridge, Staffordshire (50-200)
This Roman steelyard had two fulcum points consisting of loops above and below the lozenge-sectioned bar. These, combined with two sets of notched gradations, allowed the steelyard to be used over two ranges of weight. The object to be weighed was placed in a pan suspended from the two hooks on the chain beneath the arm, then a counter balance was slid along the gradated long arm to measure its mass. The lead weight on the suspension chain may have been used to increase the sensitivity of the balance.

BM-F5ADAA, 134mm, Piercebridge, County Durham (50-400)
Remarkably complete Roman steelyard. The object to be weighed was suspended from the short arm and a weight moved down the longer arm until it balanced.

TRADE AND COMMERCE

SUR-B894C6, 71mm, Crowmarsh, Oxfordshire (50-400)
Simple balance scale, both arms were of similar length and could swivel on the central bar.

WILT-B358AC, 41mm, Teffont, Wiltshire (1100-1400)
Complete Medieval folding beam-balance. Suspended from the terminals of each arm would have been a pan. Weights of known value would have been placed in one pan and balanced against the object to be weighed. The small pointer showing when the weights were equal.

LON-80E962, 40mm, Southwark, London (1270-1400)
This Medieval pan from a balance has three suspension holes. The engraved circles on the pan would have aided positioning of the weighed item and the weight correctly.

SOM-999EA7, 35mm, Dulverton, Somerset, (179?)
Hinge from a wooden folding ruler, usefully this object bears its owner's initials HS and the date 179?

SUR-94F953, 51mm, Cobham, Surrey (1800-50)
Post Medieval balance for checking gold sovereigns, with only the weight surviving. The other end originally had two pans; one for checking sovereigns, the other for half-sovereigns.

NLM-8D55A6, 31mm, Winterton, North Lincolnshire (1817-1918)
Part of a coin balance of the type shown on the left. This is the pan marked ½ SOVEREIGN, its counterpart, set closer to the fulcrum would have been for a gold sovereign. The half-sovereign was discontinued in 1918.

TRADE AND COMMERCE

WEIGHTS

These are often difficult to date and there is always the additional problem of distinguishing between weights used on scales and those used on fishing lines or for other purposes. Sometimes a weight can be assigned to a recorded system, for example the Roman *libra* or pound (which equalled 328.9g) – this was divided into 12 *unciae* (ounces). Crude lead blocks found on Viking sites seem to be subdivisions of a 24.4g module. Unfortunately, weights are often incomplete and corroded, making it impossible to compare them to historical standards. The PAS has recorded over 15,000 of them.

YORYM-1D9563, 44mm, North Yorkshire (50-400)
Lead weight with an iron hook. This is a type associated with Roman scales, but caution is needed in interpreting weights of this sort, as their function and date is open to question.

HAMP-079895, 61mm, Hambledon, Hampshire (50-200)
Roman copper-alloy weight with a lead core. It is in the form of a classical deity and would have been fitted with a loop to allow it to be slid along the bar of a balance scale.

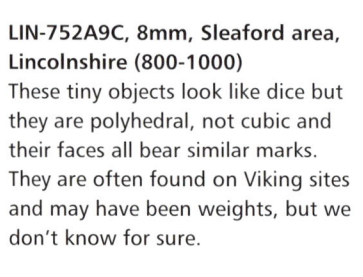

NMGW-07268F, 34mm, Wenvoe, Vale of Glamorgan (800-1000)
This Early Medieval lead block is set with a piece of enamel-decorated metalwork of Irish origin. Lead blocks set with fragments of fine metalwork were often used by the Vikings as weights in their bullion economy.

LIN-752A9C, 8mm, Sleaford area, Lincolnshire (800-1000)
These tiny objects look like dice but they are polyhedral, not cubic and their faces all bear similar marks. They are often found on Viking sites and may have been weights, but we don't know for sure.

NMS-0D47D0, 11mm, Barnham Broom, Norfolk (850-900)
As well as setting fine metalwork in lead blocks, the Vikings sometimes used Anglo-Saxon coins, like this copy of a brass *styca* of Redwulf, king of Northumbria (844-58).

TRADE AND COMMERCE

SUR-307155, 23mm, Lighthorne, Warwickshire (700-900)
This piece of fine Irish Early Medieval metalwork was probably part of a shrine. Filled with lead, it is likely to have been used as a Viking weight.

BERK-140822, 62mm, Welford, Berkshire (1250-1300)
Many Medieval steelyard weights are made of copper-alloy with a lead core; on this example the core is missing. It bears pseudo-heraldic arms, suggesting it was not an official issue which, for some unknown reason, bore the arms of Earls of Cornwall.

SF-8D5727, 63mm, Thelnetham, Suffolk (1100-1500)
The date of this lead and iron steelyard weight is not certain but its shape suggests it is Medieval.

LIN-A33593, 40mm, Minting, Lincolnshire (1000-1500)
This conical lead object with eight vertical ribs is thought to be a Medieval weight. Some of these objects, however, could have been gaming pieces (see page 193).

GLO-4F77CF, 33mm, Hamfallow, Gloucestershire (1100-1800)
This lead disc was probably a weight, but its date is uncertain.

TRADE AND COMMERCE

LVPL-F4F117, 56mm, Whissendine, Rutland (1350-1600)
Shield-shaped weights are not uncommon detector finds with almost 600 of them recorded on the PAS database. They are widespread across the country but are most common in the north. This example exhibits the royal arms of England

YORYM-5C1B40, 43mm, Catterick, North Yorkshire (1350-1700)
This acorn-shaped late Medieval or Post Medieval weight has a loop for suspension so it can be used on a balance without a pan.

WMID-30ABD3, 32mm, Brewood and Coven, Staffordshire (1300-1700)
Not all lead weights were used for weighing. This pyramid shaped object could have been a fishing weight.

WMID-F2364A, 30mm, Church Eaton, Staffordshire (1685-88)
Some trade weights can be identified by their markings. This example bears a ewer, the mark of the Founders Company used on approved weights. The crowned 'I' is the Royal cipher for King James (I or II). The sword represents St Paul, for London.

NMS-046A1A, 28mm, Deopham, Norfolk (1400-1540)
Some weights are cup-shaped, so that they can be stacked within each other. This example, is decorated with punched dots around its rim, and is probably late in date.

FAKL-6A8102, 12mm, Brough on Humber, East Yorkshire (1700-1900)
Small weights were used by apothecaries for measuring out drugs. This example has on both of its faces the apothecary's symbol for two scruples, part of a system of measurement that remained in use until the late 1960s.

TRADE AND COMMERCE

SWYOR-2F0735, 45mm, South Stainley with Cayton, North Yorkshire (1500-1700)
Set of weights, nesting within another and placed in a brass box. The three weights within the box are for an ounce, half ounce and quarter ounce, and are stamped with a fleur verification mark.

JETTONS

These are common metal detecting finds, and therefore not always studied carefully by their finders. The main purpose of these tokens was as reckoning counters, for counting money and keeping accounts, but they might also have been used for other activities, such as gaming. With almost 11,000 jettons on the PAS database we might wonder why all these counters were needed; they were perhaps also used as informal halfpennies and farthings.

PUBLIC-FE6EAD, 20mm, Wareham, Dorset (1280-1340)
English Medieval jetton with the same design on both sides, a cross patonce over a cross fleury.

BERK-8E6C45, 19mm, Fawler, Oxfordshire (1282-88)
The obverse of this Medieval jetton follows the design of coinage of Edward I, and has the English royal arms on the reverse. It was probably made at the Royal Mint, which was, at the time, in the Tower of London.

TRADE AND COMMERCE

BH-329DC3, 23mm, Kingsey, Buckinghamshire (1437-50)
Medieval jetton showing, on its obverse, a crown, surrounded by an inscription inspired by the Ave Maria prayer. Its reverse has an elaborate cross design. It was probably struck in Paris.

BUC-DF5839, 25mm, Hanslope, Buckinghamshire (1448-95)
Late Medieval jetton of Tournai type which is pierced, possibly so several of them can be kept together on a loop of string. It has upon it the inscriptions VIVE LE ROI VIVE LE ROI VIVE (Long live the king, repeated) and GETTES BIEN PAIES BIEN (cast well, play well).

LON-21DE03, 24mm, City of London (1500-50)
Nuremberg type jettons are common Post Medieval finds. This one has a nonsensical legend mixing Roman and Lombardic letters.

DOR-884F6A, 25mm, Tarrant Rushton, Dorset (1500-70)
Post Medieval jetton, of anonymous stock type, with the Lion of St Mark on its obverse. The reverse design, the imperial orb inside a three arched tressure, is typical of Nuremberg jettons.

IOW-C46C31, 22mm, Arreton, Isle of Wight (1586-1635)
Some jettons identify their maker. The obverse of this example identifies Hans Krauwinckel II, member of a famous family of jetton makers in Nuremberg. Its reverse has the inscription *GOTES•SEGEN•MACHT•REICH (God's blessing brings riches).

278

TRADE AND COMMERCE

TOKENS

There are over 16,000 tokens on the PAS database. Not all of them will have had a purely commercial role – this is particularly true of those dating from the Middle Ages. Some could have been tallies, one being given for each piece of work done and then exchanged for money or goods at the end of the day. Post Medieval tokens, especially those of the mid-17th century, are clearly for trading, and identify not only the issuers, but also their type of business and where they were based. Such tokens appeared when there was a shortage of regular coins fulfilling the need for small change.

SF-DCF30D, 19mm, Kenninghall, Norfolk (1284-1314)
This Medieval object is a *piedfort* 'heavy measure' striking of a *denier tournois* of King Philippe IV of France. Although the object is modelled on a coin used in circulation it is notably thicker than a regular coin. Their exact purpose is unknown, but they could have been used by officials.

HAMP-5E8048, 27mm, Owslebury, Hampshire (1300-1400)
On one side of this token is the sword of St Paul with the letters PP, and on the other are the keys of St Peter. It seems likely to be an ecclesiastical token of unknown purpose, perhaps linked to a Medieval payment of a dole of bread and ale.

SF-DB4C46, 15mm, Lackford, Suffolk (1470-1539)
It was tradition in some Medieval villages for a chosen boy to be made bishop for the day, and tokens were produced and distributed. This example shows St Nicholas' mitre on the obverse, and a long-cross on the other. There are over 400 'boy bishop' tokens on the PAS database, with most finds being from central East Anglia.

LVPL-AD3E32, 23mm, Burscough, Lancashire (1600-1700)
This token only has decoration on one side, a letter W, surmounted by three pellets and a semi-circular line below. Its dating is uncertain.

WILT-47479A, 15mm, West Lavington, Wiltshire (1400-1800)
Many lead tokens are decorated with symmetrical motifs, such as this eight petalled flower, with a central pellet, and a pellet in each petal. While described as tokens, many of these objects may have been used as tallies, such as by a worker being given a tally for each basket of apples picked, these being exchanged for cash at the end of the day.

PUBLIC-5305FD, 16mm, Greenwich, London (1649)
This trader's token shows the head of King James I and was issued for use in the King's Head public house in Deptford. 1649 was the year when James' son, Charles, lost his head.

TRADE AND COMMERCE

WREX-A920C9, 19mm, Handbridge, Cheshire (1667)
This trade token is typical of the many produced in the 17th century. It was issued by HENRY WILLIAMS whose name surrounds the ironmongers' arms. The reverse tells us that he was IN CHESTER with the date 1667 and that it was HIS 1D (penny).

LON-F73FB7, 18mm, Southwark, London (1665-7)
A massive range of trade tokens, mainly farthings but also halfpence were issued between 1648-1672. Traders in many small towns and villages had their own tokens. Most are dated, often bearing the words HIS HALF PENY or, in this case, more interestingly, HER HALF PENY. The issuer in this case was Elizabeth Wright of Whits Ally in Coleman Street, London.

PUBLIC-EBCBC8, 21mm, City of London (1648-74)
An octagonal trader's token, or ticket, issued by Samuel Benet, for coach journeys between London and Windsor.

LON-B02B0E, 13mm, Tower Hamlets, London (1600-1700)
This lead token follows the form of many mid-17th century traders' tokens, but it is notably simplified. On one side are some unidentified arms, with the issuers' initials I M (bottom left and top) and his spouse's initial, M, (bottom right).

IOW-B7999C, 34mm, Brighstone, Isle of Wight (1500-1850)
This lead token has only initials on both sides. Some smaller letters, that are less clear to read, can be seen above the GH side.

LON-A79B59, 20mm, Southwark, London (1667)
Heart-shaped tokens might have been used as love-gifts, though this example was issued as a trader's token by William Baldwin of Milton, Kent. Tokens often record the issuer's trade but the nature of William's business is unknown.

CLOTH SEALS

Cloth and bag seals are an important artefact type. From the Medieval period the cloth trade was regulated, with officials representing the cloth makers, dyers and others requiring a mark (normally a lead seal) to be applied to traded cloth of specified standards. Such seals shed light on the cloth trade across north-west Europe, particularly between England and the Low Countries. Other seals were used to show the contents of bags of traded goods, of which Russian bag seals are relatively common finds. Seals were also used to show that duty had been paid on the cloth or the contents of a bag. There are over 5,000 seals on the PAS database most of which are made of lead and are of Post Medieval date.

PUBLIC-30CD06, 18mm, Elvet, County Durham (1300-1400)
This two-part Medieval cloth seal is distorted, but enough of it survives to see that it has the mark for Malines (in modern-day Belgium) – the letters M and U – which produced Brabant cloth. In this case the cloth was presumably exported to Durham.

LON-51226C, 42mm, Kensington and Chelsea, London (1571)
Post Medieval cloth seal with an inscription showing that that it was once attached to cloth traded by the Dutch merchants of Colchester, Essex.

LON-490B94, 23mm, City of London (1657)
Norwich cloth seals are interesting as they contain important information about the issuers. This example was issued by the Norwich Weavers Guild in 1657, and gives the initials of both the Norwich and County wardens for the year: these are William Hardingham, Jehosephat Davy and Samuel Rawling (all Norwich), and John Knight and Chris Lym (Norfolk).

WILT-00AC3D, 24mm, St Paul Malmesbury Without, Wiltshire (1600-1700)
The shield on this cloth seal represents the arms of the Dutch city of Haarlem, with the number 20 showing the length of the fabric in Dutch *ells*.

SOM-BA9512, 32mm, Merriott, Somerset, (1838)
Lead seal from a bale of flax exported from the Russian port of Archangel in 1838. Port Inspector Ivan Mitropolov certified that it was 'select grade'.

Chapter 10
Horses and Transport

Horses were first used during the Bronze Age. Initially, they were not ridden, but pulled carts and wagons. Nowadays it is difficult to imagine how important horses and other working animals were in the past, even into recent times. They provided transport and essential muscle power for heavy agricultural work. Horses also had great military importance, allowing rapid deployment, reconnaissance and a hard-hitting impact in battle. This led to some horses having great social significance; they were expensive and were mostly ridden by the elite. It is no surprise, therefore, that horse harness fittings are common detector finds.

HORSESHOES

Horseshoes are essential for animals worked hard or being used on metalled surfaces where they would otherwise suffer damage to their hooves. There are 290 horseshoes on the PAS database and 9 Roman hipposandals. Most of them (167) have been assigned to the Medieval period, with a further 109 Post Medieval and 5 Early Medieval examples.

WILT-A3591B, 168mm, Chiseldon, Wiltshire (50-400)
This elaborate piece of ironwork is a 'hipposandal' (Latin: *soleae ferreae*) and was strapped over a horse's hoof to protect it when it was working on paved roads.

HORSES AND TRANSPORT

LANCUM-1FFE71, 118mm, Grassington, North Yorkshire (700-1100)
Its wavy edge and narrow section, along with associated finds, suggests that this horseshoe is Early Medieval.

SUSS-973667, 109mm, near Lewes, East Sussex (1050-1225)
This is an orthopaedic horseshoe, designed to support a damaged hoof. Its form suggests that it is of unusually early date.

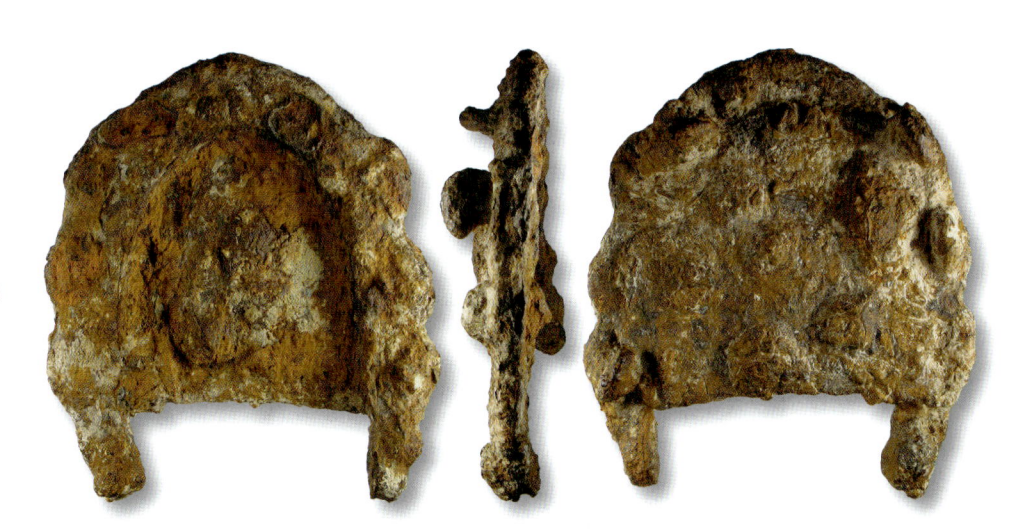

SOM-B81875, 130mm, Nunney, Somerset (1250-1500)
Its broad web and the wide margin between the nail holes and the outer edge place this horseshoe in the 'transitional' type, linking Medieval and Post Medieval shoes.

HORSES AND TRANSPORT

SUR-AF0F85, 140mm, Burghfield, Berkshire (1300-1600)
Medieval to Post Medieval horseshoe with an angular inner profile. It only has a right-angled calkin (lip) on one heel, suggesting that it was made for a horse with a hoof problem.

LANCUM-6A6326, 43mm, Sturminster Newton, Dorset (1400-1900)
The feet of oxen are quite different from those of horses, having two cleats instead of a hoof. These had to be shod separately to allow an ox's foot to flex.

SPURS

As well as being used to control horses, spurs took on an important social role; for example, to be knighted was for a knight to have 'won his spurs' They allowed equestrian status to be displayed and were often very finely decorated.

Spurs take a variety of forms of which the prick spur and the rowel spur are the basic types. The PAS has recorded over 2,500 spurs, 800 of which are Medieval, most of the rest (over 1,600) being Post Medieval.

GLO-C94D8E, 54mm, Tytherington, Gloucestershire (200-400)
This Roman spur was strapped around the heel of the rider's boot. The actual prick was made of iron and is only represented by a rust stain.

HORSES AND TRANSPORT

NCL-92C411, 23mm, Corbridge, Northumberland (300-400)
This object is probably the prick from a Roman spur. Surprisingly, there are 50 Roman spurs on the PAS database.

SF4685, 62mm, Gooderstone, Norfolk (750-900)
Both the form and decoration suggest that this spur is Early Medieval; the leathers and the prick are missing.

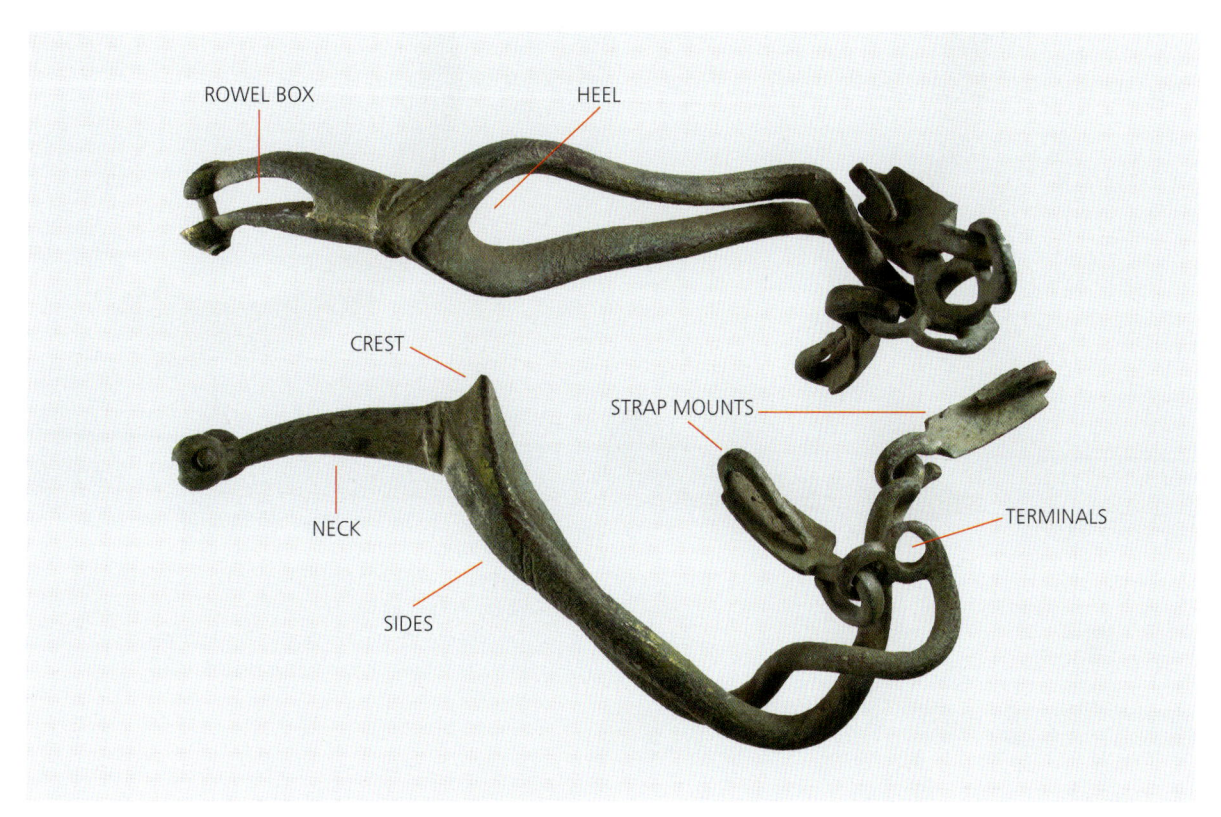

ROWEL BOX HEEL
CREST
STRAP MOUNTS
TERMINALS
NECK
SIDES

WAW-7D1368, 121mm, Bickmarsh, Worcestershire (1200-1400)
Though mangled, this Medieval rowel-spur is almost complete, with only the rowel missing. Still joined to the terminals are the attachment mounts for a leather strap.

SF-A715F6, 43mm, Fornham All Saints, Suffolk (1350-1600)
Rowels are often found alone. This example, with 12 points, is still attached to part of one arm of the spur. It shows signs of being gilded.

285

HORSES AND TRANSPORT

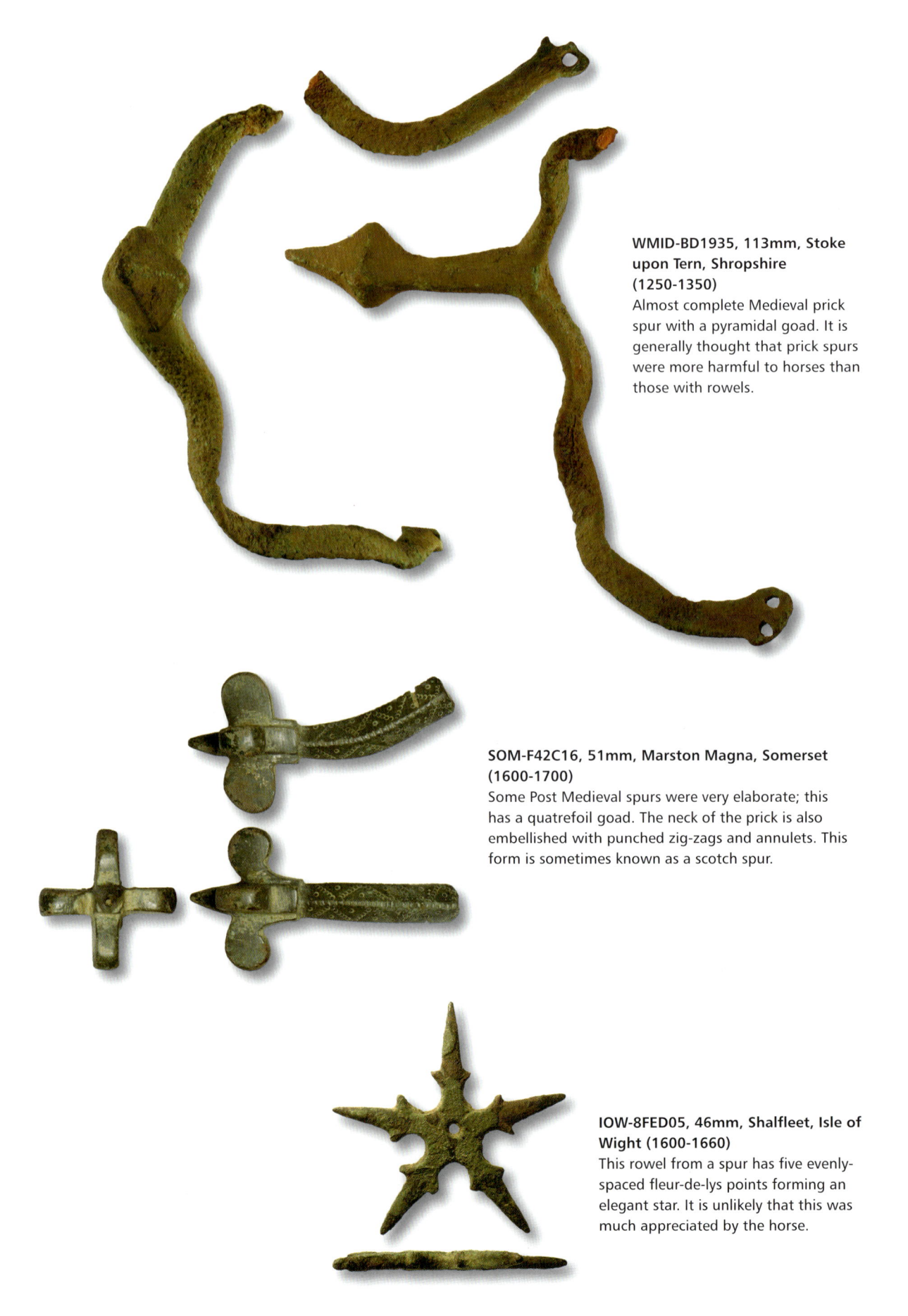

WMID-BD1935, 113mm, Stoke upon Tern, Shropshire (1250-1350)
Almost complete Medieval prick spur with a pyramidal goad. It is generally thought that prick spurs were more harmful to horses than those with rowels.

SOM-F42C16, 51mm, Marston Magna, Somerset (1600-1700)
Some Post Medieval spurs were very elaborate; this has a quatrefoil goad. The neck of the prick is also embellished with punched zig-zags and annulets. This form is sometimes known as a scotch spur.

IOW-8FED05, 46mm, Shalfleet, Isle of Wight (1600-1660)
This rowel from a spur has five evenly-spaced fleur-de-lys points forming an elegant star. It is unlikely that this was much appreciated by the horse.

HORSES AND TRANSPORT

LON-63444A, 34mm, Tower Hamlets, London (1600-1700)
Attached to this fragment of a spur arm is the buckle and other fittings for a leather strap to secure the spur to the rider's boot. The profuse use of buckles and fittings was typical of the Post Medieval period.

YORYM-33A9C3, 86mm, Cawton, North Yorkshire (1650-1850)
The outer surface of this spur is heavily embellished with incised patterns and was once heavily gilded. Such items emphasise that the spur was not just a functional object, but also an emblem of status.

SADDLES

DEV-F84055, 59mm, Loddiswell, Devon (1500-1700)
Saddles were common, but little survives of them as they were constructed of wood, leather and hair packing. Exceptions are the distinctive pommels from Post Medieval saddles, of which there are more than 100 on the PAS database. This example consists of two parts soldered together and has wings with holes so that it could be fixed to the saddle's wooden frame.

HORSES AND TRANSPORT

STIRRUPS

Stirrups were not used by the Romans whose saddles had shaped projections which held the rider's thighs. It appears that stirrups were introduced into Europe from the east by the barbarian horsemen who ousted the Romans. There are almost 2,000 stirrups on the PAS database of which most are Early Medieval. This comes about through a fashion, in the 11th century, for stirrups with copper-alloy fittings, many decorated in Anglo-Scandinavian styles. These seem to have been lost with monotonous regularity suggesting that horses were ridden much more than was previously thought.

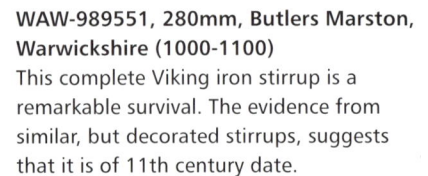

WAW-989551, 280mm, Butlers Marston, Warwickshire (1000-1100)
This complete Viking iron stirrup is a remarkable survival. The evidence from similar, but decorated stirrups, suggests that it is of 11th century date.

WAW-43A0F2, 41mm, Worfield, Shropshire (1000-1100)
This Anglo-Scandinavian stirrup terminal is decorated in the Urnes style; the animal's slit-like eyes can be seen at the bottom left. The areas of rust show where the side bar (top) and tread emerged from the copper-alloy casting.

KENT-FA174E, 45mm, Lyminge, Kent (1000-1100)
Terminal from an Anglo-Scandinavian stirrup decorated in the Ringerike style. The jaws of a crested beast form the smaller of the two rings on the inner faces. The terminal fitted where the sides of the stirrup met the tread. It has a U-shaped section into which the iron side pieces were secured with cast lead.

HORSES AND TRANSPORT

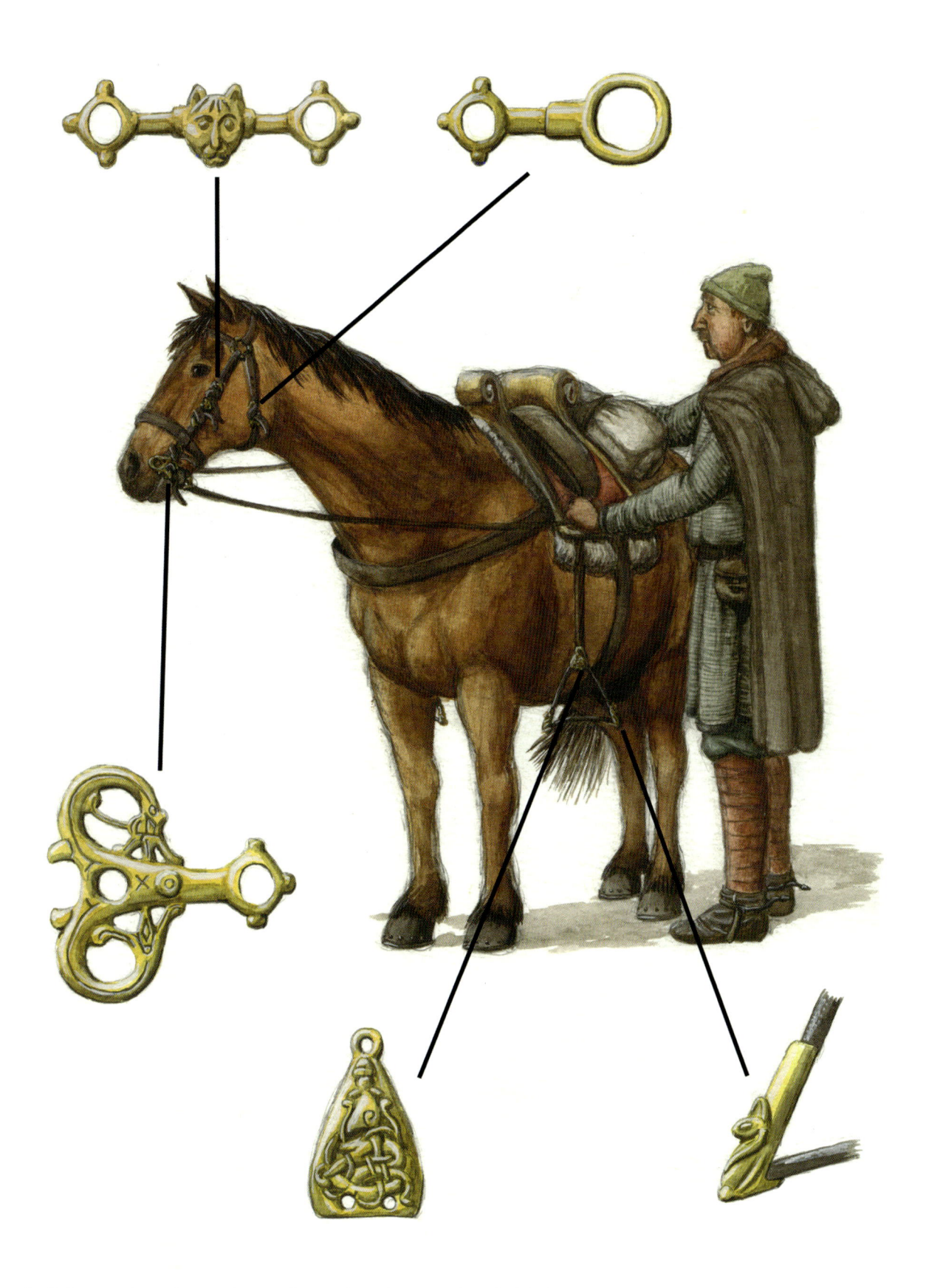

The fittings used on a late Anglo-Scandinavian horse harness. These highly distinctive metal fitments were easily lost and explain why 11th century harnesses are so well represented on the PAS database. (Image courtesy of Dom Andrews-Wilson)

289

HORSES AND TRANSPORT

HESH-EADCB1, 45mm, Bridgnorth, Shropshire (1000-1100)
Not all stirrup strap mounts were decorated. This plain example bears traces of the iron stirrup.

BH-AFA0EA, 59mm, Sherington, Buckinghamshire (1000-1100)
Stirrup strap mount decorated with an animal surrounded by interlace in the Anglo-Scandinavian Urnes style. Mounts like these, and the other examples shown here, were riveted to the leather strap where it passed through the slot at the top of the stirrup. Often decorative, they served to protect the leather from wear.

HAMP-9DA925, 52mm, Cheriton, Hampshire (1070-1140)
Stirrup strap mounts decorated with lion-like animals may have spanned the Norman Conquest. Their form looks Anglo-Scandinavian, but the decoration appears Romanesque.

WMID-8A18A6, 45mm, Aldwincle, Northamptonshire (1300-1400)
Only the top part of this Medieval stirrup survives. Its rectangular top plate is decorated with carefully cut-out trefoils.

HORSES AND TRANSPORT

WILT-B72FF6, 140mm, Chisledon, Wiltshire (1400-1500)
This iron stirrup is complete, but very corroded. Its rectangular plate masks the attachment loop. The downward pointing tongue where the foot rests helps date it.

BUC-EFD315, 130mm, Quarrendon, Buckinghamshire (1400-1500)
This late Medieval stirrup is like the example from Chisledon shown above but made of copper-alloy.

HORSES AND TRANSPORT

LVPL-EF4D47, 174mm Holt, Wrexham (1300-1700)
The top of this late Medieval or Post Medieval stirrup has a cover in the form of a faceted dome, its sides are ribbed, and three bars form the footplate.

DENO-D6F7E9, 143mm, Barnby in the Willows, Nottinghamshire (1600-1800)
Post Medieval stirrup of simple construction, formed of a single iron rod, shaped into an oval. The foot-rest is also oval.

HORSES AND TRANSPORT

BRIDLES AND BRIDLE BITS

The bridle was an important development, as it allowed a puny human to control an animal as large and powerful as a horse. Antler bridle cheek pieces are known from the Late Bronze Age, but the first evidence of bridles recorded by the PAS comes from the Iron Age. The PAS has recorded 600 bridle fittings of which 50 are Iron Age, 380 Early Medieval and 115 Post Medieval.

BH-9EDAF7, 117mm, Melbourn, Cambridgeshire (100 BC-AD 80)
Late Iron Age three-link bridle bit. One end is broken and would have originally ended in a cylinder like that seen on the left. The rings to which the reins were attached would have passed through these cylinders.

LVPL-495C15, 35mm, Scunthorpe, North Lincolnshire (100 BC-AD 100)
One end of an Iron Age bridle bit which interestingly shows signs of heavy wear. Iron Age bridle fragments recorded by the PAS are widespread but with clusters in East Anglia and North Lincolnshire.

WILT-13C344, 79mm, Salisbury, Wiltshire (AD 1-100)
Side piece from an Iron Age bridle bit. A pair of these would have been attached to the ends of the bit and would have held the reins.

WMID-F11707, 71mm, Penkridge, Staffordshire (AD 1-100)
Pair of side plates from a Roman bridle bit. Only 15 Roman bridle fittings have been recorded with the PAS although this might reflect the difficulty in telling the difference between Late Iron Age and Early Roman metalwork.

HORSES AND TRANSPORT

SF-59F6E2, 58mm, Snetterton, Norfolk (1000-1100)
Bit link from an Anglo-Scandinavian bridle. These are not uncommon and would have been the type used at the time of the Norman Conquest. Early Medieval bridle fittings are widespread in England but with concentrations appearing in East Anglia and around the important Anglo-Saxon centre at Winchester.

SF8198, 70mm, Hitcham, Suffolk (1000-1100)
Four-way Anglo-Scandinavian strap distributor. The form of the loops is typical of these fittings.

NMS-482554, 81mm, Barsham, Suffolk (1000-1100)
Bridle bit cheek piece decorated in the Anglo-Scandinavian Ringerike style. On each side of the central hole is an outward facing animal, their beaked heads are on the outer edges. Intertwined with these are serpents, their heads visible each side of the highly stylised central boss.

SUSS-9A83B4, 59mm, near Berwick, East Sussex (1000-1100)
Fragment of an Anglo-Scandinavian bridle cheek piece decorated in a highly devolved version of the Ringerike style. Comparison with some of the other pieces illustrated here shows the the copying of this style.

HORSES AND TRANSPORT

ESS-4E9F4C, 53mm, East Tilbury, Essex (1000-1100)
Further variant on the Anglo-Scandinavian bridle cheek piece, with the beast looking back over its own shoulder. The knobs on the loops are typical of these bridle fittings.

LIN-7C2052, 92mm, Saxilby, Lincolnshire (1000-1100)
This bridle cheek piece is a striking example of the Anglo-Scandinavian Ringerike style and shows what the more crudely made versions were trying to copy. The animal looks back over its own shoulder to bite its tail and has a characteristic curled crest. Its hip and shoulder joints are marked by spirals.

PUBLIC-DEB4D3, 270mm, near Wimborne, Dorset (1300-1500)
Iron harness equipment can be hard to date, but this snaffle bit is probably late Medieval or Post Medieval. The mouth piece is in two linked sections.

HORSES AND TRANSPORT

STRAP FITTINGS

Strap-fitting covers a wide range of objects that were fitted to leather belts, horse harness, bags and luggage and it is often impossible to say on to what a strap had been fitted. Some strap fittings, such as buckles and strap ends, are discussed in chapter 2. Many strap fittings were plain, but others provided a way to decorate horses and people, showing prestige and political allegiances. Nearly 14,000 objects are described as strap fittings on the PAS database, most being Medieval or Post Medieval. They are widespread, but show a marked concentration in East Anglia.

ESS-B46EE5, 30mm, Lavenham, Suffolk (1100-1000 BC)
Hollow toggles, like this, have been found in Bronze Age hoards and are likely to have formed part of horse harness.

KENT-E6C2B2, 57mm, Harrietsham, Kent (950-800 BC)
These strange finds are known as 'bugle-shaped objects', a sure sign that their function is unknown. They are found in Bronze Age hoards allowing them to be dated. It is likely that they were some sort of strap fitting.

SUR-1C54E3, 28mm, Aldermaston, Berkshire (100 BC-AD 50)
Iron Age double-lunette strap union. The two holes probably contained enamel, these were set within double arcs of incised 'basket work' style ornament.

LANCUM-DC3370, 65mm, Over Kellet, Lancashire (100 BC-AD 200)
This strange object is described by the bizarre name of 'pressure tectonic', implying that they were used to apply force. The three spikes may have been driven into the coachwork of a vehicle, but their function remains a mystery.

HORSES AND TRANSPORT

BERK-C6DAA3, 55mm, Hampstead Norreys, Berkshire (70 BC-AD 50)
This studded ring bears Celtic style decoration on the top of the stud. Fittings of this sort have been found associated with swords suggesting that they were baldric fittings.

YORYM-6385E8, 37mm Aislaby, North Yorkshire (100 BC-AD 100)
Another variant on what are likely to be baldric fittings. Its decoration, while simple, is in an assured Iron Age style.

SWYOR-6EE012, 47mm, Wakefield, West Yorkshire (100 BC-AD 200)
While the enamel inlay on the strap union is Celtic in style, it could date from after the Roman Conquest. It has lost one of the two bars around which the strap was threaded.

SF-8C0836, 34mm, Scole, Norfolk (AD 1-100)
Strap slider with enamel inlay. Sliders like this would have been used to secure the loose end of a strap, beyond the buckle. Although much is lost, sufficient enamel survives to show that this was once a striking object.

WMID-550E46, 41mm, Rowley, East Yorkshire (100 BC-AD 100)
Romano-Celtic strap slider decorated with the petal-boss motif that often appears on this 'fusion' metal work which blends Celtic and Roman traditions. It may have originally been enamelled.

HORSES AND TRANSPORT

FAKL-19312B, 62mm, West Rainton, County Durham (200 BC–AD 200)
This graceful piece of Celtic metalwork bears three 'petal boss' motifs set around what is known as a 'muzzle' motif, as it resembles an animal's nose; but the interpretation of this, and other motifs used in Celtic art, is open to question.

LIN-643B3D, 49mm, Walcot near Folkingham, Lincolnshire (100 BC–AD 100)
The central element of this strap union is asymmetric, which is a feature often seen in Celtic decoration.

WMID410, 102mm, Kingsbury, Warwickshire (100 BC–AD 100)
Strap mount with the swirling decoration typical of Celtic metalwork.

HORSES AND TRANSPORT

HAMP-74E4F6, 43mm, Corhampton and Meonstoke, Hampshire (350-450)
Propeller-shaped stiffener of the type used on Late Roman military belts.

SUR-A8D2EA, 31mm, Itchen Valley, Hampshire (50-400)
Roman strap mount of vulvate form, perhaps representing the female equivalent of the commonly found phallic motifs.

NMS-C1F585, 19mm, Wymondham, Norfolk (120-300)
Riveted strap mounts like this are commonly found on Roman military sites.

FAKL-FA3828, 31mm, Skirpenbeck, East Yorkshire (470-570)
Early Medieval shoe-shaped belt stud, a strange, but oddly common, design.

WILT-BBB06B, 54mm, The Deverills, Wiltshire (1000-1100)
Socketed hooks, like this example, appear to have been used in sets of three, the hooks being linked to the central disc (like the example from Bradfield shown to the right). It is not known what was fitted into the square sockets. Some of these hooks bear Anglo-Scandinavian decoration allowing them to be dated.

SUR-85CB26, 30mm, Bradfield, Berkshire (1000-1100)
Early Medieval strap distributor of the type used with the socketed hook from the Deverills shown on the left. This object bears traces of Viking style decoration.

299

HORSES AND TRANSPORT

SF-5CE2A2, 65mm, Barningham, Suffolk (500-600)
This mount is decorated with the devolved animals of Anglo-Saxon Style I ornament set around a central garnet. It is likely to have been a belt fitting.

HAMP-330073, 31mm, Cheriton, Hampshire (500-570)
Anglo-Saxon gilt harness mount or strap junction.

FAKL-EB0744, 34mm, Skirpenbeck, East Yorkshire (470-570)
Anglo-Saxon strap or belt mount or stiffener. This example was found on the site of a ploughed-out cemetery.

BH-EA77E7, 29mm, Hertfordshire (550-650)
Gilded harness mount with interlace decoration of late 6th or 7th century date. The 8mm long spikes on the rear show that this object was firmly attached to something and the small hole may have been a later modification.

HAMP-408148, 35mm, Nether Wallop, Hampshire (630-700)
Anglo-Saxon gilded harness mount with a garnet set in its centre. Around its edge are highly stylised eagles' heads. It was attached to the strap by the tongue-like lugs on its back.

SOMDOR-305381, 75mm, Loxton, Somerset (470-570)
This fitting bears a gilded panel of Anglo-Saxon Style I animals with a bold animal's head at each end. It probably came from a horse harness.

300

HORSES AND TRANSPORT

HESH-5875C6, 21mm, Leominster, Herefordshire (1250-1350)
Reminiscent of shield-shaped Medieval harness pendants, this mount has a heraldic motif of three 'mullets' (stars) divided by a chevron. The arms have not been identified, but much of the red enamelling survives.

NMS-236F25, 15mm, Hevingham, Norfolk (1150-1400)
While much of the red enamel inlay is missing, what remains, together with the gilding, show that this Medieval horse harness mount was highly decorative and reflective of the tastes of the time.

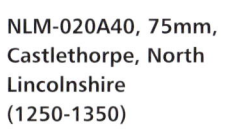

BH-3A4115, 56mm, Offley, Hertfordshire (1200-1500)
The three surviving parts remaining connected, the style and robustness of this Medieval strap fitting indicates it may have adorned a horse harness.

NLM-020A40, 75mm, Castlethorpe, North Lincolnshire (1250-1350)
This is part of an elaborate harness decoration. Its original form is unclear, though it seems likely it once contained at least another heraldic shield. A stylised beast's head adorns the fitting where its metal straps cross, cleverly hiding the join.

KENT-321A1B, 57mm, near Lenham, Kent (1250-1400)
Harness fittings of this hooked variety are not particularly common, and neither is an owl as a decorative motif. Here the beautfully executed white owl, with red feet, appears to be shown within the green leaves of an oak tree.

WAW-54B266, 75mm, Shipton-on-Cherwell and Thrupp, Oxfordshire (1200-1400)
This harness fitting is decorated with two designs; one side bearing a sexfoil flower and the other a grotesque consisting of a woman's head on a lion's body. Other finds suggest that it fitted into a sphere to form part of a composite mount.

HORSES AND TRANSPORT

LVPL-121F91, 34mm, Lyford, Oxfordshire (1200-1500)
This Medieval strap-fitting served as a distributor, so that four leather straps could be connected. On this example a single, riveted, strap attachment (which would have been joined to the end of one of the straps) still survives.

WMID-B32C92, 23mm, Harlaston, Staffordshire (1100-1700)
Too simple for accurate dating, this strap distributor may be Medieval or Post Medieval. Some distributors consist of nothing more than a loop or ring. This example has on it three strap attachments, which are folded over and still have their rivets.

WAW-0B7EE5, 28mm, Cookhill, Worcestershire (1600-1800)
Post Medieval decorative fitting, perhaps a strap slide, used to secure the loose end of a belt. This example is decorated with cross-hatching and has been gilded. It has the cluttered decoration popular in the 16th and 17th centuries.

WAW-B0ED92, 53mm, Brailes, Warwickshire (1600-1700)
It is thought that these Post Medieval lozenge strap-fittings were used as dress accessories, but they may also have been used on horse harnesses.

SUR-23EF78, 100mm, Epsom, Surrey (1603-64)
Post Medieval bridle boss bears the Stuart Arms. Charles II is known to have visited a stately home near to the findspot; it seems likely it was lost by one of his retinue.

HORSES AND TRANSPORT

SUR-2AAA52, 44mm, Farnham, Surrey (1650-1800)
The sun motif on this mount bears a striking face, with a broad nose and lips. Thickly silvered, the incised design presents a powerful image.

WMID-318F19, 56mm, Bosley, Cheshire (1700-1900)
A look at a cart-horse harness will show just how many brass decorations, like this one, were used. As well as caring for horses, the groom had a lot of polishing to do. While similar mounts were used on horse harness recent finds suggest that this object was fitted to the cover of a Medieval book.

HARNESS PENDANTS

Large numbers of horse harness pendants have been recorded, reflecting the status of the horse and horseman. Early examples are likely to have been charms worn for protection, but during the Middle Ages pendants were used to show status and political allegiances. Almost 5,300 harness pendants have been recorded by the PAS, most of which are Medieval, although a further 128 Roman pendants and 47 Early Medieval examples have also been logged. Finds are widespread discoveries for all periods.

NMGW-6368D1, 20mm, Llanasa, Flintshire (200 BC-AD 100)
These objects are known as danglers, a name which shows that their function is unknown. Their decoration shows them to be of Iron Age date.

WAW-0E5358, 48mm, Bickmarsh, Worcestershire (AD 200-300)
Roman harness pendant, probably military in nature. Its terminal is in the form of a phallus, which the Romans considered a symbol of virility and strength, as well as protection against the evil eye.

303

HORSES AND TRANSPORT

Medieval knight on armoured horse in all its finery, as dressed for tournament or battle. (Image: Michael Lewis)

HORSES AND TRANSPORT

LON-3C1941, 38mm, Southfleet, Kent (AD 50-150)
Roman military harness pendant of early type decorated with tinning and with black niello inlay.

SF-BC1C94, 45mm, Waldringfield, Suffolk (AD 50-150)
Roman harness pendant decorated with vine leaves and phalli, designed to ward off the evil-eye.

BERK-DCEB17, 27mm, Warborough, Oxfordshire (AD 50-200)
The crescent was a popular motif on Roman harness mounts perhaps representing the goddess Diana.

SF-552FD2, 28mm, Alderton, Suffolk (500-570)
The decoration on this finely gilded Anglo-Saxon harness pendant consists of two, back to back, animals. Their feet can be seen near the outer edge.

LIN-D365D2, 34mm, Sleaford, Lincolnshire (600-670)
Anglo-Saxon harness pendant, gilded with garnet inlay surrounded by interlace. On either side of the object can be seen the eye and curved beak of a stylised eagle.

PUBLIC-1FCD40, 48mm, Skidbrooke, Lincolnshire (1025-1100)
On first sight this object appears to have a plain openwork design, but a closer look shows the design to consist of the side views of two animals, facing each other and joined, on the centre line, by their tails, legs and jaws.

HORSES AND TRANSPORT

WILT-7E6C35, 47mm, Netherhampton, Wiltshire (1200-1400)
The quatrefoil is a common form for Medieval harness pendants, this example bears a cross embellished with five roses. Originally the recessed area would have been enamelled; some of the red colouring survives.

SWYOR-DA7B83, 47mm, Rathmell, North Yorkshire (1200-1500)
Medieval zoomorphic pendant, in the form of a displayed bird, probably an eagle. It is likely to be for a harness, but could also have been used on a livery collar.

LVPL-52542B, 44mm, Headon cum Upton, Nottinghamshire (1250-1400)
Medieval harness pendant formed of two parts consisting of a sexfoil frame containing a swivelling pendant. The central design is enamelled in red and blue and, while unclear, appears to depict a plant.

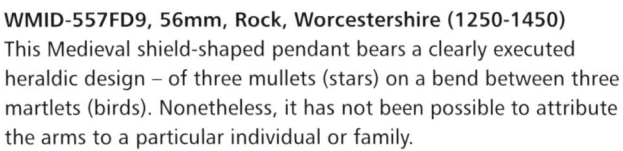

WMID-557FD9, 56mm, Rock, Worcestershire (1250-1450)
This Medieval shield-shaped pendant bears a clearly executed heraldic design – of three mullets (stars) on a bend between three martlets (birds). Nonetheless, it has not been possible to attribute the arms to a particular individual or family.

KENT-D7CCF3, 43mm, Hastingleigh, Kent (1300-50)
Medieval 'banner' harness pendants have a hollow tube so they could pivot from a mount. This example has an elaborate peacock on both sides in blue, red and white enamel.

HORSES AND TRANSPORT

BH-3FF1E6, 42mm, Melbourn, Cambridgeshire (1321-77)
This lozenge harness pendant has a complicated array of arms, combining, almost certainly, those of Aylmer de Valence, 2nd Earl of Pembroke and Montgomery with those of Marie de St Pol, his wife. The arms are borne by Pembroke College, Cambridge, which Marie founded in 1347.

YORYM-F1D245, 55mm, Yapham, East Yorkshire (1500-1800)
Not of heraldic type, the form of this Post Medieval harness pendant is reminiscent of the rowels on spurs, which might have been the inspiration for its design.

IOW-C7DA88, 32mm, Havenstreet and Ashey, Isle of Wight (1800-1900)
This highly elaborate harness mount is of recent date. It is decorated with deer suggesting that it once embellished the harness of a horse used in the chase.

VEHICLE FITTINGS, TERRETS AND LINCH PINS

Of the many vehicles made, and used, in the past, all that survives are their metal fittings; their wooden and leather parts usually long gone. Terrets, of which the PAS has recorded over 1,000, were metal rings through which the reins controlling carriage horses were guided; most of them are dated to the Iron Age and Roman periods. Linch pins were inserted into the ends of a vehicle axle to hold the wheels in place, and over 100 of them have been recorded by the PAS.

YORYM-E60DC4, 51mm, Coniston Cold, North Yorkshire (100 BC-AD 100)
Plain terret ring of Iron Age or early Roman date. These were mounted on the wooden shaft, between the horses, and acted as a guide for the reins.

HORSES AND TRANSPORT

SWYOR-884DAA, 66mm, Lindrick with Studley Royal and Fountains, North Yorkshire (1-150)
A more elaborate terret ring. At one time these were described as 'chariot fittings' but we are now more cautious and use the less exciting, but safer term, 'vehicle fittings'.

WILT-E46DB7, 93mm, East Knoyle, Wiltshire (300 BC-AD 100)
This magnificent and elaborate Iron Age terret must have been used on a vehicle of some quality, dare we say chariot?

HORSES AND TRANSPORT

NMS-D36060, 62mm, Suffield, Norfolk (100 BC-AD 100)
Lipped terrets, like this, are a common Iron Age type. Terrets, and other Iron Age vehicle fittings, are found throughout England but are most common in the eastern counties from East Anglia up into North Yorkshire.

NMS-6599B4, 67mm, Sporle with Palgrave, Norfolk (100 BC-AD 100)
This terret, with its Celtic decoration and enamel inlay, dates to around the Roman conquest and could be either Iron Age or Roman.

YORYM-363195, 24mm, Welton, East Yorkshire (200 BC-AD 100)
This tiny object looks like a terret, but has a D-shaped (rather than round) section. In the East Yorkshire Iron Age chariot graves they are found associated with linch pins, suggesting that they were not terrets but instead helped secure the wheels, perhaps on straps over the linch pins.

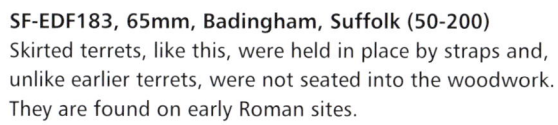

SF-EDF183, 65mm, Badingham, Suffolk (50-200)
Skirted terrets, like this, were held in place by straps and, unlike earlier terrets, were not seated into the woodwork. They are found on early Roman sites.

HORSES AND TRANSPORT

GLO-B172CF, 87mm, Stretton Grandison, Herefordshire (50-200)
Very fine skirted Roman terret, its style and decoration quite unlike that seen on Iron Age examples. Wear within the loop shows the action of the reins.

HAMP-E88954, 46mm, West Ilsley, Berkshire (50-100)
While this eagle-headed mount may have been a vehicle fitting, it could have been used on a piece of furniture.

LIN-CB11E5, 31mm, near Sleaford, Lincolnshire (100 BC-AD100)
Head from an Iron Age linch pin with red enamel inlay and retaining traces of its iron pin.

HORSES AND TRANSPORT

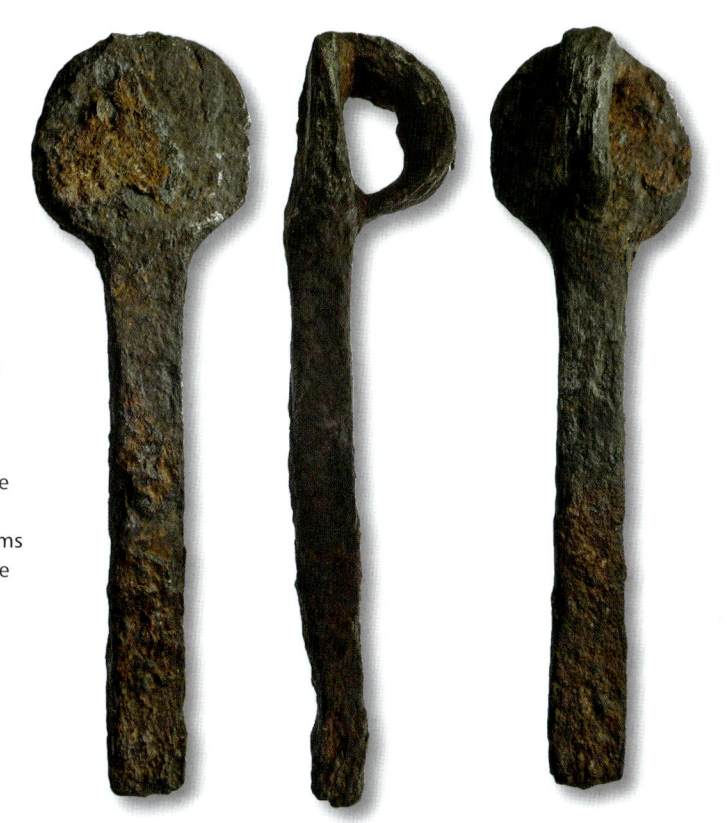

NMS-F36EDA, 142mm, Wymondham, Norfolk (100 BC-AD 100)
Fine linch pin combining an iron pin with copper-alloy terminals and enamel inlay. The punched background decoration is in Celtic style.

SUR-9319F4, 152mm, Crowthorne, Berkshire (50-400)
Plain iron linch pin of Roman date. While the finer linch pins may have been associated with chariots, this object seems more likely to have come from a farm cart.

Chapter 11
Warfare and Hunting

Two of the less desirable aspects of human society are warfare and hunting, but both continue to fascinate. Battle and the hunt had important social and ritual aspects and were a necessity for most cultures. Warriors needed to impress their friends, intimidate their foes and boost their own skills and confidence. History has seen a constant arms-race; warriors needed up-to-date weapons and changes in their form and style allows us to date them. Hunting was, for many millennia, a matter of survival and failure to make kills meant starvation. However, the hunt retained its allure even after food supplies became secure and was an important social symbol. It is ironic that weapons, designed to destroy, have survived in such large numbers. The practice of ritual deposition of weapons was long established and continued over time. Perhaps this is why so many weapons survive, often showing the highest levels of skill and craftsmanship.

SPEARHEADS

The spear was a ubiquitous weapon through most of the past, with more than 1,000 of them on the PAS database. It is an effective weapon, allowing an attack to be made while keeping the opponent at a distance. It can be difficult to tell the difference between spears (that were held) and javelins (that were intended to

Display formed an important part of warfare, boosting morale and intimidating enemies. These re-enactors show the magnificent way in which 7th century aristocratic warriors were arrayed. (Image: Paul Mortimer)

WARFARE AND HUNTING

be thrown); we cannot assume that all small weapons were javelins. Spearheads are well represented in some periods, such as the Bronze Age, from which the metal survives well, and the Early Anglo-Saxon period, where they were commonly placed in graves of free men – slaves not being allowed spears. The PAS has recorded 820 Bronze Age spears, reflecting the survival properties of bronze and the way in which they were deposited. The second largest group are Anglo-Saxon spears, with 96 finds, of which most came from ploughed-out graves.

SF-0BE51F, 197mm, West Stow, Suffolk (40,000-36,000 BC)
Magnificent early Upper Palaeolithic flint point, perhaps a spearhead. While in this work we have tried to avoid complex terminology it is impossible to resist saying that this implement belongs to the impressively named Lincombian-Ranisian-Jerzmanowician (LRJ) techno-complex!

NMGW-0BF252, 229mm, Penllyn, Vale of Glamorgan (1700-1500 BC)
Early Bronze Age spearheads were fitted with tangs, not sockets, with a rivet driven through the spear shaft to hold it in place.

WARFARE AND HUNTING

CAM-D2EF15, 126mm, Holywell cum Needingworth area, Cambridgeshire (2000-1550 BC)
Early form of socketed spearhead fitted with side loops, but with a blade still reflecting its tanged predecessor.

WILT-B7296D, 139mm, Grafton, Oxfordshire (1500-1150 BC)
The two loops set either side of the socket to secure the spearhead to its shaft are typical of British Middle Bronze Age spearheads.

SUR-49AF85, 203mm, Ufton Nervet, Berkshire (1100-900 BC)
A fine Late Bronze Age spearhead with lunate openings in its blade. Like many other Bronze Age weapons this spearhead was found near a river suggesting that it was a ritual deposit.

DENO-F70BF6, 172mm, Rufford, Nottinghamshire (1100-800 BC)
Later Bronze Age spearheads are typified by peg holes, used to secure them to their wooden shafts, rather than the side loops used on earlier weapons.

WARFARE AND HUNTING

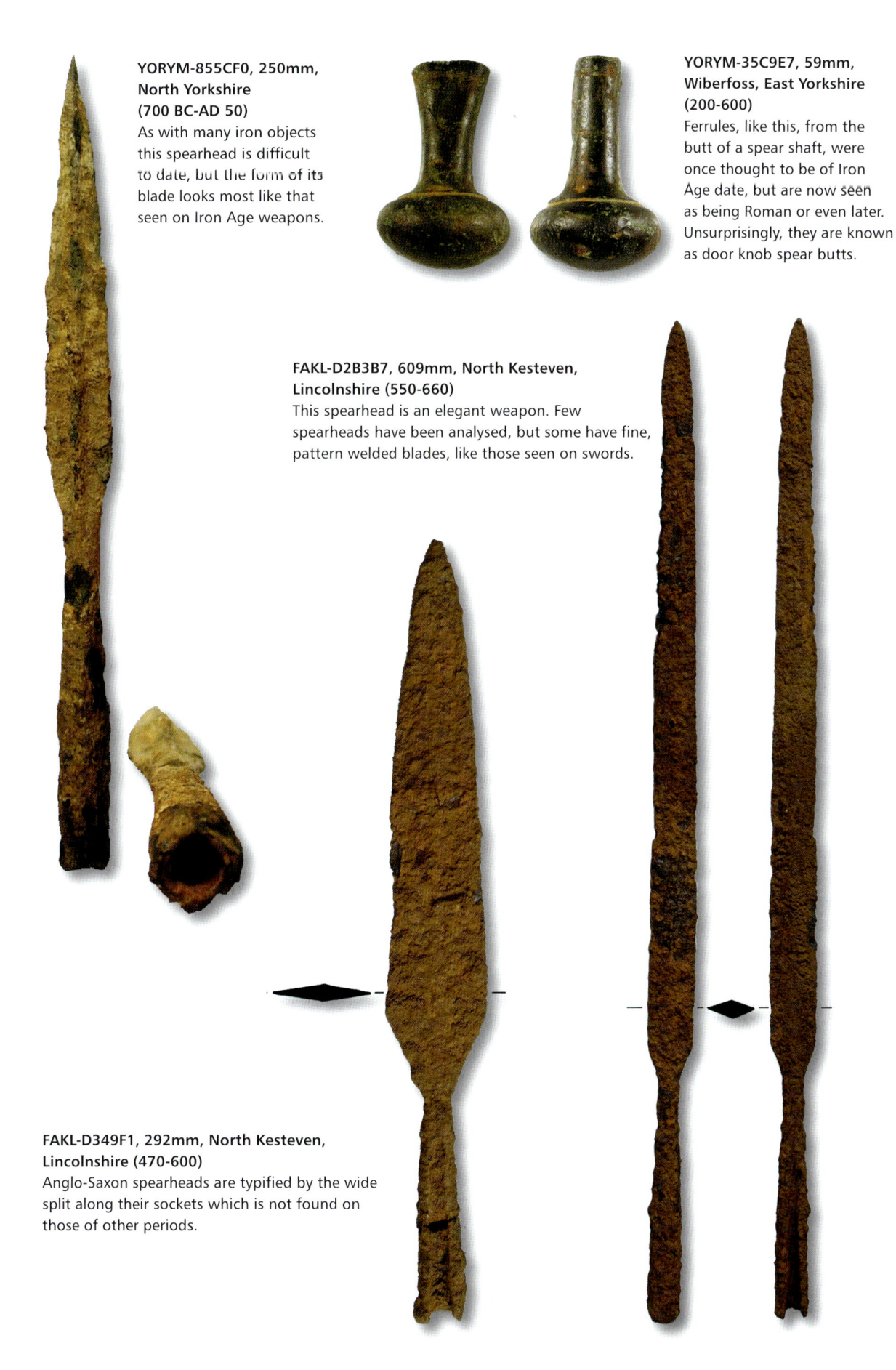

YORYM-855CF0, 250mm, North Yorkshire (700 BC-AD 50)
As with many iron objects this spearhead is difficult to date, but the form of its blade looks most like that seen on Iron Age weapons.

YORYM-35C9E7, 59mm, Wiberfoss, East Yorkshire (200-600)
Ferrules, like this, from the butt of a spear shaft, were once thought to be of Iron Age date, but are now seen as being Roman or even later. Unsurprisingly, they are known as door knob spear butts.

FAKL-D2B3B7, 609mm, North Kesteven, Lincolnshire (550-660)
This spearhead is an elegant weapon. Few spearheads have been analysed, but some have fine, pattern welded blades, like those seen on swords.

FAKL-D349F1, 292mm, North Kesteven, Lincolnshire (470-600)
Anglo-Saxon spearheads are typified by the wide split along their sockets which is not found on those of other periods.

WARFARE AND HUNTING

LON-920814, 413mm, Hammersmith and Fulham, London (800-900)
Spearhead of Middle Anglo-Saxon type. As they were not placed in graves these are far less common than the early weapons.

LON-7B7537, 174mm, City of London (1300-1500)
Part of the wooden shaft is preserved within this Medieval iron spearhead. It was probably fitted to a long pike rather than a spear. This, and the many other finds from London, reflect the activities of the 'mud-larks' who search the bed of the Thames at low tide.

LON-0A640E, 126mm, Tower Hamlets, London (1500-1700)
This post Medieval spearhead is noteworthy for its small, rounded lozenge point. Projecting from its socket are strips, known as langets, one of which has a nail to secure it to a wooden shaft. Spears remained in use in the British Army into the 19th century when 'half-pikes' were carried by sergeants as a mark of rank.

HESH-1A7B44, 209mm, Leintwardine, Herefordshire (1600-1800)
Multi-pronged spears were used for catching freshwater fish such as eels. This object was made from a single sheet of iron.

WARFARE AND HUNTING

LON-5193AA, 196mm, Tower Hamlets, London (1500-1700)
The triangular cross section of this iron weapon shows it to be a pike-head. The airless river muds have left It remarkably well preserved.

ARROWHEADS

The bow represented a technological breakthrough, making it possible to kill at a distance. While bows rarely survive, the flint or metal heads from arrows are relatively common finds, their shapes allowing them to be assigned to periods of history with some certainty. Oddly, we have no evidence for the use of the bow in the Iron Age, during which the sling appears to have been the common projectile weapon. The PAS has recorded over 1,900 arrowheads of which more than 1,600 were made from flint.

DENO-8C977B, 69mm, Tetford area, Lincolnshire (11,000-8,300 BC)
Dating from the end of the last Ice Age, this arrowhead was used by hunters moving across a tundra landscape. Flaking down its two sides produced shoulders, which would have helped fix it in an arrow shaft. A sharp point was made by abrupt flaking across one end.

WARFARE AND HUNTING

LON-CBB3E8, 293mm, Greenwich, London (1650-80)
The flints we see are only a small part of what was being made and used during the Stone Age. This find from the Thames was thought to be a Mesolithic harpoon head made of bone, which only survives in waterlogged conditions like the Thames foreshore. However, analysis showed it to be Post Medieval showing the use of a similar material and technology in two widely different periods of the past.

IOW-E18C53, 32mm, Brighstone, Isle of Wight (9000-8000 BC)
Early Mesolithic, obliquely blunted, flint point. The careful flaking used to form this arrowhead can be clearly seen.

YORYM-476B94, 24mm, Wykeham, North Yorkshire (8000-4000 BC)
The later Mesolithic period saw extensive use of tiny microliths made in geometric shapes. They were mounted in wood or bone to form sharp points and edges.

SOM-8D9385, 22mm, Bishop's Lydeard, Somerset (8000-4000 BC)
Not all Stone Age implements were made from flint. This microlith was made using chert, a coarser material.

BH-82314E, 27mm, Redbourn, Hertfordshire (4000-3300 BC)
Leaf-shaped arrowheads were typical of the Neolithic period. There has been some dispute as to when they went out of use, some seeing them being produced into the Bronze Age. The PAS has recorded 200 specimens.

WILT-843076, 43mm, Chiseldon, Wiltshire (4000-3300 BC)
Many Neolithic, leaf-shaped, flint arrowheads are of gem-like quality. Examples found embedded in human skeletons show them to have been highly effective.

SF-A53A82, 48mm, Mildenhall, Suffolk (3300-2300 BC)
Chisel-ended arrowheads were used during the Late Neolithic period. It is possible that they were designed for maximum stopping, rather than killing, power. The intention was to immobilise the prey to stop it escaping.

WARFARE AND HUNTING

IOW-9EDE55, 26mm, Brighstone, Isle of Wight (3300-2300 BC)
Hollow-based arrowhead, one of the many variants in use during the Late Neolithic period.

SF-F4C324, 36mm, Brandon, Suffolk (3300-2300 BC)
The length of the barb on this flint arrowhead exceeds any practical need and looks like an exercise in artistry.

SWYOR-14538A, 23mm, Kettlewell with Starbotton, North Yorkshire (2400-1600 BC)
Barbed-and-tanged arrowheads were introduced into Britain around 2400 BC along with Beaker pottery and metal working. There are almost 300 of them on the PAS database.

LEIC-9CCE27, 49mm, Eaton, Leicestershire (2000-1600 BC)
This large barbed and tanged flint arrowhead appears to be a more developed type than the smaller example also shown.

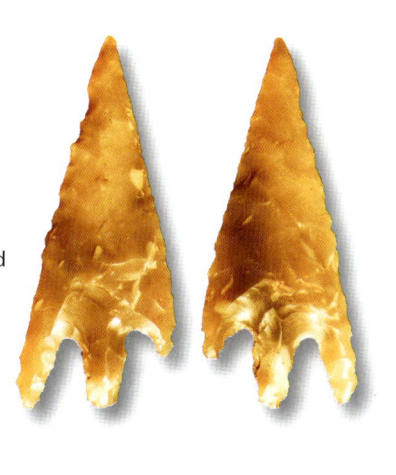

WILT-807272, 42mm, Salisbury, Wiltshire (1275-1140 BC)
At one time Bronze Age metal arrowheads were almost unknown in Britain, but they are now starting to be found; 34 of them are recorded on the PAS database.

SF-5A266B, 67mm, Mildenhall, Suffolk (1200-1400)
Barbed and tanged iron arrowheads, like this one, were used during the Medieval period. Almost 150 Medieval arrowheads have been recorded by the PAS.

NCL-D53584, 77mm, Rochester, Northumberland (AD 50-400)
Fired from a large Roman crossbow, darts tipped with heads like this were effective at long range.

BM-CAB596, 40mm, Piercebridge, County Durham (AD 50-400)
Three-edged iron arrowhead, of a type associated with the Roman army.

319

WARFARE AND HUNTING

LON-94A1F4, 41mm, City of London (1400-1500)
Crossbow bolts, or quarrels as they are also known, are of an easily recognisable form.

LON-CEFFCD, 48mm, City of London (1200-1500)
Arrowheads that retain part of their wooden shaft are always of interest. This type of military arrow, often known as a short bodkin, would have been particularly lethal against fighting-men not wearing armour.

GAT-79B088, 96mm, Llaneilian, Isle of Anglesey (1300-1500)
This iron arrowhead is especially well preserved, given it was found in the grassland of North Wales. Iron arrowheads were a lot more common than finds of them would suggest.

DAGGERS AND DIRKS

Used in combination with the spear, a dagger was a highly effective weapon. However, improvements in casting techniques allowed it to be superseded, first by the bronze rapier, then by the sword. The first examples of daggers appear in the Early Bronze Age. Daggers reappeared in the early Iron Age, perhaps due to the weakness of iron; long swords only becoming effective with the use of steel blades. It is often difficult to distinguish between daggers (weapons) and knives (tools), and it is likely that knives would be used offensively in time of need. The PAS has recorded over 850 daggers and 40 dirks, the latter term being used for Bronze Age weapons. Of the daggers, 90 are Bronze Age, over 500 Medieval and over 200 Post Medieval.

CORN-726021, 159mm, Sudbury, Suffolk (2700-1700 BC)
Some of the finest examples of flint working post-date the introduction of metal. This superb flint dagger is carefully flaked on both faces and a beautifully symmetrical object with a thickness of only 4mm.

WARFARE AND HUNTING

LVPL-55F121, 153mm Nercwys, Flintshire (1600-1350 BC)
This dagger or dirk dates from the end of the Early Bronze Age or the start of the Middle Bronze Age. The two large rivets originally held it in a wooden or bone hilt.

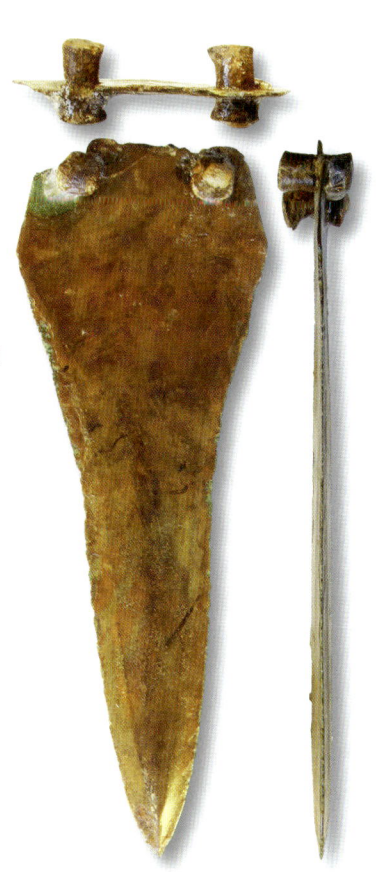

DENO-B364C6, 53mm, Clipston, Nottinghamshire (300 BC-AD 100)
This object was the lower part of an Iron Age dagger hilt. Originally, an iron blade extended down from between the two horizontal arms, and above it is the remains of the iron hilt. It is noteworthy for its Celtic style decoration. The hilt's missing upper part was an inverted version of what survives, giving it an anthropoid (human-like) form.

WMID-93EFC8, 39mm, Thorpe, Staffordshire (50-400)
The copper-alloy fittings from weapons often survive when the iron blades have gone. This object was one of a pair of fittings from which a Roman soldier suspended his dagger.

YORYM-160156, 74mm, Newbald, East Yorkshire (1200-1400)
The 'quillon dagger' got its name from the quillon, a cross guard that protected the hand. These daggers usually had double edged blades and they were purely weapons. They were most popular in the 13th and 14th centuries.

LANCUM-DC7805, 46mm, Galgate, Lancashire (1400-1600)
A more complex guard from a quillon dagger. Extra guards further protected the hand; some quillon guards were curved to prevent an opponent's blade slipping onto the user's arm.

PUBLIC-8C243F, 17mm, Fletching, East Sussex (1200-1500)
Often simple in form, but of essential function, the role of the pommel was to counterbalance the weight of the blade, helping to secure the weapon in the hand.

WARFARE AND HUNTING

BUC-75E9BD, 370mm, Waddesdon, Buckinghamshire (1400-1500)
This dagger, with its ornate copper-alloy hilt terminating in an expanding flower-like terminal, is an impressive survivor. Although corroded and fragile, part of its iron blade remains.

GLO-93A176, 278mm, Brockworth, Gloucestershire (1400-1550)
Late Medieval 'rondel' dagger. These are named from their disc-shaped pommels and guards. This dagger is double edged; others had thick-backed, triangular blades or simple spikes. Rondel daggers are purely weapons.

LIN-BF66F2, 44mm, Welton, Lincolnshire (1600-1800)
The scene on this possible dagger handle is not certain, but appears to show a man in Tudor dress accompanied by other figures. It is suggested they could be dancing.

WARFARE AND HUNTING

RAPIERS

The rapier was a stabbing weapon. The way in which the hilt was attached to the blade meant that an attempt to slash would cause it to break off; in battle, a controlled stabbing action is far more deadly than slashing. Combat with these rapiers would have resembled modern fencing.

Almost 180 rapiers have been recorded by the PAS, 170 of which are Bronze Age with a strong concentration of them in central Norfolk.

HESH-4CD185, 285mm, River Alyn, Wrexham (1500-1150 BC)
The hilt of this rapier was secured by the two large rivets leading to the weakness common to these weapons.

SWYOR-7A4C37, 345mm, Hackforth, North Yorkshire (1300-1140 BC)
On this Bronze Age rapier the rivets are set either side of the hilt ruling out any slashing action.

NLM-A23E77, 116mm, Barnoldby le Beck, North East Lincolnshire (1550-1650)
The square aperture for the tang on this hilt-guard suggests the blade was that of a Post Medieval rapier, rather than the wider blade of a sword or dagger.

WARFARE AND HUNTING

HAMP-6B8E64, 44mm, Itchen Valley, Hampshire (1600-1700)
In relief around the outside of this pommel cap is a series of figures executed in neo-classical style. A hole in its side would have held a curved guard.

DEV-D44F21, 95mm, Alwington, Devon (1690-1715)
Silver guard bar from a small sword decorated with what look like cherubs' heads. The guard has a maker's mark, reading either VC or WC.

DUR-1B4737, 61mm, near Edlingham, Northumberland (1600-1800)
Both sides of the hilt of this early Modern rapier or 'small sword' are decorated with the figure of a warrior, standing with spear and shield. While 'small swords' mark the end of the sword as a civilian weapon they were formidable in the hand of a master.

NARC-866487, 360mm, Grendon, Northamptonshire (1700-1760)
In the late 17th century 'small swords', such as this, replaced the rapier. Whilst the iron parts of this weapon are corroded, it still retains all its copper-alloy fittings, showing how the object fitted together.

WARFARE AND HUNTING

SWORDS

The sword was a weapon of status, being both expensive and requiring skill and training in its use. Its introduction may have been due to the use of the horse in warfare as fighting from a vehicle (an aristocratic practice) required greater reach. From the earliest times swords have been thrown into bogs and rivers as offerings, and these have been found and recorded with the PAS. We know that in the Early Medieval period, swords were given names and could be treasured heirlooms, but even so could be stripped for their precious metal fittings, as in the case of the swords found as part of the Anglo-Saxon Staffordshire Hoard. In later times, although the sword lacked the rapid killing power of other Post Medieval edged weapons, such as the rapier, it still would have been useful in a melee. There are over 1,200 swords on the PAS database, of which just over 500 are Early Medieval. This total is, however, distorted by the Staffordshire Hoard from which over 300 items are recorded on the PAS database. The numbers of finds are otherwise unsurprising: 244 Bronze Age, 241 Medieval and 166 Post Medieval examples. It must, however, be remembered that many of these records relate to sword parts and fittings, not complete objects.

NLM-F5AEB0, 522mm, Brigg, North Lincolnshire (950-800 BC)
The two rings were found with this sword and are likely to have come from a baldric. Like many weapons, this sword was damaged before it was deposited next to a spring, suggesting a ritual practice.

SUSS-761CD0, 84mm, near Lewes, Sussex (1150-800 BC)
This sword hilt is of Continental type and will have been imported into Britain. While it may have arrived into Britain with a warrior it could have also been imported as scrap metal which is known from the discovery of Bronze Age ship wrecks.

WARFARE AND HUNTING

LVPL759, 254mm, Quernmore, Lancashire (1150-1000 BC)
Originally the hilt of this Bronze Age sword would have been covered with wood or bone plate, riveted through the holes.

SOM-088DFF, 33mm, Ruishton, Somerset (150-1 BC)
Pommel cap probably from a late Iron Age anthropoid sword. On these, the head is placed at the top of the hilt with projections on the upper and lower guards representing arms and legs.

NMS-C4D772, 52mm, Attleborough, Norfolk (100 BC-AD 100)
Hilt guard from an Iron Age sword, the graceful curve being typical.

BUC-FA09D7, 18mm, Newton Bromswold, Northamptonshire (470-670)
Ring from the hilt of an Anglo-Saxon sword. These have been found attached to sword hilts and probably had a symbolic meaning.

HAMP-6B4136, 43mm, Bishops Sutton, Hampshire (410-720)
Anglo-Saxon cocked-hat type pommel cap. These were fixed over the hilt's upper guard to cover the riveted end of the blade's tang.

WARFARE AND HUNTING

BH-B72FCB, 15mm, Crowmarsh, Oxfordshire (550-650)
Chip-carved Early Medieval sword pyramid. These objects are pyramid-shaped with a bar across their hollow undersides. At Sutton Hoo they were found either side of the sword and it is thought that they were attached to straps securing the weapon in its scabbard.

BUC-87B54A, 13mm, Upton Grey, Hampshire (600-650)
Anglo-Saxon copper-alloy sword pyramid covered with gold filigree. This is decorated with zoomorphic interlace with two intertwined snakes on the right-hand panel and an animal on the panel to the left. The centre of the apex is inlaid with a garnet set on waffle-patterned gold foil.

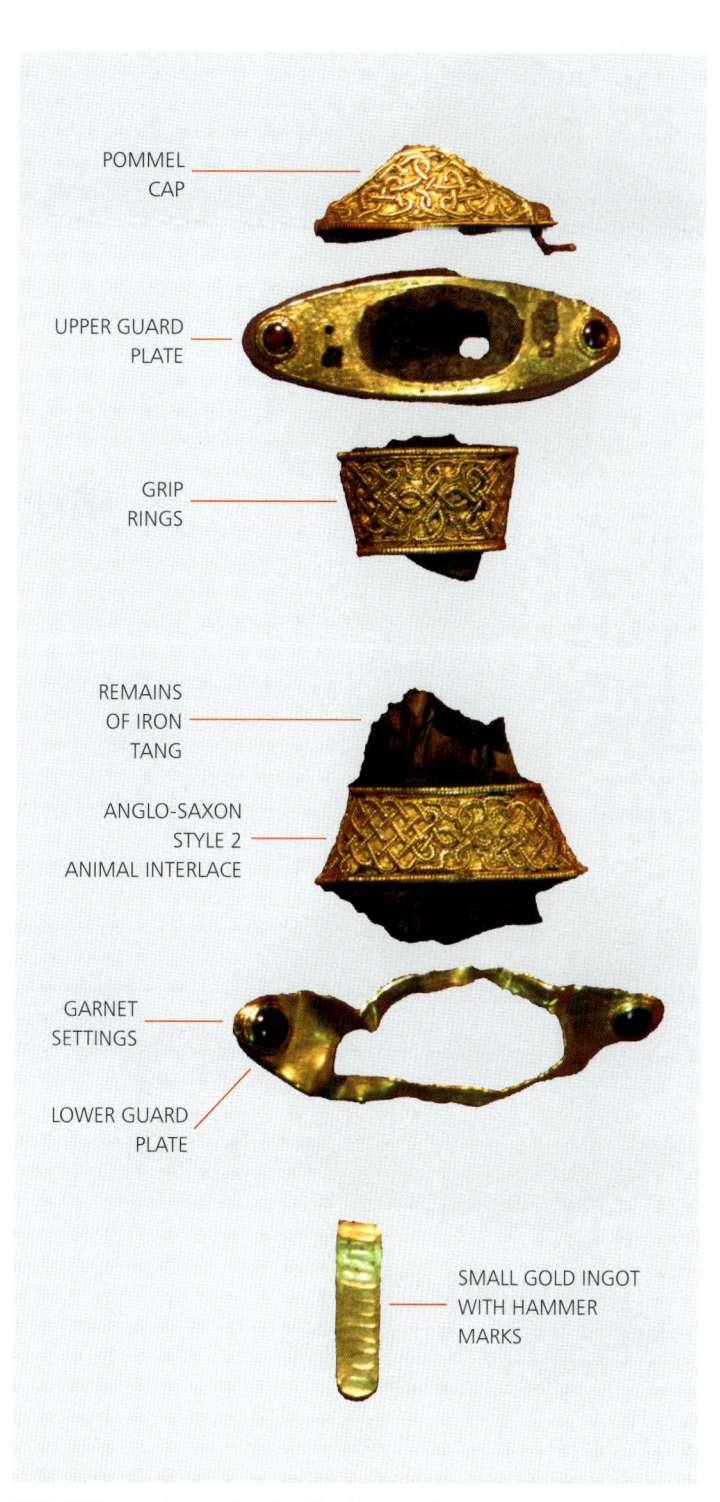

POMMEL CAP

UPPER GUARD PLATE

GRIP RINGS

REMAINS OF IRON TANG

ANGLO-SAXON STYLE 2 ANIMAL INTERLACE

GARNET SETTINGS

LOWER GUARD PLATE

SMALL GOLD INGOT WITH HAMMER MARKS

NLM6885, Scothern, Lincolnshire (600-650)
Gold fittings from an Early Medieval sword consisting of a pommel cap, parts of the upper and lower guard plates set with garnets, and two grip rings. Also found with the fittings was a small gold ingot with hammer marks, as often seen on ingots of this period. Decorated with zoomorphic filigree and garnets, these fittings represented an aristocratic weapon related to those found in the Staffordshire Hoard in 2009 but, unlike that find, this weapon appears to have been associated with an iron blade.

WARFARE AND HUNTING

LVPL-701468, 34mm, Mouldsworth, Cheshire (700-800)
Anglo-Saxon pommel cap decorated with the animals and interlace decoration typical of the 8th century. On each side, two animals gaze over their shoulders at each other and the surviving side-piece bears a beast's head.

ESS-D45534, 394mm, Colchester, Essex (800-900)
Viking iron sword found in mud dredged from the River Colne. Weapons of all periods are remarkably common finds in rivers. Many seem to have been ritually deposited, but this weapon could relate to the English recapture of Colchester from the Vikings in 917.

WMID-054E94, 52mm, Tong, Shropshire (900-1100)
Pommel cap from an Early Medieval sword, which originally fitted over the curved upper guard. This guard is of an English type also commonly used by the Vikings.

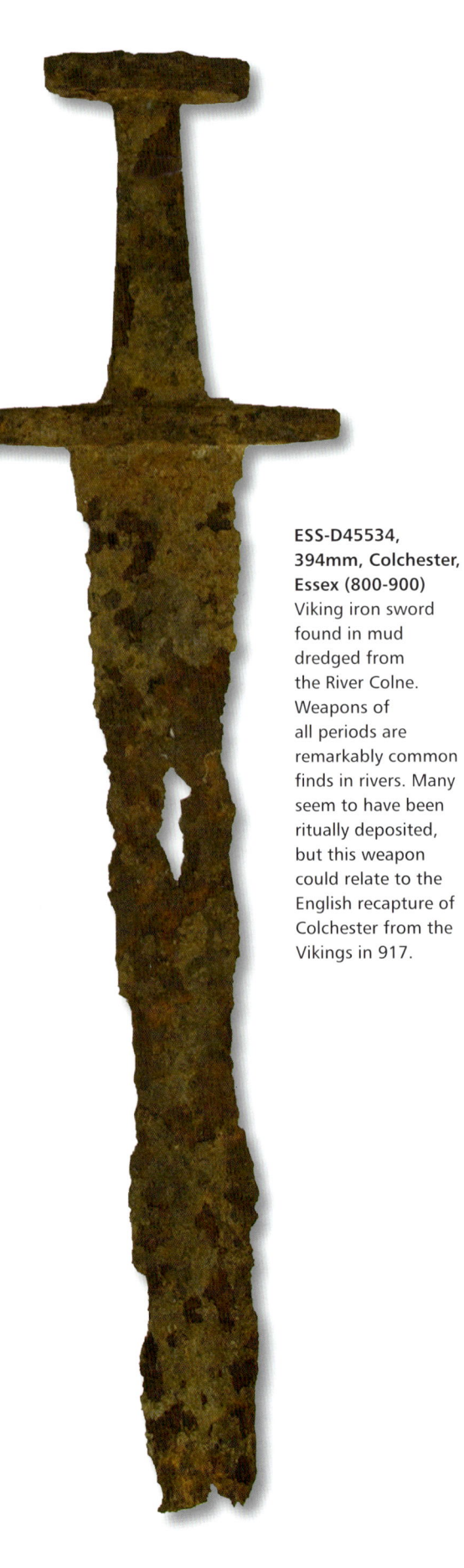

WARFARE AND HUNTING

SF-730C82, 59mm, Fressingfield, Suffolk (1200-1500)
This sword terminal is impressively crafted in the form of an eagle's head and probably served as a pommel.

NCL-DA9B37, 53mm, Hebron, Northumberland (1275-1475)
This simple, Medieval pommel has a lead core, to give it more weight.

KENT-D52E6B, 52mm, Brookland, Kent (1300-1400)
These are sometimes called wheel pommels. While not aristocratic, it has a pleasing elegance.

329

WARFARE AND HUNTING

IOW-551789, 133mm, Calbourne, Isle of Wight (1400-1600)
The downwards curving quillon (sword guard) is designed to protect the sword-hand and to foil the opponent's blade. This is a feature of 15th century swords.

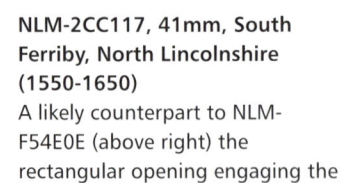

NLM-2CC117, 41mm, South Ferriby, North Lincolnshire (1550-1650)
A likely counterpart to NLM-F54E0E (above right) the rectangular opening engaging the T shaped bar. The sword probably hung from the ring.

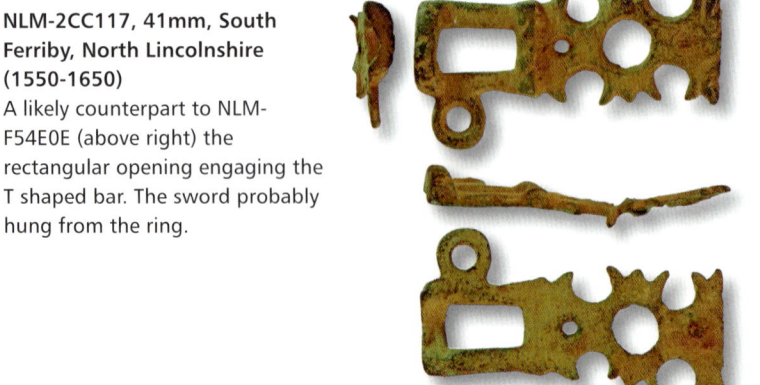

NLM-F54E0E, 45mm, South Ferriby, North Lincolnshire (1550-1650)
This complicated looking object is likely to be a sword belt fitting, the T shaped bar on the right hand side engaging in an aperture as seen on NLM-2CC117 (below left). A study of Post Medieval probate inventories in South Ferriby shows that most yeoman householders owned weapons, which was seen as an important part of their civic duties.

SUR-2FD5A4, 29mm, Cobham and Downside, Surrey (1400-1500)
A simple double looped fitting for a sword belt, the weapon being suspended from the small loop at the bottom.

NMS-C3D6AD, 72mm, Ickburgh, Norfolk (1550-1700)
The composite parts of this type of Post Medieval belt fitting are often found apart, so it is rare and informative to find them joined together.

330

WARFARE AND HUNTING

SF-1FD852, 369mm, Framlingham, Suffolk (1640-1750)
Basket hilt of a Civil War iron broad sword. Its form was designed to protect the sword-hand and was inspired by swords made in Scandinavia and Germany.

WARFARE AND HUNTING

CHAPES

The chape is the pouch-like fitting from the end of a scabbard used to protect the end of the blade and prevent accidental stabbings. As iron blades often fail to survive, the copper-alloy sword and scabbard fittings are usually all that are left. Some caution is needed when counting the numbers of chapes recorded with the PAS, as it is often difficult to tell the difference between sword scabbard and dagger chapes, and chapes from the ends of straps.

WILT-D4F151, 26mm, Rockbourne Hampshire (1000-800 BC)
Late Bronze Age purse-shaped chape, which was originally fixed to the end of wooden or leather scabbard.

CORN-AC1453, 55mm, Padstow, Cornwall (100 BC-AD 100)
This gracefully decorated Iron Age object is probably a 'locket'; the mount from the upper part of a scabbard.

GLO-7C86FA, 96mm, Hanham Abbots, Gloucestershire (1150-800 BC)
Part of a Late Bronze Age tongue-shaped scabbard chape which would have accommodated a broad, leaf-shaped blade.

HAMP-0219F8, 25mm, Ropley, Hampshire (800-400 BC)
This object is a characteristic 'anchor-shaped' chape from an Iron Age dagger scabbard. On earlier chapes the arms of the anchor are separated from the chape, but these evolve and on later examples the arms curve up to join the body of the chape as seen here.

NMS-CB328A 34mm, West Acre, Norfolk (120-300)
Finds from excavations suggest that this chape is of Roman date.

WARFARE AND HUNTING

HAMP-4CBF82, 39mm, Micheldever, Hampshire (400-600)
This chape is decorated with a human face and two eagles. It is of Frankish type and was probably imported from the Continent.

NMS-914554, 46mm, Quidenham, Norfolk (450-550)
This chape may be an Anglo-Saxon copy of a Frankish original.

SF-0E88A2, 29mm, Snetterton, Norfolk (1100-1200)
This Medieval chape is in the form of a highly simplified horse and rider based on the type from Cassington (shown to the right). This interpretation is supported by intermediate, less stylised, chapes.

BERK-2C6116, 33mm, Cassington, Oxfordshire (1100-1200)
Medieval scabbard chape in the form of horse and rider; the shield of the rider can be clearly seen.

IOW-DC61A8, 49mm, Calbourne, Isle of Wight (1450-1600)
All that survives of this Late Medieval or Post Medieval chape is the openwork front plate. Its central rib is noteworthy for its crenelated and grooved decoration.

WILT-0ECA02, 53mm, Ogbourne St George, Wiltshire (1450-1600)
This neat and simple chape still retains part of its thin, sheet metal back plate.

WARFARE AND HUNTING

WILT-D3A593, 50mm, Kington St Michael, Wiltshire (1400-1600)
The asymmetric, triangular form of this chape's front-plate is of interest. It appears to have been used on a single-edged weapon like a falchion.

WILT-5C0331, 36mm, Ogbourne St Andrew, Wiltshire (1450-1600)
Almost complete, except for part of its back-plate, this chape is formed like a scallop-shell, with an openwork heart and trefoil above. It may have come from a belt not from the scabbard for a weapon.

MACES

The mace was a simple, but highly effective, weapon, but one that was not necessarily better than a wooden cudgel. Prehistoric stone 'mace heads' have been recorded by the PAS but their interpretation as maces is open to question. Some examples, however, were finely made in naturally patterned stone and may have been weapons, or had a ceremonial role. A series of spiked, copper-alloy mace heads were at one time dated to the Bronze Age, but are now seen as Medieval; although their crudeness seems to fit into neither period. The PAS has recorded 44 objects that can be confidently described as mace heads. Of these, 38 are made from copper-alloy, and are Medieval, five are stone, and one is made of antler, all of Prehistoric date.

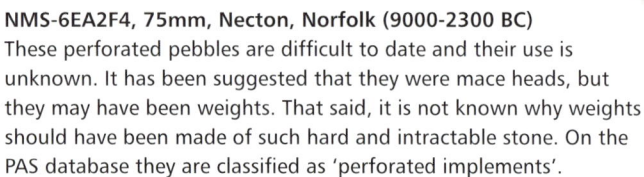

NMS-6EA2F4, 75mm, Necton, Norfolk (9000-2300 BC)
These perforated pebbles are difficult to date and their use is unknown. It has been suggested that they were mace heads, but they may have been weights. That said, it is not known why weights should have been made of such hard and intractable stone. On the PAS database they are classified as 'perforated implements'.

WARFARE AND HUNTING

LIN-871975, 58mm, Fiskerton, Lincolnshire (1100-1300)
Knobbed maceheads were once uncommon finds, but the PAS has now recorded 37 of them. They appear to have been based on a type that originated in Kiev and southern Russian cities, first spreading across Eastern Europe, and then further westwards. This example still contains part of its wooden shaft.

DUR-B9D6B8, 60mm, Lanchester area, County Durham (1250-1400)
It is not certain that this mace form, with knobs on a cylinder, is military; it could have served as a staff terminal instead (see page 103), but its crude form suggests a less sophisticated function.

BATTLEAXES

Any axe will form a highly effective weapon and it is not always possible to distinguish between tools and wargear; some tools are likely to have been used in warfare. In view of this problem, the PAS has recorded only four objects as battleaxes, all of which are stone and of Early Bronze Age date. The rest of them are included amongst the axeheads, though there are some axes for which a military use seems especially likely.

CORN-70CDC7, 110mm, Saxton with Scarthingwell, North Yorkshire (2100-1500 BC)
Battleaxe, made from polished stone. Objects like this are found in Early Bronze Age graves.

WARFARE AND HUNTING

SF-1D7E43, 171mm, Drinkstone, Suffolk (400-700)
The strange drooping blade on this axe shows it to be a *'francisca'*, an Early Medieval Frankish throwing axe, although similar axes are known from the Roman period.

BUC-B7ACE2, 260mm, Longwick area, Buckinghamshire (950-1100)
This lightly-made axe would have been unsuitable for woodworking but highly effective as a weapon. It is the sort of weapon wielded by the Vikings.

WARFARE AND HUNTING

SHIELDS

A shield formed a warrior's first line of defence, playing a vital role in combat with most blows being either dodged or caught on the shield. It is unlikely that the magnificent sheet metal shields that survive from the Bronze Age and Iron Age were intended for use in battle, as contemporary weapons would have easily penetrated them. They were probably used for display, with real shields being made from wood, leather or a combination of both. The practice of placing shields in graves resulted in there being a disproportionate number surviving from the Early Medieval period, but, in most cases, only their fittings remain. The PAS has recorded 70 shields, or to be more accurate, one shield and a number of fittings. Of these, the 42 Early Medieval fittings are probably from shields, but some of the others are more questionable.

SF-E0D9C8, 600mm, near Lakenheath, Suffolk (1300-975 BC)
Bronze Age shields, like this, would have been used for display, not protection. Bearing in mind that it was beaten from a single ingot of bronze, the size and thinness of the metal shows a remarkable level of skill.

WARFARE AND HUNTING

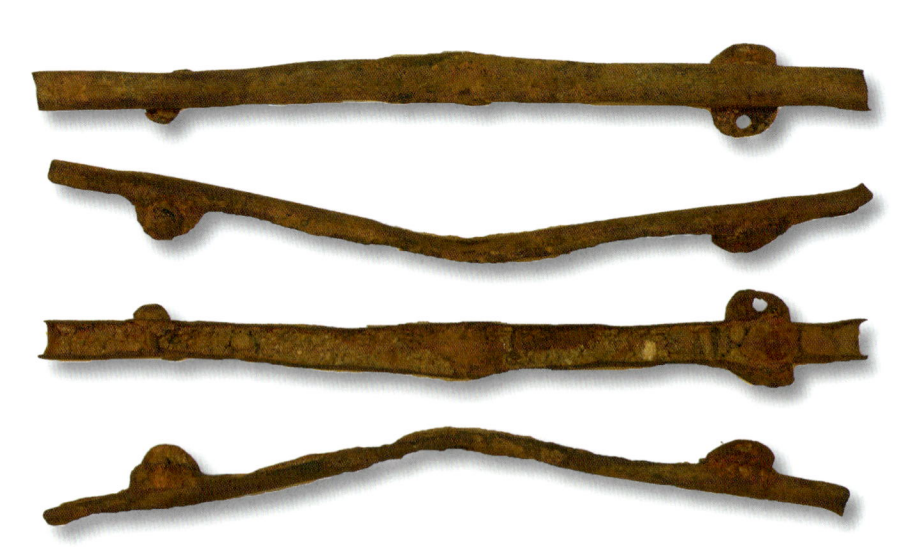

BM-015A2B, 115mm, Piercebridge, County Durham (50-200)
Sheet metal edging strip, probably from a Roman shield. The metal is bent around to form a channel and is fitted with attachment points. In the case of this find, the circumstances of discovery and its associations support it being from a Roman shield, but similar channelled strips have been used as an edging in recent times.

FAKL-92C831, 158mm, North Kesteven, Lincolnshire (470-550)
Now in two pieces, this iron strip formed the handle of an Anglo-Saxon shield. It would have been wrapped in leather and riveted to the shield's wooden board.

WARFARE AND HUNTING

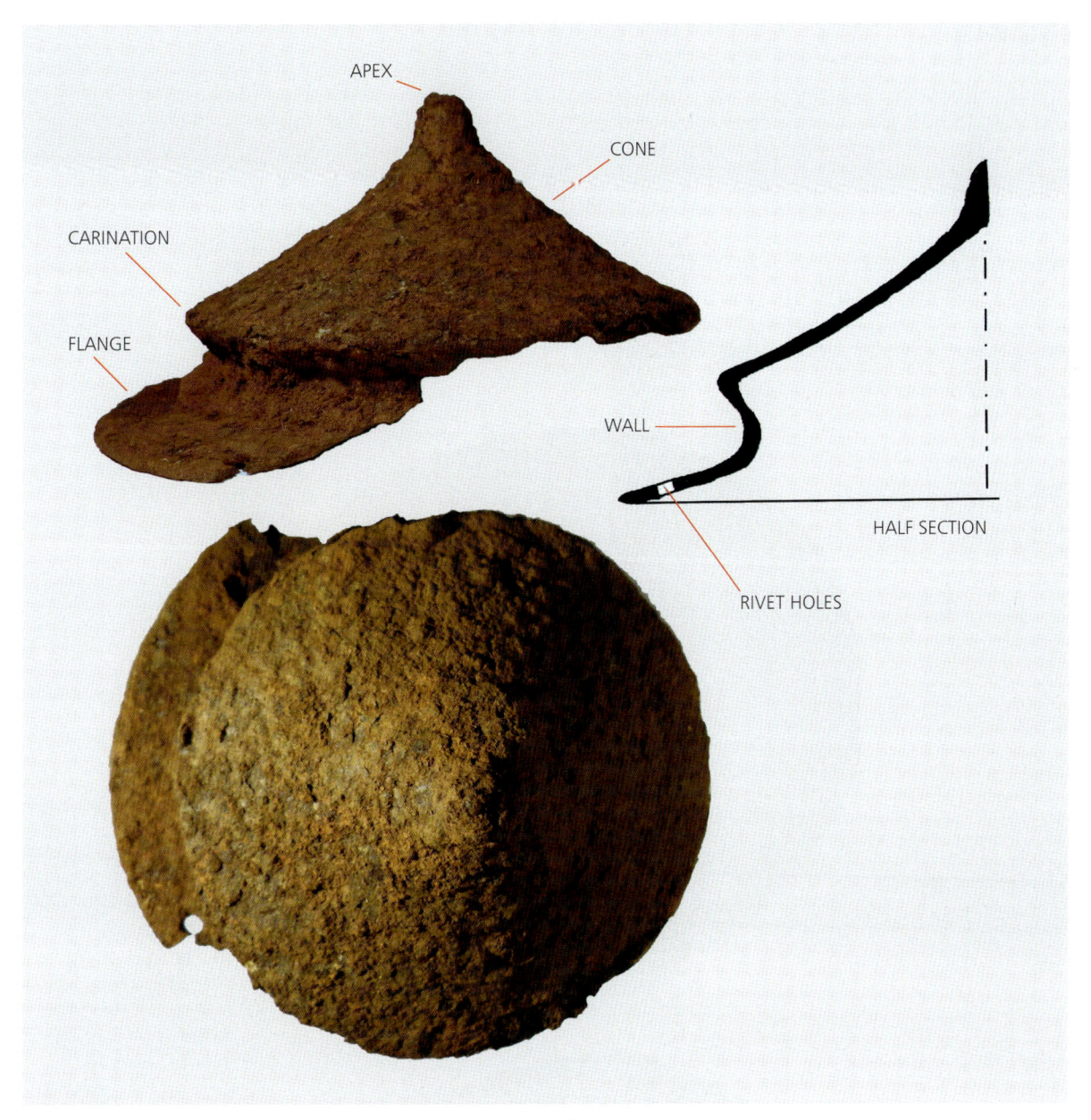

FAKL-929576, 117mm, North Kesteven, Lincolnshire (470-550)
The iron boss from an Anglo-Saxon shield. It would have been riveted into the centre of a wooden board. Early Medieval shield bosses were forged from a single piece of iron to avoid the difficulty of making hammer-welded joints.

NMS-E2B508, 112mm, Hindringham, Norfolk (550-600)
Decorative mount from an Anglo-Saxon shield; these mounts are usually in the form of fish and birds.

WARFARE AND HUNTING

HELMETS

In spite of the fact that a warrior's head was highly vulnerable, helmets are rare finds from the past. Some Iron Age helmets are known, and we also have fragments of Roman helmets, but Anglo-Saxon graves, many of which contain weapons, have only yielded three examples: Sutton Hoo, Suffolk, Benty Grange, Derbyshire and Wollaston, Northamptonshire. There are, however, many literary references to helmets from the Anglo-Saxon and Viking periods, perhaps they were used, but not placed in graves.

Many of the surviving Medieval helmets had been placed over monuments in churches. Most Post Medieval helmets appear to have been mass-produced munition issues, especially during the English Civil War. The PAS database contains 44 records of helmets of which 28 are parts of a helmet from the Anglo-Saxon Staffordshire Hoard. This is a startlingly low figure particularly as the database contains some 2,900 mentions of helmets on brooches, figurines, mounts and, most commonly, Roman coins.

KENT-FA8E56, 200mm, near Canterbury, Kent (50 BC-AD 50)
This late Iron Age helmet had been reused as an urn; when found it contained cremated human bones and a brooch. The projecting rim protected the wearer's neck, the brow protection being missing. It is unlikely that this helmet had cheek-pieces to guard the face.

WARFARE AND HUNTING

**NARC-771411, 104mm, Greens Norton, Northamptonshire
(70 BC-50 AD)**
While there is some doubt, this fragment might have been part of a helmet. It is 4.5mm thick, sufficient to provide some protection. One side is gilded, but corrosion on the other suggests that it had been attached to something organic; this could have been a helmet liner. The decoration allows it to be dated to the late Iron Age.

**SF-D21822, 27mm, Combs, Suffolk
(AD 43-100)**
This strange fitting has been identified as a plume holder from a Roman soldier's helmet.

**WMID-B2F679, 153mm, Penkridge, Staffordshire
(300 BC-AD 100)**
Cheek-piece from a helmet of late Iron Age or early Roman type. The parish where it was found contains the sites of two Roman forts, making it possible that this helmet is Roman.

**PAS-5D5B56, 40mm, Horncastle area, Lincolnshire
(600-650)**
Silver-gilt crest from an Anglo-Saxon helmet. Beowulf, the great Anglo-Saxon poem, makes constant reference to 'boar crested helmets' and it is likely this object came from one of them. The design, with emphasis being given to the head of the animal, with a small, compressed body, is ingenious.

WARFARE AND HUNTING

WILT-0BBFE7, 300mm, Durnford, Wiltshire (1630-1640)
Civil War helmets survive in museum collections, but are rare detector finds. This example, sometimes known as a lobster-pot helmet, was probably worn by a pikeman. It is likely to have been manufactured in the Netherlands.

WARFARE AND HUNTING

ARMOUR

Suits of armour do not appear amongst finds recorded by the PAS, but some fragments have been found that are of great interest. Mail appeared during the Iron Age, with examples being found in graves. Much use was made of both plate and mail armour by the Roman army and it is fortunate that Roman plate armour involved small, copper-alloy fittings that seem to have been regularly lost. No Early Medieval armour has been recorded by the PAS, although Late Anglo-Saxon wills and other literary sources make common reference to it. Mail armour continued to dominate until the 14th century when there was a move towards the use of plate armour, perhaps in face of the penetrating power of the war-bow. Armour was much used during the English Civil War (1642-51) but was not always useful; it would not stop a bullet, but could encumber the wearer when running away! There are almost 140 records of armour on the PAS database, of which 54 are Roman, 47 Medieval and 25 Post Medieval. In most cases the armour consists of a single plate from a piece of Roman scale armour and most of the Medieval armour is represented by rings from mail.

Replica Roman armour, of 1st-2nd century date. While the iron straps fail to survive, the copper-alloy buckles and fitting are represented amongst PAS finds. (Image: Kevin Leahy)

WARFARE AND HUNTING

CAM-F90F22, 32mm, Melbourn, Cambridgeshire (50-200)
Hinge from a Roman cuirass, still bearing traces of the iron strips to which it was riveted. A typical and highly recognisable find.

NCL-6F3E93, 36mm, Piercebridge, County Durham (50-400)
Sheet metal plate from Roman scale armour, the plates would have been linked by wires and fixed, in overlapping rows, to a leather jacket.

LON-BEA95E, 26mm, City of London (1350-1400)
This knuckle guard is from a Medieval gauntlet (plate mail glove). Its spike creates a menacing look.

LON-94B63C, 49mm, City of London (1500-1600)
Example of plate armour; many of these small iron rectangles would have been riveted together to create a complete garment.

LON-666316, 83mm, Wandsworth, London (1475-1525)
Finds of mail armour (not 'chain mail') are more common from the Thames foreshore than might be expected, but this is a rather splendid example, made of copper-alloy and iron riveted rings.

LANCUM-C40BC8, 28mm, Kendal, Cumbria (1550-1750)
Part of a breastplate of Japanese samurai armour of which the surviving three plates were laced together. Originally the metal would have been covered in lacquer. We cannot assume that everything found in Britain is from these shores; the PAS sees a constant stream of curios and relics of the British Empire.

WARFARE AND HUNTING

FIREARMS AND GUN RELATED FINDS

The first firearm known in England appears in an illustration dated to around 1300. Developments over the centuries that followed improved the effectiveness of guns, making firearms less dangerous for the gunners and more dangerous to the enemy. Few firearms have been recorded by the PAS and most of the 85 records on the database relate, not to guns, but to parts of them. Of these, 76 are of Post Medieval date and seven are modern. Over 230 cannon balls have been recorded, most of which are cast iron, which was introduced into England during the 1490s. Prior to this stone cannon balls were used. There are almost 3,000 lead musket balls on the database, but it is difficult to make sense of them; the examples of most interest are those found on known battlefields or skirmish sites and in this case (as with all archaeological finds) it is the exact location of the find that is important. If properly recorded, finds of musket and cannon balls can reveal the course of a battle or even tell us where an action took place.

In the 1540s Henry VIII ordered fortifications to be built to defend Hull and it is likely that they included this gun. It may have seen action in 1642 to defend the city against Royalist attack, but by 1681 it was obsolete and was abandoned, lying buried, until its discovery by archaeologists in 1997. The weapon was made from wrought iron and was stave built, long strips of iron being held together by rings like a barrel. It was a breech-loader, the gun powder and ball being rammed into the chamber (foreground) which was then wedged behind the barrel. The rings on the sides of the gun were used to secure it to a wooden carriage. The gun would have fired a 150mm diameter, 5.5kg stone ball around 500 metres.
(Image: Kevin Leahy)

WARFARE AND HUNTING

LON-8C8719, 133mm, City of London (1300-1500)
Stone cannonballs are unusual discoveries. This one was found by the Tower of London and might have been discarded without being used.

NARC-68D9C1, 142mm, Oundle, Northamptonshire (1820-40)
Much of this percussion pocket pistol survives. Before the advent of a regular police force, it was common for people to carry firearms such as this for protection.

YORYM-5379A7, 151mm, Kilham, East Yorkshire (1800-1900)
Ramrods, such as this, were used in firearms to ram the musket ball and wadding against the gunpowder.

WARFARE AND HUNTING

LANCUM-E69967, 95mm, Carlisle, Cumbria (1700-1800)
This fitting is from the underside of a firearm and held the ramrod when it was not in use.

FAKL-C33618, 91mm, Bentley, South Yorkshire (1700-1850)
This ramrod pipe was fitted nearer to the gun's muzzle; the perforated lugs, which held pins, are typical of the way that English guns were held together.

SWYOR-3B07BC, 12mm, Norton, South Yorkshire (1600-1800)
Musket balls are common finds. This example is, as is usually the case, made of lead; its neatly clipped casting seam can be seen.

BH-E474B0, 47mm, St Albans, Hertfordshire (1450-1700)
Cannon balls are hard to date, but this lead example was found close to the site of the second Battle of St Albans (1461).

WARFARE AND HUNTING

DENO-C478D9, 94mm, Barton Blount, Derbyshire (1600-1700)
The association of this iron cannon ball with a skirmish in the English Civil war helps date it. Caution is needed when recording cast iron cannon balls as many of them may have been used, not in guns, but in ball-mills for grinding pigments.

DEV-FC5606, 28mm, Buckland Tout Saints, Devon (1600-1700)
Post Medieval lead powder holder cap. A musketeer carried the charges for his gun in 12 wooden tubes, each covered by one of these lead caps. The PAS database contains over 530 powder holder caps – these are widespread finds, but finders should always consider whether their discoveries are centred around areas of conflict during the English Civil War. It is important to record them accurately as they can provide vital information on the course of a battle.

SUR-E8DF02, 39mm, Tichborne, Hampshire (1680-1780)
Grotesque butt plate from a flintlock pistol.

PUBLIC-429706, 36mm, Newnham, Worcestershire (1625-75)
This complete, but damaged, powder flask nozzle allowed the accurate pouring of a charge of gunpowder into the firearm.

SUR-955671, 48mm, Dorking, Surrey (1680-1820)
This Early Modern frog stud would have been used to attach a bayonet scabbard into a 'frog' – a leather loop on the soldier's belt.

WARFARE AND HUNTING

HUNTING AND HAWKING

The material described below relates to hunting, not primarily as a method of obtaining food, but as sport. Hunting often reflected the position of the landed gentry and aristocracy who hunted or flew falcons and their need to show their status. As with horse harness (see page 301) the animals and birds used in the chase bore ornaments reflecting their owner's place in society. Vervels or hawking rings were attached to the leather jesses that secured a hunting bird's legs to a leash which tied it to a perch or block. A vervel bore the owner's name or insignia allowing an escaped bird to be identified. The PAS has recorded 89 silver vervels which contain information relating to their owners. Also recorded are 74 small metal bells of which 45 were silver and may have been hawking bells. Falconry ceased to be popular towards the end of the 17th century, probably as a result of improvements in shotguns. While it is impossible to assign a use to many of the 268 whistles recorded by the PAS some of them will have been used in hunting. Most whistles are Post Medieval. Dog collars, usually being made of leather, are poorly represented but some of the many buckles recorded by the PAS may have been used to secure dog collars. Over 90 swivel fittings have been recorded which are likely to have come from dog-leashes but, again, other interpretations are possible.

During the Medieval and Post Medieval periods, falconry was a popular aristocratic pastime, falcons being used to hunt fowl and small game. The type of bird you owned depended on your your status; an emperor had an eagle but a knave was only allowed a kestrel. The Harris Hawk, shown here, is an American import but the falconer is using traditional equipment. (Image: Michael Lewis)

WARFARE AND HUNTING

NMS-F2EEC6, 23mm, Colney, Norfolk (1514-45)
Silver hawking vervel of ring and shield type bearing the arms of Charles Brandon, 1st Duke of Suffolk. He married Henry VIII's sister, Mary Tudor, without the king's permission, an act seen as treason.

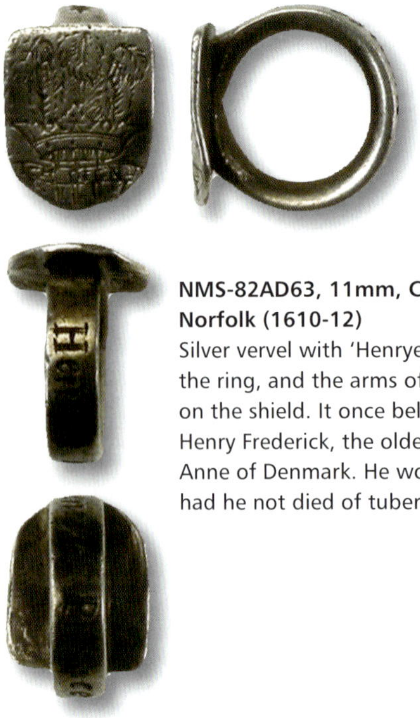

NMS-82AD63, 11mm, Cley-next-the-Sea, Norfolk (1610-12)
Silver vervel with 'Henrye Prince' inscribed on the ring, and the arms of the Prince of Wales on the shield. It once belonged to the bird of Henry Frederick, the oldest son of James I and Anne of Denmark. He would have been king had he not died of tuberculosis.

BUC-88AA68, 11mm, Burcott, Buckinghamshire (1600-42)
Washer type silver vervel bearing the name of Andrew Pitcairn, who was Chief Falconer to King Charles I.

BH-01EC33, 9mm, North Hertfordshire (1600-50)
Silver vervel of ring form inscribed with the name of Sir Edmond Lucy, who owned land near to where the object was found. By the end of the 17th century, falconry declined, perhaps as improvements in firearms made hunting with guns more popular.

DENO-CE6811, 9mm, Fenton, Lincolnshire (1400-1600)
This possible hawking bell appears to have been made with a piece of silver sheet, folded in the middle and bent to form two hemispheres.

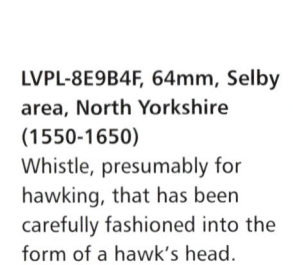

LVPL-8E9B4F, 64mm, Selby area, North Yorkshire (1550-1650)
Whistle, presumably for hawking, that has been carefully fashioned into the form of a hawk's head.

350

WARFARE AND HUNTING

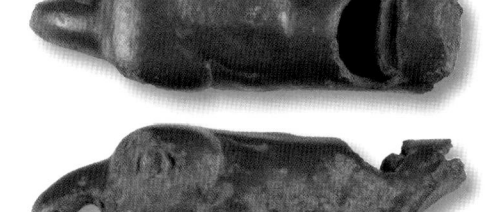

WILT-32FEA4, 52mm, North Bradley, Wiltshire (1550-1650)
This pewter whistle was made to look like the head of a bird with its open beak forming a suspension loop.

SOM-DAD21E, 164mm, Ashcott, Somerset (1676)
Collar, probably worn by a hunting dog. It bears the name of the animal's owner, Samuel Birch, who has been identified from historical records.

HESH-132E83, 100mm, Bronington, Wrexham (1250-1300)
Such complicated swivel strap distributors are of Medieval date, this one probably being used on a dog leash of particularly fine quality.

KENT-7A8B78, 17mm, Barham, Kent (1600-1950)
Although this object has not been identified with certainty it appears to be the trigger from a gin trap for catching small animals. These cruel traps are now illegal.

Chapter 12
Where to Find Out More

This book shows only a few of the more than 1.3 million items found by metal detector users and recorded with the Portable Antiquites Scheme which is available online. If you want to know more about any of the finds included here, go to the PAS website: https://finds.org.uk/database. You don't need to log in, just type the PAS record number (for example WAW-3F0491) into the 'Search our database' box and click 'Search'. This will take you to its listing; click on this to go to the full record which gives a full account of the find, details of its size, condition, dating, references to publications and, importantly, links to similar finds recorded by the PAS.

Object type.
PAS record number.
How certain is the identification?

BROOCH
Unique ID: WAW-3F0491
Object type certainty: Certain
Workflow status: Published

Roman (c. AD 60 to 80) Aesica type brooch: The wings of the cast copper alloy brooch are almost semi-cylindrical. Within the wings there is a copper alloy axis bar with a spring coiled around it. The spring has 14 coils and a fragment of the pin. The external coils join forming a horizontal bar which loops under the upper portion of the bow. At the centre of the upper edge of the wings there is an integral hook. The bow head/upper portion of the bow is an elongated trapezoidal shape in plan with concave sides and the lower corners terminating with a bulbous knop. In the centre of the bow head there is a vertical ridge which tapers towards the wings as decoration. This portion of the bow is 'C' shape in profile. The lower portion of the bow is integral to the lower edge of the upper portion. It is narrowed and is triangular in plan and has two very small knops on the lower edge. The outer surface is decorated with a triple-stranded vertical line and borders. The reverse of this portion there is a central vertical solid catchplate which has an abraded edge. The surface of the brooch has an incomplete dark green patina.

Object image: you can zoom in or download the image.

Rights Holder: The Portable Antiquities Scheme
CC License:

Image use policy
Our images can be used under a CC BY attribution licence (unless stated otherwise).

The brooch measures 38.43mm long, and is 29.12mm wide across the wings, weighing 25g.

Description: this contains information and observations on the object and a discussion of its use and significance.

The brooch is a Roman Aesica type. Hattat (1987) illustrates a similar brooch No. 794, and he dates these brooches, Aesica brooches, to the 1st century. Snape (1993) comments that Aesica type brooches were derived from continental thistle or rosette brooches and their findspots are concentrated in the Midlands and central southern England. Macreth (Macreth, 2011) suggests they date to c. 60 to c. 80AD.

Sources quoted.

Hattat, R. 1987 Brooches of Antiquity, Oxford: Oxbow

Mackreth, D. F. 2011 Brooches in Late Iron Age and Roman Britain Volume 1 Oxford: Oxbow Books

Snape, M.E. 1993 Roman Brooches from North Britain B.A.R. 235

Class: Aesica

Classification.
What we have done with the object.

Subsequent actions
Subsequent action after recording: Returned to finder

Chronology:
Period and dating.

Chronology
Broad period: ROMAN
Period from: ROMAN
Period to: ROMAN
Date from: Circa AD 60
Date to: Circa AD 80

Dimensions and weight: everything measured and recorded in detail

Dimensions and weight
Quantity: 1
Length: 38.43 mm
Width: 29.12 mm
Weight: 25 g

Date when the object was found.

Discovery dates
Date(s) of discovery: Sunday 1st April 2007 - Thursday 26th April 2007

Personal details: restricted but you can see who recorded the object.

Personal details
Found by: This information is restricted for your login.
Recorded by: Ms Angie Bolton
Identified by: Ms Angie Bolton

Materials and construction: From what was it made? How was it made? How complete is it? Is there any surface treatment?

Materials and construction
Primary material: Copper alloy
Manufacture method: Cast
Completeness: Incomplete

WHERE TO FIND OUT MORE

It is also possible to search the PAS database for particular types of object, then, using the on-screen filters, to focus in on what you want to see.

The map shows the area from which the find came, the details being restricted for security.

It is possible to click between layers to get a satellite view or 'Imperium': a Roman map.

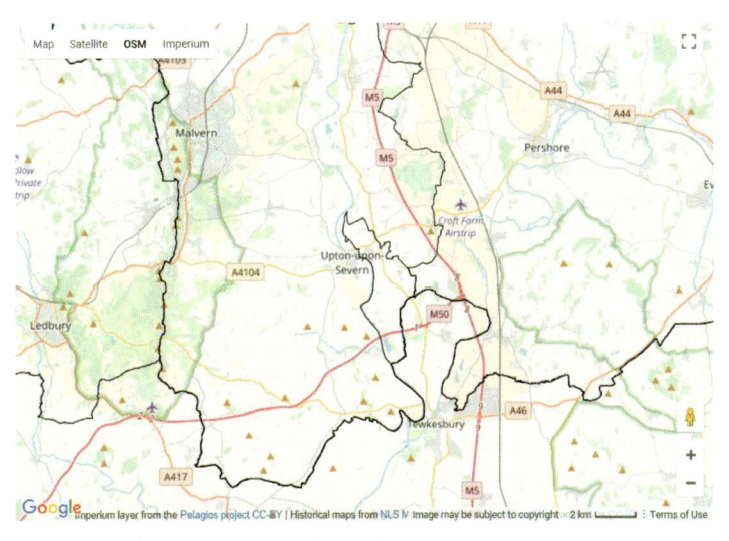

Findspot detail, restricted to kilometre square.

Spatial metadata
Region: West Midlands (European Region)
County or Unitary authority: Worcestershire (County)
District: Malvern Hills (District)
Parish or ward: Ripple (Civil Parish)

Spatial coordinates
4 Figure: SO8640
Four figure Latitude: 52.058201
Four figure longitude: -2.205603
1:25K map: SO8640
1:10K map: SO84SE
Grid reference source: From a paper map
Unmasked grid reference accurate to a 100 metre square.

Bibliography listing sources cited.

References cited
- Hattatt, R., 1987 *Brooches of Antiquity: a third selection of brooches from the author's collection* Oxford: Oxbow Books , No. 794
- Snape, M.E., 1993 *Roman Brooches from North Britain: A classification and a catalogue of brooches from sites on the Stanegate* Oxford: British Archaeological Reports 235 ,
- Mackreth, D.F., 1973 *Roman Brooches* Salisbury: Salisbury and South Wiltshire Museum

Similar objects on the PAS database.

Similar objects

Find number: WAW-922386
Object type: BROOCH
Broadperiod: ROMAN
A cast copper alloy Roman brooch. The wings of the brooch are almost semi-cylindrical, and the terminals are abraded. Within the wings there i...
Workflow: Awaiting validation

Find number: WAW-443934
Object type: BROOCH
Broadperiod: ROMAN
A cast copper alloy Roman brooch. The wings of the brooch are almost semi-cylindrical terminating with perforated wing caps. The caps support ...
Workflow: Awaiting validation

Find number: WAW-2CFE82
Object type: BROOCH
Broadperiod: ROMAN
A cast copper alloy Roman brooch. The wings of the brooch are almost semi-cylindrical. Within the wings the axis bar, spring and pin are usual...
Workflow: Awaiting validation

Timeline of associated dates

Timeline.

Associated dates for WAW-3F0491

Dates mentioned in this record

353

WHERE TO FIND OUT MORE

While detailed find spots are restricted to registered researchers you can still see the geographic spread of particular types of object. You can see the national pattern or look at a particular area by postcode or a map square set by you. From 'Advanced Search' you can look at a particular county, district or parish.

You can see different maps including Ordnance Survey, satellite images and 'Imperium' which shows Roman Britain. The whole historic landscape, as represented by finds is there for you to see and explore.

The Portable Antiquities Scheme is a community archaeology project involving

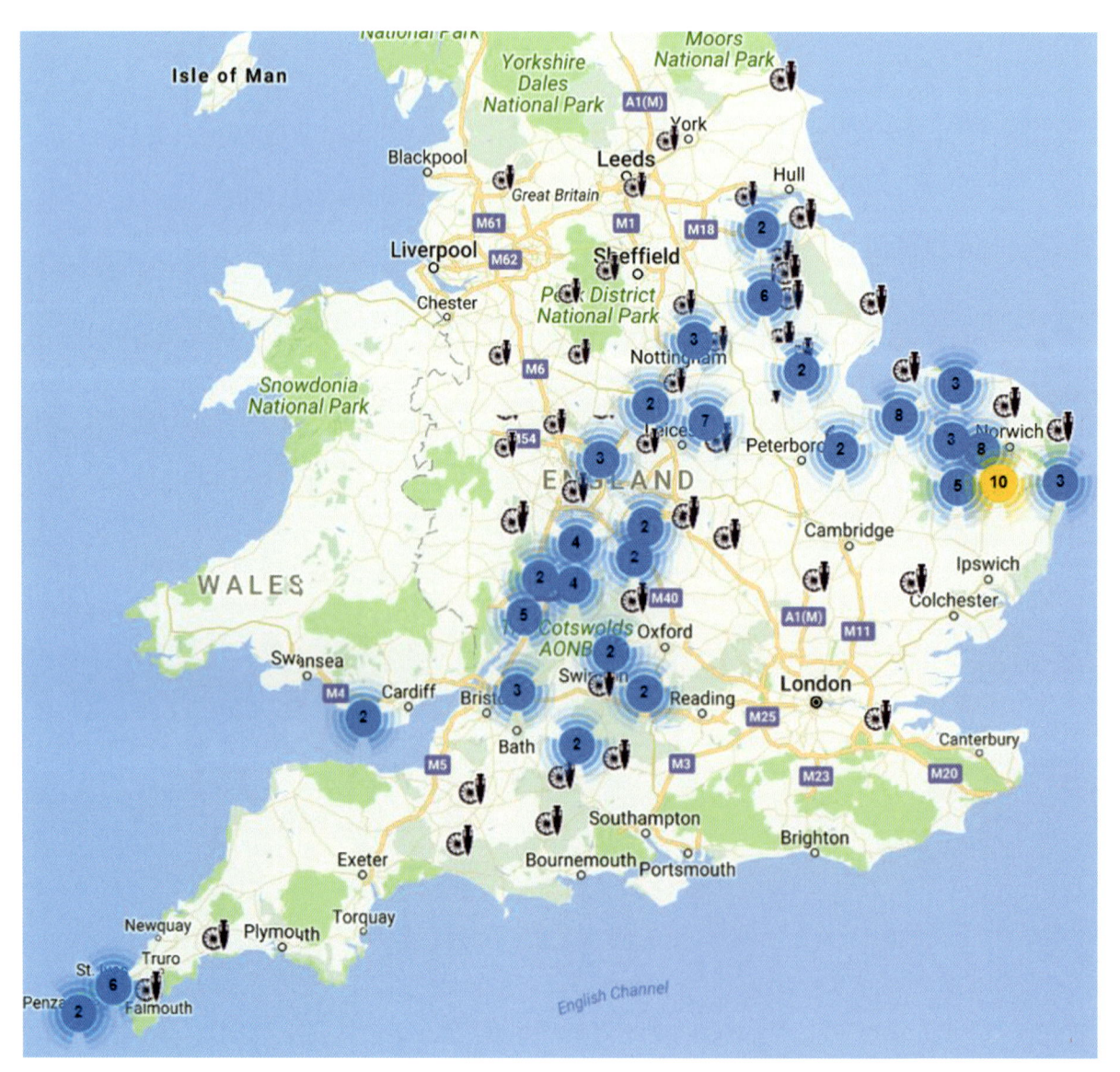

Distribution of Roman Aesica brooches.

WHERE TO FIND OUT MORE

thousands of people. The Scheme's staff, along with interns and volunteers (including metal detectorists), continue to enhance the record. Academics in universities are making increasing use of the data produced by the Scheme and are adding to our understanding of it. Importantly, some European countries have started their own projects for recording archaeological finds. This remarkable project continues to grow and develop and is producing a unique virtual model of the history of England and Wales.

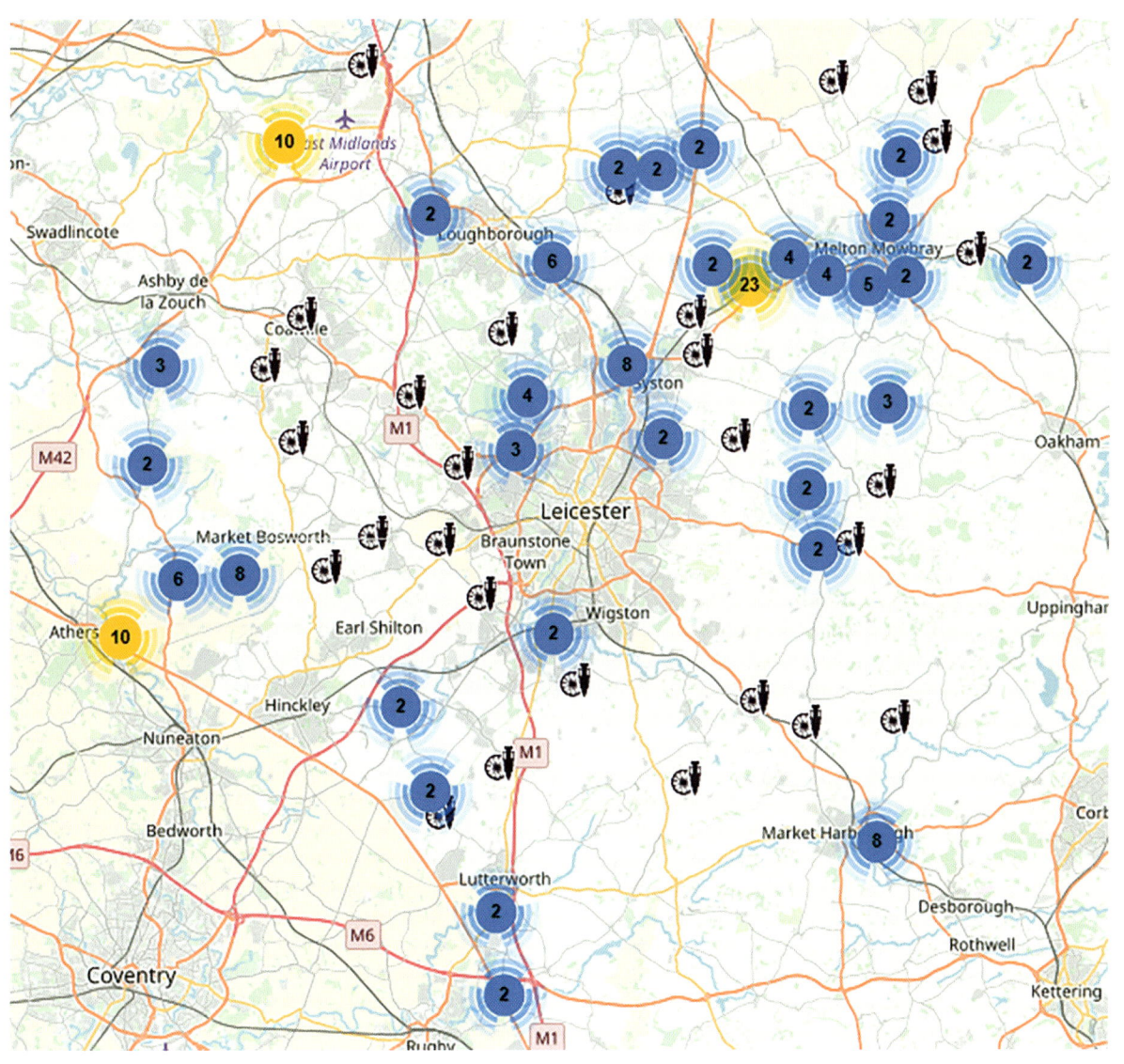

Early Medieval Leicestershire.

Chapter 13
Further Reading

Much of the information on archaeological finds is dispersed through excavation reports and not easy to find. Listed below are some of the most useful and easy to find books. As well as these there is the PAS database and the finds guides that you will find there. All of the PAS Annual Reports and Treasure Reports can be downloaded from the Scheme's web-site and provide invaluable research.

Adkins, L and R, 1998, *The Handbook of British Archaeology*, London, Constable.
An over-view of a large amount of material.

Bishop M and Coulston JCN, 1993, *Roman Military Equipment*, Batsford, London.
The place to look if you think you have something belonging to the Roman army.

The British Museum Guides, although old, contain a lot of illustrations and remain useful and not difficult to obtain. Of particular interest are:
A Guide to the Antiquities of the Bronze Age, 1920. *Guide to Early Iron Age Antiquities*, 1925.
Antiquities of Roman Britain, 1958. *Guide to Anglo-Saxon Antiquities*, 1923.

Egan, G, 2010, *The Medieval Household: Daily Living. c. 1150-1450*, 2nd Edition, Boydell Press, Woodbridge. *A look at dated Medieval finds from London.*

Egan, G, and Pritchard, F, 2018, *Dress Accessories, Medieval Finds from Excavations in London*, London HMSO. *An excellent account of the dated Medieval dress fittings found in London.*

Hattatt, R, *A Visual Catalogue of Ancient Brooches*, Oxford, Oxbow Books.
A very useful quick guide to brooches.

Hinton, D, 2005, *Gold, Gilt, Pots and Pins, Possessions and People in Medieval Britain*, Oxford, OUP.
A fascinating account of Medieval finds and what they meant to the people who made and used them.

Hobbs, R, 2003, *Treasure: Finding our Past*, British Museum Press, London.
The background to metal detecting.

Kelleher, R, 2015, *A History of Medieval Coinage in England*, Greenlight Publishing, Witham, Essex.
An excellent overview of Medieval coins.

Leahy, K A, 2007, *The Anglo-Kingdom of Lindsey*, Tempus, Stroud.
A good guide to Anglian (but not Saxon) culture.

London Museum, 1940, *Medieval Catalogue, London Museum Catalogues: No. 7.*
Old, but contains a lot of material.

Moorhead, Sam, 2013, *A History of Roman Coinage in Britain*, Greenlight Publishing, Witham, Essex.
An excellent overview.

Spink, *Coins of England and the United Kingdom*, Spink, London.
Updated each year, this book gives an excellent overall view.

Swift, E, 2003, *Roman Dress Accessories*, Shire, Princes Risborough. *A short, but useful account.*

Webster L and Backhouse J 1991, *The Making of England Anglo-Saxon Art and Culture, AD 600-900*, London. *An excellent account of Anglo-Saxon England.*

In addition to these there are also many excellent web-based resources and many old excavation reports are now available as downloads.

Other books published

Advanced Detecting *Norfolk Wolf (John Lynn)* 250mm x 190mm, 108 pages

Beginner's Guide to Metal Detecting *Julian Evan-Hart & David Stuckey* 250mm x 190mm, 92 pages

Benet's Artefacts 3rd Edition *Brett Hammond* 220mm x 140mm, hardback, 864 pages

Benet's Medieval Artefacts *Brett Hammond* 220mm x 140mm, hardback, 432 page

Benet's Roman Artefacts *Brett Hammond* 220mm x 140mm, hardback, 472 pages

British Artefacts Volume 1 – Early Anglo-Saxon *Brett Hammond* A4, 132 pages

British Artefacts Volume 2 – Middle Saxon & Viking *Brett Hammond* A4, 148 pages

British Artefacts Volume 3 – Late Saxon, Viking & Norman *Brett Hammond* A4, 128 pages

British Buttons 19th-20th Century *Dennis Blair* A5, 92 pages

Buttons & Fasteners 500BC-AD1840 *Gordon Bailey* 250mm x 190mm, 116 pages

Buckles 1250-1800 *Ross Whitehead* A4, 128 pages

Celtic & Roman Artefacts *Nigel Mills* A4, 152 pages

Cleaning Coins & Artefacts *David Villanueva* 250mm x 190mm, 116 pages

Detector Finds 1 *Gordon Bailey* A4, 100 pages

Detector Finds 2 *Gordon Bailey* A4, 100 pages

Detector Finds 3 *Gordon Bailey* A4, 96 pages

Detector Finds 4 *Gordon Bailey* A4, 100 pages

Detector Finds 5 *Gordon Bailey* A4, 100 pages

Detector Finds 6 *Gordon Bailey* A4, 116 pages

Detector Finds 7 *Gordon Bailey* A4, 125 pages

An A-Z of 1001 Field Names *Peter G. Spackman* A5, 352 pages

www.greenlightpublishing.co.uk

by Greenlight Publishing

History of Medieval Coinage in England *Richard Kelleher* A4, 216 pages

History of Roman Coinage in Britain *Sam Moorhead* A4, 224 pages

How to Find Britain's Buried Treasure Hoards *David Villanueva* A4, 152 pages

Identifying Metal Artefacts – Volume 1 *Brian Read* A4, 144 pages

Leaden Tokens & Tallies *Ted Fletcher* 250mm x 190mm, 116 pages

Medieval Artefacts *Nigel Mills* A4, 116 pages

Medieval English Groats *Ivan Buck* A4, 68 pages

Metal Detecting – All you need to know to get started *Dave Crisp* 235mm x 150mm, 150+ pages

Pottery in Britain 4000BC to AD1900 *Lloyd Laing* 250mm x 190mm, 136 pages

Reading Beaches *Ted Fletcher* A5, 80 pages

Reading Land *Ted Fletcher* A5, 100 pages

Reading Tidal Rivers *Ted Fletcher* A5, 84 pages

Roman Buckles and Military Fittings *Andrew Appels & Stuart Laycock* 250mm x 190mm, 284 pages

Saints and Their Badges *Michael Lewis* 250mm x 190mm, 168 pages

Site Research *David Villanueva* 250mm x 190mm, 160 pages

Successful Detecting Sites *David Villanueva* 250mm x 190mm, 238 pages

Saxon & Viking Artefacts *Nigel Mills* A4, 108 pages

The Tribes & Coins of Celtic Britain *Rainer Pudill & Clive Eyre* 250mm x 190mm, 84 pages

Tokens & Tallies 1850-1950 *Ted Fletcher* 250mm x 190mm, 100+ pages

Tokens & Tallies Through the Ages *Ted Fletcher* 250mm x 190mm, 100 pages

☎ 01376 521900